ART

Jacket illustrations
Inside the letters:
Leonardo da Vinci, *Mona Lisa* or *La Gioconda*, 1503-1506 and 1510 (?). Oil/wood, 77x53 cm. Musée du Louvre, Paris (see page 245 b.)
Picture as background:
Claude Monet, Nympheas, (left wing of a triptych), 1920, Oil/canvas, 200×425 cm. Museum of Modern Art, New York (see page 370 b.)

Chapter opening pages
pp. 24/25: Negative of a hand, ca. 22,000–18,000 BCE, Grotte du Pech Merle, France

pp. 36/37: Standard of Mari, Ishtar Temple, Mari, Syria, ca. 2500–2400 BCE. Shell/slate. Musée du Louvre, Paris

pp. 52/53: Funeral procession, mural painting, ca. 1391–1337 BCE, Tomb of Ramose, el-Qurna, Western Thebes

pp. 78/79: Tholos, Sanctuary of Athena Pronaia, 4th century BCE, Delphi

pp. 104/105: Forum Romanum, ca. 490 BCE–313 CE, Rome

pp. 132/133: Mosaic (detail), ca. 549, Sant'Apollinare in Classe, Ravenna

pp. 158/159: Bayeux Tapestry (detail with feast), ca. 1080. Embroidery/linen, 50×6840 cm. Musée de la Tapisserie de Bayeux, Bayeux

pp. 192/193: Apostles, west façade, main portal, Cathedral of Notre Dame d'Amiens, ca. 1220–1240, Amiens

pp. 226/227: Titian, *Sacred and Profane Love*, ca. 1513/14. Oil/canvas, 118×279 cm. Galleria Borghese, Rome

pp. 276/277: Giovanni Battista Tiepolo, ceiling fresco (detail), ca. 1752. 19×32 m. Residenz, Würzburg

p. 314 left: Antonio Canova, *Self Portrait* (detail), 1790. Oil/canvas, 68×54.5 cm. Galleria degli Uffizi, Florence

p. 314 right: Francisco de Goya, *Self Portrait* (detail), 1790–1795. Oil/canvas, 42×28 cm. Real Academia de Bellas Artes de San Fernando, Madrid

p. 315 left: Eugène Delacroix, *Self Portrait* (detail), ca. 1842. Oil/canvas, 66×54 cm. Galleria degli Uffizi, Florence

p. 135 right: Vincent van Gogh, *Self Portrait* (detail), 1889. Oil/canvas, 65×54.5 cm. Musée d'Orsay, Paris

pp. 390/391: Jackson Pollock, *Number 2*, 1949. Oil/automobile paint/aluminum paint, 97×481 cm. Munson-Williams-Proctor Arts Institute, Utica, NY

pp. 500/501: Friday Mosque, Isfahan, Iran

pp. 538/539: Bas-relief, Terrace of the Lepra King, 1150, sandstone, Angkor Wat, Cambodia

pp. 568/569: Mochizuki Gyokkai, *Shobikan-fusuma-e* (four sliding panels). Paint/gold leaf/paper, 191×560 cm. Heian-jingu, Kyoto

p. 612 left: Breastplate, Kiribati, Micronesia. Coconut fiber, 92×69×22 cm. Musée du Quai Branly, Paris

p. 612 middle: Ornamentation of a pirogue, Solomon Islands, Melanesia. Wood, 228×40 cm. Musée du Quai Branly, Paris

p. 612 right: Ceremonial shield, Papua New Guinea. Wood, 165.5×38.5×7.5 cm. Musée du Quai Branly, Paris

p. 613 left: Ceremonial support of a house, Solomon Islands, Melanesia, 17th century. Wood, 211×30×36 cm. Musée du Quai Branly, Paris

p. 613 middle: Anthropomorphic sculpture of a deity, Gambier Islands, Polynesia. Wood, 106 cm. Musée du Quai Branly, Paris

p. 613 right: Image of a *Wandjina* (cloud or rain spirit), Kimberley, Australia, 20th century. Bark painting. Private collection, New York

p. 636 left: Ritual scene, rock painting, San, Zimbabwe

p. 636 right: Shield (detail: chief dressed for battle), Oba Palace, Benin. Brass. The British Museum, London

p. 637 left: Insignia of the god of thunder, Shango, Yoruba, Benin. Wood, 19th–20th century. Musée du Quai Branly, Paris

p. 637 right: Shield (detail). Woodcarving, Yoruba, Nigeria. Ernst Anspach Collection, New York

pp. 666/667: Two-headed serpent as pectoral, Aztec, ca. 1400–1521. Turquoise/wood/shell, 20.5×44 cm. The British Museum, London

This edition published by Parragon in 2011

Production: Frechmann Kolón GmbH
Design: Rheinische Umbrechereien, Werk Düsseldorf Süd
Picture credits: See page 702
ISBN: 978-1-4454-5585-3
Printed in China

ART

ARCHITECTURE • PAINTING • SCULPTURE • GRAPHICS • TECHNICS

Bath • New York • Singapore • Hong Kong • Cologne • Delhi
Melbourne • Amsterdam • Johannesburg • Auckland • Shenzhen

Contents

Archaic—Academic—Abstract

About 40,000 years ago, mankind invented art... or perhaps art invented mankind? Although art was at first used for tool making, the possibility and the urge to recreate the world, humanity's complex individual needs, fears, or simply intellect—with color on stone or wood and in sculpture—presented themselves with more and more frequency.

With art, the individual could now leave an undying witness to his or her existence.

The creative urge and the artistic power of expression can be found all over the world. They vary according to ethnological and geographical basis as well as the societal development of different cultures.

Art can be archaic, academic, or abstract. It can be motivated by religion, politics, or simply by creativity, and it serves as a mirror of its time. In any case, art requires a personal, intellectual, or emotional dialogue between the creator and his environment. Artists make use of certain techniques, sometimes perfecting them or even inventing completely new ones, but without spiritual individuality, art could never be more than kitsch.

In addition, art constantly challenges the viewer to open and train his or her own emotions—and

◁ **Archaic**
African, Statue of a
Woman, Baoulé
→ p. 653

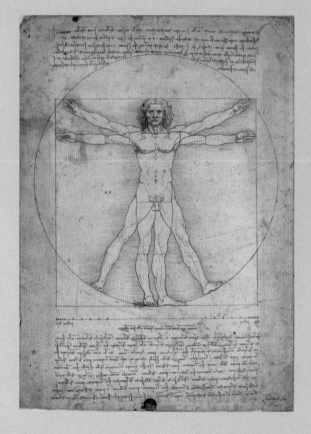

▷ **Academic**
Leonardo da Vinci,
The Vitruvian Man
→ p. 230

eyes. Personal interaction with art can be hard work, but it always provides a glimpse into culture(s), and it imparts wisdom.

Can a survey of art replace this interaction? Fortunately, the answer to that question is a resounding "No." A survey can, however, help us understand central concepts, and it can formulate a terminology that makes it possible to communicate more easily about art. This terminology can be used to describe techniques, details, styles, or perhaps the general spirit of an entire era. Art historical knowledge is first and foremost a system of classification for basic similarities and comparable traits, and in this regard, it is certainly of help.

This book will attempt to provide such help without focusing on the concepts so much that it distracts from the art itself. It will therefore intentionally avoid the more detail-oriented vocabulary that the discipline has created.

Our goal is to provide the tools necessary for the understanding of the visual arts. We will also avoid any self-promoting mention of brilliant images and other superlatives, because a reproduction on paper can never convey the experiential reality of the original work of art. Our intention is to provide a survey of world art, combined with a linguistic toolbox as well as an invitation to address the works of art of the world's cultures.

Ludwig Könemann

Abstract
Malevich, Black
Square
→ p. 436

Art and History at a Glance

Prehistory (40,000–5000 BCE)

40,000 years ago, during the last ice age, the continents were still connected by land bridges. "Modern" humans (*Homo sapiens*) had long before left their home in Africa and set out to populate the world. They reached Australia over the Torres Strait; the settlement of the Americas would first occur tens of thousands of years later.

At about this time, an artist in what is today southern Germany carved a mammoth, while another carved a lion-headed man. The artifacts found in the Vogelherd Cave are the oldest known works of art. Presumably, other "first" works that did not survive the ravages of time were created elsewhere.

Most examples of prehistoric art—sculptures, carvings, and cave paintings—have been found in central and southern Europe. Its main themes are hunting and fertility. These creations are astonishing not only for their expressive precision, but also because of their aptitude for abstraction.

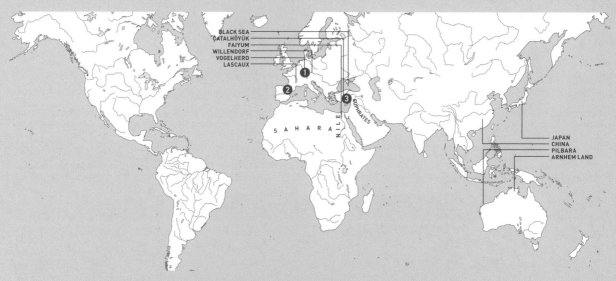

160,000 BCE The first Homo sapiens live in eastern Africa.

110,000 BCE From there, Homo sapiens set out to conquer the world, first heading north (Europe) and east (Asia). It will be 100,000 years before they reach South America.

35,000 BCE The brains of Homo sapiens are larger than those of their predecessor, *Homo habilis*. Tools are not the only evidence of their inventiveness. The first works of art are created simultaneously in Europe (Vogelherd carvings) and Australia (Aboriginal drawings in Arnhem Land and Pilbara).

25,000 BCE The Venus of Willendorf (Austria) attests to an early cult of femininity.

16,000 BCE The caves at Lascaux (France) and...

12,000 BCE Altamira (Spain) are decorated with animal and hunting scenes.

12,000 BCE The end of the ice age brings environmental change. In the following years, the sea level rises by almost 328 ft (100 m). The continents drift apart, and a great flood transforms a depression into the Black Sea. Humankind is ensnared in its continental cultures.

11,000 BCE The first Neolithic Revolution occurs along the Euphrates River. Hunters and gatherers become herders and farmers, and the first permanent settlements are established.

10,000 BCE The first cultures develop; the settlement of Japan begins with the Jōmon culture, and the first traces of pottery are detectable.

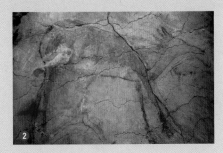

1 Mammoth from Vogelherd → p. 30
2 Altamira, cave painting → p. 35
3 Animal sculpture, 9500–8000 BCE, Göbekli Tepe, Turkey

9500 BCE The Clovis culture spreads across North and South America, marking its extent with flint spearheads.
In what is today Turkey, the temple complex of Göbekli Tepe is built; older even than the first settlements, it is evidence of the worship of higher beings.

8500 BCE As the earth becomes warmer, the dry Sahara develops into a lush, subtropical landscape. Humans push further north. 2000 years later, the land dries out again, and settlers move into the fertile Nile Valley.

7000 BCE Artful petroglyphs are carved in the Sahara.

5400 BCE Çatalhöyük, a city with several thousand inhabitants, is founded in Anatolia.

5000 BCE The first traces of Chinese ceramic art date from this time.

4800 BCE Farmers from the East migrate to Europe's fertile regions, later mixing with Eurasian nomads to become the ancestors of the European peoples.

4500 BCE The Faiyum culture establishes the first of the larger village communities in Egypt, which will later serve as the basis for the kingdom.

The First Empires (5000–1000 BCE)

The first settlement patterns arose in Anatolia and the Eastern Mediterranean between 7000 and 10,000 years ago. The Neolithic Revolution, or the transformation from hunters and gatherers to herders and farmers, heralded the end of the Stone Age (which in some corners of the world, such as Papua New Guinea and parts of South America, would not end until the twentieth century). A new order and distribution of labor characterized this social coexistence: an increasing urbanizing tendency began to take hold.

Soon, the first states developed along fertile river valleys: Mesopotamia, Egypt, India, China, and the first cultures of Central America. Centralized governments and armies were formed. Larger bureaucracies regulated daily life. With increasing prosperity, palaces and monumental tombs appeared.

Countless gods ruled the heavens, and deified monarchs such as the pharaohs ruled the earth. Life and riches after death were of central importance. Temples and cult sites gave expression to reverence for the gods.

The tombs of the pharaohs contained breathtaking artistic treasures. Rather than taking his flesh and blood soldiers with him to the grave, one Chinese emperor had an entire army of clay soldiers buried with him.

Art now also served historical purposes: images, writing and sculpture provide us with a detailed depiction of daily life in the first empires.

4000 BCE Handicrafts emerge from simple tool making. The first wheels are used in Mesopotamia.

3600 BCE The first Minoan settlement on Crete

3500 BCE Hieroglyphics are created in Egypt, and the potter's wheel is invented in Sumer.

3000 BCE Menes establishes the first united and organized Egyptian empire. The Egyptians use papyrus and discover ink.

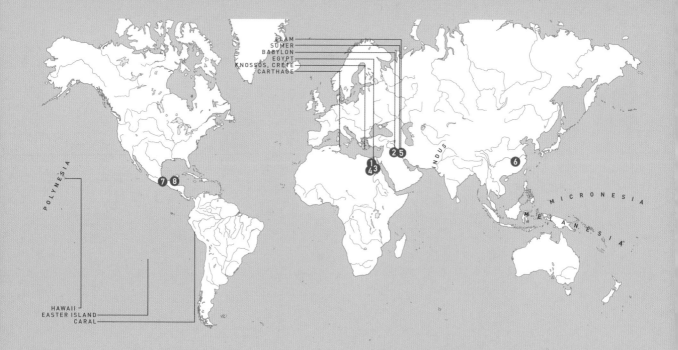

ELAM
SUMER
BABYLON
EGYPT
KNOSSOS, CRETE
CARTHAGE

HAWAII
EASTER ISLAND
CARAL

In Sumer, the first ziggurats are built. Cuneiform, a forerunner of the alphabet, is developed in Mesopotamia.

2800 BCE An advanced civilization arises in the Indus Valley (Pakistan), using a writing system that has yet to be deciphered.

2620 BCE Important monuments are constructed in Egypt; Snefru, for example, builds the Meidum, Bent, and Red Pyramids.

2600 BCE Caral, one of South America's oldest cities, is founded.

Ink is produced in China.

2400 BCE The Elamite empire is founded in Persia.

2100 BCE On Crete, the Minoans build great palace complexes.

1766 BCE End of the Xia dynasty in China

1760 BCE Under Hammurabi, Babylon becomes the most important city in the ancient Near East. His code of laws ensures his undying fame.

1500 BCE Aryan nomads destroy the Indus culture. India becomes "vedic."

Settlement of Polynesia and Micronesia: over

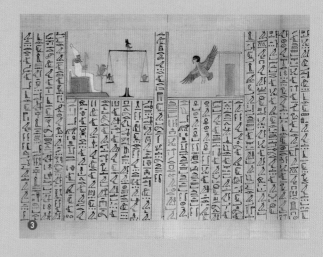

1 Hieroglyphs → p. 64
2 Cuneiform → p. 46
3 Papyrus → pp. 58/59

the next 2000 years, brave seafarers reach the most isolated islands, including Hawaii and Easter Island.

1327 BCE   Tutankhamun dies at the young age of eighteen and is buried with stunning treasures.

1200 BCE   The Olmecs are the first advanced civilization in Central America.

1000 BCE   Using Carthage as their base, the Phoenicians colonize large sections of the Mediterranean, which will lead to the Punic Wars 800 years later.

The first Maya settlements are founded in Central America.

Bronze vessels are produced in China.

950 BCE   The Old Testament is written in answer to the question, "Where do I come from?"

❹

4 Tutankhamun → p. 75
5 Code of Hammurabi, Diorite, Susa, 1792–1750 BCE, Musée du Louvre, Paris
6 Chinese bronze → p. 574
7 Olmecs → p. 673
8 Maya → p. 677

❻

❼

5

8

Antiquity (1000 BCE–400 CE)

In the Mediterranean and the Middle East, the great empires of the Greeks, Persians and Romans arose. In the Far East, the Chinese empire formed, and the Central American civilizations experienced their first zenith. Art became academic, following precise anatomical studies, and the Romans executed the first portraits and monuments that truly represented reality. A rich mythological heritage fueled the creative process. Abstract decorative forms developed alongside objective representation.

Thanks to its timeless nature, the art of antiquity is often referred to as classical, and 1500 years later it served as an inspiration for the Renaissance as well as for neoclassicism.

SUSA
EGYPT
GREECE
POMPEII, HERCULANEUM
ROME

EL MIRADO , NAKBE
CHICHEN ITZA

2500 BCE	The Cycladic harpist marks the artistic beginning of antiquity.
1500 BCE	The Minoan culture makes the bull its religious symbol.
1000 BCE	Abstraction with right angles—the geometric style rules in Greece.
800 BCE	The Greek polis (city-state) emerges.

753 BCE	Date of the legendary founding of Rome
750 BCE	Homer composes the *Odyssey*.
700 BCE	The archaic supplants the geometric style.
650 BCE	The Maya settle Chichén Itzá.
500 BCE	Confucius founds Chinese philosophy. The bronze art of the Etruscans (in northern Italy) is rather academic in nature.

540 BCE	The Pythagorean theorem: $a^2 + b^2 = c^2$
539 BCE	The Persians take Susa, the Elamite capital, and build Persepolis with its palaces.
528 BCE	Buddha attains enlightenment. Spirituality and philosophy experience their symbolic birth.
500 BCE	The Mayan cities of El Mirador and Nakbe reach their peak. The Nok in Nigeria create some of the oldest extant African sculpture.
480 BCE	Greek artists devise the classical style, a modular art based on timeless ideals of beauty and harmonious proportions.
380 BCE	Plato asserts the immortality of the soul.
338 BCE	Hellenistic art appears, emotionally exaggerating classical art's formal language.
332 BCE	Egypt falls to Alexander the Great.
270 BCE	The Greek mathematician and astronomer Aristarchus of Samos is the first to postulate a heliocentric model of the solar system (sun at its center).
207 BCE	The end of the Qin dynasty is documented by the terracotta army of more than 7000 clay soldiers.

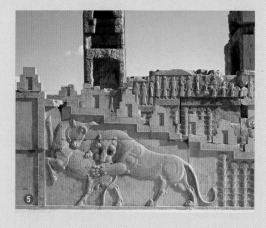

The succeeding Han dynasty experiences a type of social revolution through the division of land and lowering of taxes.

200 BCE	Roman sculptors create the first portrait busts that are true to life.
130 BCE	Antipater of Sidon describes the Seven Wonders of the Ancient World.
22 BCE	Vitruvius writes his ten volumes on architecture; 1500 years later, his ideas still inspire Dürer and da Vinci.
33 CE	Jesus Christ dies on the cross. The New Testament is written in answer to the question, "What comes next?"
70 CE	The Colosseum is built in Rome.
79 CE	Pompeii and Herculaneum are buried by an eruption of Mt. Vesuvius.
380 CE	The Roman emperor Theodosius I decrees Christianity the state religion.

1 Harpist from Keros, 2500 BCE. National Archaeological Museum, Athens
2 Minoan Bull rhyton. Ceramic. Heraklion Archaeological Museum, Crete
3 Vase with Geometric Pattern, 730–720 BCE. Ceramic, 19 in (50 cm) high. Museo Archeologico, Pescia Romana, Grosseto
4 Mars of Todi → p. 113
5 Persepolis
6 Sitting Figure, Nok → p. 645
7 Terracotta Army, Qin → p. 576

The Middle Ages, Islamic Expansion, the Great Periods of China and Japan, and the End of South American Cultures (400–1500 CE)

Barbarian invasions and the end of the Western Roman Empire led to a "dark" age when developments in art and culture came to a dramatic standstill. For almost 500 years, there was little artistic activity in the North and West. Only with the early Romanesque did a new style emerge; architecture, sculpture, and painting were now entirely at the service of the Christian church. Until the late Gothic period, classical forms made way for frightening chimeras. Then Italian and French artists studied antiquity and built on ancient achievements. Their groundbreaking success led to the Renaissance and the beginning of the Modern Era.

While the Byzantine Empire expanded in eastern Europe, an immense Islamic empire ruled the Middle East and North Africa. These were tolerant societies, boasting the most important early universities and stunning architectural monuments. For a long time, the Arab world was the cultural and intellectual power of the Western world.

In China and Japan, carving, porcelain, painting, and calligraphy reached their greatest heights. The great civilizations of Central and South America experienced their last centuries of power before the Catholic Church granted Spanish and Portuguese invaders leave to destroy their cultures.

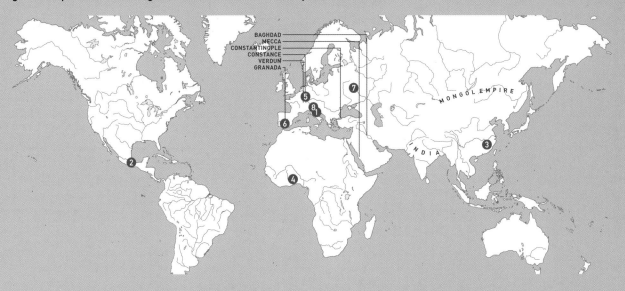

395 The Roman Empire is divided permanently into East and West. Barbarian invaders overrun western Europe.

450 With 200,000 inhabitants, Teotihuacán (Mexico) is the largest city in the Americas, and one of the largest in the world.

476 Under the Ostrogoths, the Italian city of Ravenna becomes a cultural center.

505 Benedict of Nursia establishes Christian monasticism, demanding strict celibacy from its practitioners.

537 In Constantinople, the dome of the Hagia Sophia is completed.

610 Islam is founded. Allāh imparts the Qur'ān to Muhammad through the archangel Gabriel.

618 Porcelain is invented in China.

632 The first Ka'bah is built in Mecca. Islam will be an intellectual world power for 1000 years.

730 Iconoclastic controversy in the Byzantine Empire: icons, proclaimed idolatrous, are banned.

785 Construction begins on the Great Mosque in Córdoba (Spain).

798 The Palatine Chapel, a masterpiece of early Romanesque architecture, is built in Aachen.

843 The Treaty of Verdun: the Frankish Empire is split up among Charlemagne's grandsons, and the map of Europe takes a significant step toward assuming its current shape.

850 The University of Baghdad is the world's most important center of knowledge.

1000 Leif Eriksson casts off in Greenland, headed for North America.

1 Mosaic, Ravenna → p. 144
2 Teotihuacán → p. 674
3 Porcelain → p. 592
4 Yoruba → p. 648
5 Palatine Chapel, Aachen → p. 165
6 Great Mosque, Córdoba → p. 516
7 Icon → p. 513
8 Giotto, *The Lamentation of Christ* → p. 214

1200 The Yoruba in Nigeria create magnificent sculpture in wood and bronze.

1206 Genghis Khan establishes the Mongol empire, the largest in world history.

1250 India is largely under Islamic rule.

1252 Pope Innocent IV allows the Inquisition to use torture.

1306 Giotto paints *The Lamentation of Christ* in late Gothic style.

1350 The Nasrids construct the Alhambra, a tiled jewel of decorative simplicity.

1415 The Czech church reformer Jan Hus is burned with his writings in Constance.

1450 Johannes Gutenberg invents printing with movable type.

1453 The Ottoman armies take Constantinople, soon ending Arab dominance in Muslim territories.

1492 Spanish Catholics defeat the last Muslims in Granada. Columbus reaches the Americas.

The World in the Early Modern Era (1500–1900 CE)

The Europeans discovered their expansive tendencies. Within two centuries, they had occupied and colonized immense portions of the Americas, Africa, Southeast Asia, and Australia. The Arab world had been dominated since about 1500 CE by the Turks, who at their height ruled a territory about the size of today's European Union. China and Japan remained isolated in the East.

Within the space of just a few years, Italy produced about ninety percent of its artistic heritage, exemplified by the geniuses Michelangelo, Raphael and Leonardo da Vinci. The Ottoman court architect Sinan transformed Istanbul into perhaps the world's most architecturally delightful city. In India, the Mughals bequeathed to the world magnificent structures like the Taj Mahal. The peoples of the Ivory Coast and Nigeria created powerful, archaic art, and Japanese artists perfected minimalism.

In this flood of influences, fashions and styles alternated with increasing speed. Whereas the Romanesque and Gothic styles continued for hundreds of years, and the Renaissance and the baroque each prevailed for about 150 years, in the nineteenth century, dozens of styles often not lasting more than twenty years evolved: impressionism, art nouveau, neoclassicism, romanticism, the Nazarenes, Pre-Raphaelites, realism... The arts in the later part of the Early Modern Period forged their own paths, exploding around the turn of the twentieth century into the Modern Era.

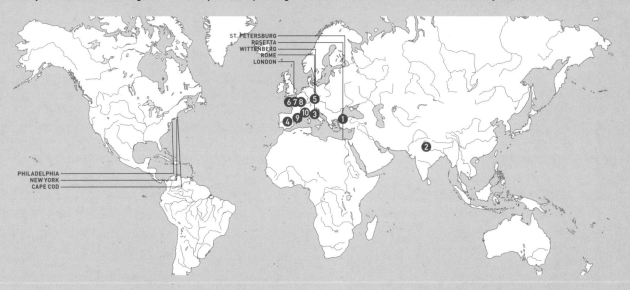

1500 The humanists herald an intellectual turning point— a precondition of the Renaissance.	North American Indians will become the largest genocide in history. In art historical terms, the first 250 years of "settlement" in the New World are largely insignificant.
1508 Michelangelo begins to paint the frescoes in the Sistine Chapel—a bit too revealingly, in fact, as his work would posthumously endure (under overpainting) one of the first instances of censorship in art history.	
	1650 Europe is dominated by absolutism, or as Louis XIV states it, *"L'État, c'est moi."* Art (baroque) is created at and for the courts.
1517 Martin Luther begins the Protestant Reformation.	
1550 Giorgio Vasari publishes his *Lives of the Artists*.	**1656** At the Spanish Royal Court in Madrid, Diego Velázquez paints *Las Meninas*.
1557 The Sultan Süleyman Mosque in Istanbul is completed.	**1703** In Russia, Peter the Great has St. Petersburg built. The art and architecture borrow heavily from absolutist Europe (eclecticism).
1606 William Shakespeare writes *Macbeth*.	
1620 The Mayflower brings the "Pilgrim Fathers" to North America. The expulsion and partial eradication of the	**1748** Johann Sebastian Bach composes *The Art of the Fugue*.

1 Sultan Süleyman Mosque → p. 532
2 Taj Mahal → p. 530
3 Leonardo, *Mona Lisa* → p. 245
4 Francisco de Goya, *The Nude Maja*, 1797–1800. Oil on canvas, 38 x 75 in (97 x 190 cm). Museo del Prado, Madrid

1776 The United States of America declares its independence from Great Britain.

1779 Gotthold Ephraim Lessing takes up the idea of religious tolerance with the "Parable of the Ring": a father presents his three sons three replicas of the one true ring (i.e., Judaism, Christianity, and Islam) and tells each that his ring is the real one. It becomes a key work of the Enlightenment.

1785 The Marquis de Sade publishes The *120 Days of Sodom* as a foil to Boccacio's *Decameron* (1353), in which people stuck together tell bawdy stories to each other. But in de Sade's work, the characters act out the most horrible perversities.

1789 The French Revolution ends the era of absolutism, and with it the baroque.

1791 Shortly before his death, Wolfgang Amadeus Mozart composes *The Magic Flute*, which takes its inspiration from Freemasonry.

1793 Art for the general public: after the Revolution, Paris's Louvre is opened as a museum.

1799 Napoleon's Egyptian campaign leads to the discovery and speedy decoding of the Rosetta Stone.

1800 Goya paints nude and clothed versions of his *Maja*.

1823 Caspar David Friedrich paints *The Sea of Ice*, an allegory of dashed social hopes. It is an essential work of German romanticism.

1830 Eugène Delacroix enters a new mode of genius free of aristocratic and religions tendencies with his *Liberty Leading the People*.
Frédéric Chopin composes his *Revolutionary Étude*.

1835 Louis Daguerre develops the daguerreotype, a forerunner of modern photography.

1837 Samuel Morse invents the telegraph.
Charles Dickens's *Oliver Twist* is a social manifesto.

1848 Karl Marx publishes the *Communist Manifesto*.

1850 Richard Wagner completes his multimedia spectacle, or "*Gesamtkunstwerk*," *Lohengrin*.

1859 Charles Darwin's *The Origin of Species* shakes the Old Testament conception of the world.

1863 Édouard Manet paints *Luncheon on the Grass*.

1866 Gustave Courbet ignites a scandal with his painting of a woman's genitalia, entitled *The Origin of the World*.

1870 The Metropolitan Museum of Art opens in New York.

1873 Claude Monet paints *Impression, Sunrise*.

5 Friedrich, *The Sea of Ice* → p. 338
6 Delacroix, *Liberty Leading the People* → p. 335
7 Monet, *Impression, Sunrise* → p. 357
8 Manet, *Luncheon on the Grass* → p. 354
9 Gaudí, *Sagrada Família* → p. 383
10 Vincent van Gogh, *Sunflowers*, 1888. Oil on canvas, 36⅜ x 28 in (92.4 x 71.1 cm). Philadelphia Museum of Art, Philadelphia

1876 Pierre-Auguste Renoir paints *Ball at the Moulin de la Galette*
Nikolaus Otto patents his combustion engine.
The Industrial Revolution reaches its height. People can travel by machine, communicate over vast differences, and electricity is flowing. Art must react.

1877 Peter Tchaikovsky composes the ballet *Swan Lake*, a Viennese waltz with Russian romantic thoughtfulness. It is the swan song of the romantic era.

1882 Antoni Gaudí begins construction on the *Sagrada Família* cathedral, which remains unfinished to this day.

1888 Vincent van Gogh, an otherworldly Dutchman living in the south of France, combines impressionistic colors and expressionist forms in his *Sunflowers*.

The Modern Period

Barcelona and Paris were the first centers of modern art, followed by Berlin, Moscow, and later New York. Picasso's work of the century, *Les Demoiselles d'Avignon*, signaled the start of cubism, the Bauhaus revolutionized architecture and design, Malevich and Kandinsky established abstraction in modern art. Other important movements like expressionism and Dada were also developed.

About one hundred styles emerged, often represented by a handful or even one artist. Sometimes just a name stood for a style. Technique and form became the "signature" or trademark of the artist: Christo wrapped, Yves Klein painted monochrome works in blue, Warhol (re)produced portraits in different color combinations, Uecker nailed, and Jeff Koons left the production of his wood, porcelain, and metal works to professional manufacturers. Borders disintegrated. Art became world art, and the art market became a world market.

But such global creativity was not always allowed to prosper. The Nazis condemned "degenerate art," communist regimes permitted only ideologically pure realism, and the Taliban demolished the artistic masterworks of other religions.

The classical modern period was supplanted by the postmodern, and at the turn of the millennium, art was being created in all available media.

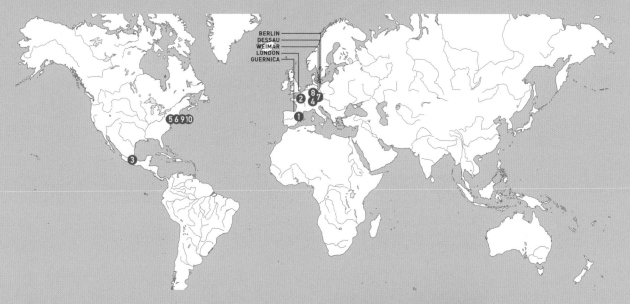

BERLIN
DESSAU
WEIMAR
LONDON
GUERNICA

1900 New artistic styles are described as "avant-garde."

1903 Picasso quotes the mannerist formal language of El Greco. One color—blue—dominates his pictures of extended bodies.

1905 Expressionism, especially in Germany, becomes the leading artistic movement of the early twentieth century.

1907 Artists such as Picasso discover the archaic power of the "primitive" sculpture of Africa and Oceania.

1911 The *Mona Lisa* is stolen from the Louvre—the most significant artistic booty in history, with a value today of well over one billion dollars.

1912 The *Titanic* sinks.

1 Pablo Picasso, *The Old Guitarist*, 1903. Oil on canvas, 47¾ x 32½ in (121.3 x 82.5 cm). The Art Institute of Chicago, Chicago

1914 The industrialized slaughter of World War One begins.

1915 Kazimir Malevich paints a *Black Square*.

1916 Tristan Tzara, Hans Arp, and others found Dada in Zurich. Parodying the bourgeoisie becomes art.

1917 Artists are at first inspired by the ideals of the Russian Revolution.

1919 Walter Gropius founds the Bauhaus.

1920 The immense cultural dynamism after the war's end in Berlin, London, Paris, and of course in the USA goes down in history as the "Roaring Twenties."

1922 Diego Rivera and José Clemente Orozco explore fresco technique for their large, socially critical murals in Mexico and the USA, establishing muralism as the national style of Mexico.

1928 Walt Disney's Mickey Mouse character becomes world famous.

1929 The MoMA opens in New York.

1937 "Degenerate Art" (including Dadaism, surrealism, and expressionism) goes against National Socialist party ideology, and is singled out by the Nazis for condemnation in a traveling exhibition.
With his painting *Guernica*, Picasso treats the destruction of the Spanish city of the same name by the German Condor Legion. The picture hangs from 1931 to 1981 in the MoMA, at which point it is given to the new Spanish Republic (as Picasso had stipulated in his will).

1939 World War II and the Holocaust begin in Europe. Many Jewish collectors are dispossessed. The return

2 Picasso, *Les Demoiselles d'Avignon* → p. 404
3 Rivera, *Sugar Cane* → p. 459
4 Arp, *Birds in an Aquarium* → p. 439
5 The Museum of Modern Art, New York

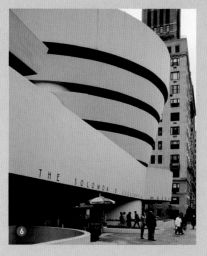

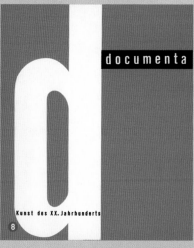

6 The Solomon
R. Guggenheim
Museum, New York
7 Poster for
the Exhibition
"Degenerate Art"
→ p. 452
8 documenta
Catalogue → p. 396
9 Warhol, *Marilyn*
→ p. 475
10 Rothko, *No. 3/No.
13* → p. 463

of works of art to the heirs of the dispossessed
continues to this day despite often-incomprehensible
laws that inhibit the exportation of art to the heirs'
new home countries.

1949 With his color field painting, Mark Rothko is one
of the most important proponents of abstract
expressionism.

1950 Jackson Pollock makes action painting world-
famous.

1955 The first documenta opens in Kassel.

1958 Advertising and consumerism become artistic
subjects, and pop art emerges in England and the
United States.

1959 New York's Solomon R. Guggenheim Museum is built
according to plans by Frank Lloyd Wright.

1990 The fall of communism: art is by and large free.

1991 Damien Hirst preserves a tiger shark in formaldehyde, calling the work *The Physical Impossibility of
Death in the Mind of Someone Living.*

1992 Kitsch is art: Jeff Koons shows his *Puppy*, a 39-ft
(12-m) high dog made of flowers.

2006 Jackson Pollock's *No. 5* and Gustav Klimt's *Adele
Bloch Bauer I* are sold for 140 and 135 million
dollars, respectively.

Periods

	40,000 BCE –5000 BCE Prehistory	5000 BCE –1000 BCE First Empires	1000 BCE –400 CE Antiquity
Europe	40,000 BCE Upper Paleolithic (Late Stone Age) 8000 BCE Mesolithic (Middle Stone Age) 5500 BCE Neolithic (New Stone Age) 5000 BCE Chalcolithic (Copper Age)	2200 BCE Bronze Age 2000 BCE Minoans 1400 BCE Mycenae	1000 BCE Geometric Style in Greece 800 BCE Etruscans 753 BCE Romans 700 BCE Archaic Greece 480 BCE Classical Greece 336 BCE Hellenistic Greece
Near and Middle East		3500 BCE Uruk 3200 BCE Kish 2400 BCE Akkad 2400 BCE Elam 2000 BCE Babylon 1800 BCE Hittites 1380 BCE Assur 1000 BCE Phoenicians	800 BCE Nabataeans 539 BCE Persians
North Africa	7000 BCE Tassili n'Ajjer, Sahara	3000 BCE Egypt: Early Dynasties 2665 BCE Old Kingdom 1991 BCE Middle Kingdom 1554 BCE New Kingdom	713 BCE Egypt: Late Period
Africa			1000 BCE Ife 500 BCE Nok
East Asia	10,000 BCE Jomon Period, Japan 7000 BCE Hemudu Culture, China	2205 BCE Xia Dynasty, China 1600 BCE Shang Dynasty, China 1045 BCE Zhou Dynasty, China	221 BCE Qin Dynasty, China 206 BCE Han Dynasty, China 220 CE Three Kingdoms Period, China 250 CE Yayoi Period, Japan 300 CE Kofun Period, Japan
South and Southeast Asia		2800 BCE Harappa Civilization	321 BCE Maurya Empire, India 50 BCE Kushan Empire, India 320 CE Gupta Empire, India
Australia and Oceania	40,000 BCE Pilbara, Australia	1800 BCE Maori, New Zealand 1500 BCE Lapita, Melanesia	
North and Central America		3000 BCE Early Mayan Preclassic Period 1200 BCE Olmecs 1000 BCE Zapotecs 1000 BCE Huastecs	900 BCE Middle Mayan Preclassic Period 400 BCE Late Mayan Preclassic 300 BCE Hopewell Tradition, USA 100 CE Teotihuacán 200 CE Early Mayan Classic
South America			900 BCE Chavín Culture, Peru 400 BCE Nazca Culture, Peru 100 CE Moche Civilization, Peru

400–800 Late Antiquity	800–1400 Middle Ages	1400–1900 Early Modern	1900→ Modern
300 Early Christian Art 400 Byzantium 650 Insular Art 756 Umayyads, Spain	800 Carolingian Renaissance 920 Ottonian Art 1050 Romanesque 1150 Gothic 1200 Flamboyant 1230 Nasrids (Moors), Spain	1420 Renaissance 1500 Mannerism 1575 Baroque 1720 Rococo 1750 Historicism 1750 Neoclassicism 1790 Romanticism 1830 Realism 1860 Impressionism 1880 Art Nouveau/Jugendstil 1880 Post-Impressionism 1890 Symbolism	1901 Expressionism 1904 Fauvism 1908 Cubism 1909 Futurism 1913 Constructivism/Suprematism 1916 Dada 1917 De Stijl 1918 Surrealism 1919 Bauhaus 1923 New Obectivity 1940 Abstraction 1956 Pop Art 1960 Minimalism 1970 Conceptual Art 1980 Postmodernism
600 Byzantium 661 Umayyads, Syria 750 Abbasids	909 Fatimids 1038 Seljuks 1060 Almoravids 1300 Ottomans 1370 Timurids		
800 Coptic and Early Christian Art 800 Umayyads	900 Abbasids 1000 Fatimids	1450 Ottomans	
800 Yoruba	800 Ghana 1100 Great Zimbabwe 1200 Benin 1235 Mali	1600 Dahomey 1680 Ashanti	
552 Asuka Period, Japan 618 Tang Dynasty, China 668 Silla Kingdom, Korea 710 Nara Period, Japan 794 Heian Period, Japan	936 Goryeo Kingdom, Korea 960 Song Dynasty, China 1115 Jin Dynasty, China 1192 Kamakura Period, Japan 1279 Yuan Dynasty, China 1333 Muromachi Period, Japan 1368 Ming Dynasty, China 1392 Joseon Dynasty, Korea	1644 Qing Dynasty, China 1603 Edo Period, Japan	
350 Champa Kingdom, Vietnam 800 Khmer Empire, Cambodia	950 Classical Champa, Vietnam 1238 Sukothai Kingdom, Thailand 1351 Ayutthaya Kingdom, Thailand	1526 Mughal Empire, India	
400 Rapa Nui (Easter Island)			
600 Late Mayan Classic Period 700 Anasazi, USA 720 Toltecs, Mexico	900 Mayan Postclassic Period 1300 Aztecs, Mexico	1885 American Impressionism	1914 American Realism 1922 Muralism 1946 Abstract Expressionism 1958 Pop Art 1965 Minimalism 1966 Conceptual Art 1968 Photorealism 1968 Land Art
	1200 Inca, Peru		

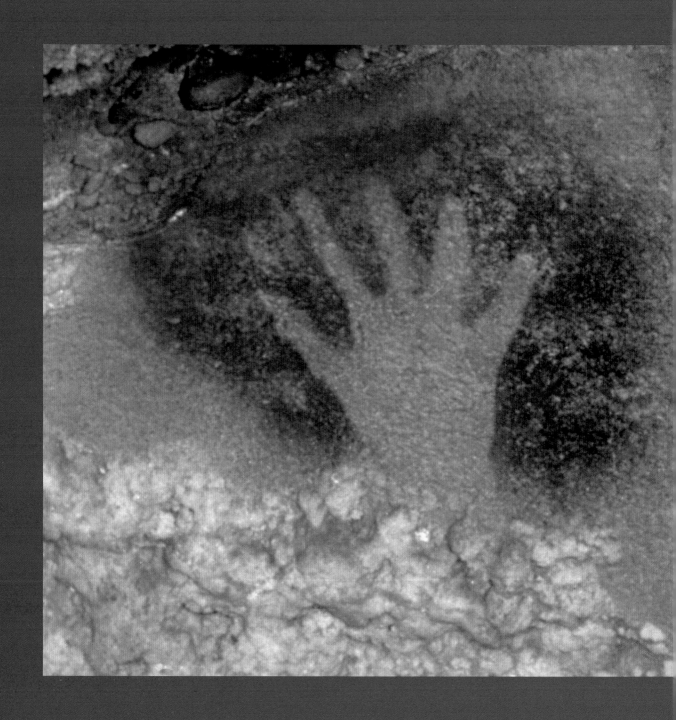

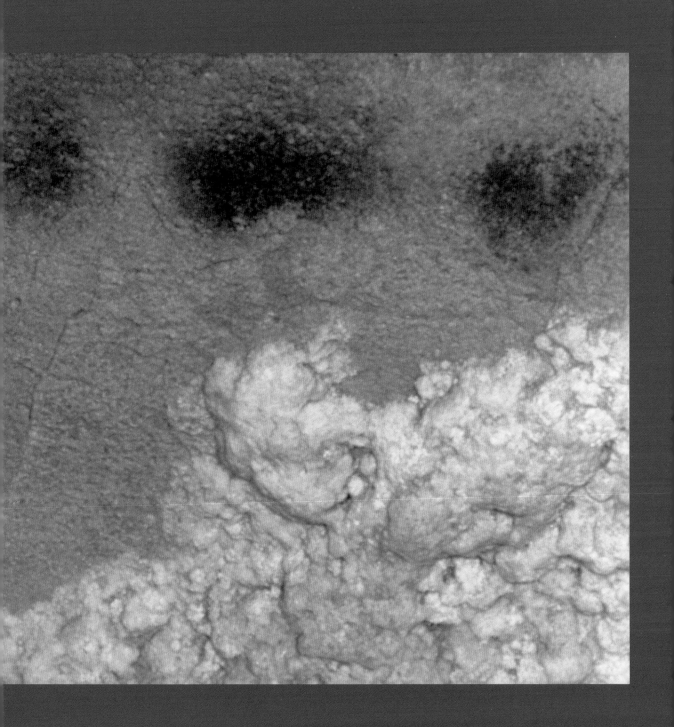

Prehistory

ATLANTIC

Rhine

Danube

Vogelherd/Hohle Fels/
Hohlenstein-Stadel

Willendorf

ALPS

Rhône

Danube

Laussel
Lascaux

Pech Merle
Ardèche
Chauvet

La Madeleine

Altamira

PYRENEES

APENNINES

BALKANS

MEDITERRANEAN

Addaura

SICILY

Artifact

Cave

Cave painting

Rock engravings

Historical development
ca. 2,000,000–10,000 BCE
The Paleolithic (Old Stone Age),
the longest period of prehistory.
Its latest phase is

ca. 40,000–10,000 BCE known as
the Upper Paleolithic period.
This is subdivided into several
sub-phases named after important
sites in France.

ca. 38,000–28,000 BCE The Aurigna-
cian period. Art includes the Venus
of Hohle Fels, mammoth and horse
figures from Vogelherd, and the Lion
Man found at Höhenstein-Stadel.

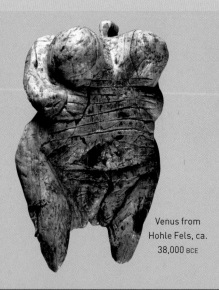

Venus from
Hohle Fels, ca.
38,000 BCE

Mammoth from Vogelherd, ca. 33,000 BCE

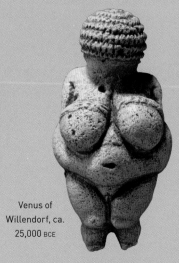

Venus of
Willendorf, ca.
25,000 BCE

40,000

35,000

30,000

Prehistory (40,000–5500 BCE)

The Origins of Art

Early humans first made stone tools over 2 million years ago in Africa, and later in other regions as well. They were made to help them survive. The Paleolithic period (Old Stone Age) of prehistory includes all phases of human activity prior to the development of writing and founding of the first cities. It ended ca. 10,000 BCE, depending on the region. The final phase is called the Upper Paleolithic period (ca. 40,000 - 10,000 BCE), which began toward the end of the last ice age. The Neanderthal populations "disappeared" around this time. According to finds from a cave in Swabia, southwestern Germany, the evolved, creative prehistoric period dominated by *Homo sapiens sapiens* began suddenly. Using sharpened flints and scrapers, the inhabitants of the cave fashioned the small bone figures that are the earliest known examples of artistic expression. Later, extensive series of cave paintings executed with exceptional technique and high aesthetic values appeared in what is known as the Franco-Cantabrian triangle, ranging from southwestern France to northern Spain. These might well excite more fascination and wonder today than at the time of their creation, when the audience for some of them presumably consisted of the painter alone. This was the first time that humans stepped outside basic survival activities and created objects and pictures of past events, like a hunt. This reflection of their own dealings with the world foreshadows future creative endeavors, marking the beginning of a long series of artistic development that continues today.

ca. 28,000–20,000 BCE Gravettian period. Art includes the Venus of Willendorf, Chauvet Cave, Pech Merle, France.
ca. 20,000–14,000 BCE Solutréan period, the first rock engravings
ca. 16,000–10,000 BCE Magdalénian period. Bison from La Madeleine, Lascaux and Altamira caves

ca. 8000–5500 BCE The Mesolithic period. The first complex cultures begin to form.

The first historical period begins **ca. 5500–2300 BCE** with the Neolithic period (New Stone Age). The Neolithic revolution marks the transition between pre- and proto-historical times. Complex civilizations develop in Mesopotamia and Egypt. Writing develops in the fourth millennium, and written transmission of information begins.
ca. 4000–2000 BCE The Megalithic cultures flourish, marked by monumental arrangements of monolithic stone blocks.

Red cow and horses, Lascaux, ca. 16,000-12,000 BCE

Figure group from Addaura, ca. 8000 BCE

20,000   10,000   5500

At a Glance

◁ **Venus from Hohle Fels**, Swabia, south-western Germany, ca. 38,000 BCE. Mammoth ivory, ca. 2½ in (6 cm). Institute for Prehistory, Protohistory and Medieval Archaeology, Tübingen University. Found in 2008, this small figure is the oldest sculpture in the world.

▷ **Venus of Willendorf**, Austria, ca. 25, 000 BCE. Limestone, 4½ in (11.5 cm). Museum of Natural History, Vienna. Traces of color indicate that the figure was once painted.

Women and Goddesses

Figures dating to the Paleolithic period were made by Homo sapiens who immigrated to Europe some 40,000 years ago. Many of these figures are women, and in most of these representations, the sculptors emphasize the essential physiology. As with animal representations, it is important to make the figures easily recognizable. With human figures, however, it is not the species that needs to be clear, but the parts of the body that have to do with fertility. That said, gender characteristics are not the only aspects given attention. Details like the hairstyle are also carefully rendered. Whether all these female figures are also fertility idols remains unclear. Gestures and attributes can aid in interpretation. The female figure from Laussel holds her hand over her belly, a gesture that has clear and complex symbolic meaning. Very likely an early mother goddess, she holds a bison horn shaped like a crescent moon with thirteen gouges, perhaps indicating a lunar calendar or some other kind of cycle. At first, there seemed to be no particular system for human representation. Images showing action and movement only appeared at the very end of the Paleolithic period, and then as rock engravings.

▷ **Figure group from Addaura Cave**, Monte Pelligrino, Sicily, ca. 8000 BCE. The figures are ca. 10–15 in (25–38 cm) tall. Carved with clear, strong lines, the engraved figures from Addaura are much more naturalistic and active than earlier sculptures. Dating to the very beginning of the Mesolithic period, their dance-like movements may represent a ritual event.

◁ **Mother goddess from Laussel**, Drodogne, France, ca. 23,000 BCE, 18½ in (47 cm) tall, sculpted in high relief. Musée d'Aquitaine, Bordeaux

△ **Mammoth from Vogelherd Cave**, Swabia, southwestern Germany, ca. 33,000 BCE. Mammoth ivory, ca. 1½ in (4 cm) long. Institute for Prehistory, Protohistory and Medieval Archaeology, Tübingen University. This is the oldest sculpture of an animal in the world. The eyelet between the mammoth's front legs suggests that it was once worn as an amulet.

▷ **Lion man from Höhenstein-Stadel Cave**, Swabia, southwestern Germany, ca. 30,000 BCE. Mammoth ivory, 11½ in (29.6 cm) tall. Ulm Museum. Zoomorphic human figure or anthropomorphic animal?

▷ **Bison from La Madeleine**, France, ca. 12,000 BCE. Reindeer horn, 4 in (10.2 cm) wide. Musée des Antiquités Nationales, Saint-Germain-en-Laye. Although this is a sculpture in the round, the artist rendered this bison in motion using relief sculpture techniques that incorporate the natural features of the horn.

Hunted Animals and Mythological Creatures

The skilled hands of Homo sapiens sapiens produced naturalistic images of animals as well as women. Subsistence was based on the hunt, and the animal figures reflect early man's belief in hunting magic. Did they ensure their luck on the hunt with self-made mammoth amulets, or did they gain power over animals via amulets made by someone else?

The question remains open. Many of the figures have gouges representing wounds. Perhaps these were models used to teach hunting skills, or were stand-ins with the power to conjure up the real thing.

Composite animal-human figures can be interpreted in two ways. One of the earliest preserved is the lion man. Did the hunter or shaman who carved it acquire the speed and power of the lion? The piece is carved from mammoth ivory, not a lion bone, so the image alone must be enough. Could this be a god represented in the form of an animal? Composite creatures are common in many cultures, from Egypt and ancient Greece to the present.

Lascaux

The paintings discovered in the caves of Lascaux in the Dordogne region of France in 1940 have been dated from between 16,000 and 12,000 BCE. Since many of the paintings are located in the least accessible corners of the caves, the images must have served as more than mere decoration, especially since people only lingered in the frontmost sections of caves or under overhanging rocks while on the hunt.

As with the ivory figures, they were likely intended to magically invoke success in future hunts, even if a place of complete darkness seems odd for that purpose. The colors consist of mineral-rich soil with iron oxide, while black is manganese oxide and charcoal. Binding agents are animal blood and fat. The paintings were made with bare hands, or with a stick in hard-to-reach spots.

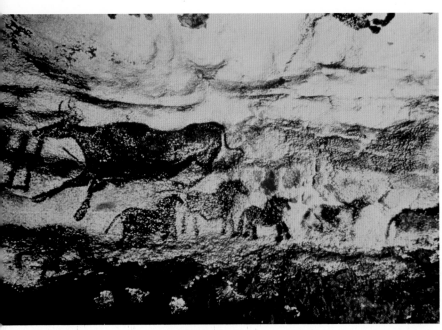

△ Cow and small horses, Lascaux, France. A leaping cow flees from danger, while the horses stand calmly beneath her. As is often the case with cave paintings, the individual motifs cannot be understood as parts of larger compositions.

Chauvet Cave

In 1994, Jean-Marie Chauvet discovered the oldest cave paintings known so far in the Ardeche Valley of southern France. The painted cave named after him dates to ca. 28,000 BCE, and is distinguished by its naturalistic representations of rhinos, lions, bears and horses.

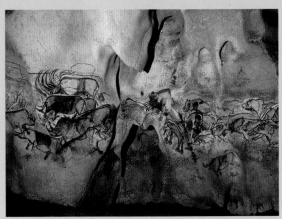

◁ **Unicorn and horse, Lascaux,** France, Hall of the Bulls. The spotted unicorn seems odd in a cave noted for its overwhelmingly naturalistic depictions of animals. The antenna-like projections on its head suggest it was a mythological creature.

△ **Red cow and horse, Lascaux,** France, Ceiling of the Axial Gallery. From the imposing figure of the red cow onward, each animal comes across first and foremost as an individual work of art. Indications of plant life suggest cattle grazing in a meadow.

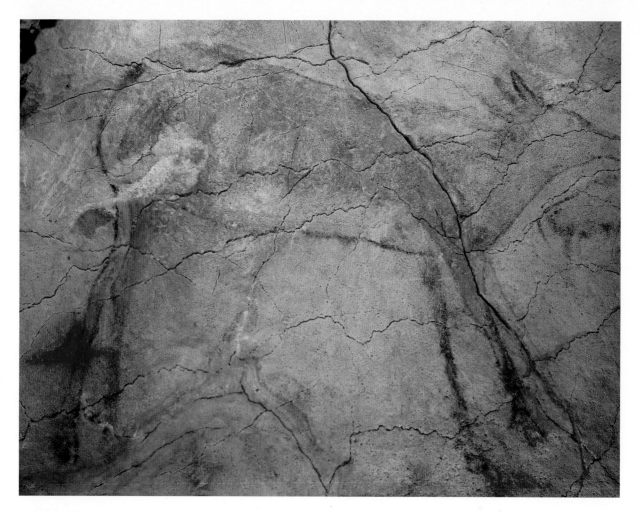

Altamira

Although known since 1868, the cave paintings of Altamira, located in the Cantabrian region of northern Spain, have only been systematically investigated since 1979. As is the case with all cave paintings, their authenticity was at first doubted. The skillful rendering and high degree of preservation—the latter due to the utter inaccessibility of the paintings for centuries as well as the mineral content of the pigments—made an ancient date seem impossible. What some perceive at Altamira as a Stone Age interest in abstraction continues to ignite controversy.

What one person might think is simply not possible for a Stone Age painter is celebrated by another as an archetype of modern art, in the same lineage as Picasso's images of bulls, making Altamira the site of the birth of art itself. Although images like the Altamira bulls can be found all over the world, they tend to be rare, chance discoveries where any interpretation of the intentions of the artist and function of the images amounts to pure speculation—and there is always plenty of that to go around.

◁ + △ **Bison and doe, Altamira Cave,** Spain, ca. 16,000-14,000 BCE, Great Hall. Each of the animals depicted on the roof of the great hall is in a different pose, demonstrating the different stages of the hunt. Perhaps hunters used the painting to mentally prepare for the experience, or perhaps it was used to pass on skills to young boys. The tendency to paint over earlier figures without any reference to the complete composition suggests that the individual figures were most important.

Mesopotamia

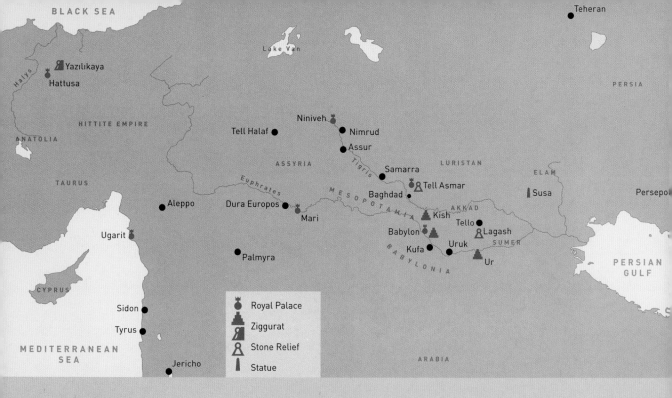

BLACK SEA

Teheran

Lake Van

PERSIA

Yazılıkaya
Hattusa

Halys

HITTITE EMPIRE

ANATOLIA

Niniveh
Nimrud
Tell Halaf
Assur

ASSYRIA

Samarra

LURISTAN

Tigris

ELAM

TAURUS

Euphrates

MESOPOTAMIA

Tell Asmar

Susa

Baghdad

Persepol

Aleppo

Dura Europos

AKKAD

Mari

Kish

Tello

Babylon

Lagash

Ugarit

Kufa

Uruk

SUMER

BABYLONIA

Ur

Palmyra

PERSIAN
GULF

CYPRUS

ARABIA

Sidon

Tyrus

MEDITERRANEAN
SEA

Jericho

🏰	Royal Palace
🔺	Ziggurat
🗿	Stone Relief
▮	Statue

Chronology

ca. 3700–3500 BCE The Tell Halaf culture

ca. 3500–3200 BCE Early Sumerian period; Uruk period; cuneiform writing develops

ca. 3200–2400 BCE Early Dynastic period; first dynasty of Kish in Sumeria

ca. 2400–2200 BCE Akkadian Empire; reign of Sargon I from ca. 2334–2279 BCE

ca. 2200–2000 BCE Neo-Sumerian empire; reign of Gudea from ca. 2144–2124 BCE

ca. 2000–1800 BCE First Babylonian dynasty: reign of Hammurabi (ca. 1930–1888 BCE)

Votive figurine, Tell Asmar, Iraq, ca. 3000 BCE

Cylinder seal and imprint showing a hunting scene, Iraq, 2250–2150 BCE

Gudea, Telloh, Iraq, ca. 2200 BCE

3700   3000   2500   2000

Mesopotamia (3700–332 BCE)

Culture in the Fertile Crescent

Like the Nile Valley, the Fertile Crescent attracted settlers from the earliest times. Between the Tigris and Euphrates, the two great rivers that flow from the Anatolian highlands into the Persian Gulf, villages grew into city-states, and then into the highly developed societies that characterized the entire region. Like its archrival Egypt, Mesopotamia was among the earliest of the advanced civilizations. It is considered one of the primary sources of European culture. The Sumerians laid the foundations of this civilization in the fourth millennium BCE around the southern Mesopotamian city of Uruk. Subsequently, various ethnic and linguistic groups would establish the empires of Akkadia, Babylon, and Assyria. Always in contest with each other for highly prized areas of settlement, these states succeeded each other in establishing their dominion over the entire area. The cultural identities of these empires thus became so interwoven that they cannot be observed independently from one another. In addition, their governmental structures were similar, with religiously legitimized god-kings wielding power. Mesopotamia's relations with the Hittite empire on its northwestern borders were especially close; both civilizations used the same system of writing, and on Mesopotamia's northern edge, territories with overlapping borders were consensually ruled by both powers. There were also points of contact with the Elamites and the Persians, who lived in what is today Iran. Between 539 and 332 BCE, a satrap of the Persian Empire ruled the region. Alexander the Great crossed the Tigris and Euphrates in 331 BCE, and took Babylon the next year. After his death, the territories he conquered were split up into the kingdoms of the Diadochi. Among these was the Seleucid empire, which extended from the Indus Valley to the Mediterranean, and which remained a power in the region into the second century BCE.

ca. 1800–1200 BCE Hittite empire; its capital is Hattusa
ca. 1520–1270 BCE Kingdom of Mitanni in northen Mesopotamia
ca. 1380–909 BCE Middle Assyrian empire

ca. 909–625 BCE Neo-Assyrian empire; reign of Ashurbanipal from 668–631 BCE
ca. 625–539 BCE Neo-Babylonian empire; reign of Nebuchadnezzar II from 604–562 BCE

ca. 539–332 BCE Cyrus the Great (559–529 BCE) conquers Babylon; Persian (Achaemenid) Empire
ca. 332 BCE Alexander the Great (336–323 BCE) conquers Babylon.
from 312 BCE Seleucid empire

Lion Gate, Hattusa, Turkey, fourteenth–thirteenth century BCE

Lioness Devouring an African, Nimrud, Iraq, eighth century BCE

Terrace Relief, Persepolis, Iran, sixth–fifth century BCE

1500   1000   500   300

At a Glance

Votive figurine, Tell Asmar, ca. 3000 BCE. National Museum of Iraq, Baghdad

Votive statues

Statues of standing or kneeling figures were placed in temples to "pray" for those who commissioned them.

Standard of Mari, 2500–2400 BCE

Standards

Ivory, mother-of-pearl, lapis lazuli and other stone inlays on wood panels and boxes, found in royal tombs.

Cuneiform

Developed by the Sumerians, this writing system insured Mesopotamia's economic and cultural preeminence (see p. 46). The illustration shows the evolution of cuneiform from pictograms: 1. steer; 2. grain; 3. person; 4. woman; 5. mountains; 6. woman + mountains = slave woman; 7. head.

1				
2				
3				
4				
5				
6				
7				

Hanging Gardens of Semiramis

Upon his marriage to a Median princess, Nebuchadnezzar II decided to welcome his new bride to the drab plain of the Euphrates with a reminder of the forested mountains of her homeland. The Hanging Gardens that bore her name, presumably terrace-like beds of vegetation surmounting powerful layers of columns and arches, was one of the Seven Wonders of the Ancient World.

Johann Georg Schmidt, *The Hanging Gardens of Babylon*. Copperplate, ca. 1730

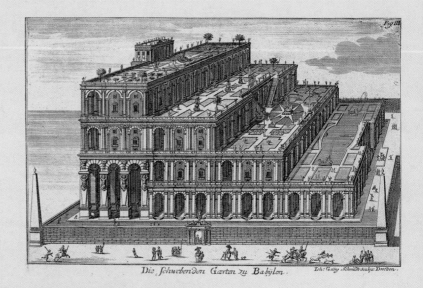

Die schwebenden Gaerten zu Babylon.

Mesopotamia (3700–332 BCE)

Ziggurat

The typical ziggurat was built out of mud bricks and consisted of several layers of construction, culminating in a temple. Priests and priest-kings could thus elevate themselves, approaching the level the gods. The ramps of the ziggurat of Ur (ca. 2100 BCE) have been preserved. The concept of an architecture that strives for the heavens—the realm of the gods—and the hubris manifest in this style is reflected in the Old Testament story of the Tower of Babel (Genesis 11).

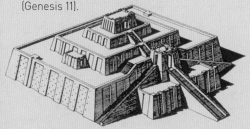

Reconstruction of the Ziggurat of Ur

Coronation of a King, copy of a mural from the Palace of Mari, eighteenth century BCE

Murals

The most significant murals still extant are from the Sumerian palace at Mari (eighteenth century BCE).

Guard lion, Hittite

Guard statues

Guard statues were usually placed before city gates and walls, taking the form of monumental animals or composite beings made of ceramic or stone.

Orthostats

Orthostats are upright stone slabs covered with reliefs, and were intended to protect the wall and building foundations made mostly of unbaked mud bricks.

Glazed bricks

Sometimes decorated with relief and color, glazed bricks were used to protect and ornament palace and city walls, especially in Assyrian and Neo-Babylonian architecture. One of the most famous examples is the Ishtar Gate of Babylon, now in the Pergamon Museum in Berlin (see below).

Lion from the Ishtar Gate, Babylon, ca. 604–562 BCE

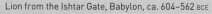

Victory Stele of Naram-Sin, ca. 2300 BCE

Steles

Steles are upright stones decorated with reliefs and/or inscriptions.

Key Terms

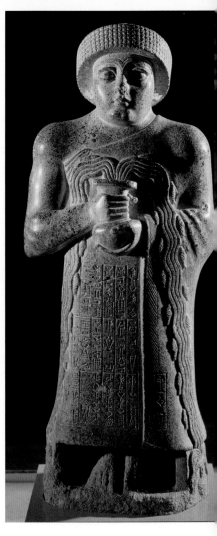

Sumer and Akkad

Oversized, wide-open eyes with a fixed gaze characterize the statuary of early Sumer (ca. 3000 BCE), the first great civilization of the Fertile Crescent. Perhaps it is a stylized means of depicting the all-seeing or clairvoyant powers of those represented, who were perhaps addressed as idols or gods. If the figures were meant to represent people, placed in temples to pray in lieu of the patrons who commissioned them, then their gaze might be intended to depict the fervor of their belief.

Around 2200 BCE, Neo-Sumerian art shows a more direct relationship with the real world, with portrait statues of princes and kings, their deeds described on their bodies in cuneiform. The Akkadians, who established the first great empire between the Tigris and Euphrates, discovered the narrative advantages of bas-relief. This art form was perfectly suited to depicting rulers' heroic deeds on steles, works meant to celebrate and solidify the power of the Akkadian empire.

△ **Gudea Holding the Vase from Which Flow the Waters of Fertility**, Telloh, Iraq, ca. 2200 BCE. Dolerite, 24¾ in (63 cm) high. Musée du Louvre, Paris.
Inscriptions on the robe praise the deeds of Gudea, *Ensi* ("Prince") of Lagash.

▽ **Votive Figurine Holding a Vase** (detail), Tell Asmar, Iraq, ca. 3000 BCE. Alabaster, hair and beard blackened with bitumen, eyes made from mussel shells and black limestone in bitumen, 28⅜ in (72 cm) high. National Museum of Iraq, Baghdad

▷ **Victory Stele of Naram-Sin**, Susa, Iran, ca. 2300 BCE. Sandstone, 78¾ in (200 cm) high. Musée du Louvre, Paris.

This stele depicts Naram-Sin, King of Akkad (ca. 2300 BCE), subjugating the Lullubi people of the Iranian border region. It is unclear if the three stars are meant to symbolize deities. When the Elamite king Shutruk-Nakhunte II (ruled 1185–1155 BCE) sacked Akkad, the stele was part of the war booty he took back to Susa. There, the original inscription was replaced with one in the Elamite language.

Babylon and Ashur

At the beginning of the second millennium BCE, Hammurabi secured Babylon's ascendancy in Mesopotamia, making his city the center of a powerful state. This turn of events marked the genesis of a Babylo-Assyrian iconography of power, with the lion playing the main role. The image of the lion attacking its prey symbolizes the ruler defeating his enemy. At the same time, the ruler enjoys the privilege of hunting the lion, which his divinely ordained power him alone permits to kill. After the fall of Ashur, the Neo-Babylonian empire under Nebuchadnezzar II (seventh century BCE) became the most magnificent city in the world. The lion dominated the arts here as well: sixty of them parade as guard animals along the processional way that leads to the Ishtar Gate (today in Berlin's Pergamon Museum).

▽ **Lioness Devouring an African**, Nimrud, eighth century BCE. Ivory, gold, colored stones, ca. 2⅜ in (6 cm) high. National Museum of Iraq, Baghdad

◁ **Lion from the Processional Way**, Babylon, ca. 570 BCE. Glazed brick, ca. 78¾ in (200 cm) long. The Metropolitan Museum of Art, New York

△ **Lion Hunt**, Relief from the palace of Ashurbanipal, Nineveh, ca. 645 BCE. Alabaster, ca. 61¾ in (157 cm) high. The British Museum, London

Babylonian Mythology

The oldest extant poetry in the world was composed between the Tigris and Euphrates around 2500 BCE. It is the *Epic of Gilgamesh*, the mythical king of Uruk. His (not always) heroic deeds and the search for immortality that leads him into the underworld are preserved in different versions on clay tablets. The eleventh tablet tells of a catastrophic flood reminiscent of the biblical story of Noah. In the Old Testament, the Babylon of Nebuchadnezzar II is reviled as the city of sacrilege and moral degradation, although it was in reality the cultural and scientific center of a highly civilized state. But Nebuchadnezzar II had conquered Jerusalem and forcibly resettled segments of the ruling class, an act which—as is known today—was falsely perceived as slavery. With the Tower of Babylon, the Bible presents a timeless story of man's hubris that has inspired artists into the Modern era.

◁ **Gilgamesh, Subduer of Lions**, Palace of Sargon II of Ashur in Khorsabad/Nineveh, Iraq, ca. 710 BCE. Alabaster, 185 in (470 cm) high. Musée du Louvre, Paris. This relief of Gilgamesh originally stood between two winged bulls with men's heads at the entrance of the Assyrian palace.

▷ Pieter Bruegel the Elder, **The Tower of Babel**, 1563. Oil on wood, 45 x 61 in (114 x 155 cm). Kunsthistorisches Museum, Vienna

Cuneiform, Clay Tablets, and Cylinder Seals

The Sumerians' most significant invention was the cuneiform writing system (ca. 3000 BCE). Originally derived from pictograms, the characters developed through abstraction into ideograms, phonograms, and determiners. Using wedge-shaped wood styluses, scribes pressed the characters into soft clay tablets that were subsequently dried and baked. Thus were contracts, laws, scientific treatises, and poetry recorded and preserved. Cuneiform was also used to write in other languages, among them Hittite.

Cylinder seals were made of stone and most often inscribed with images of animals and people. They were pressed into and rolled across soft clay, serving as personal seals for contracts and trade documents.

Baked clay tablet with cuneiform writing

Cylinder seal with imprint
showing a hunting scene,
Iraq, 2250–2150 BCE

The Hittites

Roughly contemporaneous with the Babylonians (at the beginning of the second millennium BCE), the Hittites rose to power in Anatolia, eventually expanding their territorial holdings into northern Mesopotamia and Syria. The site of their capital at Hattusa, founded around 1650 BCE, is located near the modern Turkish village of Boğazkale. Hattusa possessed monumental temples and palaces, and was later protected by a mighty city wall, one of whose gates is guarded by an enormous pair of lions. The most significant find at Hattusa was a state archive consisting of about 3000 cuneiform clay tablets documenting the lively trade relations between the Hittites and Egypt in the fourteenth and thirteenth centuries BCE. During the reign of King Tudhaliya IV (ca. 1250–1220 BCE), the rock sanctuary of Yazılıkaya with its two roofless chambers was decorated with reliefs. To date there are no known documents attesting to the purpose of this natural sanctuary, first dedicated in the fifteenth century BCE. One can only assume that New Year's and spring festivals were celebrated here under the open sky and the gaze of the gods depicted in procession (sixty-six in Chamber A alone).

◁ **Lion Gate of Hattusa**, Anatolia, fourteenth–thirteenth century BCE. Limestone. Apart from the Lion Gate (seen here from outside the city wall), the King's Gate has also survived into the present. It shows a warrior in mid-stride.

▷+◁ **Tudhaliya IV with the God Sharruma / Procession of the Twelve Gods.** Stone reliefs in Chamber B in the rock sanctuary of Yazılıkaya, ca. 1250–1220 BCE

◁ **Enthroned Goddess with Child**, Anatolia, fourteenth–thirteenth century BCE. Gold, 1¾ in (4.3 cm) high. The Metropolitan Museum of Art, New York. This representation recollects statues of the Egyptian goddess Isis, usually depicted with a solar disc over her head and the child Horus on her lap.

Persepolis

When the Persians under Cyrus the Great took the city of Susa in 539 BCE, the state of Elam, which had flourished in southwestern Iran since ca. 2400 BCE, ceased to exist. Shortly thereafter, the construction of Persepolis began under Darius I (reigned 522–486 BCE). The first building project was the raising of a great terrace. It was on this artificially created level surface that the palaces of Darius and Xerxes, as well as a great throne room, were built. It is not known if this palace complex ever served as a residence, or if it was intended solely as a venue for the games of the New Year's festival. The great processional reliefs commissioned by Darius and his successors for the outer walls and stairways could support either interpretation.

△ **Relief showing fighting animals**, Stairway to the so-called Tripylon, a small gatehouse in the center of the terrace, Persepolis, Iran, sixth–fifth century BCE

▷ **Lion rython**, Hamadan, west-central Iran, 500–450 BCE. Gold, 8¾ in (22.3 cm) high; diameter of opening 5 in (12.8 cm); 2 lbs (892 g). National Museum of Iran, Teheran

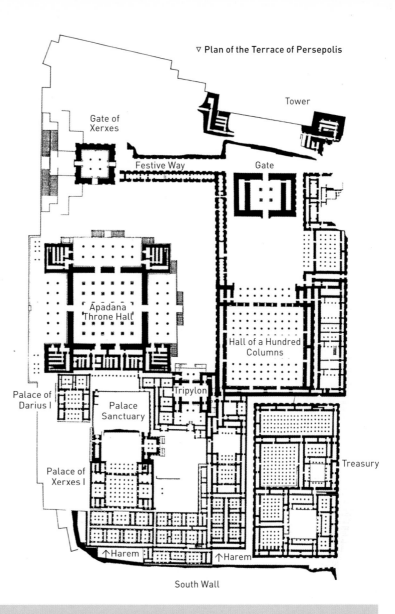

▽ Plan of the Terrace of Persepolis

Tower

Gate of
Xerxes

Festive Way

Gate

Apadana
'Throne Hall'

Hall of a Hundred
Columns

Tripylon

Palace of
Darius I

Palace
Sanctuary

Palace of
Xerxes I

Treasury

↑Harem

↑Harem

South Wall

Gold Tableware of the Persians

Drinking horns ("rytha") with sculpturally realized mythical animals on the base were commonly produced in the Near East from the first millennium BCE until into the Islamic period. The size of the golden drinking vessel and its rich ornamentation of lotus blossoms and palmettes indicate that it most likely belonged to the royal tableware. The front half of a winged lion's body has been soldered onto the actual cup. The lion's facial expression, as well as the richly detailed mane and curved feathers show an exceptionally high standard of artistic skill.

Ancient Egypt

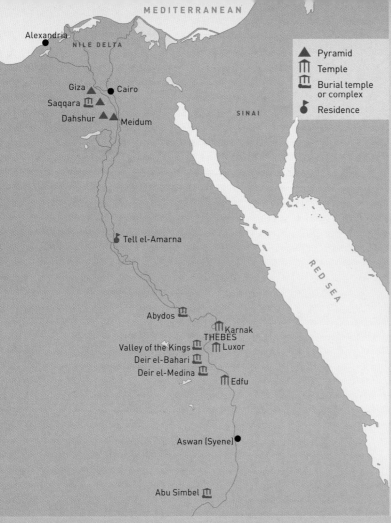

Legend:

▲ Pyramid
🏛 Temple
🏛 Burial temple or complex
🏺 Residence

Art for the Afterlife

No other advanced civilization ever lasted as long as that of ancient Egypt. This accounts for the vast number of art objects that survive. The great majority of these come from tombs and are closely related to ancient Egyptian concepts of the afterlife, which remained essentially unchanged over thousands of years. This also explains why Egyptian art itself changed surprisingly little over such a long stretch of time. The portion of Egyptian art which was not intended for the living resisted change, so as not to endanger the deceased in the afterlife. How members of the nobility decorated their villas in this life remains virtually unknown. Art for the gods was also largely tied to tradition. Their images and those of their sons, the pharaohs, always followed the same ideal. The only exception was Akhenaten (1365–1348 BCE), the "heretic king," who abolished all the gods with the exception of the sun god. In the light of Aten, which took the form of a solar disk, Akhenaten was endowed with almost individual traits.

Narmer Palette (front), ca. 2950 BCE. Slate, ca. 25 in (64 cm) high. Egyptian Museum, Cairo

Prince Rahotep and his wife Nofret, ca. 2500 BCE

Grazing and hunting scenes, ca. 2350 BCE. Saqqara, tomb of Nefer and Kahai

3000   2500   2000

Ancient Egypt (3000–332 BCE)

Chronology

ca. 3150–3000 BCE Predynastic

ca. 3000–2665 BCE Early Period (dynasties 1–2). Menes, 1st king of the first dynasty, is credited with inventing writing, founding Memphis, and uniting the empire. Later kings wore a striped head scarf to honor him.

2665–1991 BCE Old Empire and First Intermediate Period (dynasties 3–11)

ca. 2620–2600 BCE Djoser (2nd king, dynasty 3) commissions the Step Pyramid at Saqqara.

ca. 2570–2545 BCE Snofru (1st king, dynasty 4), builds the Bent and Red Pyramids.

2545–2520 BCE Cheops (2nd king, dynasty 4)

ca. 2510–2485 BCE Chephren (4th king, dynasty 4)

ca. 2485–2457 BCE Menkaura (6th king, dynasty 4): he, Chephren, and Cheops commission the Pyramids of Giza.

after 2155 BCE Collapse of the Old Empire. In the First Intermediate Period, the country splits: the northern kingdom has its capital in Memphis, the southern capital is near Thebes.

ca. 2040 BCE Successful reunification under Mentuhotep II.

1991–1554/44 BCE Middle Kingdom and Second Intermediate Period (dynasties 12–17)

1991–1971/62 BCE Amenehet I (1st king, dynasty 12) founds a new capital near Memphis; Thebes remains the center of the Cult of Amun. During the Second Intermediate Period, Asian mercenary leader Schalik occupies the capital near Memphis in ca. 1650 BCE. Hyksos (EN: foreign) rule lasts about 100 years.

1554/44–1080 BCE New Kingdom (dynasties 18–20)

1529/26–1508/05 BCE Amenophis I (2nd king, dynasty 18)

1508/05–1493 BCE Thutmose I (3rd king, dynasty 18.): the Valley of the Kings begins with his tomb.

1488–1470/68 BCE Hatshepsut (5th king, dynasty 18)

1365–1348 BCE Amenophis IV/Akhenaten (10th king, dynasty 18) and his queen, Nefertiti. Akhenaten decrees the sun, Aten, the only god and founds a new capital, el-Amarna.

1345–1327 BCE Tutankhamun (12th king, dynasty 18)

1290–1224 BCE Ramses II (2nd king, dynasty 19). His reign is long, his building activities extensive (Abu Simbel, among others).

ca. 1080 to 714/12 BCE Third Intermediate Period (dynasties 21–24). Egypt comes under Libyan and Nubian rule from time to time.

713/12–332 BCE Late Period (dynasties 25–30). The First Persian Domination begins with Cambyses in **525 BCE** (27th dynasty), lasts until ca.

404 BCE Second Persian Domination from 342 to 332 BCE.

332 BCE–395 CE Greco-Roman Period

332–305 BCE Egypt becomes a province within the empire of Alexander the Great.

305–30 BCE The Ptolemaic dynasty (51–30 BCE: Cleopatra VII)

30 BCE Roman domination begins under Emperor Octavian.

Death mask of Tutankhamun, ca. 1345 BCE

Rock temple of Ramses II, Abu Simbel, 13th century BCE

Vizier as scribe, ca. 500 BCE

1500   1300   1000   300

At a Glance

Luxor: Temple of Amun-Mut-Khonsu, view of Ramses II Pylon

Temples

These were built not only for gods, but also for kings, who became gods after death. The most important was the Temple of Amun at Karnak, a complex that was augmented by various kings from the Middle Kingdom through the Late Period. Other well-known temples include Amun-Mut-Khonsu in Luxor (Amenophis III), Abu Simbel (Ramses II), and the Temple of Horus in Edfu (Ptolemy III).

Cartouche

These included the names of royalty rendered in hieroglyphics. The oval or circular loop was a symbol for "all that orbits the sun."

Hieroglyphic cartouche of Ramses II

Pharaoh

The Egyptian king was only called a pharaoh (literally: royal palace) from ca. 1000 BCE onwards. In the Early Period, "Horus names" identified kings as earthly representatives of the sky god. They later carried the name, "Son of Re," who was the sun god.

Djoser, the oldest monumental statue of a pharaoh (detail)

The Ebers Papyrus

The main source of ancient Egyptian medical knowledge was written ca. 1520 BCE, during the ninth year of the reign of Amenophis I. The papyrus, acquired in 1873 by Egyptologist George Ebers, is mostly a collection of remedies and formulas.

Cosmetic Palettes

The depression on the front held ceremonial make-up. Like the Narmer Palette (see p. 54), these also recounted the deeds of the pharaoh. Front: interlacing mythical beasts as a symbol of unification. Reverse: defeat of an enemy.

Ship of the Dead

After death, the deceased mounted the barque of the sun god and undertook the dangerous journey to eternal life. His earthly life would be judged in the process.

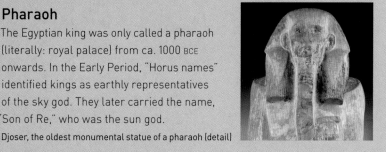

Reverse side of the Narmer Palette

Geography

The curvature of the earth was calculated between Aswan and Alexandria. Eratosthenes, head of the Great Library at Alexandria around 240 BCE, knew that on June 21 at noon, the sun would stand directly above the surface of the water in a well at Syene near Aswan, whereas an obelisk would cast a shadow in Alexandria. He realized this was only possible if the earth was spherical. Using the distance between Alexandria and Syene, and measuring the angle of the sun's shadow, he calculated the earth's circumference with remarkable precision.

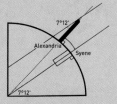

Ancient Egypt (3000–332 BCE)

Pyramids

These are mastabas resting on a rectangular base that decrease in size as they are stacked atop one another, as can be seen in the Step Pyramid at Saqqara. It was built by Imhotep for King Djoser in ca. 2600 BCE. The design of these tombs, reserved for kings of the Old Kingdom, reached its peak in the Pyramids of Giza (▷). Pyramids are not enclosed spaces, but monumental artificial burial mounds that represent the primeval mound upon which the creator god once brought the world into being. The grave chambers lie beneath or within the pyramid.

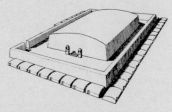

Abydos: Meryneith's mastaba tomb, ca. 2900 BCE

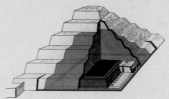

Saqqara: section drawing of the Step Pyramid of Djoser

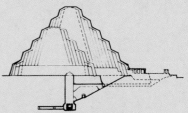

Saqqara: Step Pyramid of Djoser, cross-sectional view

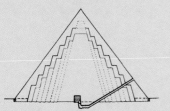

Meidum: Step Pyramid of Huni, ca. 2670 BCE

Dahshur: Bent Pyramid of Snofru, ca. 2650 BCE

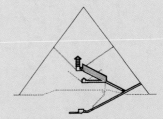

Giza: Pyramid of Cheops, ca. 2580 BCE

Mastabas

These flat, rectangular structures were built above ground over smaller, subterranean burial grounds, accessible via vertical shafts. This basic form of tomb construction in the Early Period remained typical throughout the Old Kingdom. Important mastabas are found in Saqqara and Abydos.

Rock Tombs

Unlike their man-made counterparts, "natural pyramids" had the advantage of being hidden within the landscape, as in the Valley of the Kings. This should have ensured the eternal peace of the wealthy deceased in the New Kingdom—unfortunately it did not.

Grave chamber in the rock tomb of Tutankhamun in the Valley of the Kings

Key Terms

Pictorial Representation

Murals, painted bas-reliefs, and illustrated papyrus rolls tell us a great deal about the everyday life of the ancient Egyptians. They describe various artisanal activities, offer insight into the duties and pleasures of kings and high officials, and explain medical procedures and rituals. As vivid as the content is, the characters look stiff, their movements awkward. Were the artists incompetent? Not at all! The figures were simply depicted in a systematic way. The first rule

△+▷ **Papyrus harvesting, pastures and hunting scenes**, ca. 2350 BCE. Painted limestone relief, Saqqara (grave of Nefer and Kahai)

◁ **Scene from a book of the dead**, 715–332 BCE, Egyptian Museum, Berlin. The instructions and incantations were intended to help the deceased on their journey to life on the other side.

▷ **Scene from a book of the dead (papyrus roll)**, Egyptian Museum, Cairo. The soul of the deceased is weighed in the presence of Osiris.

was that of documentary clarity: the profiled head allowed the nose to show; the frontal eyes revealed the irises and pupils, the frontal torso revealed both shoulders, and the walking-position profiled legs revealed both feet. Clarity was the crucial point of these representations, and they were intended to help the tomb owner continue his earthly life, uninterrupted, on the other side. In one form or another, the tomb contained everything its owner would need in the afterlife. But he first had to reach the other side, and the tomb had many pictures to lead him safely there. What the owner of the tomb did not need in the afterlife was a grave. And that is why the subject of pyramid building was not covered. Egyptologists are therefore still forced to speculate about this.

Image and Text

Images in themselves were ineffective and only fulfilled their purpose with the addition of texts. In order for people, animals, and objects to materialize, they had to be spoken as incantations. The owner of the tomb had to be able to read them aloud. Thus, an important element of the funeral ceremony was the ritual opening of mouths of his mummy and other portraits. All texts were accessible to the Ba, comprising all of the tomb owner's non-physical personality, which moved freely both inside and outside the tomb. The Ba appeared as a bird with a human head. Only by keeping together the Ka and Akh (earthly and heavenly life forces), his shadow, and his name was it possible for the tomb owner to live forever.

Images of People

Full-length, sculpted depictions of people survive from both tombs and temples. They had specific functions, and their design was subordinate to these. That is why statues of kings did not represent individuals, but the institution of the monarchy itself. Its implacably idealized form became a symbol of continuity. The same applied to members of the royal family and to members of respected professions.

◁ **Ka-Aper, Priest and Official**, grave in Saqqara, ca. 2300 BCE, 43 ¼ in (110 cm) high. Egyptian Museum, Cairo. The statue was originally plastered and painted.

The scribe's formulaic posture also expressed abstract concepts, such as dignity and reliability. However, senior officials and priests could be shown standing or striding. A bit of a paunch or a double chin can be seen on figures of private individuals, because strict idealization was not mandatory in their case. Burial objects in the form of doll-like figures served to illustrate the various professions. Cube stools found in temples attested to a person's permission to participate passively in ritual activities.

△ **Woman grinding corn**, wood
▷ **The vizier Nespakashuti in the formal posture of a scribe**, Karnak, ca. 500 BCE
▷▷ **Chamberlain of Hatshepsut with his daughter**: cube stool used as an educational device, ca. 1490 BCE.

All of the above: Egyptian Museum, Cairo

△ **Great Sphinx of Giza** (ca. 2500 BCE): a lion's body with the head of the Pharaoh Khafre was intended to protect the tombs and temples. This figure also served to enhance the power of the king.

▷ **Prince Rahotep and his wife Nofret,** tomb at Meidum, ca. 2500 BCE. Egyptian Museum, Cairo

Animals of the Gods

Animals were predominantly shown in three dimensions. They were either honored as manifestations of deities or associated with gods through their behavioral patterns. They could serve as burial objects, votive offerings or amulets. Their form was always characterized by the careful observation of nature, which led to naturalistic interpretations and unerring reduction to essentials.

As the son of Amun, the king required special protection. And Horus, the falcon god of heaven and sky, took on that role beginning in the first dynasty. The Ibis was Thoth's animal,

△ Ibis, sacred animal of the god Thoth, ca. 600 BCE. Limestone and bronze, 13 ¼ in (34 cm) high. Egyptian Museum, Cairo

and he, as the god of science, historiography and chronology, was present at the Judgment of the Dead—so it was better not to anger him. The Apis bull represented fertility and generative power and was initially associated with the creator god Ptah. It was incumbent upon sphinxes (mythical lions with human heads) to keep watch in pairs at the sides of avenues or in front of portals. Very ancient hippopotamus figures are less easy to classify. Male animals embodied Seth, enemy of the gods, while females represented Thoeris, the protector goddess of pregnant women.

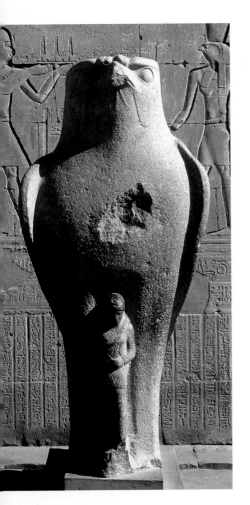

◁ The God Horus in the shape of a falcon, ca. 250 BCE. Courtyard of the Temple of Horus, Edfu

△ **The Lion of King Nectanebo I**, ca. 370 BCE. Rose granite, 77 ½ in (197 cm) high. Vatican Museums, Rome

▽ **Apis bull of the god Ptah**, Saqqara, ca. 600 BCE. Bronze, 12 in (31 cm) high. Egyptian Museum, Cairo

▽ **Hippopotamus**, faience with painted water plants, ca. 2000 BCE. Egyptian Museum, Cairo

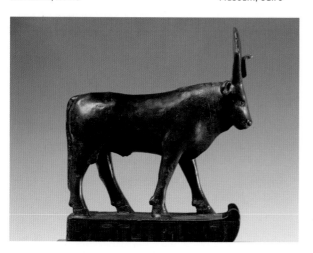

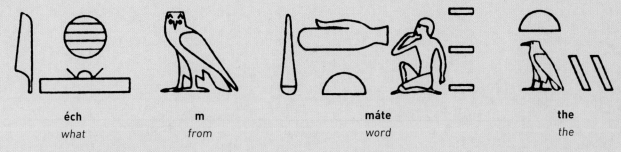

éch	m	máte	the
what	from	word	the

But What Does it Mean?

The discovery of the Rosetta Stone made it possible for Jean-Francois Champollion (1790–1832) to ultimately succeed in deciphering its hieroglyphics. But he first had to abandon the notion of picture-writing and understand that he was dealing with an alphabetical script. He started with the name Ptolemaios (Ptolemy), mentioned in the Greek text. He compared it to the same spot in the hieroglyphic text, and thus translated his first word. When combined with the equally verifiable translation of the name Cleopatra, he worked out the first letters.

By ca. 2000 BCE, when hieroglyphics had been in use for about 1000 years, they comprised about 700 characters. Many of these characters were letters, i.e., one, two, or three-consonant letters, as vowels were not written. Certain characters were determinatives that defined the preceding characters and could provide additional information about a pictograph. The signs could be read in various directions, and the direction in which animals or people were facing pointed to the beginning of the text.

Hieroglyphics were reserved almost exclusively for religious purposes. In tombs, the magical effect of the texts was so powerful that it awakened all the creatures portrayed. Ideographs in the form of dangerous animals such as snakes, therefore, were deliberately left incomplete so that the onset of magic did not bring them to life and allow them to cause harm.

The Hieroglyphic Alphabet

Hieroglyphic	Image and meaning	Romanization	Hieroglyphic	Image and meaning	Romanization
	vulture	a (aleph)		?	h (soft as in Houston)
	reed leaf	j		animal body with teats	h (seh)
	forearm	a		door latch	s (voiced: zero)
	quail chick	u		folded cloth	s (sharp, voiceless)
	leg	b		pond	s (seh)
	stool	p		sandbank	k (q or k)
	viper	f		basket	k(k)
	owl	m		jug stand	g
	water	n		loaf of bread	t
	mouth	r		rope	t (ch)
	courtyard	h		hand	d
	cord	h (gutteral ch)		cobra	d (dj or dge)

It was not mandatory for characters in the texts to be written one after another. Rather, they were nested according to the spatial and aesthetic aspects of words.

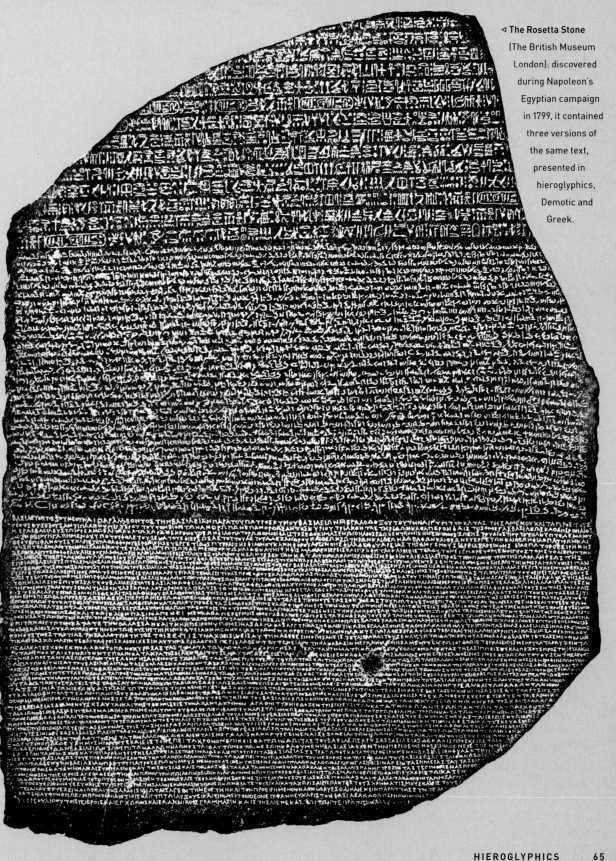

▷ **Statue of Hatshepsut in the form of the Sphinx**, ca. 1480 BCE, Egyptian Museum, Cairo: in contrast to the Sphinx of Giza, which is 1000 years older, the head of the ruler is no longer shown with the Menes headdress. The lion now has a human face and king's beard, surrounded by the mane.

Costuming

In order to prove her legitimacy and live up to the monarchical image, the controversial ruler of the eighteenth dynasty, Hatshepsut (1488–1470/68 BCE), had to be pictured with the same attributes and in the same posture as male rulers.

She commissioned a temple at Deir el-Bahri in honor of Amun and for her own cult of the dead. It was faced with columned halls that not only made it look like a step pyramid, but caused the steep cliff behind it to become a visual part of the architectural concept. The temple was not simply a building in front of a cliff, but the basis of the rock itself. The tomb of Hatshepsut was located in the Valley of the Kings (KV 20).

△ Wall painting in the Mortuary Temple of Hatshepsut: located beneath the vulture-goddess Mut, Hatshepsut's image was eradicated by her successor.

▽ Temple of Hatshepsut, Deir el-Bahri: view of the first terrace facing west. The Valley of the Kings is behind the cliff.

▷ Hatshepsut in the form of the god Osiris: statue fragment, Egyptian Museum, Cairo

Paths to Eternity

At death, the deceased began the dangerous journey to a second material and eternal life. During the trip, his earthly life would be judged; he had to placate the gatekeepers and be received onto the barque of the sun god. Even if all went well, he could not feel safe, because his body had to remain intact in order to provide a domicile for his creative power, called the Ka here on earth and Akh in the heavenly abode, and for his non-physical personal characteristics or Ba. If this was no longer possible, he was could fall back on a life-size statue in his tomb, a replacement body that sometimes even came with an extra head. Further more his name could not be allowed to fade into obscurity. Thus his eternal life depended on the kindness of the living. And if they destroyed his body or his name, he was—effectively—dead.

◁◁ **Sarcophagus and mummy of a priestess**, dynasty 21 (ca. 1080–946 BCE), The British Museum, London

◁ **Canopic jars for the burial of organs**, dynasty 26 (664–525 BCE), Egyptian Museum, Turin

◁ **Back of a heart scarab**, Christie's (London): the text reminds the heart not to testify against the dead in court. Scarabs like these were wrapped within the mummy's bindings.

▷ **Wall painting in the tomb of Inherkha**, eighteenth dynasty, Deir el-Medina: a priest fills the mouth of the mummy with holy water during the Opening of the Mouth ceremony.

Mummification

The embalmers first removed the fatty tissue and internal organs, but not the heart. Part of the brain was also removed through the nose. The skin-covered skeleton was then allowed to dry in natron for seventy days, then filled with fragrances and anointed. The body was wrapped in impregnated linen bandages, and protective amulets were placed between the layers.

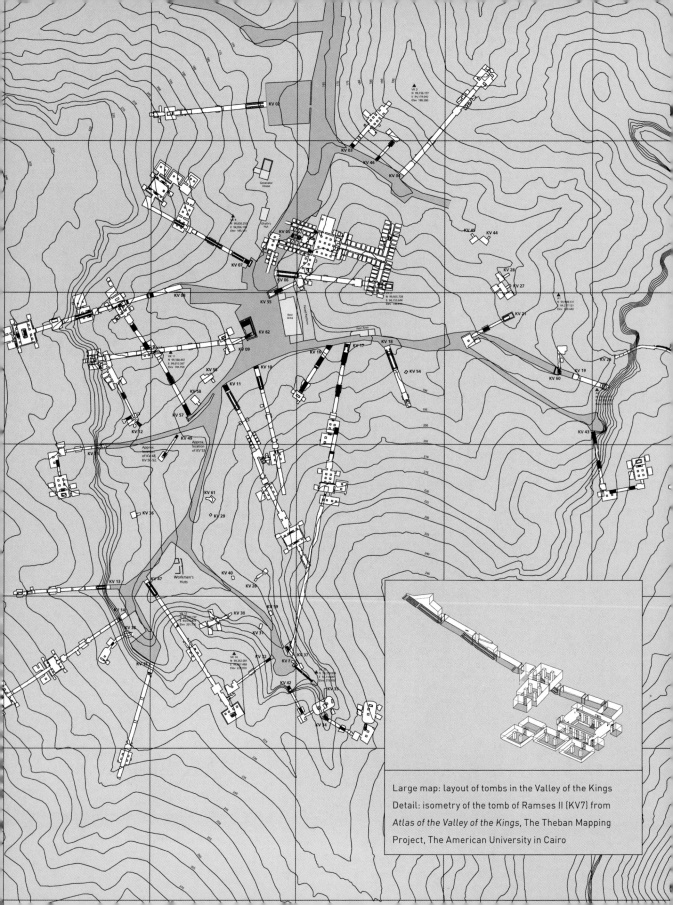

Large map: layout of tombs in the Valley of the Kings
Detail: isometry of the tomb of Ramses II (KV7) from
Atlas of the Valley of the Kings, The Theban Mapping
Project, The American University in Cairo

In the Valley of the Kings

The necropolis was located in the west to be near to the setting sun, as, in order to live forever, the tomb owner eventually had to reach the solar barque. From 1500 BCE onwards, the builders decided to construct "invisible" tombs for urgently-needed, albeit useless, protection from robbers. These tombs were completely hidden in the solid rock of El-Quorn west of Thebes.

For a period of around 500 years, rulers intended to spend eternity largely among themselves in the Valley of the Kings. Mothers, sisters, wives, and daughters would forever remain in a neighboring valley. Rock tombs for well-to-do subjects consisted of a sealed tomb and a walk-in cult chamber. Royal tombs, on the other hand, were inaccessible, since there was ample opportunity to practice the pharaoh's cult in nearby funerary temples. The construction basically led deep into the earth via several corridors, and shafts hindered accessibility. An anteroom opened into the (usually) pillared main chamber containing the sarcophagus. These rooms could branch off to an indeterminate number of adjoining rooms. The quality of the limestone varied and played a role in site selection. With more than sixty tombs, confusion set in over time. And the builders repeatedly ran into the forgotten graves of ancestors while excavating the new ones.

△ Ceiling painting in the tomb of Sethis I (KV17): Nut as personification of the star-studded firmament of heaven.

◁ Grave chamber in the rock tomb of Tutankhamun (KV 62): the indispensable Opening of the Mouth ceremony is performed on the dead king in the guise of Osiris.

Akhenaten

In the fourteenth century BCE, a king, the hereditary guarantor of order, broke with tradition. Amenhotep IV decreed the sun god Aten to be the sole god. By disempowering Amun, the "king of the gods," he also stripped the priests at Thebes of power. From that point onward, he called himself Akhenaten. To honor Aten, he built a new capital at Amarna amidst fertile lands. In accordance with the ideological significance of sculpture, Akhenaten expanded his overhaul of tradition to the arts, which experienced a programmatic and stylistic "coup." No longer idealized, his portraits show individual features almost to the point of caricature. Ostensibly private family portraits were a popular theme, depicting the royal family basking in the rays of the sun god, who served to emphasize their legitimacy. Even representations of nature became more vivid, such as startled ducks flying out of realistic thickets.

◁ Bust of Nefertiti, wife of Akhenaten, dynasty 18, ca. 1340 BCE: limestone, 19½ in (50 cm) high. Egyptian Museum, Berlin. In contrast to the usual white skin of upper-class Egyptian ladies, her complexion is naturally tanned. But the eyes remain emphasized, as before, and black makeup served to protect and adorn.

▷ Ducks in a papyrus thicket, floor painting, dynasty 18: Tell el-Amarna, Egyptian Museum, Cairo

▽ Head of one of the 13-ft (4-m) high statues of Akhenaten from the colonnades of Aten's temple on the eastern edge of Karnak, dynasty 18: sandstone, Egyptian Museum, Cairo

▷ Stele with the royal family in the light of Aten, dynasty 18: limestone, Tell el-Amarna, Egyptian Museum, Cairo

Tutankhamun

Akhenaten's ideas only had a temporary impact on the Egyptian Empire.
Under his successor, the ten-year-
old Tutankhamun, the priests of
Amun were back in power. Yet
there remained visible traces of the
more natural Amarna style in the
decorative arts. The backrest of the
throne from Tutankhamun's tomb is
crowned with a radiant sun disk, for
example. The king's posture, with
his right arm casually propped up,
is unconventional. Thanks to clever
design his wife meets him at eye
level, and the scene seems rather
private despite the abundant regalia.
One detail is interesting to note: the
typical Amarna-style rendering of all
ten toes.

By contrast, the famous gold
mask shows a royal image with traditionally idealized facial features.

Napoleon, Carter and Egyptology

Napoleon's 1798 Egyptian
campaign to weaken the
British not only triggered a
craze for all things Egyptian,
but also stimulated a new
science (archaeology).
It ignited a gold rush
mentality, and anyone
who could afford it went in
search of treasure. From
1907 on, Lord Carnarvon
financed Howard Carter's
excavations, and these
resulted in the discovery of
Tutankhamun's intact tomb
in 1922.

◁ **Tutankhamun and his wife
Ankhesenamun**, backrest of throne,
ca. 1345 BCE. Gold, silver and enamel
on wood, 20 ¾ × 20 ¾ in (53 × 53 cm).
Egyptian Museum, Cairo

△ **Death mask of Tutankhamun with Nemes
headdress**, ca. 1345 BCE. Embossed gold
inlaid with precious stones and glass flux,
21 ¼ in (54 cm) high. Egyptian Museum,
Cairo

Egyptian Temple Construction

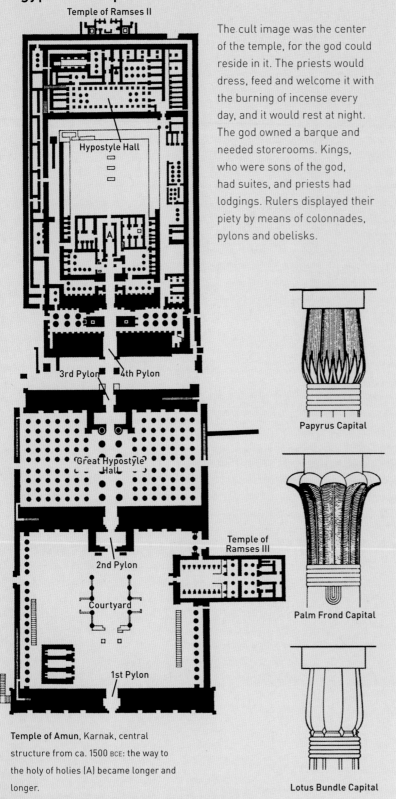

Temple of Ramses II

Hypostyle Hall

A

3rd Pylon   4th Pylon

Great Hypostyle Hall

Temple of Ramses III

2nd Pylon

Courtyard

1st Pylon

Temple of Amun, Karnak, central structure from ca. 1500 BCE: the way to the holy of holies (A) became longer and longer.

Papyrus Capital

Palm Frond Capital

Lotus Bundle Capital

The cult image was the center of the temple, for the god could reside in it. The priests would dress, feed and welcome it with the burning of incense every day, and it would rest at night. The god owned a barque and needed storerooms. Kings, who were sons of the god, had suites, and priests had lodgings. Rulers displayed their piety by means of colonnades, pylons and obelisks.

The Period of Ramses II

A king assumed the role of creator god on earth. This meant that building was among his ceremonial duties. Because it was incumbent upon him to perform rituals, he made building and expanding temples a priority. His third role was military strategist, and he adorned the temple walls with images of war. The buildings and grounds were furnished with obelisks and pylons. The latter were high hollow columns that made up the gate, towered above the temple, and served as symbols of the two mountains between which the sun rose in Egypt. Some contained unspecified chambers.

Ramses II carried out countless building projects, and no Egyptian ruler erected more monuments than he. Among the most spectacular were the rock temples of Abu Simbel, whose massive exteriors were graced with four monumental statues of the seated king. In Thebes, the remains of Ramses II's building activities include his tomb in the Valley of the Kings (KV7) and the Ramesseum, his monumental funerary temple. The Amun Temple in Karnak is indebted to Ramses II for the Avenue of Sphinxes in front of the first pylon and for decorating the southern wing of the Great Hypostyle Hall, among others. Ramses II also expanded the Temple at Luxor with an Avenue of Sphinxes, sixteen colossal statues, two obelisks, and the first pylon, with the First Court of Ramses II behind it.

The buildings were accompanied by statues up to 65 ft (20 m) tall that portray the ruler with a lion's body in sitting, standing or reclining position. Though the faces of these figures are programmatically idealized, they are by no means uniform and show slightly different facial expressions.

▷ **Temple of Amun-Mut-Khonsu**, Luxor: view of the first pylon in the First Court of Ramses II. The missing obelisk now stands in the Place de la Concorde in Paris.

◁ **Rock temples of Abu Simbel:** on the façade are four statues of Ramses II. At the foot of each are portraits of his favorite wife, his mother and some of his children. The falcon-headed sun god Re-Harakhti stands between the monumental statues. The temple was moved to make way for the Aswan Dam. In the original location on solstice days, the light went through the portal and fell directly onto images of the gods on the rear wall of the holy of holies, about 150 ft (45 m) away.

▽ **Temple of Amun-Mut-Khonsu**, Luxor: view of the Avenue of Sphinxes with the head of Ramses II.

Ancient Greece

Map legend:

- Shrine, temple
- Castle, palace
- Theater
- Wall painting
- Mountain

ca. 1000–ca. 700 BCE Geometric style was named after a style of ceramics that were covered by small-scale, ornamental bands.

ca. 700–ca. 480 BCE Large-scale sculpture developed in the archaic period.

ca. 480–ca. 338 BCE The classical period was characterized by the timeless ideal of beauty and the canon of harmonious proportions that are representative of Greek art.

ca. 338–ca. 30 BCE During the Hellenistic period, the language of classical forms became dramatically exaggerated.

The importance that the Greeks attached to the arts led to the fact that, for the first time in Western history, artists and their works were known by name, even if only mentioned in literature, e.g. in the works of Pliny the Elder (first century BCE) or Pausanias (second century BCE). Famous potters and painters of Greek vases even signed their work.

From Minos to Hellas

Ancient Greek art did not suddenly start out with geometric style around 1000 BCE, but had previously assimilated Mycenaean, Minoan, and Cycladic elements. The Dorian immigration in ca. 1200 BCE was always thought to be a turning point in the decline of Mycenaean civilization and took place so smoothly that post-Mycenaean and pre-geometric styles of pottery flowed into one another completely unhindered.

Fisherman from Thera, ca. 1500 BCE

Mycenaean Lion's Gate, ca. 1400 BCE

Dipylon vase, ca. 750 BCE

Archaic Kouros, ca. 580 BCE

| 1500 | 1400 | 800 | 600 | 500 |

Ancient Greece (ca. 1500–146 BCE)

Chronology

ca. 2000–500 BCE Minoan civilization on Crete and Thera (Santorini)

ca. 1400–200 BCE Height of Mycenaean civilization

ca. 1200 BCE Immigration of Doric tribes

8th century BCE Emergence of the Greek polis (city state), settlement of lower Italy and Sicily

7th–6th centuries BCE Greek supremacy in the eastern Mediterranean, tyrannical political system

5th–4th centuries BCE Individual city-states adopt democratic constitutions.

500–479 BCE Greco-Persian Wars

490 BCE Greek victory at Marathon

431–404 BCE The Peloponnesian War between Athens (democracy) and Sparta (aristocracy) ends in victory for Sparta.

371 BCE The Battle of Leuctra marks the end of Sparta's power.

328 BCE The Macedonian king Philip II, father of Alexander the Great, becomes the ruler of Greece.

336 BCE onward Expansion of the empire under the leadership of Alexander the Great

146 BCE Greece becomes a Roman province.

Sculptors

Apollonius of Athens: 1st century BCE, *Belvedere Torso*

Lysippos: 4th c. BCE, court sculptor to Alexander the Great

Myron: 5th c. BCE, sculpted the body in motion, *Discobolus*

Phidias: ca. 500–432 BCE, antiquity's most famous sculptor. Only copies or reconstructions survive, e.g., *Olympian Zeus, Athena Parthenos*.

Polyclitus: ca. 480–end 5th c. BCE, invented contrapposto; only copies of his *Doryphorus* survive. His son Polyclitus the Younger was also an architect (Epidaurus).

Praxiteles: ca. 390–320 BCE, whose works emphasized naturalism

Painters

Apelles: ca. 375/370–end 4th century BCE, the most important painter of antiquity, known only through literature

Brygos: active in Athens ca. 480–470 BCE, red-figure vases

Douris: late 6th c.–mid-5th c. BCE, Athens, red-figure vases

Euphronios: ca. 535–470 BCE, Athens, pioneer of red-figure vase painting

Exekias: active in Athens ca. 550–530 BCE, black-figure vases

Polygnotos: active in Athens ca. 450–420 BCE, red-figure vases of the high classical period

Polyclitus, *Doryphoros*, ca. 440 BCE

Temple of Athena Pronaia, Delphi, Theodoros of Phocaia, ca. 370 BCE

Relief from the Pergamon Altar, ca. 180 BCE

400   200   150

At a Glance

Demeter

Goddess of the harvest and sister of Zeus, who dispatched Triptolemos with ears of grain. Demeter and Zeus had a daughter, Persephone.

Demeter relief, ca. 440 BCE, National Archaeological Museum, Athens

Aphrodite relief, ca. 470 BCE, Museo Nazionale, Rome

Aphrodite

Greek goddess of love, beauty, and eroticism, was born from the sea foam that gathered around the genitals of the castrated Uranus. Paris declared her the most beautiful goddess.

Zeus

God of lightning, sky and thunder, was the supreme ruler of the gods, son of Chronos and Rhea. He married his sister, Hera.

Hera

Goddess of women and marriage. She bore Ares (war) and probably Hephaestus (fire) as sons of Zeus.

Metope from Selinus, ca. 460 BCE, Museo Archeologico, Palermo

Marble relief, ca. 27 BCE, The Metropolitan Museum of Art, New York

Hermes

God of commerce. The herald and messenger of the gods and the son of Zeus and the nymph Maia. He guided the souls of the dead to Hades and also protected travelers.

Pan

Son of Hermes, god of shepherds and flocks. The word panic is derived from Pan's method of frightening his opponents.

Prometheus

Son of the Titan Iapetus. Stole fire from the gods and gave it to mortals, thus drawing Zeus's ire.

Ancient Greece (ca. 1500–146 BCE)

Dionysos

God of wine, grapes, theater and ecstasy. Son of Zeus and the Theban king's daughter Semele

Exekias, drinking bowl with the sea journey of Dionysus, ca. 535 BCE, Staatliche Antikensammlungen, Munich

Cella frieze, east side of the Parthenon, Acropolis, Athens, ca. 440 BCE, The British Museum, London

Poseidon

Brother of Zeus (left) and god of the sea and earthquakes, among others, distinguished from Zeus by the trident, a fish spear.

Apollo

God of youth, music, prophecy, and healing (center). Son of Zeus and Leto, father of Asclepius

Artemis

Goddess of the wilderness, hunt and wild animals (right). Daughter of Zeus and Leto, who fought against the Titans

Eros

God of love and beauty. The son of Aphrodite, he was in charge of sexual rapprochement and intercourse. At the time the world began, the Eros of early antiquity was a primordial god.

Athena

Goddess of wisdom, warfare and crafts, favorite daughter of Zeus. She sprang forth from Zeus's head in full armor at birth, and her bird is the owl. She was the patron goddess of Athens and protector of Odysseus.

Relief, ca. 470 BCE. Marble, 19 in (48 cm) high. Acropolis Museum, Athens

Hades

God of the underworld and brother of Zeus. Abducted Persephone, daughter of Zeus and Demeter, but had to bring her back. After that, Persephone spent winters in the underworld, often called the House of Hades or simply Hades.

Relief with Hades and Persephone, ca. 470 BCE, Museo Nazionale, Reggio Calabria

Key Terms: Gods

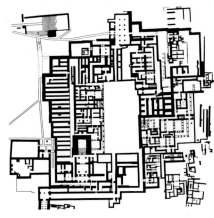

△ **Plan of Knossos Palace**, Crete, ground floor, ca. 1600 BCE (Middle Minoan III, New Palace period): the confined spaces of the rooms reflect the Greek myth of the Labyrinth. The Cretan Minotaur lived at its center and was defeated by Theseus.

◁ The reconstructed **North Propylaeum (entrance) to Knossos Palace** with characteristic red columns that taper downward.

The Fall of the Minoans

From about 2000 BCE onwards, the Minoans were an economic powerhouse in the eastern Mediterranean with trade links to the Near East and Egypt. They were sailors and merchants, not warriors, and they conquered markets, not territories. Around 1700 BCE, their island was struck by a devastating fire that was probably the result of an earthquake. But they were so sure of the merits of their island that they rebuilt their cities and palaces in even more magnificent style, and successfully expanded their trade contacts until the next disaster hit.

Current theory holds that in 1650 BCE there was a massive volcanic eruption on Thera (Santorini) that

probably generated giant tsunamis. An older theory dates the eruption to 1500 BCE and attributes the disappearance of the Minoan culture to the volcanic eruption itself.

But the current theory disputes the old one. The Minoan culture survived for at least another 100 years, albeit weakened. Perhaps additional earthquakes and economic failures were responsible for the final demise of Minoan society. The scientific debate continues to this day.

What is certain, however, is that the eruption on Santorini preserved the finest Aegean frescoes within its ashes.

△ **Landscape with lilies and swallows**, ca. 1500 BCE, wall painting from Thera (Akrotiri, Santorini), National Archaeological Museum, Athens: this mural combines naturalism and stylization.

◁ **Marine-style bottle with octopus**, ca. 1500 BCE (Late Minoan I, New Palace period). Clay, 11 in (28 cm). Archaeological Museum, Heraklion: the winding arms of the relaxed octopus fill the space without regard to the shape of the vessel.

◁ **Fisherman**, ca. 1500 BCE, wall painting from Thera (Akrotiri, Santorini), National Archaeological Museum, Athens: the combination of frontal and profile views is reminiscent of Egyptian painting.

The First Greeks

The Minoans established their commercial empire on Crete and the Aegean Islands around 2000 BCE. They were neither linguistically Greek nor of Greek origin. Meanwhile, the warlike Achaeans settled in the Peloponnese. While the Minoans lived in open cities, Greek Achaeans preferred fortified castles. In the fifteenth century BCE, they benefited from the weakening of the Minoan economy. Shortly thereafter, they inherited what belonged to the Minoans, and the Achaean realm, named after its center at Mycenae, reached its peak around 1400–200 BCE.

It is fitting that we also encounter warlike motifs on Mycenaean wall ornaments and ceramics. This is true despite the fact that both styles seem so dependent on peaceful Minoan art that we might expect the Minoans to have expanded their repertoire.

The Mycenaeans lost their importance around 1200 BCE, although the archeological record does not show that they were conquered by another Greek tribe.

◁ **The Lion Gate of Mycenae**, ca. 1400 BCE. A typical Minoan column stands between the two lions.

▷ **Two Phi idols** (possibly divine nurses) **with child**. Grave goods, ca. 1250 BCE. Clay, 5 in (13 cm) high. Musée du Louvre, Paris

Schliemann's Agamemnon

Heinrich Schliemann's (1822–90) 1873 discovery of the golden treasures of Troy had already provoked many questions when, in 1876, he again stumbled onto gold inside the shafts of Mycenaean graves and deemed it to be Agamemnon's treasure. It was hard to believe anyone could have so much luck, and Schliemann was even suspected of planting the masks himself. Today, it seems certain that he discovered the graves of Mycenaean princes who had died some 300 years before Agamemnon. The graves date to the period around 1500 BCE.

Mask of Agamemnon, ca. 1500 BCE, 12 in (31.5 cm) high.
National Archaeological Museum, Athens

Increasingly Lifelike

The majority of Cycladic idols come from tombs and are females in reclining positions with arms crossed over their stomachs. But each one is different in some respect, showing unexpected variation within a form whose language has been reduced to a minimum. This particular type of marble sculpture reached its highpoint in the Cyclades around 3000 BCE, yet would continue to be found there for another 1500 years. In view of the differing find contexts, the most convincing interpretation is probably that these figures represent deities.

Some 1700 years later, the highly stylized figures of Attic geometric vases would depict humans rather than gods. These were the first timid signs of figurative portrayal since the vibrant animal, plant, and human decoration on Minoan and Mycenaean ceramics. They were still firmly integrated as short dramatic narratives in the vessel's shoulders, although they are less inconspicuous than the animal sequences set on the neck of the vessel between carefully crafted, small-scale ornamental friezes.

A very similar style of figure can be seen in bronze statuettes from the same period.

▷ Heracles (?) and Centaur, ca. 760 BCE. Bronze, 4½ in (11.3 cm) high. The Metropolitan Museum of Art, New York

◁ Female idol with folded arms (Spedos style), Cyclades, ca. 2500 BCE. Marble, 25 in (63.5 cm) high. The Metropolitan Museum of Art, New York

▷ Dipylon vase, ca. 750 BCE (Attic geometric). Clay, 5 ft 1 in (155 cm) high. National Archaeological Museum, Athens

◁ **Temple of Poseidon**, apparently dedicated to Hera, peripteral, ca. 460 BCE, 80 × 197 ft (24.31 × 59.93 m), columns 6 × 46 ft (1.9 × 14 m). Paestum, Italy

▷ **Façade design of a Doric temple**

▷▷ **Erechtheum**, 421–406 BCE, north side of the **Acropolis**, Athens: as a multi-purpose religious building, the unfinished Erechtheum broke with the canon. There were four differently proportioned columns at four different levels, as well as three structures, each with a different roof.

▽ **Parthenon, Temple of Athena Parthenos**, peripteral, 447–432 BCE, 100 × 228 ft (30.88 × 69.5 m), columns 8 ft 6 in × 60 ft (2.54 × 17 m). Acropolis, Athens

Greek Temples

These were regarded as places to house statues of deities, not as centers of worship. Rituals took place at the altar in front of the temple within view of the sacred image. Frequently, priestesses were the only ones who had access to the temple's interior (naos).

The most popular temple design was the peripteros, in which a series of columns completely surrounded the rectangular naos that had a vestibule at one or both of its narrow sides. Ancient architects placed particular value on mathematically harmonious proportions. Their favorite ratio of front to side columns was n:2n + 1. The ratio of the column height to the separating space (intercolumniation), was also rigorously defined. The slenderness of the columns could be visually manipulated by the amount of fluting, which consisted of semi-cylindrical vertical grooves along the length of the column shafts. The best Greek architects did not build geometrically perfect structures but made optical adjustments to make them appear straight.

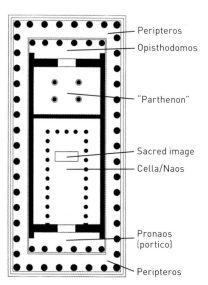

- Peripteros
- Opisthodomos
- "Parthenon"
- Sacred image
- Cella/Naos
- Pronaos (portico)
- Peripteros

△ **Peripteral** (Parthenon)

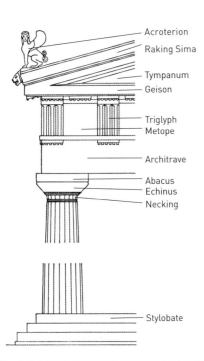

- Acroterion
- Raking Sima
- Tympanum
- Geison
- Triglyph
- Metope
- Architrave
- Abacus
- Echinus
- Necking
- Stylobate

Narrative Architectural Sculpture

The figural sculpture of a temple was mainly found on the exterior pediments and in the metopes between the triglyphs in the load-bearing zone, as well as on the interior frieze at the upper end of the cella walls. In the archaic period, pediment figures had an apotropaic function, i.e., to ward off evil. The oldest surviving example is the Temple of Artemis at Kérkyra (Corfu). The Gorgon, a monster with serpents for hair whose gaze turned all to stone appears to come rushing down from the pediment with all the horror of her entwined snakes. The rapid movement is conveyed by the kneeling-running position, and her head overlaps the cornice, which detaches her visually from the background. The miniature scenes in the corners bear neither formal nor substantial relation to the central group of figures. This additive pictorial concept was later abandoned in favor of newer images in a significantly more didactic, narrative style.

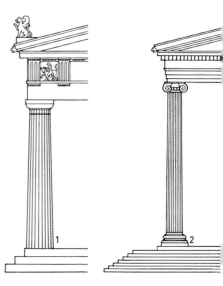

△ Reconstruction of tympanum relief

▽ Dying warrior (from the east pediment), ca. 490 BCE, Glyptothek, Munich

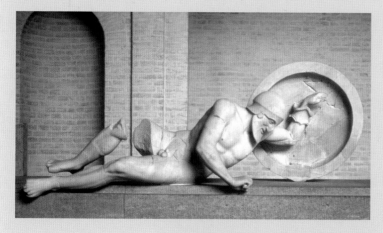

Temple of Aphaia at Aegina

All the figures on the tympanum relief from the east pediment are involved in a scenic event, and the posture of the individual figures and their arrangement relates to the triangular frame. Athena at the center is actively engaged in the Trojan War. Traces of paint on the marble can be reconstructed into a decorative image that tells a good and memorable story.

▷ **Water bearers**, scene from the cella frieze on the north side of the Parthenon, ca. 440 BCE. Marble, 42 in (106 cm) high, total length 525 ft (160 m). Acropolis Museum, Athens

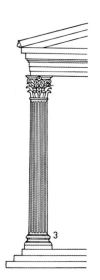

◁ Archermos, **Nike (Winged Victory)**, fragment from Delos, ca. 550 BCE. Marble, 3 ft (90 cm) high. National Archaeological Museum, Athens

◁ **Archaic Kouros**, ca. 580 BCE. Marble, 6 ft (184 cm) high. The Metropolitan Museum of Art, New York. To ensure stability, the sculptor did not allow the arms to completely separate from the body.

From Standing to Contrapposto

To represent movement, archaic sculptors developed a running motif with one knee touching the ground. The abdomen was shown in profile, legs in lunging position with one knee on the ground, and the frontal torso with arms reaching out was added to this.

This "windmill" stance allowed Nike to part the air and "fly" with flowing locks and skirt riding high. On the other hand, an archaic Kouros stands with both feet on the ground, although one foot is slightly forward. He holds his arms at his sides, somewhat relaxed but with his hands clenched into fists. Strictly frontal and block-like, his nude, ideal body is

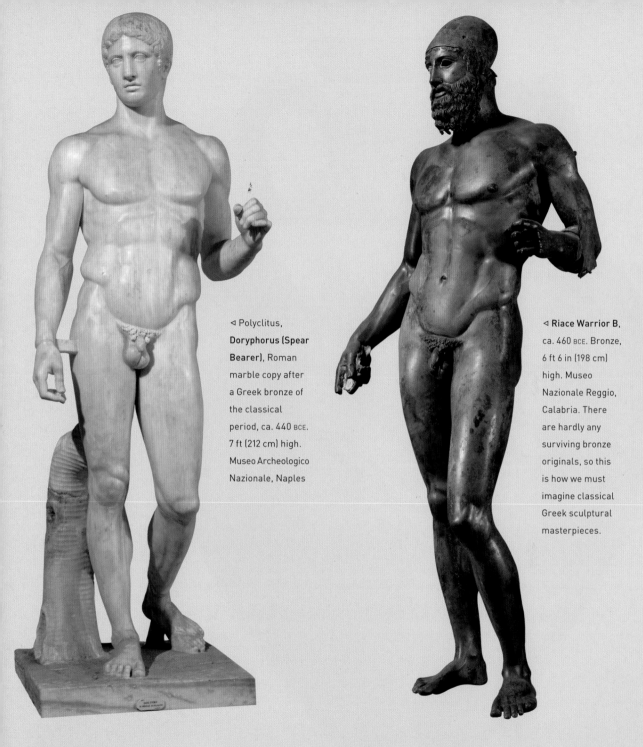

◁ Polyclitus, **Doryphorus (Spear Bearer)**, Roman marble copy after a Greek bronze of the classical period, ca. 440 BCE. 7 ft (212 cm) high. Museo Archeologico Nazionale, Naples

◁ **Riace Warrior B**, ca. 460 BCE. Bronze, 6 ft 6 in (198 cm) high. Museo Nazionale Reggio, Calabria. There are hardly any surviving bronze originals, so this is how we must imagine classical Greek sculptural masterpieces.

completely symmetrical apart from the legs. His focused energy suggests restrained power.

During the classical period, Polyclitus (active from 450 BCE) developed a more comfortable stance. We can observe the balanced and anatomically precise alternation of tension and relaxation, raising and lowering, turning forward and away as they unfold in contrapposto and in the distribution of standing and free legs.

Like many Greek bronze sculptures, Polyclitus' *Doryphorus* survives only in Roman marble copies, with supports and struts of the same material that can also be disguised as a tree stump.

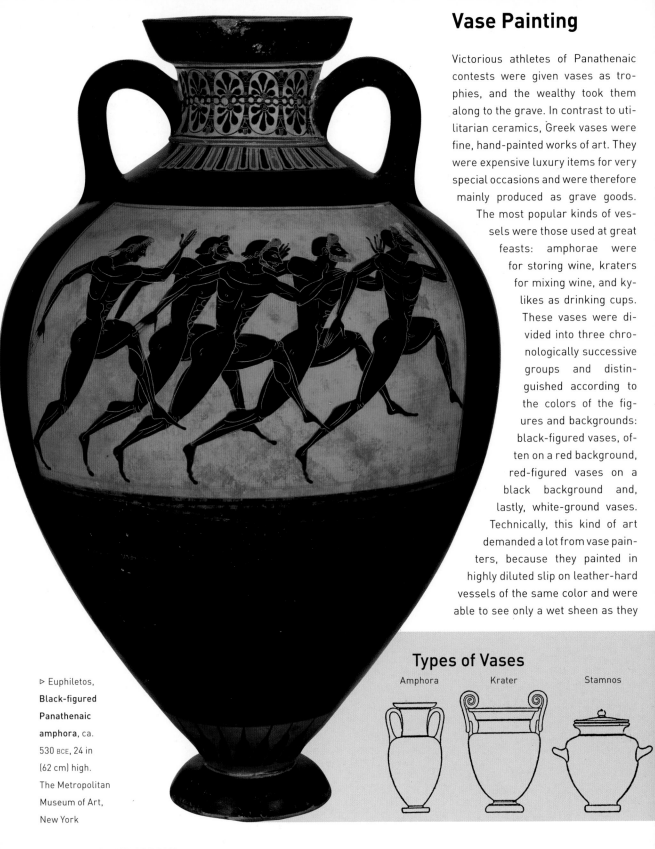

Vase Painting

Victorious athletes of Panathenaic contests were given vases as trophies, and the wealthy took them along to the grave. In contrast to utilitarian ceramics, Greek vases were fine, hand-painted works of art. They were expensive luxury items for very special occasions and were therefore mainly produced as grave goods. The most popular kinds of vessels were those used at great feasts: amphorae were for storing wine, kraters for mixing wine, and kylikes as drinking cups. These vases were divided into three chronologically successive groups and distinguished according to the colors of the figures and backgrounds: black-figured vases, often on a red background, red-figured vases on a black background and, lastly, white-ground vases. Technically, this kind of art demanded a lot from vase painters, because they painted in highly diluted slip on leather-hard vessels of the same color and were able to see only a wet sheen as they

▷ Euphiletos,
Black-figured
Panathenaic
amphora, ca.
530 BCE, 24 in
(62 cm) high.
The Metropolitan
Museum of Art,
New York

Types of Vases

Amphora   Krater   Stamnos

worked. Colors resulting from a regulated supply of oxygen only appeared during reduction firing, when the thin clay slip turned black and the compact clay turned red. Thus, everything was painted black, but the red sections were left alone. Only white-ground lekythoi were painted after firing. Filled with oils or creams, they served in burial rituals. That is why a popular motif on grave steles was the meeting of the mourner and deceased.

△ Macron, **Red-figured Kylix**, 490–480 BCE, 11 in (28.6) cm diameter. The Metropolitan Museum of Art, New York

▷ Achilles Painter, **White-ground Lekythos**, ca. 430 BCE, 14¾ in (37.4 cm) high. The Metropolitan Museum of Art, New York

Hydria   Oinochoe   Kylix   Kantharos   Lekythos

Expressions of Grief

A grave monument was indispensable for an honorable burial. In the archaic period, this might have been a fully sculpted kouros or a kore, his female counterpart. Grave steles developed into an independent sculptural genre and would later become the exclusive means of depicting a dead person as he or she was in live. On older steles, the person depicted appeared in a strictly archaic walking stance and fully erect. Less than one hundred years later, the standing posture was more natural with the weight resting on one leg. In general, reliefs had become less flat, certain details had been removed from the background, and the effect was more sculptural. Along with single persons, steles with two or more figures began to be produced. In the late classical relief of the lady with her servant, the deceased has already been carried away from the earthly realm, and her little jewelry case is no longer of value to her. She remains lost in thought and does not notice her servant or the jewels.

◁ Aristocles, **Grave stele of Aristion**, ca. 510 BCE. Marble, 7 ft 8 in (240 cm) high. National Archaeological Museum, Athens

▷ **Grave stele of a Girl with Doves**, ca. 450 BCE. Parian marble, 31½ in (80 cm) high. The Metropolitan Museum of Art, New York

▷▷ **Grave stele of an unknown woman from Piraeus with her servant**, ca. 380 BCE. Marble, 4 ft (121 cm) high. National Archaeological Museum, Athens

Theater and Place of Worship

Epidaurus was considered the mythical birthplace of Asclepius. An unwanted child, the result of Apollo's affair with a princess that ended in scandal, he was raised by the centaur Chiron, who taught him the art of healing. Asclepius could soon bring the dead back to life, whereupon Zeus killed him with a bolt of lightening and made him into a god.

Beginning in the fourth century BCE, the Sanctuary of Asclepius at Epidaurus grew into one of the major religious and healing sites of classical antiquity. Successful treatment was based on the idea that Asclepius visited patients during sleep in order to cure them personally or to tell them what was needed for their recovery. Before a patient underwent divine treatment, he had to go through various purification rituals. It was crucial for him to experience his visit to the

sanctuary as a complete withdrawal from everyday life. The god could appear to the patient immediately or after he had been asleep for some days, so it was possible for a person to stay until he felt cured. Outside of healing sleep, the patient took part in water cures and [mineral] baths, busied himself with sports, made sacrifices to the god, studied in the library, marveled at the solemn inscriptions of cured patients, or attended the theater.

The sanctuary came with a 160-bed guesthouse, but also had a theater with 12,000 seats. Thus, the spa facility was largely organized for outpatient treatment, and the theater functioned independently from it. Archeological finds prove that the complex was, in fact, repeatedly plundered by the Romans, but it was only the Christians who ultimately closed it down.

◁ The **Tholos**, a circular building erected from 360 to 320 BCE, continues to baffle us. The outer ring of twenty-six Doric columns attaches to an inner one with fourteen Corinthian columns, some of the earliest surviving examples of this order. The floor was covered with a black and white spiraling diamond pattern. At the center point of the portico, one could descend into the underworld of a basement labyrinth.

△ Polyclitus the Younger, **Theater at Epidaurus**, displaying all the characteristics of a Greek theater, i.e., the inclusion of the landscape, the extended half-circle of the auditorium, and the open, variable stage.

▷ View into the **Adyton**, an area of the temple usually accessible only to priests. Curative sleep almost certainly took place here in the Sanctuary of Asclepius, and the patient's dreams or visions would then be reported to the priests for prescription.

The Altar at Pergamon

The altar, 115 ft (35 m) wide, was built by order of Eumenes II (reigned 197–58 BCE), king of Pergamon, which is located in contemporary Turkey. This famous Hellenistic construction was less an expression of piety than a stage for representative acts of state in which the gods were offered sacrifices for proven blessings in general rather than for specific victories. The dominant element of this structure, which is not a temple, was the 90-inch (230-cm)-high circular frieze that shows the victory of the Olympian gods over the giants. After some 400 years of Greek sacred architecture, decorative figures no longer "acted" far from viewers on the metopes and friezes below temple roofs, but were tangibly present at eye level. And never before did sculpted scenes portray motion so dramatically.

△ **West side of the Pergamon Altar**, ca. 180 BCE, Pergamon Museum, Berlin

▷ **Eastern Frieze, Pergamon Altar**, Pergamon Museum, Berlin: **Athena overcomes Alcyoneus**, and tears him away from his mother, the earth goddess Gaia. As a long as he remains in contact with her, he is invincible.

Ancient Rome

Chronology

753 BCE Legendary founding of Rome by Romulus.

ca. 510 BCE The last Etruscan king is overthrown: Rome becomes a republic.

264–241/218–201/149–146 BCE Rome defeats the Carthaginians (Phoenicians) in the three Punic Wars.

90/89 BCE All free-born Italian males are granted Roman citizenship.

44 BCE Gaius Julius Caesar (100–44 BCE) appoints himself dictator for life; he is assassinated.

27 BCE Octavian (63 BCE–14 CE) becomes Augustus Caesar, the first

Etruscan grave monument at Cerveteri, ca. 520 BCE

The Ficoroni Cista, ca. 320 BCE

Wall painting in the Third Pompeian style, Pompeii, 20/30 BCE–ca. 50 CE

750	500	400	100	50

Ancient Rome (753 BCE–395 CE)

Imperial Culture

By the time of the legendary founding of Rome in 753 BCE, the Etruscans had already left their mark on Italy. Their metallurgists devised a bronze alloy from which sculptors made works of art through lost-wax casting. Their architects developed new vault technology. Their priests perfected the art of prediction by observing viscera and interpreting bird flight and lightning.

Artists from Greece worked for the wealthy upper class. As the Roman ascent to unify Italy under their rule began, they integrated many aspects of Etruscan culture. With the expansion of their territory into Greece, the Romans took over much of Greek art, philosophy and mathematics. From that time onwards, the great Roman libraries consisted of two buildings, one for Latin scrolls, the other for Greek.

As the expansion of empire would suggest, the Romans were more strategists and engineers than poets and artists. They specialized in constructing water systems, bridges and highways. The first window panes appeared in their homes. The Romans are also credited with raising their legal system to a science.

Cultural History

54–51 BCE Cicero's philosophical work, *De re publica*, describes the Roman Republic as the ideal state.
ca. 50 CE Roman army surgeon Pedanios Dioscorides (ca. 20–90 CE)

writes the pharmacology text, *De materia medica*, which will remain in use throughout the Renaissance.
ca. 150 CE Roman jurist Gaius writes *Institutiones*, a comprehensive legal textbook.

161 CE Galen (Galenus of Pergamum) works as a physician in Rome; his text, *Four Elements and Humors*, will survive well into the Middle Ages.
244 CE Plotinus founds the neo-Platonic school of philosophy in Rome.

emperor of Rome, ending 100 years of civil war.
66–70 CE The Jews are subject to Roman occupation; Jerusalem is destroyed.

84 CE Emperor Domitian begins to build the Limes Germanicus (Germanic frontier).
98–117 CE The largest expansion of the Roman Empire takes place

during the reign of Emperor Trajan.
380 CE Christianity, which has been tolerated since 313, becomes the state religion under Theodosius I (347–395 CE).

Roman noblewoman, ca. 90 CE

Arch of Trajan, Benevento, 114–120 CE

Palmyra, Hadrian's Gate, 200 CE

The Via Latina Catacomb, Rome, ca. 350 CE

| 0 | 100 | 200 | 300 | 400 |

At a Glance

Ara Pacis Augustae, 13–9 BCE, Rome

The Origin Myth

The Vestal Virgin Rhea Silva bore the twins Romulus and Remus to Mars, the god of war. King Amulius, who ousted Rhea's father Numitor, ordered them drowned in the Tiber. But they landed at the foot of the Palatine in their basket, where a she-wolf found and suckled them, and they were then raised by shepherds. In the end, they killed Amulius and restored Numitor to his rightful place. Following the creation of the new city in 753 BCE, they could not agree on the division of power. A fight ensued, and Romulus killed his brother Remus. He then named the city after himself and became the first King of Rome.

Art as Propaganda

In the relief on his Ara Pacis (Altar of Peace) in the Campus Martius, Augustus combined the saga of the city's founder Romulus with that of peace hard-won through his father, Mars. This peace, maintained by the army, legitimized the rule of Roman emperors thenceforward. Imperial statues were erected in public places throughout the empire to keep the ruler present for the people; their facial expressions, gestures, and dress were highly significant. Augustus's breastplate, for example, features a celebration of victory over the Barbarians above the reclining earth goddess to symbolize a perfect world order and the dawn of a golden age.

Places of Worship

The Sanctuary of Fortuna Primigenia was built into hillside terraces on massive substructures with long colonnades. These opened onto the surrounding landscape and provided anyone approaching the sanctuary with an impressive display of how the Romans also ruled over nature.

Trivulzio cage cup, diatreta glass, 4th century, Museo Archeologico, Milan

Grave Goods

The Romans also liked to spend money. In addition to weapons and jewelry, large numbers of *diatreta* (cage cups) were discovered in the Rhineland. Impractical for daily use, these vessels were made of multi-colored, double-walled glass blanks that were polished and drilled, resulting in a perforated (Greek: diatreton) basket or net with a toast on one of the cups.

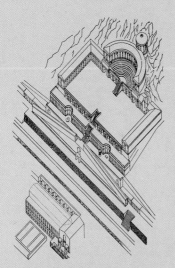

Sanctuary of Fortuna, ca. 80 BCE, Praeneste, reconstruction

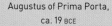

Augustus of Prima Porta, ca. 19 BCE

Ancient Rome (753 BCE–395 CE)

City Planning

In contrast to the "wild growth" of Rome itself, the newly founded towns were built systematically, especially in the provinces. Street grid plans dated back to military camps. Entering through the city gate (1), one arrives at the main axis running north-south (cardo, 2), which crosses the center of the east-west axis (decumanus, 3). The forum (4) was located in the center, and almost all major towns had a theater (5).

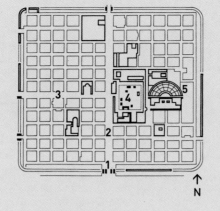

Prototype of a Roman city layout, Timgad, Algeria (founded 2nd century)

Opus Caementicium (Roman Concrete)

For eons, natural stone has been valued as a durable material for important monuments. But it is very heavy, and thus could only span limited spaces. The Romans developed a technique for spanning great widths by using lightweight concrete: a mixture of cast rocks, sand, mortar and water was poured between two layers of natural stone or brick. Such distances were not attained again until the twentieth century. The dome of the Pantheon, for example, spanned a stunning 141 ft (43 m).

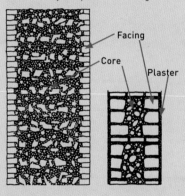

Opus caementicium: shown with visible masonry on the left, an additional layer of plaster on the right.

Mummy Portrait

In the first to fifth centuries, the ancient Egyptian practice of preserving dead bodies for the afterlife benefited from Roman portraiture. Thanks to the dry desert climate of northern Egypt, a large number of these mummy portraits have been preserved, particularly in the Fayum Oasis. Wooden tablets with faces painted in tempera or encaustic (pigment mixed with beeswax) covered the heads of the mummies and preserved the appearance of the dead.

Portrait of a young woman, 2nd century, Fayum, Museo Archeologico, Florence

The Forum

Although occasionally referred to as "market places", Roman fora were the most important public gathering places in Roman cities. They were centers that consisted of temples, squares with speakers' platforms for political events, and large ornate basilicas that housed law courts, government offices, shops and banks.

Forum Romanum, Rome

Key Terms

△ Wall painting
in the burial
chamber, Tomb
of the Triclinium,
Tarquinia,
ca. 500 BCE. Dance
scenes were as
much a part of
tomb programs as
banquets, horse
races, and other
performances.

▷ Urn, second
century BCE
(around the time
mass production
began), Museo
Archeologico,
Chiusi

Italy Before
the Romans

As early as 800 BCE, Etruscan culture
was demonstrably present in Italy.
The Etruscans, whose origins
are still unclear, organized their
individual communities over time
as loose leagues of cities with city-
states ruled by monarchs. Rome was
allegedly founded in 753 BCE, but the
actual date is somewhat later. And
up until ca. 510 BCE, even Rome was
subject to Etruscan rule. When the
Romans unified Italy in 90/89 BCE by
"granting" citizenship to all free-
born males, including the Etruscans,
much of Etruscan art and religion
had already been absorbed into
Roman culture. Owing to their trade

relations with Greece, the Etruscans had come under the influence of Greek culture, and Greek artists had even settled in their cities.

The Romans later preferred to view the Greeks as their ancestors rather than the Etruscans, and placed little value on the cultural heritage of their purportedly unsuitable for-bears. Tombs, therefore, provide the greatest number of clues about the Etruscans, even if the information is contradictory. For example crema-tions as well as burials were cus-tomary. Yet the worldly orientation of their grave chambers suggests that they believed in a physical afterlife.

Sarcophagi and urns depict the deceased as living persons reclining on couches. They are the audience for the painted performances in the grave chamber. Elaborate sculptures centered on the disproportionately large upper body.

△ **Grave monument from Cerveteri,** ca. 520 BCE. Clay, 6 ft 6 in (200 cm) long (inside is a cavity for the ashes). Villa Giulia, Rome. The woman was probably holding a perfume bottle from which she trickled fragrant oil onto her husband's palm.

Etruscan Bronze

In the fifth century BCE, Etruscan bronze pieces were sought after as status symbols, even in Greece. In Italy, the finest bronzes were usually cult objects. They served as votive offerings, (e.g., the sinewy Chimera of Arezzo or the Mars of Todi); as ritual implements, like the model of the liver used for divining entrails (below), or as grave goods, such as cistas for storing toiletries. The Ficoroni Cista was cast in Rome, and its metal surface contains an engraved episode from the Greek tale of the Argonauts. According to the inscription on the base plate of the cast figures of Dionysos between two satyrs, the cista was a gift from a mother to her daughter. The perfect continuity of the surrounding frieze contradicts the theory that it was based on a lost Greek painting.

▽ **Instructional model of a sheep's liver** for divining entrails (the edges are heavenly sectors and the interior is allocated to the deities), ca. 100 BCE. Bronze, 5 in (12.6 cm) long. Museo Civico, Piacenza

◁ **Chimera of Arezzo**, ca. 400 BCE. Bronze, 4 ft 3 in (129 cm) long. Museo Archeologico, Florence. This Greek mythical creature with a lion's body, goat's head and snake's tail faces battle with the hero Bellerophon.

▷ **Mars of Todi**, ca. 400 BCE. Bronze, 4 ft 7 in (140 cm) high. Musei Vaticani, Rome. The contrapposto stance is indeed Greek. But this helmetless Etruscan warrior is much less physically toned than Greek statues of the same period.

▽ **Ficoroni Cista**, ca. 320 BCE. Bronze, 21¼ in (54 cm) high. Villa Giulia, Rome

The Faces of Rome

As marble copies of lost Greek bronzes, Roman sculptures may be more valuable as evidence of Greek art than they are as examples of Roman art. On the other hand, that Greek inspiration should be contrasted with Roman portrait sculpture. Until the late first century BCE, the Romans practiced ancestor worship, which meant portraits had to be highly realistic. Even official portraits from the period of the Republic showed individual traits, albeit somewhat refined.

Octavian, the first Augustus, used his image for propaganda purposes. With ideal beauty, his hair combed evenly over his forehead, he stands in Greek contrapposto and seems to be speaking. The breastplate tells us that, thanks to Augustus, the entire world will become Roman. Where full statues would not fit, there were busts. The clothing at the neckline of a bust was an additional opportunity to characterize the subject. In general, nouveau riche Romans preferred more realistic portrayals of themselves than those who were better educated and born wealthy.

△ + ◁ **Augustus of Prima Porta**, ca. 19 BCE. Marble, 6 ft 8 in (204 cm) high. Musei Vaticani, Rome. Traces of paint on the marble reveal that the statue was originally colored, which made the symbolic representations on the breastplate more obvious.

▷ **Head of a Roman**, ca. 75–50 BCE. Marble, 11 in (28 cm) high. Museo Archeologico, Chieti. The representation is veristic and signs of aging have not been minimized.

△ **Vespasian** (r. 69–79 CE). Marble, Museo Nazionale Romano, Rome. Emperors wanting to be seen as traditionalists embraced the realism of Republican portraits.

▽ **Portrait of a noble Roman woman**, ca. 90 CE. Marble, 15 in (38 cm) high. Musei Capitolini, Rome. The smooth neckline balances the profusion of tight curls.

◁ **Marcus Aurelius** (r. 161–180). Marble, Musei Vaticani, Rome. This emperor saw himself as a Greek philosopher. In addition to the detailed drill work of the hair, the pupils are drilled to give the eyes a sense of expression.

◁◁ **Caracalla** (r. 211–217). Marble, 20 in (51 cm) high. Musei Vaticani, Rome. The soldier emperor is seldom seen without an angry, furrowed forehead.

Illusionistic Walls

△ **House of the Gryphons**, Rome, Palatine, first style mural, also called the masonry or incrustation style

The walls of Roman villas and palaces were almost entirely painted. There were four distinct styles whose formal criteria were open to interpretation, and surviving works show that the boundaries were fluid.

First style (ca. 200–80 BCE): Painting imitated marble paneling in which the "panels" showed illusionistic shadows along the edges. The solid wall was divided into three horizontal zones: The tall, usually lighter central zone was set on the continuous base, with continuous moldings along the top.

Second style (ca. 80–20 BCE): The wall gained optical depth through the use of architectural perspective, while the three-zone organization was retained. Spaces opened onto illusionistic landscapes, and figures sometimes inhabited the architecture.

Third style (20/30 BCE–50 CE): Architectural elements increased in quantity, the organization was small-scale, and even the top moldings were interrupted. Landscapes and figures appeared in the form of pictures on the wall.

Fourth style (ca. 50–120 CE): Uniform black, white or red fields created greater calmness, yet the style remained richly detailed, markedly delicate and boldly illusionistic.

△ **Villa of the Mysteries**, Pompeii, second style mural, also called the architectural style

△ **House of M. Lucretius Fronto**, Pompeii, third style mural, also called the ornamental style

▷ **House of M. Fabius Rufus**, Pompeii, fourth style mural, also called the fantasy style

Illusionistic Floors

Floors with patterns of colored clay inlays were already known to the Babylonians in the fourth century BCE. Finds near Ankara date to the eighth century. The Greeks used this practical flooring (pebble mosaic) from the fifth century BCE onwards. Motifs consisted of simple geometric patterns or figurative line drawings. According to a Roman description from the first century CE, Sosos of Pergamon was the first to have laid an "unswept floor" mosaic in the second century BCE. From then on, this was a popular motif in luxury villas of the Roman upper classes. Not only could they afford to bring culinary delights to the table that littered the floor with illusionistic embellishments; they could obviously also afford enough

▷ **Nile flood**: apse mosaic from the Sanctuary of Fortuna Primigenia at Praeneste near Rome, ca. 80 BCE, Museo Nazionale Prenestino, Palestrina

▽ *Asarotos oikon* (unswept floor) mosaic from a villa on the Aventine Hill, second century, Musei Vaticani, Rome

slaves to remove the remains of carelessly discarded food.

In both public and private life, wall and floor mosaics matched content to the function of the rooms. Aquatic themes predominated in spas. The flooded Nile in the Sanctuary of Fortuna Primigenia at Praeneste emphasized the goddess as provider, who gives not by chance but quite intentionally. The landscape representation was based on a model from Alexandria and was said to have been executed by guest workers.

◁ *Cave Canem* **mosaic**, House of the Tragic Poet, Pompeii. The appropriate place for a mosaic with a good guard dog is, of course, the hallway.

Casa and Villa

Casas were inseparable from the typical Roman rectangular city plan and opened inward to the atrium and peristyle. Villas, on the other hand, lay outside the city walls and often had outward oriented floor plans. They were either freely structured or designed with three or more symmetrical wings. The villa rustica, a country estate with individually designed rooms for the processing and storage of particular agricultural products, was very different from the villa urbana with its urban luxury. If the cumulative effect of reception, dining, bed and bathrooms was not prestigious enough, then sports arenas, theaters and temples could be included in the plans. If the owner wanted to show his cosmopolitan outlook in addition to his wealth, he could enlarge his villa into an amusement park with copies of exotic architectural forms.

The deliberate use of a succession of open and closed, bright and dark areas was characteristic of urban residential buildings and, to an even greater extent, of country houses as well.

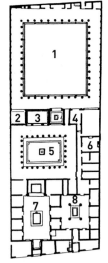

The House of the Faun, 2nd century BCE, Pompeii, floor plan and view of atrium: (1) peristyle/colonnade, (2–4) reception rooms, (3) room with Alexander mosaic, (5) fountain with faun plus atrium (6) office, (7) atrium, (8) living room and baths

△ **Teatro Maritimo, Hadrian's Villa**, construction began in 118 CE. The "small" (3,230 ft²/300 m²) circular island apartment was an independent residence with sleeping and dining rooms, bathrooms and latrines, and was often thought of as the emperor's private hideaway.

◁ **Hadrian's Villa at Tivoli** was unique among Roman villas. Covering an area of 741 acres (300 ha), the above-ground portion combined innovative and traditional Roman designs with Greek-inspired landscapes and occasional Egyptian touches. Underground, there was another entire realm of passageways for servants and service rooms.

Lasting Tribute

△ **Arch of Trajan, Benevento**, 114–120,
view of the city-facing side and detail
(right middle zone): Trajan regulates
Roman trade.

Until 27 BCE, a spectacular victory procession through the capital was granted
to military commanders by the Roman
Senate, and Roman emperors took
the liberty of allowing themselves the
same honor. By their nature, triumphal
processions provided only fleeting
satisfaction. Marble monuments were
a different story.

Together with the Via Appia Nuova
in Benevento, the Arch of Trajan (single

arched) provided a better connection
to the port of Brindisi, which was the
starting point for all military campaigns
in the East. The relief in the passageway
shows Trajan's good government. His
domestic activities are displayed on the
city side, and his foreign policy on the
state side.

A single, albeit exhaustive, theme
adorns Trajan's column in Rome. A
frieze 656 ft (200 m) long filled with

images in praise of Trajan's triumphant campaigns against the Dacians spirals to the top. The idea of a continuous narrative has been ascribed to Trajan's architect, Apollodorus. The walk-in column was both a tomb and a monument, since the base housed the ashes of the emperor. Today, in place of Trajan's gold-plated statue, there is a statue of St. Peter at the top.

△+▷ **Trajan's Column** in Rome was dedicated in 113. The band of reliefs about the Dacian wars widens upward to compensate for foreshortening. The figures are frequently contoured with grooves in order to bring out the shadow effects.

Baths and Theaters

The outlay that clever emperors lavished on their subjects to generate good will was as stupendous as it was self-indulgent. The Baths at Caracalla were among the largest and most luxurious of all the public baths in ancient Rome, as can still be felt today on seeing the ruins. Admission was free, and about two thousand visitors could relax well into the night in cold, lukewarm or hot water tubs, enjoy steam baths in other rooms, have ointments applied, get a massage or have their hair styled. The large dome over the caldarium (warm-water bath) was a lightweight construction of clay pipes fitted into each other. The Colosseum, an amphitheater, differed considerably from ancient classical theaters, both architecturally and functionally. Inside the closed, oval amphitheater

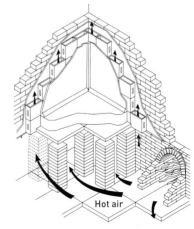

Hot air

△+▷ **Colosseum**, Rome, 70–80. Exterior and view into the still visible basement. The columns are ordered in a horizontally organized façade with Doric columns below, Ionic above and Corinthian at the top, a practice that has continued into the present.

▷ **Baths of Caracalla**, Rome, 206–216

◁ **Hypocausts** (Greek: heat from below) were used in the spas, and there was floor and wall heating fed by hot air.

bloody battles were fought on land and water. The arena could be flooded for naval and galley battles. Up to 50,000 spectators found seating in the rising rows that were not built on a slope here, because there were none on the Campus Martius. Instead, they were divided into superimposed arched tiers, a design that can still be seen today on the façade.

Provincial Architecture

Rome was developed on seven hills over the course of centuries, and urban chaos was its chief characteristic. In the provinces, on the other hand, newly established Roman cities were planned according to a rectangular grid pattern (see p. 109). After integration into the Roman Empire, existing cities took on the look of reworked Roman towns with triple-arched gates dedicated to the currently reigning Roman emperor, two intersecting colonnaded streets, a forum that served as the central square, as well as theaters and spas. Such testaments to Roman urban culture were fashionable accomplishments in cities along distant trade routes that were not yet Roman. However, the ubiquitous Roman and Greek-inspired architectural forms beyond the limits of Roman frontiers are difficult to date.

▽ **Palmyra**, Syria (Roman since 106 CE): view through Hadrian's Gate (ca. 200 CE) to the colonnaded street. Well before 106, Roman merchants were represented by the Office for Eastern Trade that was so important to overland transport.

◁ **Sbeitla**, Tunisia (Roman since 67 CE): view of the forum and Capitoline temple through the Arch of Antoninus Pius. The olive oil trade made the town prosperous.

▷ The Monastery, Petra, Jordan (Roman from 106 CE), probably second century. The divided pediment is not of Nabataean origin, but Roman.

▽ The Theater at Sabratha, Libya (Roman since 46 BCE), built ca. 190 CE. Architectural fly towers and semi-circular auditoria distinguished Roman from Greek theaters.

For All the Gods

The widest dome in antiquity was dedicated to all the gods, which might either have meant all the gods of Olympus or all planetary deities. The lighting of the hall was organized against a backdrop of the heavenly bodies and their movements. The only direct light fell through a hole in the apex of the dome, so the light could be seen moving through the hall. In clear contradiction to the concept of a Roman temple, this structure, commissioned by Hadrian (r. 117–138), focused on the interior instead of the façade. This fascinating interior was based on a technically necessary deception. What is most astonishing

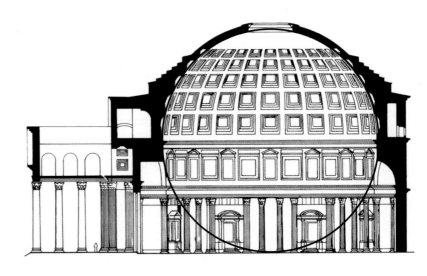

△ This longitudinal section reveals that only the inner dome could be extended to form a sphere. The exterior has a flatter dome supported on a higher drum.

on the inside is not apparent from the outside: the circular drum was "lowered" to accommodate the steep inner dome. Both dome and drum were made of opus caementicium, a kind of poured concrete (see p. 109). The dome was composed of ever lighter components towards its top. Only in this way, and by leaving a hole at the top, could the dome be supported by the 20-ft (6-m) thick walls.

◁ **Pantheon**, Rome, 118–125 CE: Colonnades originally integrated the Pantheon into the rectangular courtyard so that you could not see the rotunda and the interior came as a complete surprise.

▷ Interior view: as a result of the coffered ceilings, the dome is lighter and the illumination from above is more dramatic.

Christians "Infiltrate" Rome

Followers of a religion that proclaimed the resurrection of the flesh would clearly decide against cremation. Consequently, Christians buried their dead in walls or in niche graves located in underground tunnels. Legally, the property also had to belong to them, which thus required that they have permission to buy it. So originally, wealthy Romans provided for their own final resting places and then, out of a sense of community, for those of fellow Christians. Later, Christian communities tended to these cemeteries. And although everyone was equal before God, wealthy Christians preferred to wait for their resurrection in larger, more richly furnished graves. Beginning in the first half of the third century, figurative murals became part of the furnishings. They included themes from the Old and New Testaments and even from Greek and Roman mythology. But there are no depictions of Christ's Passion, because only criminals were crucified at that time.

◁ **Catacomb on the Via Latina**, Rome, ca. 350. Christ raising Lazarus on the wall of a tomb leaves no doubt as to what also awaits the deceased.

▷ **Catacomb on the Via Latina**, Rome, ca. 350. Hercules brings Alcestis back from the realm of the dead to her husband who awaits her. The demigod is accompanied by the hellhound Cerberus on a leash. Peacocks symbolize the Resurrection, as their flesh was considered incorruptible. The deceased rests in the base below.

◁ **Bust of Constantine the Great** (ca. 280–337 CE). He helped win recognition for Christianity in 313 CE. The document stating that he gave Rome and the Western Roman Empire to Pope Sylvester I and his successors is a medieval forgery.

Late Antiquity
& Byzantium

Map legend:
- † Church/basilica
- ⚕ Monastery
- ♜ Castle
- ✥ Mosaic
- ▲ Mountain

could appear openly. But the "secret signs" were already established and retained their value within the young religious community. Sparked by the question of whether God could be depicted and worshiped through images, the iconoclastic controversy caught fire in the eighth century.

In the Mediterranean area, **late antiquity** encompassed the period of transition after the fall of the Roman Empire. It began in 284 with the accession of Diocletian. Based on the continuance of Roman administrative structures, late antiquity ended in the West with the Lombard invasion of Italy in 568 and was followed by a gradual transition to the early Middle Ages. In the East, late antiquity lasted longer, parallel to early Byzantium.

The **Byzantine Empire** refers to the Eastern Roman Empire. It began in 395 with the final division of the Roman Empire among the sons of Emperor Theodosius I and ended in 1453 with the Ottoman conquest of Constantinople.

Early Christianity

In the beginning, Christianity established itself underground. As persecuted followers of a banned religion, early Christians used signs and symbols to communicate with one another, which either had no meaning to or were understood differently by outsiders. Cross, wreath, fish, lamb, palm, and grapevine: all these symbols were handed down along with the allegorical texts of the new faith. Under Constantine the Great, Christianity was accepted from 313 CE onward, and Christian images

Passion sarcophagus with Christ's monogram in the victory wreath, 4th century, Rome

Hagia Sophia, 532–537, Constantinople

Codex Purpureus Rossanensis, 6th century, Syria

| 250 | 350 | 500 | 550 | 700 |

Late Antiquity & Byzantium (284–1453)

Chronology

284 Diocletian becomes Roman emperor. He tries to rule the empire with three co-rulers (tetrarchs).

311/313 Christianity is first recognized in the Edicts of Nicomedia and Milan.

324 Constantine the Great achieves autocratic rule as Roman emperor.

326 Constantinople is established as the new capital of the Roman Empire.

375–568 Period of intense migration: the Huns drive the Ostrogoths into Roman territory; Goths and Vandals plunder Rome repeatedly. The Lombards finally destroy the Western Roman Empire.

395 The Roman Empire is divided: birth of the Byzantine Empire.

402–476 Ravenna, principal residence of Western Roman emperors, is taken over by Teutons, then in 493 by Ostrogoths led by Theodoric.

450 Empress consort Galla Placidia dies at Rome; her mausoleum remains empty.

527–565 Justinian rules over the Eastern Roman Empire.

540–571 After the reconquest of Italy, Ravenna becomes the seat of the [Praetorian] Prefecture.

632 Islamic expansionism begins with the death of Muhammad.

730–843 The iconoclastic controversy

1096–1099 During the First Crusade, French and German knights occupy Jerusalem, which becomes an independent state.

1204 Crusaders and Venetians conquer and plunder Constantinople in the Fourth Crusade.

1261 The Byzantines reconquer Constantinople.

1453 Ottoman conquest of Constantinople marks the end of the Byzantine Empire

Cultural History

383-406 (?) Church scholar St. Jerome translates the Hebrew and Greek versions of the Old and New Testaments into Latin. This Vulgate Bible becomes the generally binding textual basis of Christianity.

524 Unjustifiably accused of treason, just before his execution Boethius writes *Consolation of Philosophy*. It is one of the most important texts of late antiquity, early Christian philosophy and theology.

529 Benedict of Nursia founds the monastery at Monte Cassino, Italy. By means of the Benedictine Order, he lays the cornerstone for European monasticism.

600 Isidore of Seville writes an encyclopedia of all the sciences.

731 The Benedictine monk Bede the Venerable introduces the counting of years beginning with the birth of Christ.

ca. 814 The Arabs adopt Indian numerals, including zero. From the twelfth century onward, these are known in Europe as Arabic numerals.

Icon of Michael the Archangel, ca. 1100, Constantinople

The Last Judgment, 13th century, Torcello

San Marco, interior mosaics, 13th century, Venice

| 1000 | 1100 | 1200 | 1300 | 1450 |

At a Glance

Continuity or Change?

Historically, there have been two theories concerning the period between antiquity and the Middle Ages. The first posits a downfall of ancient culture during the storms of mass migration and radical changes in the wake of the fall of the Roman Empire. The second claims that all Western cultures developed side by side with continuous cross-fertilization of style and content.

Church of the Holy Sepulcher

According to ancient tradition, Helena, mother of Constantine the Great, found the places where Jesus Christ was crucified, buried, and resurrected beneath a Roman temple in 325 CE (today in the Old City of Jerusalem). Constantine commissioned the Church of the Holy Sepulcher in ca. 326. It was dedicated on September 13, 335, and is recognized as one of the most important shrines in Christendom.

Church of the Holy Sepulcher in Jerusalem: dedicated 335, destroyed 1009, rebuilt 1140–1149.

The Tetrarchs

Diocletian's solution to crisis was to appoint two senior ruling emperors (Augustus) and two junior emperors (Caesar) who would rule as four equals in the Western and Eastern Roman Empires. The symbol of this harmonious policy was made of Egyptian porphyry by a local Roman artist. It consciously avoided mighty Roman posturing so that the first Christians could view it as "love your neighbor as yourself."

Tetrarchs, ca. 300, San Marco, Venice

Lady of Carthage mosaic, ca. 500

The Vandals

Germanic Vandals were Christianized and ferried across from Spain to Africa in 429. They made Carthage their capital, led a Roman lifestyle and built Christian basilicas. Their rule ended in 534, when they were conquered by Justinian I and after being attacked by the Moors, they subsequently disappeared without trace.

The Copts

The art of Christian descendants of the ancient Egyptians (Greek: *Aegyptus*) shows a curious mixture of Egyptian tradition along with Hellenistic, Roman Christian and Byzantine elements. The flatness and schematic positioning of the characters is reminiscent of the Egyptian style, and the design of the garment folds tends to be ornamental. Rigid yet expressive images of the deceased on grave steles look at observers out of eyes that are frequently oversized.

Portrait of a woman with palm branch, grave in Antinoe, ca. 300–350, Egypt

Late Antiquity & Byzantium (284–1453)

Constantinople

In 326, construction work began in the provincial city of Byzantium on the Bosphorus. Constantine the Great wanted to turn his city, Constantinople, into a second Rome. Realizing that his fractured realm would be better ruled from a central location, he retreated from Rome, and Constantinople grew exponentially as a result. Fortifications to the west of the city had to be extended several times in order to ensure peace over the course of centuries.

In the sixth century, the population was estimated at around half a million. In order to supply water for the inhabitants, huge cisterns were built and numerous aqueducts fed wide columned halls. The port facilities were expanded to accommodate an ever-increasing number of grain deliveries.

Despite waves of Arab sieges in the seventh and eighth centuries, the city's highly developed infrastructure astonished the first Crusaders. They arrived from their home countries in the eleventh century knowing nothing of such things as baths, hospitals or sewage systems. The city's splendor also aroused envy. The Ottomans made several attempts before taking the stronghold in 1453. Istanbul has been the official name of the city since 1930.

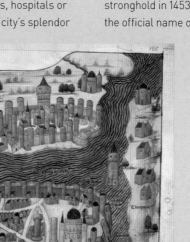

◁ **Map of Constantinople** from the Liber Insularum Cycladum by Cristoforo Buondelmonti, ca. 1485, British Library, London. Fortifications still dominate the cityscape.

▽ Crac des Chavaliers Crusader fortress, 1150–1250, Order of Saint John, Syria

Gregorian Chant

Sung liturgy originated in Rome from the fourth to eighth centuries. This form of unaccompanied liturgical music is sung in unison, in Latin.

Text and musical notation of a Gregorian chant

The Crusades

After Caliph Omar I (634–644) took control of the entire Middle East as his Islamic empire, sacred Christian locations in Palestine also came under Islamic rule. Initially the churches remained intact and untouched, and Christians were left alone. But in the eleventh century, their position grew increasingly precarious because of inter-Islamic struggles. Pilgrims were assaulted and murdered. As a result, Pope Urban II delivered an address in 1095 calling for Christians to liberate the Holy Land. Jerusalem

was conquered in 1099 and the Kingdom of Jerusalem founded. Six subsequent Crusades gave rise to four additional Crusader states. After many cruel, savage battles in which religious goals were all but forgotten on both sides, Mamluk troops finally withdrew from the Crusader kingdom for good in 1291.

Key Terms

△ **Hermes Criophoruos** (the sheep bearer), first half of the 5th century BCE. Marble, Museo Barracco, Rome

◁ **The Good Shepherd**, ca. 360. Marble, Musei Vaticani, Rome. This statue is not an image of Jesus, but the personification of Christian providence.

▽ **Passion sarcophagus**, 4th century. Marble, Musei Vaticani, Rome. At the center, the victory wreath contains a cross with the monogram of Christ flanked by doves of peace. PX (Chi-Rho for **Ch r** istus) is the symbol of eternal life.

The Good Shepherd with Sacrificial Lamb?

The Lord attended to every single lost sheep (Matthew 18:12), and Christians believed themselves to be protected. Here, the idea of the picture hearkened back (painfully, from the sheep's perspective) to its origins, corresponding to the Greek god Hermes, who shouldered a ram and mounted the walls of Tanagras to protect the entire city from plague by sacrificing the sheep.

The early Christian idea of the Good Shepherd was Greek in origin, and its realization was both Greek and Roman: the *contrapposto* stance was Greek, while the perforated surface that dramatically increased the play of shadows was Roman.

In artistic terms, the new religion often returned to earlier forms, as demonstrated by the relief sarcophagi of late antiquity, which differed

△ **The crucified Christ between two thieves**, detail, ca. 430. Cypress wood, door from the main portal of Santa Sabina, Rome

little from each other in terms of style and turned the pagan wheel of fortune into a symbol of eternal life. Overcoming death was a major aspect of Christianity, and that is why Christian imagery on sarcophagi focused on it. Since Jesus died in order to overcome death, the cross, and shortly thereafter the crucifixion itself, became the central motifs of Christian art. The hallmark of the first crucifixion scenes was not the suffering of Jesus, but the living, victorious Christ.

Basilicas Instead of Temples

Their choice was a programmatic one. The early Christians rejected Roman-style temples, where priests presented offerings to a god in the form of a religious image inside a windowless chamber. Instead they chose bright, multi-purpose, Roman-style assembly halls as their houses of worship. In the basilica, justice was pronounced, markets were held, and deities worshiped. Believers needed a spacious setting in which to pray

▷ Grave mosaic: the basilica as mother church, 5th century, Bardo Museum, Tunis

▽ Old St. Peter's, Rome, ca. 320. This five-aisled basilica, commissioned by Constantine the Great in 324, stood on the site of the present-day St. Peter's Cathedral (painting by J. Ciampine, 1693).

together in memory of their religious founder and to share bread and wine with one another.

A basilica was divided by columns or pillars into three or five parallel spaces. The middle section was wider and higher than the sides to allow for additional windows in the upper walls on either side. The central nave had a flat ceiling or was open to the truss. The semicircular niche (apse) opposite the entrance was reserved for judges in secular buildings and for the bishop in religious ones. The altar stood between the apse and the central nave. From 313 onward, Constantine the Great commissioned Christian basilicas to be built in Rome. Even then, they were furnished with a transept between the apse and nave that resulted in a cruciform floor plan.

△ **San Giovanni Evangelista**, Ravenna, first half of the fifth century, view of the apse

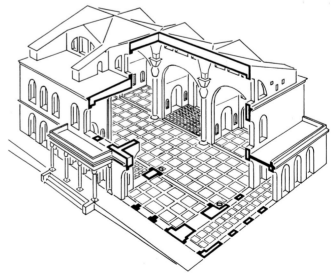

▷ **Basilica of Maxentius**, Rome. Isometric representation of the juristic basilica begun under Emperor Maxentius (reigned 306–312) and completed under Constantine the Great. The Basilica of Maxentius dispensed with the "forest of columns" typical of many Roman basilicas in favor of a vast, unified single interior. The vault was supported by just four piers and was the largest in the ancient world at 260 x 164 ft (80 x 50 m). Its vaulted space would serve as the prototype for numerous churches in the Eastern Roman Empire.

Pilgrims and Stylites

In the second half of the sixth century, in the Church of St. George at Madaba, near Bethlehem, a wide floor mosaic with a map of the Holy Land was installed to help orient pilgrims. Pilgrimages from the West had flourished since Helena, the mother of Constantine the Great, discovered Christian holy sites in Jerusalem in 325. Pilgrims also frequently sought out hermits. Streams of visitors allegedly drove the Syrian ascetic Simeon (ca. 390–459) to take refuge on top of a pillar, for which he earned sainthood. Shortly after his death, the

◁ **Mosaic map of Jerusalem** in Madaba, Jordan: second half of the 6th century.

▷ **Beta Giorgis**, Lalibela, Ethiopia, ca. 1200

▷▷ **Baptismal pool** at Sbeitla, Tunisia, 6th century. The person to be baptized walked across the monogram of Christ originally found at the bottom of the basin.

△ **Martyrionum of St. Simeon the Stylite**, Qalaat Seman (Simeon Monastery), Syria, ca. 480. The structure consisted of four cruciform pillared basilicas around a central octagon, and Simeon's 52-ft (16-m) high pillar was enshrined within it.

pillar became the site of the St. Simeon the Stylite Monastery. Prior to Hagia Sophia, it was the largest Christian structure in existence.

Early Christian believers were attentive not only to their actions, but to tradition as well. The entire body had to be cleansed in preparation for baptism, just as Jesus had once experienced it in the River Jordan. And the shape of the baptismal font was suited to its function.

When Jerusalem fell to Saladin in 1187, King Lalibela felt called by God to create a new Jerusalem in Ethiopia. The cruciform Beta Giorgis is the most elegant of the many monolithic churches he had carved out of solid pieces of tuff. Technically speaking, all of them were sculptures rather than buildings.

◁ **Theodora with followers**, ca. 540. Glass flux mosaic at San Vitale, Ravenna. Some 100 years later, the mosaic style in Ravenna changed. The figures looked more stationary, the folds of the gowns more schematized.

▷ **Christ the Good Shepherd** (with all his sheep gazing at him), ca. 440. Glass flux mosaic in the mausoleum of Galla Placidia, Ravenna

Golden Glass: More Than the Glory of God

Theodora is the tallest person in her entourage and, as an important figure, is not overlapped by any other. Opposite her, Justinian arrives on the scene from the far side of the church. The imperial couple provides the cruet for the Sacrifice of the Mass and they are highlighted by every means possible, culminating in the circle behind her head that is intentionally reminiscent of a halo. At the edge of her cloak, Theodora self-confidently carries the image of the Magi, who pay homage the Christ, though they are kings themselves.

A gold ground can strip historical figures of their reality. The Son of God thus becomes real within the spatially arranged landscape, as if viewing the blue sky through a window. In early Christian art, the beloved popular motif of the Good Shepherd underwent several interpretations in the course of the fifth century. While Christians were still being persecuted, they converted the Greek god Orpheus into the image of Christ. Orpheus tamed wild animals with his singing, just as Christ's words tamed sinners. In those days, there really were shepherds watching over their sheep. The Good Shepherd now became the King of the World, garbed in purple and his head framed with a halo. In the shape of a cross, the shepherd's staff symbolized victory over death through Christ's Passion. This once familiar interchangeability of Christ with Orpheus would continue to be cultivated in Christian iconography.

△ **Orpheus taming wild animals,** 3rd century. Part of a mosaic at Tarsus, Hatay Museum, Antakya, Turkey. In Greek mythology, Orpheus returned from the dead, and was comparable to Christ in this respect.

Hagia Sophia

With regard to technology, symbolism, and design, Justinian's architects, Anthemios of Tralleis and Isidore of Miletus, conceived the centrally planned form of this domed basilica as an architectural high point. Four massive piers support the four wide arches, above which the central dome hovers. The piers open up so skillfully into a series of half domes and colonnades that it is difficult to grasp their enormity and mass. The tightly spaced row of forty windows at the base of the dome create a circle of light that makes the vault appear to float. Contemporaries even perceived the dome as if it were suspended from heaven. The dome seemed to them like a floating canopy, the image of heaven, that was designed to enhance believers' experience of God.

△ The building, strengthened by buttresses in the early 14th century, appears squat from the outside despite the fact that the dome was elevated to just under 23 ft (ca. 7 m) after it collapsed in an earthquake in 558. The minarets are Muslim additions from after the conquest of 1453.

▷ Floor plan of the Justinian structure (532–537):
1 treasury, 2 apse, 3 and 4 east and west semi-domes,
5 baptistery, 6 supporting niches (exedrae).

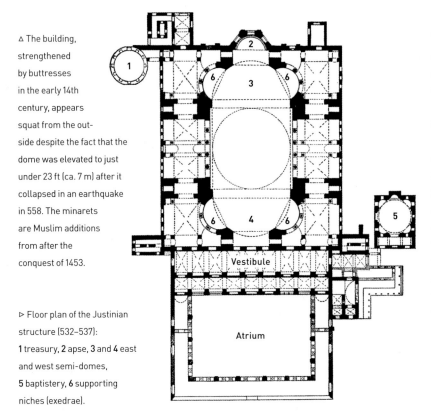

△ In order to distinguish **Hagia Sophia** (Holy Wisdom), the bishop's seat of Constantinople, as the church of all churches, marble from all parts of the Roman Empire was used for the interior.

The original decoration of the galleries and vaults consisted of mosaics, which did not include human forms, but consisted of ornaments, crosses and leaf scrolls on gold ground. Images of Mary and Christ, as well as pictures of the patriarchs and emperors, were first openly used after the end of the iconoclastic controversy in the 9th century. Since then, they have been repeatedly exposed and painted over.

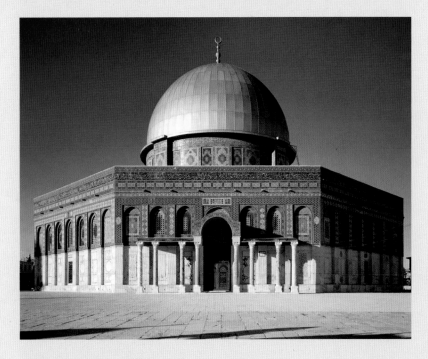

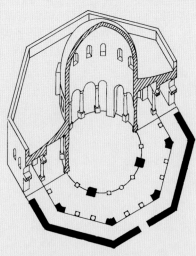

▷+△ **The Dome of the Rock** in Jerusalem (built after 690) encloses the slope where Abraham is said to have prepared to sacrifice his son, where Allah fashioned the first man at the center of Paradise, and where Muhammad began his night journey to heaven. The columns stand in a circle around the visible rock and support the pendentive dome.

▽ **Theodoric's Mausoleum**, Ravenna, ca. 525: Theodoric's architects worked according to the modular principle. The 300-ton dome was carved from a single piece of stone and rests on a cylinder.

▽ **Sergius and Bacchus Church**, Istanbul, after 527. Here, too, the rim of the pendentive dome rests directly upon the perimeter of an octagon without pendentives.

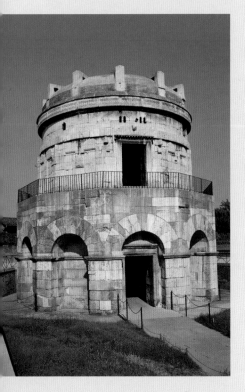

The Dome of Heaven Solution

Combining a dome with a cylinder, as at the Dome of the Rock in Jerusalem (see photo opposite), appeared relatively simple. But how does one connect a circular dome to an enclosed square, or construct a semidome over a cube? This complex task is what Byzantine architects confronted in the construction of new, sacred Christian buildings. The floor plan was a shaped like a cross. The square crossing was located in the middle of the cruciform floor plan, so the base of the dome was a cube. The placing of the dome created a deep round-arched niche (squinch) at the four corners of the cube. Through geometric simplification, an octagon was formed from the square. The transept was made to look more organic by means of spherical triangular sections of vaulting (pendentives). Imagine a semidome turned upside down over a cube. Now remove all the parts where the cube slices through it, i.e., all parts of the cube that are taller than the semidome. If the ratio has been calculated correctly, the curved pendentives will close at the circular rim of the dome, which then only needs to be bricked in.

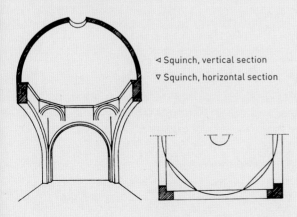

◁ Squinch, vertical section
▽ Squinch, horizontal section

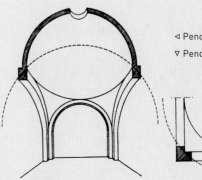

◁ Pendentive, vertical section
▽ Pendentive, horizontal section

△ **Mosaic: Constantine IX donating 7 pounds (3 kg) of gold**, 11th century, Hagia Sophia, Istanbul. Eleventh-century Byzantine mosaicists knew what was important. Human faces lost their rigidity, and ornate fabric patterns were never obscured by folds. Gold had a livelier luster when laid unevenly rather than uniformly.

◁ **Diptych of Areobindus**: ivory, Constantinople, 506, Musée National du Moyen Age, Paris. Consuls were issued such tablets upon assuming office.

Hand-crafted Works of Art

The most talented craftsmen of the period worked in Constantinople. From ivory they carved representational works of art and luxury articles, as well as fittings for furniture and reliquaries.

Even before the iconoclastic controversy (730–843), and certainly thereafter, they covered church walls with technically advanced and theo-logically sophisticated mosaic cycles. Members of imperial social circles commissioned the most sumptuous manuscripts of the Gospels, which were written with silver ink on high quality parchment dyed purple.

But the most intriguing of all these arts was glittering enamel work. Colorful glass powder (every effort was made to achieve identical melting points for each color) had to be fired up to three times to fill the tiniest depressions in gold wire frames.

Whether as gifts, dowries or loot, everything that was portable made its marks beyond Constantinople as well. And after the Fourth Crusade (1204) destroyed the art business, these arts moved toward the East with their masters.

△ **Codex Purpureus Rossanensis**, Syrian, 6th century. Museo Diocesano, Rossano. The lively presentations and anecdotal details of illuminated manuscripts are full of surprises. In the Codex, we see the Old Testament prophets authenticating the events of the New Testament from below.

△ **Icon of Michael the Archangel**, Constantinople, ca. 1100. San Marco, Venice. Icons testify to the mastery of Byzantine enameling. Except for precious stones, all colors were made from glass powder that was melted between gold wire frames, including the elaborately sculpted faces.

Powerful Images, Powerful Opponents

In 730, Emperor Leo III called for the prohibition of images (aniconism). Since 544, when the "true" image of Christ appeared in the form of an imprint of his face on a cloth, the veneration of this image and all its reproductions had risen alarmingly. There was also an image of Mary with the Christ child, allegedly by the hand of Luke the Evangelist. In the possession of influential religious orders, these icons were often thought to work miracles. They were political dynamite, and the emperor responded. According to members of Leo III's entourage, Jesus's divine nature was inexpressible, so his image would reduce him to a mere human being. Consequently, his likenesses were inadmissible.

Proponents of icons argued that one should be able to portray a person as long as the true picture was copied faithfully; one honored the venerable archetype in the image, but did not pray to it. In a hair-splitting confrontation, ecclesiastical interests finally triumphed over worldly ones, and the prohibition of images, an issue the West had hardly taken notice of anyway, was repealed once and for all in 843. Worshipping images of the Blessed Mother increased markedly as a result of the iconoclastic controversy, and many different types of images developed, beginning with the one ascribed to St. Luke.

△ As on the legendary shroud with its miraculously imprinted image, which appeared in Edessa in 544 and arrived in Constantinople in 944, only to disappear from there in 1204, **Christ Pantocrater** and ruler of the world is shown with the Gospel in one hand and his right hand raised in speech. His thick brown hair is parted in the middle, falling to both sides of his narrow face in gentle waves and down his back. The thin mustache turns downward, and the full beard ends in two rather prominent points. The intentionally asymmetrical facial features and dissimilar eyes are meant to underscore the lifelike nature of this image.

△ **Hodegetria** (she who points the way) corresponds to the portrait by Saint Luke. Mary carries the child on the left and gestures toward him with her right hand. Christ's right hand is raised in blessing, and he holds a scroll. Both regard the viewer.

△ **Glykophilusa**, the sweet-kissing mother, also called Eleusa the merciful, caresses the child, who nestles his cheek against hers and hugs his mother. The contours of his face complete the circle.

△ **Pelagonitissa**, she who plays with child, just manages to hold the squirming boy, whose posture is prescribed. Although they face one another, both look to the viewer, and Mary seems especially worried.

△ **Galaktophorousa**, she who nurses the child, is a familiar motif that not only appears in Eastern and Western churches, but also in ancient Egypt with Isis nursing her child, Horus. The resulting painting is less strictly prescribed from an artistic standpoint.

△ **Strastnaja**, Madonna of the Passion, holds the troubled child, who clings to her right hand with both of his. The instruments of the Passion are in sight. He has crossed his feet, and a sandal has come loose.

△ **Nikopoia**, she who brings victory, directly faces the viewer. The child is seated in front of her chest, held only at the shoulder and knee. Byzantine emperors supposedly carried this icon to war. Today it resides in San Marco, Venice.

1. The Crucified Christ between Mary and John: the source of life flows from his wounds.

2. In the Harrowing of Hell, the dead Christ breaks open the gates of the underworld and saves the righteous, beginning with Adam.

3. The Judge as shining light in the mandorla between Mary and John the Baptist, with archangels and Apostles. At his feet springs the river of fire for Hell.

4. Sounding horns raise the dead, whether buried or eaten by beasts. An angel unrolls the firmament. The throne has been prepared and symbolizes the presence of God.

5. and 6. The Blessed on the left, Mary orant in the center, the Damned with Lucifer and his son, the Antichrist, on the right.

◁ The Last
Judgment at
Torcello is one of
the most complete
examples of
Byzantine
iconography. From
top to bottom:
1.–2. 13th century,
3.–6. 12th century

The Church Decoration Program: From East to West, Between a Rock and a Hard Place

Theologians used images in order to protect those entrusted to them, the children of God, from ruin. They focused the attention of the faithful on the apse image as they entered the church.

In the Basilica of Santa Maria Assunta, Mary appears with the blessed Christ child, and she is the most influential advocate for humanity.

She dominates the shimmering gold celestial sphere and radiates loyalty. Upon leaving the church, the comforted ones, facing west where the sun goes down, are shown what to expect on the Last Day. These are the horrors of hell, deliberately shown at eye level, and even more imaginatively presented than the joys of heaven.

▷ Golden mosaic with the Virgin Hodegetria (she who points the way), end of the 11th century. Basilica of Santa Maria Assunta, Torcello, Italy. Mary gestures to the blessed Child. The Apostles beneath her are human witnesses to divine revelation. They stand upon the earth and appear to hold up the sky. The garments of the stationary figures show typical Byzantine folds that suggest the body underneath.

San Marco

Venice had a lucrative relationship with Constantinople in terms of trade, artistic inspiration and booty. Following the sixth-century model of the Holy Apostles in Constantinople, Doge Domenico Contarini built the Basilica of San Marco, the doges' private chapel, a five-domed, cruciform church. Upon completion in 1094, San Marco's exterior and interior were much less ornate than they are today. The mosaics adorning the five-arched façade on the Piazza San Marco date from the thirteenth century, and were largely replaced in the seventeenth and nineteenth centuries. The horses above the main entrance arrived as Crusade booty from Constantinople in 1204. They came from the quadriga of a Roman triumphal arch, and Constantine the Great had ordered their installation to adorn his new capital. The tracery, sculptures, and open towers of San Marco were fourteenth-century Gothic additions.

The interior mosaics originated mainly in the thirteenth century. They were staggered according to their theological significance: the saints below, scenes from the lives of Mary and Jesus above them, and themes including the Miracle of Pentecost and the Ascension in the dome area.

▷ The many different kinds of stone columns on the façade are striking. Like the marble slabs, they are Crusade booty.

▷▷ Windows were walled in when the mosaics were laid, which changed the lighting. The unevenly embedded gold background tesserae (colorless glass flux with melted gold foil) created a shimmering, unearthly light instead.

▽ **1** Porta di San Alippio, **2** north vestibule, **3** baptistery, **4** Chapel of St. Peter, **5** presbytery, **6** Chapel of St. Clement, **7** apse

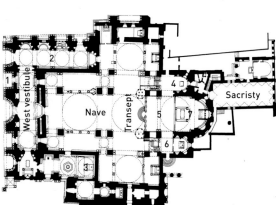

**Pre-Romanesque
& Romanesque**

NORTH SEA

ATLANTIC

Borgund †

Castle Acre †
Ely †
London ●

Bayeux

Paris ●

Aachen ●
Maria Laach

Cologne †
Hildesheim †
Gernrode †
Schwarzrheindorf †
Limburg †
Mainz
Lorsch ●
Speyer

Fontenay ●
Vézelay †
Autun
Cluny ●
Cîteaux ●

Reichenau †
St. Gallen †
Zillis †

Saint-Savin-
sur-Gartempe

Santiago de
Compostela ●

Oviedo †

Toro †

Moissac ●

PYRENEES

Conques ✕

Saint-Martin-
du-Canigou

CORSICA

Florence †

Pisa †

Rome ●

Bari †

SARDINIA

MEDITERRANEAN

SICILY

† Church
● Monastery
♟ Palace
✕ Reliquary
🧵 Tapestry

Images of Salvation

"Anyone can see that this ponderous, raw architecture is opus romanum… at the same time developed out of the mutilated Latin a Romance language." Even as the antiquary Charles de Gerville created a stylistic term out of a negative description in 1818 (as has often happened in art history), his observation is correct. The key feature of the architectural style that emerged during the Carolingian Renaissance is the return to the aesthetic forms and traditions of ancient Rome, such as the Roman arch that can (in extended form) act as vault over interior spaces, connect columns to form arcades, and adorn the façades of clearly ordered structures. The Roman Catholic Church—especially in its monasteries—undertook almost all of its artistic endeavors not only in order to depict salvation but also to serve the representational needs of a strictly organized clergy. Regional developments such as the evolution of the Gothic style were organic and idiosyncratic.

Gatehouse, Lorsch Abbey, 767–774

Evangelary of Archbishop Ebo, Hautvillers (Reims), 816–835

Fresco: Storm on Lake Tiberias, late tenth century, St. Georg, Oberzell on Reichenau

750　　　　800　　　　850　　　　900　　　　950

Pre-Romanesque & Romanesque (750–1200

Chronology

For artistic purposes, the pre-Romanesque and Romanesque periods in the history of the Holy Roman Empire are often divided into sub-periods according to the ruling dynasty:

751–918 Carolingian
919–1024 Ottonian
1024–1125 Salian
1138–1250 The genesis of the Gothic period also took place during the rule of the Hohenstaufen dynasty.
800 Coronation of Charlemagne as emperor

910 The Abbey of Cluny is founded.
962 Otto I becomes the emperor of the Holy Roman Empire.
1009 First meeting of the *Reichstag* at the Imperial Palace in Goslar
ca. 1020 The Normans establish a Christian state in southern Italy.
1054 The Great Schism separates the Roman Catholic and Greek Orthodox Churches.
1066 Anglo-Saxon England falls to William the Conqueror, Duke of Normandy.
1075–1122 Investiture controversy: conflict between Pope Gregory VII and Emperor Henry IV over secular versus church power to appoint bishops and abbots
1077 Henry IV makes his "Walk to Canossa" to beg the pope's forgiveness
1095 The First Crusade begins.
1098 Foundation of the Cistercian Order
1099 The armies of the First Crusade conquer Jerusalem.
1152 Frederick Barbarossa becomes Holy Roman emperor.
1194 Richard I the Lionheart is ransomed.

Cultural History

ca. 800 Carolingian minuscule—a basis for today's "Roman" alphabet—is developed in Charlemagne's palace school and scriptorium.
ca. 850 Early scholasticism gives rise to a revival of classical dialectics and academic debate—albeit in accordance with Christian dogma—in the fields of science, philosophy, and theology.
ca. 900 The stave is introduced to musical notation at the Abbey of St. Gall.

ca. 935–1000 The nun Roswitha of Gandersheim composes holy legends, dramas and a history of the Ottonian Dynasty, thus becoming the first German poetess.
ca. 950–1022 Notker III "the German" translates Roman and Greek texts into Old High German—the first scientific use of German.
1086 William the Conqueror commissions *The Domesday Book*, a property survey of England's 2.5 million inhabitants. It will not be updated until the seventeenth century.

ca. 1100 *The Song of Roland*, an Old French epic poem—its subject is the heroic death of Roland on one of Charlemagne's campaigns against the Moors in Spain.
ca. 1140 The epic *El Cid*, celebrating the deeds of the Castilian knight El Cid, marks the beginning of the Spanish heroic epic.

St. Michael, Hildesheim, 1010–1033

Bayeux Tapestry, ca. 1080

Dream of the Magi, ca. 1120–1130, Saint-Lazare, Autun

1000	1050	1100	1150	1200

At a Glance

Romanesque Church

Choir

Westwork

Pyramidal roof

Choir tower

Crossing tower

Central nave (aisle)

Transept

Clerestory

Side aisle

Rhenish helm roof

Triple window

Eaves

Pyramidal roof

Pitched roof

Double window

Dwarf gallery

Trefoil arch

Lombard band

Apse

Pilaster strip

Atrium

At the western end of Maria Laach Abbey (see p. 172) are the portals of an atrium porch called the "Paradise," which contains a fountain for performing ritual ablutions. At the other end of the nave is the choir, the section of the church in which the clerics sang. It is flanked by two choir towers.

Fontenay Abbey, ca. 1139–1147. Fontenay provides an early example of the sublime purity of design that Bernard of Clairvaux advocated for Cistercian abbeys.

Vaulted or Flat Roofs?

In pre- and proto-Romanesque church architecture, the flat roof reflected a link to the tradition of early Christian basilicas. But in High Romanesque churches, the barrel vault, known since antiquity, became the principal type of ceiling. This change was due not simply to aesthetic reasons; stone vaulting lasts longer than flammable wood ceilings.

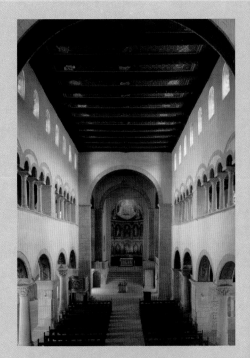

St. Cyriacus, Gernrode, ca. 970–1000. This abbey church is one of the best-preserved monuments of Ottonian architecture. The coffered ceiling is only one of the elements imitated at St. Michael in Hildesheim.

Pre-Romanesque & Romanesque (750–1200

Madonna

The Madonna and Child (∇ France 1150–1200) is, after the crucified Christ, the primary motif in Romanesque woodcarving.

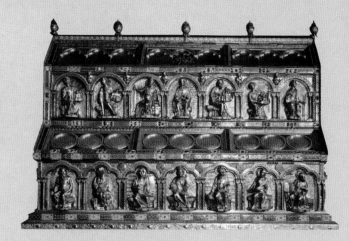

Shrine of the Three Holy Kings, 1190–1220

Reliquaries

Originally, the relics of saints and other holy people were buried underneath the altars of the first Christian churches. By the early Middle Ages, journeys of pilgrimage had contributed to a considerable expansion of the cult of relics. In order to emphasize the growing significance of relics for the churches that housed them, the clergy began to commission exquisite and expensive containers for these revered artifacts known as reliquaries or shrines.

Crucifix

The crucified Christ became the central theme of Christian art (see p. 180f.).

Herimann Cross, ca. 1050. Gilded bronze, lapis lazuli head, 16¾ x 18½ in (42.5 x 47 cm). Kolumba, Cologne

Portal

As seen at Vézelay, Christ in Judgment often dominates the tympanum that crowns a Romanesque church's central portal (see p. 182f.)

Archivolt

Tympanum

Jamb figures

Jamb pedestal

Trumeau

Lintel

Capital

Key Terms

Carolingian Renaissance

When Charlemagne was crowned Holy Roman emperor by the pope in 800, he filled a post that had been vacant since the the last Western Roman Emperor was banished in 476. This title made it easier for Charlemagne to enact reforms necessary to revive the empire. Most important were an efficient bureaucracy and an educational program for the nobility and the clergy. The first of these goals was made possible through the development of Carolingian minuscule, a simplified but standardized official script. To accomplish the second goal, Charlemagne transformed monasteries into centers of learning. Charlemagne's ideals were heavily influenced by those of ancient Rome. It is no coincidence that the

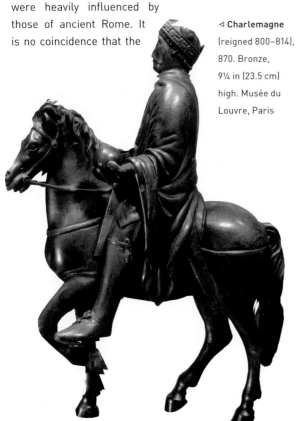

◁ **Charlemagne** (reigned 800–814), 870. Bronze, 9¼ in (23.5 cm) high. Musée du Louvre, Paris

gatehouse at Lorsch Abbey makes use of the Roman arch, recollecting a triumphal arch. Here, however, simple Ionic capitals crown complex composite capitals as opposed to the other way around.

The newly crowned emperor and protector of Western Christendom did not settle in Rome. He chose Aachen (Aix-la-Chapelle) as his capital, but he and his entire retinue were constantly moving from palace to palace (there were fifty imperial "way stations" in total). One part of the (destroyed) palace complex at Aachen is the chapel, an octagonal central-plan structure that mirrors Byzantine models from Constantinople or Ravenna. The term "palace" derives from "Palatine," the hill on which the emperor's palace in Rome had been situated, and whence the new emperor had the Corinthian capitals adorning the galleries delivered.

△ **Gatehouse of the destroyed abbey complex at Lorsch**, 767–774

▷+▽ **Palatine Chapel**, finished 798, dedicated 805. Aachen Cathedral. The eight sides of the octagon represent a new beginning, as eight people were saved on Noah's Ark.

Bernward's Ottonian Hildesheim

Bernward, Bishop of Hildesheim from 993–1022 and educator of Otto III, had ambitious plans for his bishopric. With the abbey church of St. Michael, he created a prototype for the clearly ordered constructions of Ottonian architecture. The proportions are based on the square of the crossing, where the nave and transepts cross. In order to arrange the nave as a chain of squares, each pair of columns is set off with one pilaster.

According to the Revelation of John (21:16), the New Jerusalem, the

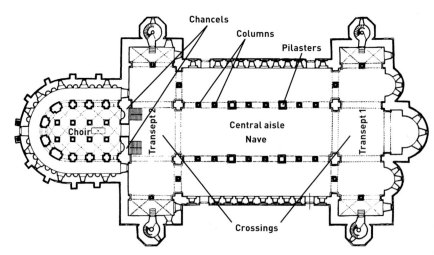

city that God would build to house His people after the Final Judgment, is laid out "foursquare." Well-balanced proportions also determine the length, breadth, and height of St. Michael's, as well as the distribution of its four towers.

The bronze doors commissioned by Bernward (today at the cathedral of St. Mary, also in Hildesheim), show, in eight panels, humanity's fall from grace (on the left side) and its salvation through Christ (on the right). The figures are executed in differing degrees of relief; their lower bodies remain in bas-relief, while their upper bodies, shoulders, and heads often spring from the panels in high relief, as if they were striving toward redemption, spiritually as well as formally. At Hildesheim, Bernward set new standards for Ottonian art, not only in architecture but also in sculpture.

◁ + △ **St. Michael**, 1010–1033, Hildesheim. View from the southeast and floor plan.

◁ **Bernward's Door**, ca. 1015, Hildesheim Cathedral. Bronze, each panel 185 x 49¼/45 in (472 x 125/114.5 cm). Detail of the left panel showing the expulsion from paradise, the life of Adam and Eve, and the sacrifices of Cain and Abel.

Cubiform capital

▽ **Chancel in the west crossing**, St. Michael, Hildesheim, 1194–1197. The columns in the background are crowned with Bernward's cubiform capitals.

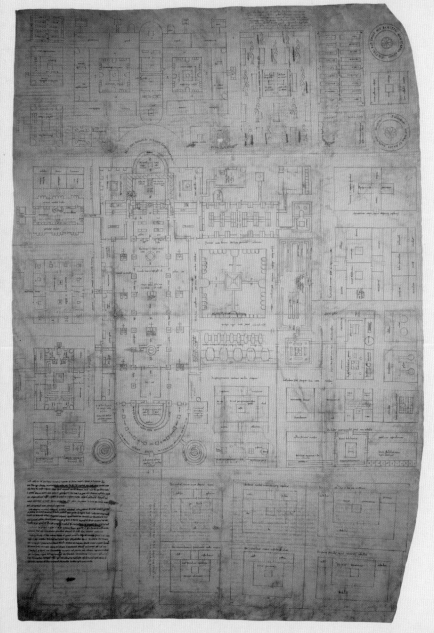

Ora et Labora

Benedict of Nursia founded the Benedictine Order at Monte Cassino, between Rome and Naples, in 529 CE. In establishing the dictum of *ora et labora* ("pray and work") as the Benedictine Rule's main principle, he continued a tradition begun by the hermits and early desert monasteries of fourth-century Egypt. Charlemagne especially fostered the foundation of new monasteries, whose scriptoria and libraries became treasuries of knowledge, meanwhile supporting his educational reforms. Benedictine abbeys thus sprang up all over Europe at this time. The Plan of St. Gall, probably drawn up on the island of Reichenau in Lake Constance, shows what a Benedictine Abbey needed in order to be economically independent, as well as all the features necessary for a communal life dedicated to faith. As the earthly splendor and power of some abbeys (especially Cluny) reached heights deemed by many to be excessive, Bernard of Clairvaux called for a return to the more modest Benedictine Rule. The Cistercian Order, which renounced all luxury, was founded at the Burgundian abbey of Cîteaux in Burgundy in 1098.

◁ **Cistercian Abbey of Fontenay,** 1139–1147, France. This abbey, founded by Bernard of Clairvaux in 1118, is one of the best-preserved of its kind in Europe.

△ A monk cutting grain forms an **initial Q** in a manuscript from Cîteaux.

◁ **The Plan of St. Gall** (ca. 820), a manuscript on parchment in the Library of St. Gall, details the ideal design for a self-contained abbey complex.

▷ **The Benedictine Abbey of Saint-Martin-du-Canigou,** ca. 1009, France

▽ **Former Benedictine Abbey Church of Saint-Pierre,** cloister, ca. 1100, Moissac, France. The cloister—a place for solitary contemplation—marks the center of many abbeys. Usually accessible from the abbey church, the cloister also often borders on the chapter house, refectory and dormitories.

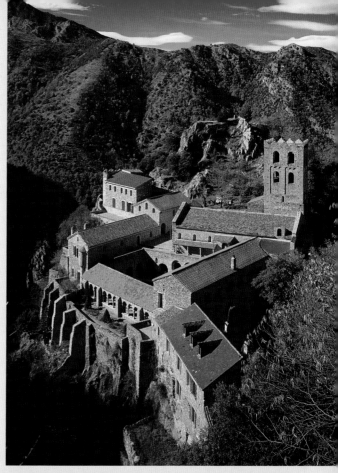

The Bayeux Tapestry

Around 1070, hundreds of soldiers —on foot and on horseback, in ships on the English Channel, wounded or lying dead on the ground—were patiently stitched onto canvas. 223 ft (68 m) long and 21 in (53 cm) high, this colossal work of embroidery portrays the events leading up to William the Conqueror's conquest of England (1066), culminating with his victory at the Battle of Hastings. The "tapestry" formerly adorned the walls of Bayeux Cathedral, but can be seen today in Bayeux's *Centre Guilllaume le Conquérant*. Like illuminated manuscripts, it combines image and text.

Book Illumination as Worship

◁◁ **Ebbo Gospels**:
St. Mark the
Evangelist, 816–
835, Hautvillers
(Reims). Ink
and tempera
on vellum,
Bibliothèque
municipale,
Épernay

◁ **Gospels of
Otto III**: Otto III
Enthroned, after
997, Reichenau (or
Trier). Ink, gold
leaf and tempera
on vellum

All Romanesque manuscripts, from exceptional specimens to simple work material, were made exclusively by hand. The monks who carefully copied these books in monastic workshops (scriptoria) considered their work a form of prayer. According to the nature of the manuscript, they adorned their work with historiated initials (from Latin *initium*: beginning), decorative borders, and painted images often containing gold, called miniatures (from *minium*, a vermilion ink used in these pictures). The manuscript leaves were most often made of parchment (usually vellum), a specially prepared animal hide. (The word "parchment" is derived from the ancient city of Pergamon, where it was invented.) Miniaturists took older works of illumination as

their models, then further developed or reinterpreted them.

While the atmospheric and illusory style of the Ebbo Gospels is indebted to painting of late antiquity and thus an example of Carolingian illumination, the drapery and hierarchically determined scale of the figures in the Gospels of Otto III reflect Byzantine influences in Ottonian book art. Copies of the *Commentary on the Apocalypse* of Beatus, a monk who expected the final judgment around 800, display a unique style that is perfectly suited to their content. And in order to do justice to the visions of Hildegard von Bingen (1098–1179), Abbess of Rupersberg, the illuminator used an especially allegorical visual language.

▷ **Beatus
of Liébana,
Commentary on
the Apocalypse**:
Beatus Facundus
(for Ferdinand I
and Doña Sancha),
1047. Biblioteca
Nacional, Madrid

▽ Hildegard von
Bingen, **Liber
Divinorum Operum:
Universal Man**, ca.
1230. Manuscript.
Biblioteca
Governativa, Lucca

Romanesque Architecture

The clearly ordered structuring of church buildings apparent in the design of St. Michael's in Hildesheim became a fundamental principle of Romanesque architecture. The relationships between interconnected and dependent structural elements remained visible on the exterior as well as in the interior: choirs, transepts, aisles, towers, and façades with hierarchically organized volumes of architectonic features. The Roman arches that dictated the interior form also ordered the façades with blind arches, windows and galleries. Special characteristics included the formation of the choir at the east end of the church, situated above the crypt and containing an ambulatory with radiating chapels, or—as was especially common in the Rhineland—a triconch choir, which was modeled on the Church of the Nativity in Bethlehem.

▽ Maria Laach, Benedictine Abbey Church.
Begun 1093, choir completed 1170, atrium at
west façade ("Paradise") 1230/40

△ Limburg Cathedral, Limburg an der
Lahn, formerly the Abbey Church of St.
George. 1215–1235, with late Romanesque
two-towered façade

◁ Church of the Holy Apostles, 1020–1030,
Cologne, dwarf gallery of the triconch choir

▷ St. Pantaleon, 984–ca. 1000, Cologne,
westwork

At the west end of some churches, an architecturally and liturgically
independent, seemingly defensive
structure called a westwork was
added. In the westwork's galleries, a
visiting king or emperor could attend
mass in a private setting, undisturbed
and unseen by the congregation.

With its more finely organized
interior and exterior design, Limburg
Cathedral signaled a shift from the
heavy, massive walls characteristic
of the Romanesque to the lighter
constructions of the Gothic.

Arches and Vaults

After proto-Romanesque church architecture had established a link to the tradition of early Christian basilicas through its flat roofs, the barrel vault, known since antiquity, became the principal type of ceiling in High Romanesque churches. As a rule, vaulting of stone or masonry lasts longer than flammable wood ceilings.

Two types of vaulting exemplify Romanesque construction. The line-supported barrel vault consists of a load-bearing shell;

ribs or transverse arches running perpendicular to the longitudinal axis could also provide support. If three-aisled structures were designed with parallel barrel vaults, the partition walls could be opened up with columned or pilastered arcades, or arcades with alternating supports.

If two barrel vaults of equal height intersect at a right angle, the result is a point-supported groin vault, thanks to its shape also called a cross vault. If the vault's spines are

visibly supported and emphasized with sculpted armatures, then it is called a ribbed vault.

The individual vault segments, organized into four bays, are separated from each other by transverse arches, which often serve as points of reference for the pillars of the arcade by extending to the floor. They strengthen the pillars, and simultaneously give the impression that they are shouldering some of the pillars' burden.

◁ Central aisle showing a **barrel vault** without transverse arches, resting on a columned arcade. Saint-Savin-sur-Gartempe, France, former priory church, 1065–1115

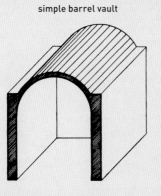
simple barrel vault

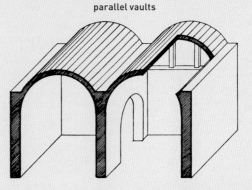
parallel vaults

▽ **Groin vault with transverse arches**, Speyer Cathedral, 1030–1106, side aisle

△ **Ribbed vault**, Mainz Cathedral, 1081–1137, central aisle

△ Cubiform capitals on thickset columns support a **cross vault**, Speyer Cathedral, crypt (oldest section of the cathedral, dedicated 1041)

single-nave ribbed vault

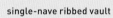
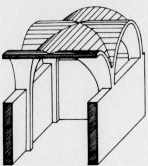

multiple-nave ribbed vault with transverse arches

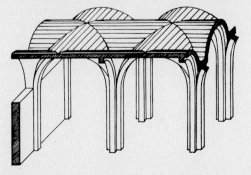

◁ **Storm on Lake Tiberias**, from the fresco cycle Christ's Miracles, late tenth century. St. Georg, Oberzell (Reichenau), central aisle, southern wall

Images on Walls and Ceilings

▷ **Scenes from the Life of Christ and the Legend of St. Martin**, ca. 1130/40, St. Martin, painted wood ceiling (detail), Zillis, Switzerland. The life of Jesus and the legend of St. Martin are portrayed on 153 panels, framed by sea serpents. Some scenes required two panels to provide enough room for all the figures.

▽ **Christ Pantocrator** (Ruler of the Universe), frescoes in the Upper Church, ca. 1180, double church of Sts. Maria and Clemens, Schwarzrheindorf (Bonn). Looking past the destruction of the Old and the foundation of the New Jerusalem in the Lower Church, the eye is drawn through the opening in the roof to the image of Christ.

A Romanesque church is brightly colored on the inside and outside. The colors are an integral part of the design, and if they are missing, then the design must be considered incomplete. Mural painting is the finishing touch that gives the interior its true look and heightens its effect. With its depictions of scenes from the Bible, the painting brought the divine closer, and provided a visual echo of the liturgy. The images were intended to educate the viewers in true belief, and therefore be comprehensible to all. The narrative qualities of painting made it preferable in didactic terms to sculptural ornament, which, due to its practical limitations, only provided for single views. Most of the figurative painting was centered on the nave, which is where the faithful would see the life, works and Passion of Jesus. In the central aisle, the space occupied by the congregation, the images are not distant as they are in the apse, but instead can be observed up close.

The entire wall surface of most Byzantine churches was covered with golden mosaics (see p. 149). In Ottonian and Romanesque churches in Germany and Switzerland, and as would later be the case in the Gothic churches of France, the subjects of the colorful murals remained the same—only the medium changed.

Furnishings

Romanesque churches, especially cathedrals, were richly decorated with sculptures and paintings. In addition to the representations of Christ and the Virgin, a lectern, occasionally serving simultaneously as a censer, was invariably among the furnishings. The bishop's throne or *cathedra* underscored his exalted position, even in his absence. And a sumptuous baptismal font lends this central sacrament of Christianity the appropriate gravity.

The most magnificent decorative elements were created in connection with the cult of relics. Increasingly costly and luxuriant shrines were built to house the numerous remains of saints (martyrs being exceptionally popular) and to impress pilgrims. The gilded reliquary of St. Foy originally contained the martyred saint's head, and Nicholas of Verdun completed an exquisite shrine to house the bones of the Magi in the Cologne Cathedral.

△ **Lectern**, ca. 1150. Painted wood, 47¼ in (120 cm) high. Evangelical Lutheran Church of Freudenstadt. Each of the four Evangelists is identified by the symbol above his head.

◁ **Bishop's throne** (cathedra), twelfth century. Marble, Basilica of San Nicola, Bari. The throne is supported by Atlases reminiscent of antiquity.

◁ Nicholas of Verdun, **Shrine of the Three Holy Kings**, 1190–1220. Silver, gold, jewels and enamel, 60¼ x 43¼ x 87 in (153 x 110 x 222 cm). Cologne Cathedral

▷ **Reliquary of St. Foy**, ca. 1000. Gilded wood, jewels, 33½ in (85 cm) high. Abbey Church of Sainte-Foy, Conques

▷▷ **Baptismal font**, ca. 1225. Bronze, 67 in (170 cm) high. Hildesheim Cathedral

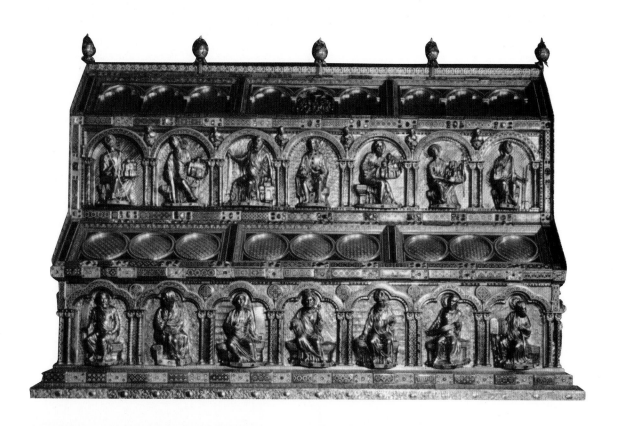

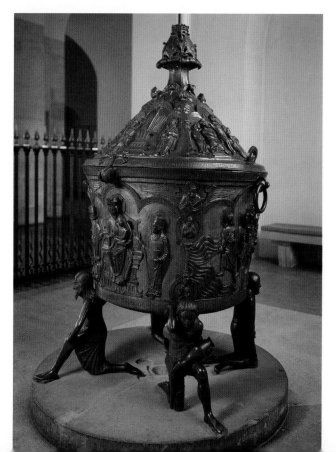

Cross and Crucifix

The Gospels offer little more than the sober statement, "And they crucified him." But the cross is nevertheless the symbol of Christianity, and the crucified Christ has long been a central theme of Christian art. This fact is difficult to comprehend; after all, no other religion has elevated to a cultic image the instrument responsible for the suffering and death of its spiritual focus. But with his triumph over fear, suffering, and death, Christ is exalted, and his divine power is revealed. Vital to the depiction of Jesus on the cross are His two aspects: the divine and the human. In early Christian and Byzantine art, the crucified Christ is represented in triumph, alive and with eyes open (see p. 139). In this way, the cross becomes a sign of victory, visible also in European art as processional crosses (2,3) or as monumental triumphal crosses (8) that were hung over the entrance to the choir. Crosses with a clothed Jesus, like the Catalonian crucifixes (7), also continued this tradition. During the Carolingian period, when the first monumental crucifixes like the Gero Cross (4) were created, a different representational convention appeared: the crucified Christ is dead, as can be seen in the light curve of his slouching, very human body. His eyes are closed, and his face is a mask of silent suffering. (St. George, 5, 6). Even the Cross of Lothair (1), with its recycled ancient cameo of Augustus, bears such a crucifix on its back.

△ **Cross of St. George**, detail, ca. 1070. Walnut, 74¾ in (190 cm). Schnütgen Museum, Cologne

▷ 1. **Cross of Lothair**, ca. 980. Wood, gold, jewels, and ancient cameo, 19⅝ in (49.8 cm). Cathedral Treasury, Aachen

▷ 2. **Cross of Gisela**, after 1006. Wood, gold, and jewels, 17½ in (44.5 cm). Residenzmuseum, Munich

▷ 3. **Ivory crucifix**, ca. 1063. 20½ in (52 cm). Museo Arqueológico Nacional, Madrid

▷ 4. **Gero Cross**, before 976. Painted oak, 73⅝ in (187 cm). Cologne Cathedral

▷ 5. **Crucifix**, ca. 970–1000. Basswood, 76 in (193 cm). Rectory of the Holy Cross, Schaftlach

▷ 6. **Ringelheim Cross**, ca. 1000. Basswood, 103⅛ in (262 cm). Diocesan Museum, Hildesheim

▷ 7. **Majestas Battlo**, ca. 1150. Painted wood, 36¼ in (92 cm). Museo de Arte Cataluña, Barcelona

▷ 8. **Udenheim Crucifix**, ca. 1150. Wood, 82⅔ in (210 cm) high. Cathedral of Sts. Martin and Stephen, Mainz

▷ 9. **Crucifix**, ca. 1220. Painted alder, 70½ in (179 cm). Holy Cross parish church, Munich

1

2

3

4

5

6

7

8

9

Sculpture in Burgundy

Only when a threshold has been consecrated is a Christian church sacred space. That explains why builders of Romanesque churches—especially those in Burgundy, along the pilgrims' way to Santiago de Compostela—dedicated so much time and energy to the design of churches' main portals. Comparable to ancient triumphal arches, the portals give expression to complex iconographic programs. Everyone who crossed the threshold was to be instructed in the Christian doctrine of salvation and thus enter the holy space as a new person. This was all the more important if people could not read. In the middle point sits Christ triumphant, passing judgment, saving the souls of the righteous and condemning sinners to the carefully detailed torments of hell. From 1100 on, even the column capitals' ornamental vegetation and other embellishments took on biblical themes, in many cases designed more with visual stimulation in mind than spiritual well-being.

All **capitals from the Cathedral of Saint-Lazare**, Autun, 1120–1150. Musée de Saint-Lazare, Autun

△ **Dream of the Magi**: With an angel as his messenger, God warns the Magi in a dream not to return to Herod after they have found and adored the Christ child.

◁ **Suicide of Judas**, after his betrayal of Christ. Demons pull on his noose.

▽ **Eve Takes the Apple**

◁ **Former Abbey Church of Sainte-Madeleine**, main portal, 1125–1130, Vézelay. In the tympanum: Christ and the Mission of the Apostles, Surrounded by the Peoples of the Earth. In the archivolt: Astrological Signs and Labors of the Months. On the trumeau: St. John the Baptist

Pisa and Florence

The once mighty Maritime Republic of Pisa took home many spoils after its 1063 naval victory over the Saracens: "Six great ships laden with treasure fell into their hands. With these avails was this building begun," proclaims the inscription on the façade of Pisa's cathedral. In its five-nave design, its builders combined early Christian and Byzantine structural elements with influences from Islamic and Romanesque architecture. The lower section of the exterior wall is dominated by tall blind arcades accented with colored marble, from which the four dwarf galleries on the façade emanate.

In contrast, the octagonal baptistry of San Giovanni as well as the church of San Miniato in the Tuscan city of Florence are encrusted with thin, colorful marble panels. With its pilasters, the lower level of the baptistry supports the blind arches that circle the structure above. A graceful attic level crowns the building. This clear ordering, reminiscent of ancient structures, became a primary influence for Italian architects of the early Renaissance, and is therefore sometimes referred to as proto-Renaissance.

Cathedral of Santa Maria Assunta, 1063–1160, and the Campanile, 1173–ca. 1350, on the Campo dei Miracoli, Pisa

△ **Baptistry of San Giovanni**, ca. 1059–1150, Florence. Octagonal central-plan building with marble cladding in white and green

△ **San Miniato al Monte**, ca. 1070–1150, Florence. Basilican structure, three aisles with flat ceilings

Romanesque in Northern Spain

The political situation on the Iberian Peninsula set narrow limits on church construction. With most of the peninsula in Muslim hands, Christian rulers managed to keep a foothold only in northern regions such as Asturias and Catalonia.

Influenced by the art of southern France, churches designed to serve the spiritual needs of the ever-increasing numbers of pilgrims appeared from Catalonia to Santiago de Compostela, which became a major pilgrimage destination in 830. These churches also had the purpose of reflecting and consolidating the political and military victories of the *Reconquista*.

◁ **San Miguel de Liño**, ca. 850. Monte Naranco, near Oviedo

▷ **Collegiate Church of Santa Maria la Mayor**, ca. 1160–1240, Toro. The apses in the choir termination of this triple-nave, cruciform basilica are ordered with blind arcades. Above the crossing rises an almost too powerful tower. The central aisle is barrel-vaulted, whereas the side aisles are topped with groin vaults.

▷ **Santa Maria del Naranco**, dedicated in the thirteenth century. Ramiro I (842–850) built a recreational palace on Monte Naranco, near the Asturian capital of Oviedo. His successor, Ordoño I, expanded the clear, cubically ordered ensemble with the triple-aisled, barrel-vaulted church of San Miguel de Liño.

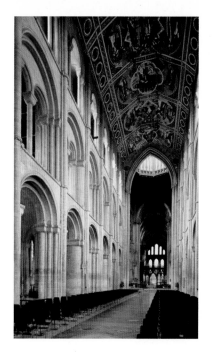

◁+△ **Ely Cathedral**, Cambridgeshire, begun 1083, west façade late twelfth century. View of the central aisle with its painted wooden ceiling

▷ **Castle Acre**, Norfolk, mid-twelfth century. The west façade of this church, part of the Cluniac priory founded here in 1089 and now in ruins, shows blind arcades with Roman arches and crossed arches in alternation.

Romanesque in England

Cultural influences from the Continent found their way to England during the reign of St. Edward the Confessor (1042–1066), who had grown up in Normandy. With the accession of William the Conqueror to the throne in 1066, Norman rule set new standards in English architecture and art.

Many abbots of extant Benedictine monasteries were replaced by Norman dignitaries. In 1081, Simeon of St. Ouen assumed the post of Abbot of Ely. Within two years of his appointment, he had initiated the construction of a new cathedral. Elements inspired by the churches of his homeland include the alternating columns and pilasters in the central aisle, and the pilaster strip that extends all the way from the floor to the painted wooden ceiling.

The exterior displays much more ornament, especially the west façade, which was built about a hundred years later, and which is replete with blind arcades.

English builders' tendency to use rhythmic repetitions of various formal elements over large swaths of wall surface is still recognizable in the ruins of Castle Acre.

Stave Churches in Norway

At the end of the tenth century, the Viking king Olaf Tryggvason became the sole ruler of Norway, where he introduced Christianity. When one sees the first churches built there, one cannot help but think of a seafaring people's indisputable skill in shipbuilding and carpentry. It is therefore no coincidence that the term "stave church" derives from the Norwegian word *staf* ("mast"). In addition, a ship is a perfect symbol for Christian purposes: from Noah's Ark to the term "nave" (from the Latin *navis*), the church is literally the "ship" that takes the faithful into its hold. The high and often rectangular central aisles of Norwegian stave churches, which rise vertically like rigged up Viking longboats, are surmounted by multilevel roofs bearing gables crowned with outstretched dragon heads. The portals and interior woodwork are artfully carved, and the ceilings and walls adorned with murals.

◁ **Borgund Stave Church**, ca. 1150. The best-preserved stave church in Norway

◁ Interior of the **Borgund Stave Church**, ca. 1150. Rectangular central aisle with twelve masts supporting the roof

▷ **Structure of a stave church** (Torpo, 1192)

▷▷ **Adoration of the Magi**, ceiling mural from the demolished stave church Ål, ca. 1200. University Archaeological Museum, Oslo

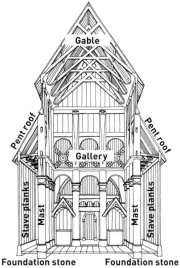

Gable

Pent roof

Pent roof

Gallery

Stave planks

Mast

Mast

Stave planks

Foundation stone   **Foundation stone**

Gothic

The Standard of Divine Order

Around 1550, Italian Renaissance artist Giorgio Vasari reviled the architecture of the period as *maniera dei Goti*—characteristic of the Goths; it had lost all sense of proportion, just as the Barbarian Goths had no sense of classical Greek order. "Gothic" master builders, on the other hand, lauded the proportions of their churches as a harmonious reflection of divine order. The architectural style of increasingly transparent walls began in France around 1140 and matured during the 1150s and 1160s into the high Gothic style (ca. 1200–1380). The late Gothic style endured sporadically until about 1550. England produced "Gothic" architecture for about 385 years (Early English 1175–1269; Decorated Style 1250–1350; Perpendicular Style 1330–1560). In Germany the Gothic period lasted less than 300 years (early Gothic 1235–1250; high Gothic 1250–1350; late Gothic 1350–1520). The chronological placement of the "Gothic" period is based on the persistence of the Gothic architectural style. Independently of this, painting developed toward the Renaissance style as early as 1400.

† Church/cathedral

♱ Monastery

▲ Secular building

／∣ Fresco

Saint-Denis, Paris,
ca. 1135–1140

Jamb figures on Chartres
Cathedral, ca. 1145–1155

Upper chapel of Sainte-Chapelle,
Paris, 1241–1248

Giotto, *Expulsion of the Merchants
from the Temple*, 1303–1305, Scrovegni
Chapel, Padua

| 1140 | 1200 | 1250 | 1300 |

Gothic (ca. 1140–ca. 1500)

Chronology

1204 Fourth Crusade, led by Venice; results in the conquest and sack of Constantinople.

1227 Pope Gregory IX appoints his own special deputies as inquisitors for the persecution of heretics.

1242 Mongol conquests reach the Adriatic Sea.

ca. 1250 Founding of the Hanseatic League, an alliance of international merchants and trade cities in the Baltic and North Sea regions

1291 Fall of Acre, the last stronghold of the crusaders in the Middle East

1337–1453 Hundred Years' War between England and France over the rights of succession to the French throne

1346 Duchy of Estonia is sold to the Teutonic Knights.

1347 Outbreak of the plague (known as the Black Death) in Europe

1356 The Golden Bull is adopted as the constitution of the Holy Roman Empire; the king is to be chosen by seven prince-electors.

1378–1417 Western (Papal) Schism; the Latin Church is divided, and two popes rule simultaneously in Avignon and Rome.

ca. 1400 Rise of the Medici family to power in Florence

May 30, 1431 Joan of Arc is burned at the stake in Rouen, France.

1452 Frederick III is the last German emperor to be crowned in Rome.

1453 Ottoman Turks conquer Constantinople; fall of the Eastern Roman or Byzantine Empire

1477 Swiss and Lorraine armies defeat the army and state of Burgundy.

1492 Arabs and Jews are driven out of Spain.

Cultural History

ca. 1200 Origin of the *Nibelungenlied* (Song of the Nibelungs), a Middle High German epic poem composed by an anonymous author.

ca. 1250 Ebstorf World Map depicts the medieval world with Jerusalem at its center.

1274 The Dominican priest, philosopher and theologian Thomas Aquinas completes his most famous work, *Summa Theologica*.

Ca. 1309–1320 Dante Alighieri (1265–1321) begins work on *The Divine Comedy*, the most influential work in Italian literature.

Ca. 1330 Compilation of the *Codex Manesse*, an illuminated manuscript of Middle High German *Minnelieder* (love songs)

1336 Petrarch (1304–1374) ascends Mont Ventoux; his written account of the natural world he observed stands in sharp contrast to the symbolic medieval perception of the landscape.

1390 Geoffrey Chaucer (ca. 1343–1400) composes the *Canterbury Tales*.

1397 Medici bank set up in Florence

ca. 1430 Development of copperplate engraving

ologne Cathedral, nave and choir, 1248–before 1322

Krumau Madonna, 1390–1400

Jan van Eyck, *Madonna of Chancellor Rolin*, ca. 1435

Michael Pacher, *St. Augustine and the Devil*, Church Fathers' Altar, ca. 1480

| 1300 | 1400 | 1450 | 1500 |

At a Glance

Rose Windows

A rose window is a circular window filled with tracery and decorated with stained glass. In Gothic churches, they were typically placed above portals and in transept gables. The tracery is usually constructed in a pattern radiating out from the center of the circle, divided by mullions into arch or lancet-shaped sections of varying complexity, all pointing outward toward the edge of the circle.

Schematic drawing of the rose window at Lausanne Cathedral, before 1235

Light

In Gothic church interiors, windows became a crucial element in the spatial structure. Because without light—that is, the manifestation of God—life cannot exist. In this way, light also became the power that infused the colorful decoration with theological content.

The Façade of a Gothic Cathedral (Amiens)

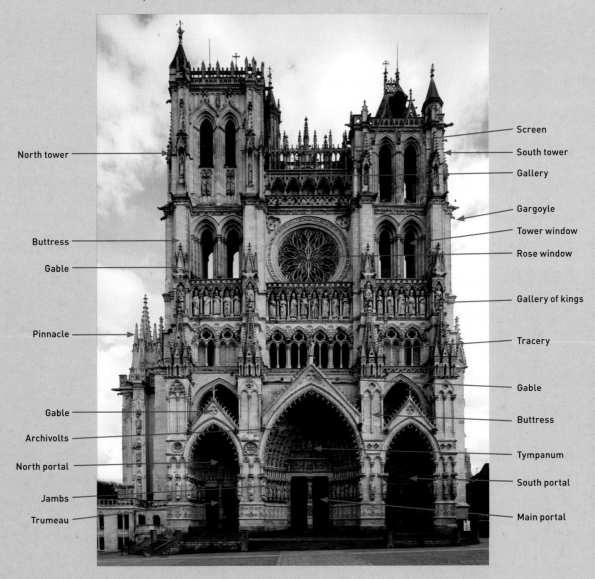

North tower — Buttress — Gable — Pinnacle — Gable — Archivolts — North portal — Jambs — Trumeau

Screen — South tower — Gallery — Gargoyle — Tower window — Rose window — Gallery of kings — Tracery — Gable — Buttress — Tympanum — South portal — Main portal

Gothic (ca. 1140–ca. 1500)

Tracery

Geometric ornamental stonework found in Gothic churches. Initially used as a means of subdividing large windows, it was later used in the decorative articulation of wall surfaces, gables, etc.

Pattern Books

Collections of (copied) drawings used by medieval master builders and artists as examples (*exemplum*) or inspirations for their own works.

Jan van Eyck, *Portrait of the Goldsmith Jan de Leeuw*, 1436

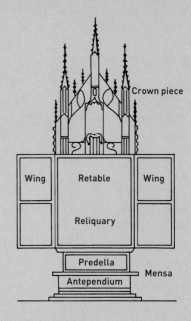

Portrait Painting

In the mid-fifteenth century, aristocrats and members of the upper middle class began commissioning paintings without religious content. Thanks to the growing trend toward naturalism and realism, portrait painting in particular flourished during this period.

Winged Altar or Polyptych

A form of shrine altar which was particularly popular during the Gothic period. Depending upon liturgical requirements, its appearance could be changed by opening or closing one or more of its wing sections.

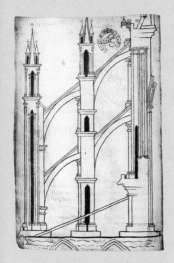

Drawing of buttresses from the master builder's book of Villard de Honnecourt, ca. 1240

Church Mason's Guild

A medieval community consisting of all the master builders and stonemasons involved in the building of a church, independent of the craftsmens' guilds. Its members were subject to the rules of the guild. A few such organizations exist even today, in part to counteract detrimental environmental changes.

Timber Frame Construction

A type of wooden skeleton construction using vertical wall posts, horizontal joists, and diagonal braces; the spaces in between were filled with doors and windows or various materials such as timber planks, wattle and daub, bricks or stones. This style of construction, which evolved from scribe-rule carpentry, was particularly common in Germany. Here, the oldest surviving houses date back to the thirteenth century. Timber frame construction experienced its heyday from the end of the Gothic period until around 1700.

Fritzlar, guild house of the Michaelsbruderschaft, ca. 1480

Key Terms

△+▷ **Amiens Cathedral**, nave, 1220–1236; west façade, 1220–1243 (rose window and towers after 1366). The vault ribs and arches rest on individual shafts of the compound piers.

◁ **Former Abbey Church of Saint-Denis**, Paris, west façade ca. 1135–1140; choir with radiating chapels 1141–1144 (the west façade was renovated in the 19th century).

Exemplary Gothic Style in France

The tomb of a saint in the royally-sponsored Abbey of Saint-Denis, a growing influx of pilgrims (and the revenue they brought), a Carolingian church that was now too small, and a visionary abbot: these are some of the factors that led to the birth of the Gothic style. Rather than ordering something entirely new, however, Abbot Suger (1081–1151) simply enhanced the most essential element: light. Suger wanted light everywhere, but especially concentrated at the altar, which he wanted to be bathed in light, since he saw it as a manifestation of God. Large windows meant less masonry and lower costs, but also less stability, and thus a construction problem to be solved. In Suger's plan, the additional light was provided by extra windows in the west façade and two rows of windows in the choir, the lower of these in a ring of chapels surrounding the choir. All the windows were placed in such a way that light could stream unimpeded onto the altar at the center of the choir.

Approximately a century later, the cathedral at Amiens demonstrated what was meant by "less masonry": the walls are layered across the space like leaves, with higher elements rising up behind lower ones. Glass replaces stone, and everything is clad in delicate stonework. In the interior, the moldings of the compound piers show which sections of the space they support. In this way, the ashlar masses of the Romanesque were transformed into the skeletal forms of the Gothic.

Relieving the Supporting Walls

A gabled roof is supported by its truss and transfers the weight vertically into the walls. In contrast, the line of a vault's thrust—which varies with the type of vault—runs diagonally outward through the wall toward the ground. If this imaginary line reaches the ground outside the wall, the wall is too thin and will not support the vault. Through trial and error, medieval master builders learned that the required thickness need not be maintained throughout the entire masonry. In late Romanesque churches, vaults over side aisle galleries were already being used to stabilize the nave vaulting.

When galleries were eliminated in favor of suffusing the nave with light, buttresses were used to support the walls.

In the case of flying buttresses, ascending half-arches conduct the thrust of the vault freely over the roofs of the side aisles and into the wall buttresses. The ribs and cells of the vaults in the building's interior combine with the flying buttresses and abutments on the exterior to create a unified support system that is essential to the building's stability, but in which the thickness of the walls is no longer an essential factor.

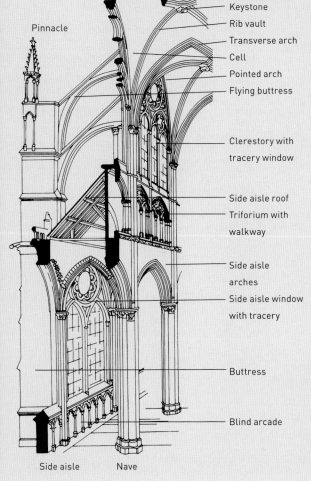

Pinnacle

Keystone

Rib vault

Transverse arch

Cell

Pointed arch

Flying buttress

Clerestory with tracery window

Side aisle roof

Triforium with walkway

Side aisle arches

Side aisle window with tracery

Buttress

Blind arcade

Side aisle

Nave

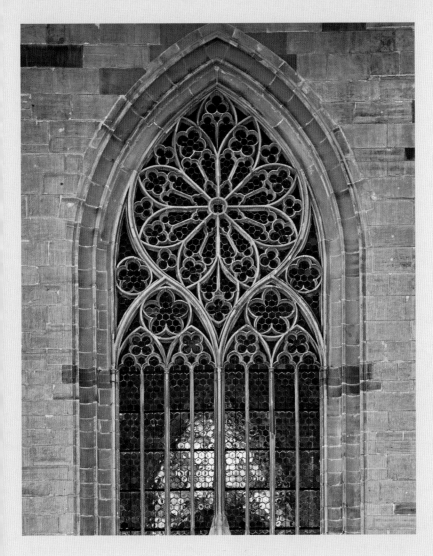

Glass medallions in plate tracery. **Lausanne Cathedral**, south transept, before 1235

Three unframed recumbent trefoils above two lancets. **Amiens Cathedral**, axial chapel in the chevet, ca. 1236–1250

One standing and two recumbent quatrefoils in lozenges above three cusped lancets, **Königsfelden, Abbey church**, choir, 1310–1330

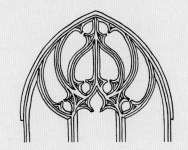

▷ **Sainte-Chapelle**, choir, Paris, 1241–1248. Buttresses without arches can support a single-aisled building.

◁◁ **Beauvais Cathedral**, choir, ambulatory with radiating chapels 1227–1245; raised choir and vault 1255–1272. Flying buttress system with piers and flying buttresses.

This saves material, and walls carrying less weight can be opened with large areas of glass. A stone framework of molded bars provides further stability for glass. The tracery consists of nothing more than segmented circles and straight lines created with compasses and straight edges, but the variety of its forms is inexhaustible. Tracery was used to secure windows from around 1215; later it was also used on walls and freestanding elements. The only architectural element not previously seen in Romanesque churches, tracery is a quintessentially Gothic building technique.

△ **Salem**, **Cistercian church**, north transept, ca. 1300–1305. Paired lancets with circles form the basic segments of the window.

▷ The fish bladder—a double-leaf shape with one long leaf, often curved in the form of an S—emerged around 1300.

Sainte-Chapelle

In 1237 Baldwin II, the last, debt-ridden emperor of Byzantium, rehabilitated his finances by selling Christ's crown of thorns—which had been enshrined in Constantinople—to Louis IX of France. Shortly thereafter, the pious French king acquired drops of Jesus' blood, pieces of the cross, the lance, the vinegar-soaked sponge, the crimson mantle, the shroud and a stone from Christ's tomb in similar manner. In a shining example of the adoration of holy relics in the Middle Ages, Louis—later Saint Louis—ordered the construction of Sainte-Chapelle for the sole purpose of housing these treasures.

As the container for the relics of the Passion, the church is furnished like a shrine made of gold, gemstones and enamel. The relics of Christ's martyrdom—both the tangible and the imaginable—appear bathed in the colored light of divine omnipotence. And on twelve piers, statues of the apostles symbolize their functions as pillars of the church.

△ **Sainte-Chapelle** was built 1241–1248 in the courtyard of the (destroyed) royal palace as a shrine for the relics of the Passion.

▷ In the single-aisled upper chapel of Sainte-Chapelle, a 40 ft (12 m) high wall of light stands above a stone plinth, telling the story of the Bible in 1,134 glistening scenes. In addition to the buttresses outside the building, four iron ring beams run horizontally around the interior, ensuring the stability of this "vision."

◁ In the lower chapel, the structure of the choir supported the golden reliquary which was originally placed above it in the upper chapel. More than twice as expensive as the building itself, the reliquary was melted down in 1793.

Colored Light

"'When the rays of the sun shine through the colorful glass in all of their brilliance, to whom would you attribute the array of colors on the wall?' 'Without a doubt, I would attribute the beautiful colors on the wall to the rays of the sun, and not to the glass.'" This comment from the *Speculum Virginum*, a widely-used theological teaching text in dialogue form dating from 1140, clearly illustrates the preference for stained glass over mural painting and mosaic in this period. The colorful window motifs depicting the history of salvation were brought to life by the light of the sun (symbolic of God). In contrast, the gold ground used in Byzantine mosaics—in Saint Mark's Basilica in Venice, for example, which, like the 176 windows in the Chartres Cathedral, was constructed in the thirteenth century, but contains very few windows—depends on candlelight for its brilliance (see p. 157).

◁ **Chartres Cathedral, southern rose window**, 1221–1230, 36 ft (11 m) diameter, *The Glorification of Christ*. With their circular shape, the rose windows interrupt the perceived upward movement of Gothic architecture, focusing attention instead on the depiction of fundamental theological truths.

▷ **Chartres Cathedral, north choir ambulatory, Charlemagne window**, ca. 1225, 29 ft 6 in (9 m) high. Detail: Charlemagne inspires the builders of a church. Colored plates of glass were cut precisely according to an original-size pattern and each piece was outlined with black paint which was then burned into the glass. Only then could the pieces be joined together with lead came to form panes.

◁ **Old Testament Precursors of Christ**, ca. 1145–1155, Chartres Cathedral, central west portal, right jamb

▷ **Bamberger Rider**, ca. 1230–1235. Sandstone, 7 ft 6 in (230 cm) high, Bamberg Cathedral, eastern choir. The following traces of color have been detected: green for the leaves, white with brown spots for the horse, red for the clothing, gold for the crown, girdle and spurs.

▷▷ Soft Style: **Krumau Madonna**, southern Bohemia, 1390–1400. Limestone, traces of original paint, 44 in (112 cm) high. Kunsthistorisches Museum, Vienna

Meaningful Statues

A church itself is an allegory for Christianity. The stones are the faithful; the columns are the pillars of the faith, like the apostles. Portals are another metaphor, leading believers to salvation. The symbolism is multilayered, and not every aspect needs to be understood by everyone. Some of it is obvious—the idea of the pillars, for example, particularly when it is expressed as vividly as at Chartres: the statues continue the shape of the columns, they hold their attributes close to their bodies, and the folds in their garments are shallow, as if engraved. We understand their meaning, even if we are not able to name each individual figure.

In contrast, the realistic form of the Bamberger Rider, sculpted barely a hundred years later, offers no clues to its interpretation; the important information about the statue's meaning has been lost. The only thing that is certain is that it was deliberately placed in the cathedral. Thus, an essential element is missing from this masterpiece.

The late Gothic "Beautiful Madonnas" created in the international soft style were intended to make an ethereal impression. Yet even though they seem to have no bodies, since their garments "stand by themselves," some purists still feared that observers might adore them in a manner that was too earthly. In contrast the Chartres figures have the architectural feature of a softer, more flowing style.

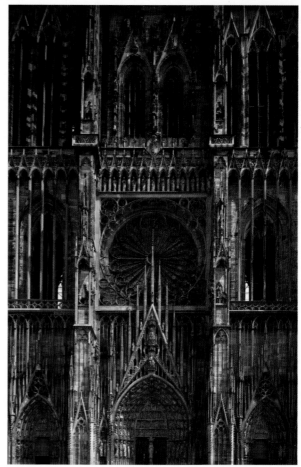

△ **Strasbourg Minster**, west façade, after 1284

◁ **Cologne Cathedral**, nave (completed 19th century), view into choir (1248–pre 1322). Portions of the compound piers extend uninterrupted from floor to ceiling, leading directly into the ribs of the vault and creating a visual impression of upward motion.

Gothic Architecture

The Strasbourg Minster illustrates the "conquest" of Gothic style in a kind of time-lapse: the choir (after 1179) is still Romanesque; moving from the transept (1125–1240) through the nave (ca. 1240–1275), the tracery and ornamentation steadily increase, until they ultimately dominate the entire west façade (1284–1365). Influential master builders and large religious orders such as the Cistercians brought Gothic architectural forms to other countries. Rather than being copied, they were adapted to regional architectural traditions, which were always influenced by the type of materials available. In the Baltic Sea region, this meant brick. Brick Gothic

△+▽ **Minster**, Bad Doberan, begun after 1291, choir and radiating chapels completed by 1336, final consecration in 1368. Interior:

painted triforium; the transept arms are separated from the nave by two-story arcades.

▽ **St. Mary's Church**, Lübeck, ca. 1260/65–1351, central aisle of the nave facing east, view into choir

architecture also includes high quadripartite rib vaults, molded pointed-arch arcades, and narrow rows of windows along with rose windows, tracery and buttress systems. These components were simply used more sparingly, and (red) brick masonry still dominates the buildings' appearance. Cologne Cathedral—the ultimate German Gothic church—is a special case. Its completion in the nineteenth century using the original plans was intended to strengthen national morale, since at the time Germans believed the Gothic style was a German invention.

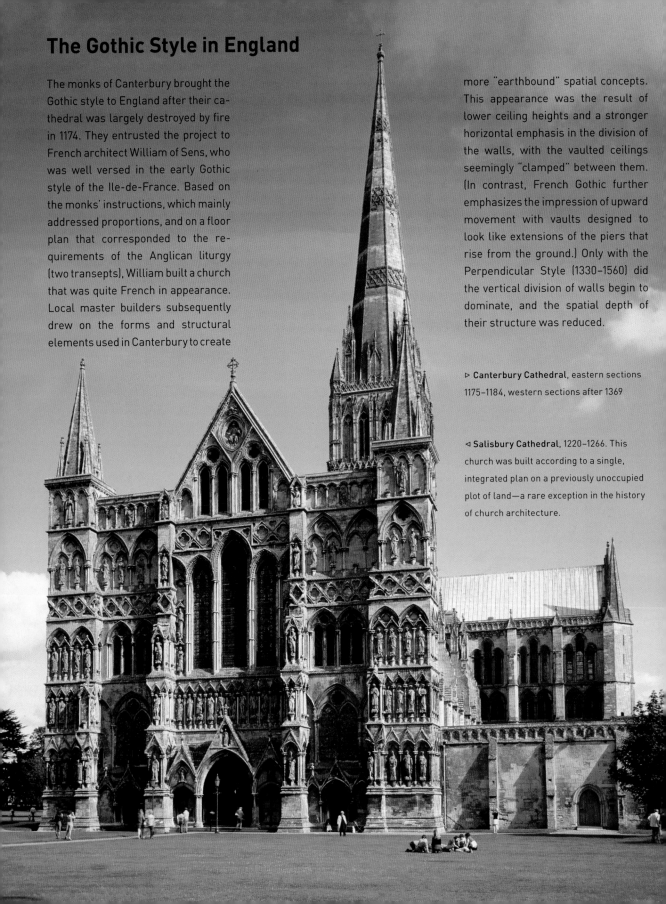

The Gothic Style in England

The monks of Canterbury brought the Gothic style to England after their cathedral was largely destroyed by fire in 1174. They entrusted the project to French architect William of Sens, who was well versed in the early Gothic style of the Ile-de-France. Based on the monks' instructions, which mainly addressed proportions, and on a floor plan that corresponded to the requirements of the Anglican liturgy (two transepts), William built a church that was quite French in appearance. Local master builders subsequently drew on the forms and structural elements used in Canterbury to create more "earthbound" spatial concepts. This appearance was the result of lower ceiling heights and a stronger horizontal emphasis in the division of the walls, with the vaulted ceilings seemingly "clamped" between them. (In contrast, French Gothic further emphasizes the impression of upward movement with vaults designed to look like extensions of the piers that rise from the ground.) Only with the Perpendicular Style (1330–1560) did the vertical division of walls begin to dominate, and the spatial depth of their structure was reduced.

▷ **Canterbury Cathedral**, eastern sections 1175–1184, western sections after 1369

◁ **Salisbury Cathedral**, 1220–1266. This church was built according to a single, integrated plan on a previously unoccupied plot of land—a rare exception in the history of church architecture.

△ **Lincoln Cathedral**, south transept, rose window ("Bishop's Eye"), ca. 1320, tracery in the Decorated Style

▷ **Wells Cathedral**, 1180–1239, Early English Style, eastern sections 1320–1369. The extended crossing tower was later stabilized by "scissor arches" inserted into the crossing on three sides.

▽ **King's College Chapel**, interior facing east, Cambridge, 1416–1515, fan vault in the Perpendicular Style of the late English Gothic

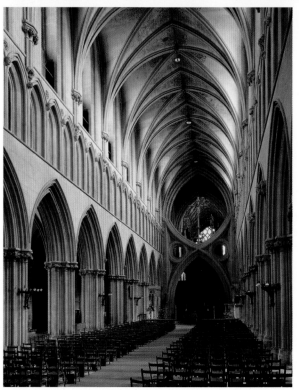

Italian Façades

Churches whose walls are thick enough to support a vault do not need an additional support structure such as an exterior buttress system. The walls are also solid enough to support a vault because the number of window openings is limited (a feature that was already part of the basic architectural repertoire in the hot southern European countries). Thus, the style that can be called Gothic by Italian standards could focus instead on decorative elements. This freedom is well represented in the elaborate decorative façades, which sometimes bear little relation to the structure itself. The façades are balanced in height and width; they are self-contained. It is telling that one's attention is not immediately drawn to the absence of a French-style twin-towered façade: it is not missed. The impression generated by the building's exterior is reiterated when entering the church from the west. Here, the central and side aisle arcades with their wide, high arrangement of arches—rather than being separated—seem to open into one another, lending an almost hall-like atmosphere to the space.

◁+▷ **Orvieto Cathedral**, begun 1290 (the building is constructed from layers of light-colored tuff and dark basalt); west façade after 1310, rose window ca. 1359, sculpture gallery 1452–1458. As evidenced by the decorative images on the façade, this cathedral, like Sainte-Chapelle, is a shrine for holy relics. Orvieto Cathedral houses a blood-soaked altar cloth, evidence of the transformation of sacrificial bread and wine into the body and blood of Christ.

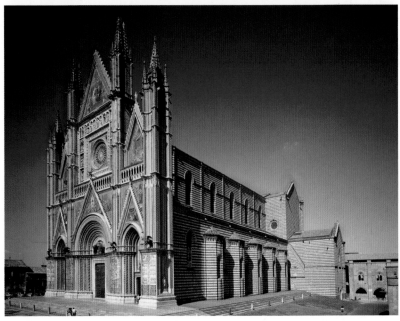

▷ **Milan Cathedral**, begun 1387, choir consecrated 1418, nave 1452–1572. Designs for the façade date back to 1537, but were not executed until 1809, under Napoleon I; all work was completed in 1890. Like Cologne Cathedral, Milan's Duomo is a vivid example of timeless Gothic style.

◁ **Siena Cathedral**, begun after 1150, nave vaulted 1256–1260, choir rebuilt after 1267, façade 1284–1377 by Giovanni Pisano

▷ **Palazzo Ca d'Oro**, Venice, 1421–1436, façade facing the Grand Canal with six-arched tracery loggias between tracery windows

SACRED AND SECULAR ARCHITECTURE   213

Frescoes

While French master builders were replacing walls of Gothic churches with glass so that images could appear in the windows, churches in Italy retained their walls for fresco painting. Giotto decorated the chapel of the Scrovegni family with scenes from the lives of the Virgin Mary and Jesus. The images appear to be embedded in illusionistically painted marble frames. Giotto played with the viewers' perception throughout the space; he was particularly successful in the case of two deep window niches topped by quadripartite rib vaults to the right and left of the altar. Both paintings contain better illusions than one would expect to see approximately 100 years prior to the development of central perspective governed by a single vanishing point. Perhaps Giotto

△ Giotto, *Expulsion of the Merchants from the Temple*, 1303–1305, fresco, 73 × 82 in (185 × 200 cm). Scrovegni (Arena) Chapel, Padua

▽ Giotto, **painted right-hand niche**, Scrovegni (Arena) Chapel, Padua

△ Ambrogio Lorenzetti, *The Effects of Good Government in the City and the Country* (detail), 1338–1339, fresco, ca. 10 × 46 ft (300 × 1400 cm). Sala dei Nove, Palazzo Pubblico (city hall), Siena. The landscape section alone, which depicts the area around Siena, is 23 ft (7 m) long.

◁ Giotto, *Lamentation Over the Dead Christ*, 1303–1305, fresco, 6 ft 1 in × 6 ft 5 in (185 × 200 cm). Scrovegni Chapel (Arena Chapel), Padua

benefited from his experience as a master builder—as evidenced by the buildings which often appear in many of his scenes as a contextual backdrop for the activities of the figures in the foreground. When the content does not call for an urban setting, the figures move in front of an implied landscape. And they actually do move: they interact with one another and display emotions. This is true not only of the human figures but of the angels as well: in their complete dismay at the sight of the dead Christ,

they are barely able to master their airy element, plummeting in and out of the heavens in all directions.

Many painters attempted to portray angels floating in the air, but the result was usually detached figures standing or kneeling in a field of blue, similar to the winged goddess Securitas in Ambrogio Lorenzetti's *Allegories of Good and Bad Government*. But Lorenzetti was the first to create a recognizable landscape panorama, long before "landscape painting" became a significant genre.

Panel Painting

To the north of the Alps as well, painters were addressing the question of
how to place their painted figures
in space. As long as the subjects of
books and panel painting remained
exclusively religious, they were
able to find a convincing approach:
"Space" was defined not materially,
but spiritually. Thus, painters could
fill the area around their figures with
gold ground and thereby do away
with the earthly problem of spatial

illusion. After all, their saints were
not presented as figures of this world.
For the paying observers, this made
the objects of their reverence all the
more believable. Nevertheless, the
gold grounds vary: in the *Division of
Light and Darkness* in the Grabow
Altar, the gold background is clearly
an image of divinity itself, which
existed even before the creation
of the world. In a later example,
Konrad Witz was able to depict an

Old Testament couple in a temporal
setting, as if they were sitting at
the next table. For contemporary
viewers, the setting for the Biblical
scene was clearly evident from the
picture's gold background.

If the earthly depth of an image
was increased while maintaining the
heavenly gold ground, the space for
interpretation was opened up as well.
The patch of grass and the leaves in
Lochner's painting of the Madonna

▷ Michael Pacher, *The Devil Presents St. Augustine with the Book of Vices*, section of the outer right wing, Church Fathers' Altar, ca. 1480. Tempera on wood, 40½ × 36 in (103 × 91 cm). Alte Pinakothek, Munich

△ Stefan Lochner, *Madonna of the Rose Bower*, ca. 1450. Tempera on wood, 20 × 16 in (50.5 × 40 cm). Wallraf-Richartz-Museum & Corboud Foundation, Cologne. The medieval concept of paradise and heaven was inextricably linked with music.

are symbols of purity. Mary is not only sitting in front of the gold ground, she is surrounded by it. The angels appear to be opening it up for the viewer along with the gold-interlaced curtain.

On the other hand, if a saint is depicted in a dispute with the devil, the setting—if not Hell itself —is earth. Over time, the backdrop often became the city, the open street leading deep into the image.

Private Devotion

The Fourth Lateran Council in 1215 irrevocably determined the way in which the Holy Mass was to be celebrated: Pope Innocent III decreed, among other things, that bread and wine were actually transformed into the body and blood of Christ—several times a day and before the eyes of the faithful. And since it is easier to believe in something one can see, the faithful were treated to elaborate spectacles in and around the churches. The ceremonies became so grandiose and multifaceted that some clerics feared they would impede true devotion more than they would foster it. Thus, various "aides to devotion" were created for members of the aristocracy, the clergy and —increasingly—of the bourgeoisie who wished to spend time in prayer outside the church, whether at home or while traveling. With folding altars, the religious experience intensified stage by stage as the user advanced to the innermost compartment. If, in addition, the shrine contained relics, the worshiper would have

▽ **Reliquary**, French, before 1350. Silver, gold plating, enamel, 10 in (25.4 cm) high, open 16 in (40.6 cm) wide. The Metropolitan Museum of Art, New York. The nursing Madonna is accompanied by angels presenting relics; the wings depict scenes from Jesus' childhood; in the gables, angels playing music; in the side panels, saints.

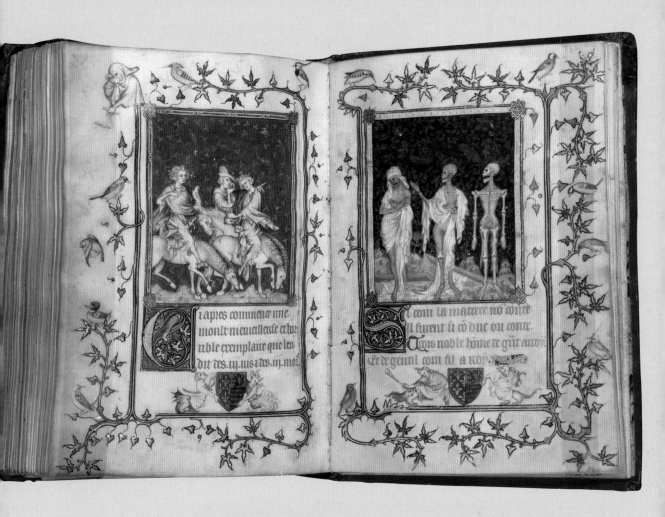

access to a tangible stimulus for devotion above and beyond the conceptual depiction. Often these were only third-order relics—that is, paper, cloth or metal foil which had briefly touched a relic of the first order (a body part of the saint being honored). Those who could read would certainly benefit even more from a book of hours. These books not only provided the appropriate texts for sessions of prayer, they also contained calendars noting religious holidays, uplifting anecdotes from the lives of the saints as well as the most important stations of the Passion. They were intended to instruct the user in leading a life pleasing to God.

Such a life was essential to achieving salvation at the Final Judgment. Death was ever-present, and one should never forget that everything earthly is transitory. *Memento mori* images were used as a vivid reminder of this fact. The book of hours made for Bonne of Luxemburg contains an image also familiar from church paintings, that of three courtly youths being addressed by three dead figures with the words, "What you are now, we once were; what we are, you shall become." We can only hope that the book's owner spent enough time in prayerful meditation over these pages: she died of the Black Death in 1349.

△ **The Psalter and Book of Hours of Bonne of Luxemburg**, 1348–1349. Tempera and gold leaf on parchment; each page measures 5 × 3½ in (12.6 × 9 cm). The Metropolitan Museum of Art, New York. The memento mori pages, with their images of three living and three dead figures (fol. 321 v/fol. 322 r) are framed by branches and leaves in which carefully-observed birds are cavorting; in the upper left corner of the left-hand page, a horrified person can be seen turning away from the terrifying beings on the opposite page.

Panel Painting in France

A gold ground was not necessarily prerequisite for depicting a glimpse into heaven—angels could also suffice. Beginning with the Church Fathers, theologians developed concepts of colored angels based on properties of the body: red for the etheric body, blue for the element of air. Against this background, Jean Fouquet painted the Virgin Mary (wearing one of the most transparent-possible veils) and child as a loftily detached, enthroned Madonna.

The figures in Quarton's *Pietà* express their pain in stony numbness, calling on the viewer (along with an inscription) to suffer with them—an appeal which the painting's benefactor (left) also follows. Rather than observing the scene, he directs his gaze, perhaps, to a real cross placed at the painting's original location; the scene becomes his own vision.

△ Jean Fouquet, *Madonna and Child*, ca. 1454–1456. Tempera on wood, 37 × 35½ in (93 × 85 cm). Royal Museum of Fine Arts, Antwerp. This painting was part of a pair (Melun Diptych) which included a portrait of the donor, Etienne Chevalier and St. Stephan to its left (the latter is now in the Gemäldegalerie in Berlin). Originally, the Christ child was pointing toward the benefactor.

◁ Enguerrand Quarton, *Pietà of Villeneuve-lès-Avignon*, ca. 1455. Tempera on wood, 5 ft 4 in × 7 ft 2 in (163 × 219 cm). Musée du Louvre, Paris. A major work of the Provençal School; at left in the picture is the donor, the canon Jean de Montagnac.

Virtuous Longing?

In a series of six wall-sized tapestries created for the occasion of a wedding in an influential Lyonnaise family in the late fifteenth century, five contain allegorical depictions of the human senses. The sixth, however, remains a mystery to this day. A maidservant holds a jewelry chest open for her mistress while a lapdog looks on; a lion and a unicorn hold up the family standard as well as the panels of the tent, atop which we read the puzzling line: *Mon seul désir* ("my sole desire"). What is her only desire? Is it the jewelry—the wedding necklace, perhaps? Is she putting it on or taking it off? What is the significance of the legendary unicorn, the symbol of purity, the animal that no hunter can capture—which can only be tamed if it lays its horn in the lap of a virgin and gently falls asleep? What is the unicorn doing in this enclosed, flower-strewn garden, the *hortus conclusus*—the place of innocence? Is this a demonstration of the bride's virtue, or, in contrast to the physical senses, a symbol of free will: "It is my wish"?

▽ *Mon seul désir (My One Desire)*, 1484–1500. Wool and silk, 12 ft 6 in × 15 ft 3 in (380 × 464 cm). From the series *The Lady and the Unicorn*, Musée National du Moyen Age, Paris

Early Netherlandish Painting

As if a curtain behind them had been opened, these paintings offer an unhindered view into the immediate and distant surroundings. The figures have even moved to the side so as to allow a better view. Chancellor Rolin commis- sioned Jan van Eyck to paint a picture not for him to pray before, but as a monument to him inside a church. The painting shows Rolin praying in front of a book of hours, so deep in his devotion that the Virgin Mary, her child and an angel have appeared in his room. The era of symbolic scale (in which the importance of figures in a painting is indicated by their relative size) had come to an end for donor portraits. Why should the chancellor hang on the

hem of the Virgin's robe as a tiny figure when it is he who has caused her to appear?

Biblical events may seem to take place in the next room—an Annunciation, for example—but this is not just any room. The vase of lilies and washing bowl symbolize purity; the New Testament lies open on the table, but the Virgin reads from the Old. The Holy Spirit, in the form of the breath of God, has not yet touched her, though it has extinguished the candle.

Similar to a carved altarpiece, areas remain unrevealed so as not to detract from the figures' emotions.

◁ Robert Campin, *The Annunciation*, center panel of the Mérode Altarpiece, ca. 1425–1428. Oil on wood, 25¼ × 25 in (64.1 × 63.2 cm). The Metropolitan Museum of Art, The Cloisters, New York

◁ Jan van Eyck, *The Madonna of Chancellor Rolin*, ca. 1435. Oil and tempera on wood, 26 × 24 in (66 × 62 cm). Musée du Louvre, Paris

▽ Rogier van der Weyden, *Descent from the Cross*, center panel of a triptych, ca. 1435–1440. Oil on wood, 87 × 104 in (220 × 262 cm). Museo del Prado, Madrid

△ Petrus Christus, *A Goldsmith in his Shop*
(St. Eligius?), 1449. Oil on wood, 38½ × 31½ in
(98 × 85 cm). The Metropolitan Museum of
Art, New York

Portrait Painting

Given that panel painting first became established in Western art in the form of painted altarpieces, as an alternative to expensive woodcarvings or metal and enamel work, it was initially limited to religious subjects. Yet, beginning even in the cycles depicting Jesus's childhood, genre-like scenes made their way into these altar paintings —for example, in an *Adoration of the Magi* where we see Joseph cooking at a campfire. "Regular" people had themselves immortalized at the feet of saints in donor paintings. And once saints began appearing in "natural" surroundings, still life elements— with symbolic significance—became increasingly prevalent as well.

Around the middle of the fifteenth century, aristocrats and members of the bourgeois middle class began commissioning paintings without religious content. The guild painting for the goldsmiths of Bruges by Petrus Christus was intended to hang in their chapel. Here, however, St. Eligius, the patron of the trade, has taken on the role of a goldsmith weighing a ring at his shop's counter. By using this image, the guild was also attesting to the honesty of its master craftsman.

The portrait genre elevated panel painting to the level of masterpieces. In contrast to the case of a *vera icon* —an image of Christ—a portrait painter's work was judged according to its resemblance to a living person. His ambition was to place the textures of various materials in the best possible light without distracting the viewer from the subject of the painting. In portraits of men (less often in those of women), painters even took on the challenge of establishing eye contact.

◁ Jan van Eyck, *Portrait of the Goldsmith Jan de Leeuw*, 1436. Oil on wood, 9½ × 7½ in (24.4 × 19.3 cm). Kunsthistorisches Museum, Vienna

◁ Rogier van der Weyden, *Portrait of a Lady*, ca. 1460. Oil-tempera on wood, 14½ × 11 in (37 × 27 cm). National Gallery, London. On the back is an image of Christ with the crown of thorns: here we see the connection to the subject's hope for resurrection and salvation. The sacred content of the painting is not renounced, but it has moved far into the background.

Renaissance

NORTH SEA

BALTIC SEA

Ebstorf

Wittenberg

London

Rotterdam

's-Hertogenbosch

Brugge

Paris

Mainz

Nuremberg

Fontainebleau

Munich

Isenheim

Vienna

ATLANTIC OCEAN

Vicenza

Milan

Venice

Cremona

Parma

Florence

Urbino

Bomarzo

Madrid

MEDITERRANEAN

Rome

Toledo

SICILY

✝ Church
🏠 Secular building
🎨 Painting/altar
📖 Books/printing

Achieving Perspective

As early as 1550, Giorgio Vasari used the term *rinascità* in his accounts of the lives of famous artists. He was referring not to an era, but to "the rebirth of good art" in contrast to the Middle Ages, which he saw beginning with the time of Giotto, around 1300. Thus, *rinascità* initially referred to the launch of a movement rather than the movement itself or a certain style. Only around 1820 did the term "Renaissance" become established in France and Germany as an art historical

Chronology

1422 As a result of the Hundred Years' War, northern France as far as the Loire River is under English rule.
1469–1492 Lorenzo I de' Medici, a patron of the arts, rules Florence.
1481 Beginning of the Inquisition in France
1492 Conquest of Granada; the Arabs are driven out of Spain.

Masaccio, *The Holy Trinity* (detail), ca. 1426/27

Leonardo da Vinci, *Ginevra de' Benci*, ca. 1478–1480

Giovanni Bellini, *Portrait of the Doge Leonardo Loredan*, ca. 1501–1504

Michelangelo, *David*, 1501–1504

1420

1450

1475

1500

Renaissance (ca. 1420–ca. 1600)

term referring to a new era that ushered in the modern age. The intellectual groundwork was laid by figures such as the poet Petrarch, who studied authors of antiquity and advocated self-confident individualism, as well as Greek scholars who had fled Constantinople after the Ottoman conquest and brought the ideas of the ancient world to the West. Centers of learning were thus established in the prosperous Italian city-states in which the human being was the measure of all things, and a universally educated human being, the *uomo universale*, was held superior to people of the Middle Ages, who remained trapped in visions of heaven and hell. This humanism, which was centered around people and their earthly existence, dealt in part with ancient art and its orientation toward ideal beauty, but it also focused on nature. The study of perspective and precise observation of human anatomy laid the groundwork for the illusionistic depiction of life in this world.

October 12, 1492 Columbus discovers the New World.
1507 Sale of indulgences for the rebuilding of St. Peter's in Rome
1571 Publication of Luther's theses against the sale of indulgences; beginning of the Reformation
1524–1526 Peasant Wars
1529 The first Ottoman siege of Vienna is repelled.

1534 Founding of the Jesuit Order; the Anglican Church breaks with Rome and the papacy.
1558 Coronation of Elizabeth I
1567 Unrest in the Spanish Netherlands; beginning of the reign of terror by the viceroy, the Duke of Alba
1598 Edict of Nantes: the Huguenots are tolerated in France.

Cultural History

1434 German polymath and philosopher Nicolas of Cusa theorizes that the Earth rotates on its axis.
1445 Johannes Gutenberg invents book printing using movable type.
1474 Italian philosopher Marsilio Ficino completes his work *Theoligia Platonica de immortalitate animae* ("Platonic Theology").
1492 In Nuremberg, Martin Behaim constructs a globe.
1502 Desiderius Erasmus publishes his critique of the Church.
1512 Nicolaus Copernicus lays the groundwork for a new, heliocentric view of the world.
1550 Adam Ries writes *Practica*, an arithmetic book for common people.
1569 Gerhard Mercator completes his isogonically projected world map.
1580 English sea captain Francis Drake completes his circumnavigation of the world.
1599 English dramatist William Shakespeare becomes co-owner of London's Globe Theatre.

ymus Bosch, hip of Fools, 1510–1515

Albrecht Altdorfer, *The Victory of Alexander at Issus*, 1529

Andrea Palladio, Villa Almerico, "La Rotonda," 1566–1567

Giuseppe Arcimboldo, *The Vegetable Gardener*, ca. 1590

1525   1550   1575   1600

At a Glance

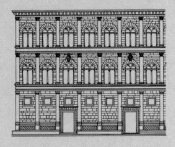

Leon Battista Alberti, proportional drawing of a façade

Architectural Theory

Alberti's architectural treatise *De re aedificatoria* (Ten Books on Architecture), 1485, was based on Vitruvius' classical theories of architecture as well as on the precise study of antique buildings (see p. 256).

The Human Being as Standard

The Middle Ages were characterized by the concept of church architecture as the image of the City of God, with the apostles as its foundation, Christ as the cornerstone which stabilizes the structure, and the shape of the cross as a reference to Christ's crucified body. With the rise of humanism, the examination of the visible world and the secular image of human beings, human proportions became the standard for artistic creation.

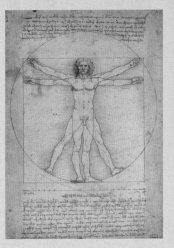

Leonardo da Vinci, *Vitruvian Man*, ca. 1490. Pen and ink with wash over metalpoint, 3½ × 24½ in (34.4 × 24.5 cm). Gallerie dell' Accademia, Venice

Patrons of the Arts

Lorenzo I de' Medici (1449–1492), called *il Magnifico*, who ruled Florence from 1469 until his death, was considered the successor to his father, Cosimo de' Medici, both as a patron of the arts and as a great connoisseur of architecture and literature.

Michelangelo, *The Last Judgment* (detail), 1536–1541

Art History

Giorgio Vasari (1511–1574), a painter, master builder and art historian, published his *Lives of the Most Excellent Painters, Sculptors and Architects* beginning in 1550. Although controversial, it was considered the essential source work for the history of European art. In addition to information about the artists, the book contains important information about contemporary concepts of art.

The Study of Antiquity

In addition to imitating nature, reconnecting with the world of antiquity was the greatest imperative for Renaissance artists. The classical world had set standards for every area of life that surpassed those of the Middle Ages. Renaissance artists also began studying the classical architecture of Rome—some of which had been plundered as stone quarries—for the first time.

Giorgio Vasari, *Lorenzo the Magnificent*, 1533/34. Oil on wood, 28 × 35 in (72 × 90 cm). Galleria degli Uffizi, Florence

Fresco Painting

Painting on the fresh (Italian: *a fresco*) lime plaster of a wall. Pigments were mixed with limewater and painted onto fresh plaster applied to the wall only a small section at a time. The pigment was then indelibly mixed with the plaster. Each section of the painting was worked from top to bottom and had to be completed in one day, since the plaster would dry within that time.

Renaissance (ca. 1420–ca. 1600)

Perspective

Renaissance artists wanted to have a clear view of things; they wanted to be able to look through them (*perspicere*). They searched for techniques with which they could depict a three-dimensional space and all of the objects in it on a two-dimensional surface in such a way that everything would be perceived as if it were in real space. They recognized that lines leading into the depth of a space needed to be depicted shorter in perspective and to meet at a vanishing point. We speak of central perspective if this vanishing point is located in the center of a drawing or painting.

Paolo Uccello, *Perspective Study*, ca. 1450, Galleria degli Uffizi, Florence

The Golden Ratio

This refers to the harmonious division of a line in such a way that the shorter distance (AE) is in the same ratio to the longer distance (EB) as the longer distance (EB) is to the undivided line. Ever since antiquity—and particularly during the Renaissance—the golden ratio was used (and documented) in attaining harmonious proportions in buildings or statues.

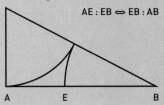

AE : EB ⇔ EB : AB

St. Peter's, Rome

St. Peter's is not only the largest sacred building in the Christian world, it is also a textbook of art history. Constantine the Great first initiated an enormous, five-aisled basilica on this site above the grave of St. Peter. When the papal residence was moved to the Vatican in 1377, St. Peter's became the most important church in Christendom. Documents dating from as early as 1451 state that it was in ruins and needed to be rebuilt. Donato Bramante (ca. 1444–1514) was

initially commissioned as its architect. He designed a central-plan church in the shape of a cross inscribed inside a square (begun in 1506) with a nave opening to the east. His successors, Raphael (1483–1520) and Antonio da Sangallo (1483–1546), who commissioned the building of a large wooden model, repeatedly changed their plans from central-plan structure to a basilica and back again. In 1546,

Michelangelo became *capomaestro* of the project; he preferred the central plan. In a modified version of Michelangelo's plan, Giacomo della Porta (ca. 1532–1602) oversaw construction of the dome (1588–1590). Only in the early seventeenth century were the final sections of Old St. Peter's torn down, and Carlo Maderna added a shorter, basilica-shaped nave. Finally, Bernini renovated the façade, and between 1656 and 1667 he built the pincer-shaped colonnades that encircle St. Peter's Square.

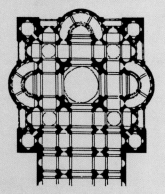

Raphael, plan for St. Peter's, after 1515

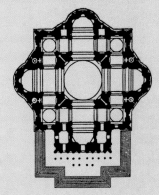

Michelangelo, plan for St. Peter's, after 1546

Key Terms

The Renaissance of Perspective

In order to create a convincing illusion of spatial reality on a painted surface, one needs to use a trick. The technique which the Romans employed perfectly in the Second Pompeian style of the last century BCE—perspective representation in wall painting (see p. 116)—had been lost along with their empire. Giotto was the first artist to attempt it again, although he did not carry it out consistently. *Perspicere*— or seeing through—was the goal of the Renaissance artists. They were concerned not only with the beauty of antiquity, but also with the example set by nature. Their desire to comprehend and imitate it was now clearly evident alongside the Christian messages of their paintings.

Masaccio (1401–1428), whose work marks the beginning of the Renaissance in art history, was the first artist to use central point perspective again in a painting. The idea is that "optical" paths of light from an object meet the observer at his or her point of view (in nature, his eyes) in a funnel formation and merge together there. If we identify this vantage point on a painted surface, it will be the point where the optical paths of an object meet. In order to depict this phenomenon in perspective on the painting's surface, all the lines that do not run parallel to the image must be oriented toward this point.

Alberti formulated this process in 1435/36 in *Della pittura* (On Painting), emphasizing the observer's point of view. Previous to this, Masaccio had already put the idea into practice in a depiction of the Trinity of God the Father, the Holy Spirit in the form of a dove, and the crucified Christ in an illusionistic chapel seen from the perspective of an observer standing in front of it on the floor of the church.

◁ Masaccio, **The Holy Trinity** (detail), ca. 1426/27. Fresco, total dimensions 21 ft 5 in × 10 ft 5 in (667 × 317 cm). Santa Maria Novella, Florence

▽ Reconstruction of Masaccio's **scheme for the construction of perspective**, the observer's lines of vision and the levels of the image in *The Holy Trinity*

▷ Piero della Francesca, **perspective diagram of a groin vault from *De prospectiva pingendi** (On Perspective in Painting)*, ca. 1472–1475. Pen and ink on paper, 11½ × 8½ in (28.9 × 21.5 cm). Biblioteca Palatina, Parma

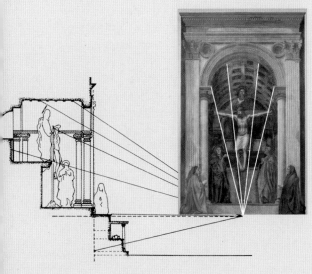

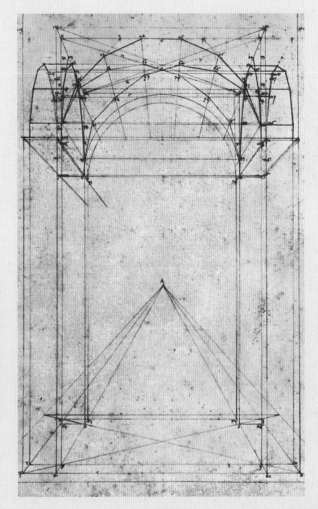

△ Piero della Francesca, *The Flagellation of Christ*, ca. 1460–1465. Tempera on wood, 23 × 32 in (58.4 × 81.5 cm). Galleria Nazionale delle Marche, Urbino

▽ Leonardo da Vinci, **perspective study for *The Adoration of the Magi*.** Pen and ink on paper, 6½ × 11 in (16.5 × 29 cm). Galleria degli Uffizi, Florence

De Prospectiva Pingendi

Piero della Francesca's (ca. 1420–1492) *Flagellation* is not only a deeply mysterious painting (perhaps a veiled allusion to an attempted political assassination of the Duke of Urbino?), but it is also one of the most mathematically precise—as though it were intended as a demonstration of Piero's *De prospectiva pingendi*, the fundamental contemporary treatise on perspective in painting. The written work describes the way in which one "can depict the shape in which one sees each thing and the distance from which one sees it," because "every line leads from the outline of the objects to the eye." Thus, the

△ Albrecht Dürer, *Draftsman Drawing a Reclining Woman.* Woodcut, 3 × 8½ in (7.5 × 21.6 cm). From his *Four Books on Measurement*, 1st edition, Nuremberg, 1525

◁ Andrea Mantegna, *Lamentation over the Dead Christ*, ca. 1480. Tempera on canvas, 26 × 32 in (66 × 81 cm). Pinacoteca di Brera, Milan

▽ Piero della Francesca, **Head studies from *De prospectiva pingendi***, 1472–1475, Biblioteca Palatina, Parma

grid pattern of a tiled floor, which Leonardo used in his spatial study for the *Adoration*, can be used as unit of measurement for shortening the space and thereby aid in achieving the correct proportions. Piero even applied his measuring process for perspective to the human head, achieving an accurate depiction by means of precise measurements from different directions. In 1525,

Dürer demonstrated in a woodcut the way in which a lattice framework placed between the artist and his model can simplify this process. It is essential that the visual focus remains unchanged; a gauging cylinder can be useful for this purpose. Andrea Mantegna (1431–1506) achieved one of the most impressive depictions of the human body in shortened perspective in his *Lamentation*.

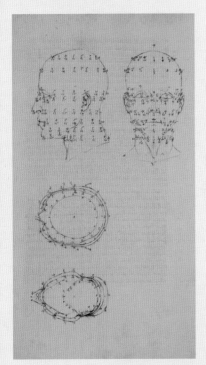

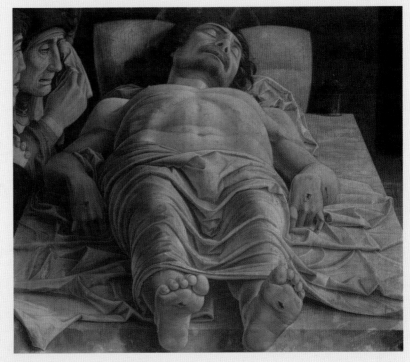

Brunelleschi's Dome

For a long time, the 135-ft (41-m) diameter dome on the crossing tower of Florence Cathedral, begun in 1296, had presented builders with an in-surmountable technical challenge. Filippo Brunelleschi (1377–1446) was the first architect to solve the problem. He studied ancient buildings such as the Pantheon in Rome, but since knowledge of Roman cast concrete construction had been lost, he had to make use of more recent building technology. The dome, which tapers slightly to a point at the top, consists of a 13-ft (4-m) thick interior and an outer shell that is only 31 inches (80 cm) thick: a double-layered structure that is held together by vertical ribs and cross beams in stone—basically a form of the Gothic buttress system. It was constructed from individual, octagonal, self-supporting rings (following the principle that bodies that lean toward each other will support one another reciprocally). As soon as one ring was closed, the next could be placed on top of it, eliminating the need for a complicated centering; Brunelleschi used lightweight bricks joined together in a herringbone pattern with a fast-drying mortar to support his innovative construction.

▷ Santa Maria del Fiore, Florence, 1296–1467; campanile by Giotto, 1359; dome by Brunelleschi, 1418–1436

◁ Diagram of the dome's construction

Ghiberti's Doors

From 1338, the Florentine Baptistery had featured a pair of bronze doors designed by Andrea Pisano (1295–1349) bearing scenes from the life of St. John the Baptist. In 1401, a contest was held for the design of a new set of doors. The young sculptor Lorenzo Ghiberti won against no less than the formidable Brunelleschi. Ghiberti's door does not differ dramatically from Andrea Pisano's; as required, he maintained the Gothic quatrefoil frames. Comparing his early *Annunciation* panel with the later *Raising of Lazarus*, however, one can see how the relief background is increasingly incorporated into the action of the image. Ghiberti's figures appear more alive; the flow of their garments emphasizes the sense of movement.

The *Gates of Paradise*, for which Ghiberti received a commission in 1424, are strikingly different. The panels are larger and no longer constrained by frames; the spaces are filled with landscape, architecture and sky. While the figures in the foreground are nearly three-dimensional, from a distance the panels seem almost painterly by design: detailed perspective is maintained throughout, and the figures in the background have become smaller and flatter. The *Creation* scene offered Ghiberti the opportunity to depict the perfect beauty of nude human figures, as in the art of antiquity.

△ *The Annunciation to the Virgin*, north door of the Baptistery, Florence, 20½ × 18 in (52 × 45 cm, inside frame); left column, third panel from bottom

△ *The Raising of Lazarus*, north door of the Baptistery, Florence, 20½ × 18 in (52 × 45 cm, inside frame); second column from left, third panel from top

△ *The Creation of Adam and Eve, The Fall, and Expulsion from Paradise*: Gates of Paradise, Baptistery, Florence, 31 × 31 in (ca. 79.5 × 79.5 cm), left column, first panel

△ *The Story of Isaac, Jacob, and Esau*: Gates of Paradise, Florence Baptistery, 31 × 31 in (ca. 79.5 × 79.5 cm), left column, third panel from top

The Art of the Bellinis

Without a doubt, one of the most influential artistic dynasties of the Renaissance was the Bellini family of Venice. As a result of his two extensive sketchbooks, which are now preserved in London and Paris (only a few of his paintings have survived), father Jacopo Bellini is among the most interesting artistic personalities of the early Renaissance. His drawings document his ongoing efforts to depict spatial depth and the improvement of his technique in perspective.

The older son, Gentile, concentrated primarily on the narrative genre: his paintings are authentic images of his home city and valuable records of Venetian life in his day. In addition, Gentile was a sought-after portrait artist and served as court painter to Sultan Mohammed II in Constantinople from 1479–1480. The most influential Bellini was Giovanni, who was also the teacher of Giorgione and Titian.

One of his major works, *Holy Allegory*, perplexes scholars to this day. On a fenced-in terrace with floor tiles arranged in the shape of a cross, putti are seen plucking fruit from the Tree of Knowledge and handing it to the seated Christ child. The Virgin Mary is enthroned on the left, surrounded by allegorical figures (Veritas or Justitia on the right, a floating figure on the left) and saints (Jerome and Sebastian). Outside the balustrade are St. Joseph (or St. Peter) and St. Paul with his attribute (a sword). A landscape of Christian and heathen wilderness extends beyond this artificial paradise: we can see human settlements and people as well as mythological beasts.

△ Giovanni Bellini, *Holy Allegory*,
ca. 1500. Tempera on wood, 29 × 47 in (73
× 119 cm). Galleria degli Uffizi, Florence.
Art historians debate: is it a *sacra
conversazione* (a meeting of saints around
the throne of the Virgin), an allegory of
Christian virtues, Paradise, or a meditation
on the incarnation of Christ?

◁ Giovanni Bellini,
*Portrait of the Doge
Leonardo Loredan*,
ca. 1501–1504. Tempera
on wood, 24 × 18 in
(61.5 × 45 cm). National
Gallery, London.
Bellini's portrait
shows us the man who
led the Serenissima
through difficult times
with unshakeable
calmness.

◁ Gentile Bellini, *Procession of the Relics
of the Cross on the Piazza San Marco*, 1496.
Tempera on canvas, 12 ft × 24 ft 6 in (367 ×
745 cm). Gallerie dell' Accademia, Venice

THE BELLINIS: JACOPO (CA. 1400–CA. 1470) · GENTILE (CA. 1429–1507) · GIOVANNI (CA. 1430–1516)

Uomo Universale

In his artists' biographies, the painter and "father of art history" Giorgio Vasari praised Leonardo's great talent but added, "in learning and in the rudiments of letters he would have made great proficience, if he had not been so variable and unstable..." As the illegitimate son of a notary, Leonardo did not have the privilege of a higher education; his command of classical Latin—an essential skill for a scholar—was only middle rate. Thus, it is his abundant legacy of drawings, completed in a multitude of different techniques, which provide us with a fascinating glimpse into his artistic and intellectual workshop: sketches for planned as well as completed works of art, architecture and nature drawings, studies of garments and movement, physiognomy and anatomy as well as drafts of technical inventions such as weapons or flying machines, often including comments in mirror writing.

△ Leonardo da Vinci, **Garment study for a seated figure**, ca. 1475–1480. Brush/grey tempera/white highlights on canvas with grey ground, 10½ × 10 in (26.5 × 25.3 cm). Musée du Louvre, Paris

◁ Leonardo da Vinci, **Study for *The Last Supper*** (James the Greater) and architectural sketches, ca. 1495. Red chalk/pen and ink on paper, 10 × 6¾ in (25.2 × 17.2 cm). Royal Library, Windsor Castle

▷ Leonardo da Vinci, **Upright flying machine**, 1487–1490. Pen and ink on paper, 9 × 6½ in (23.2 × 16.5 cm). Bibliothèque de l'Institut de France, Paris

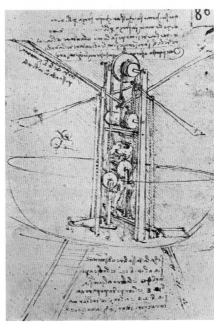

▷ Leonardo da Vinci, **The explosion of a cliff due to a burst underground watercourse; waves on the ocean caused by falling rock**, ca. 1515. Pen/black and yellow ink/black chalk, wash on paper, 6½ × 8 in (16.2 × 20.3 cm). Royal Library, Windsor Castle

▽ Leonardo da Vinci, **Five grotesque heads**, ca. 1494. Pen and ink on paper, 10¼ × 8 in (26.1 × 20.6 cm). Royal Library, Windsor Castle

◁ Leonardo da Vinci, **Depiction of a fetus in utero**, ca. 1510. Pen and brown India ink, partial wash/red chalk on paper, 12 × 8¾ in (30.4 × 22 cm). Royal Library, Windsor Castle

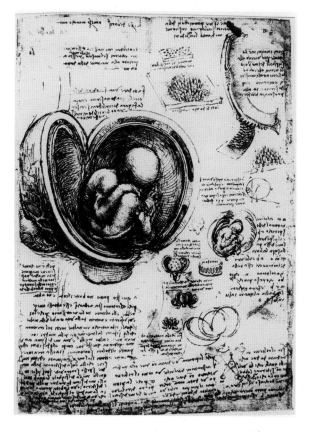

Leonardo the Painter

With the painstaking precision he had learned in the studio of his teacher, Verrocchio, young Leonardo da Vinci structured his image of *The Annunciation* based on central perspective. Symbols such as auras identify the figures depicted as divine beings. Even in the portrait painting of this period, symbols and attributes were used to emphasize the individual qualities of the people being portrayed.

Starting with his lively interest in physiognomy—which he cultivated in countless physiological and anatomical studies—Leonardo was nevertheless convinced that emotional processes and personality traits leave their mark on humans' faces

◁ Leonardo da Vinci, *Ginevra de' Benci*, ca. 1478–1480. Oil and tempera on wood, 15¼ × 14½ in (38.8 × 36.7 cm). National Gallery of Art, Washington, D.C.

▽ Leonardo da Vinci, *The Last Supper*, 1495–1497. Tempera on stucco, 15 × 29 ft (460 × 880 cm). Santa Maria delle Grazie, Milan

△ Leonardo da Vinci, **The Annunciation**, 1473–1475. Oil and tempera on wood, 39 × 87 in (100 × 221.5 cm). Galleria degli Uffizi, Florence

▷ Leonardo da Vinci, **Mona Lisa** or **La Gioconda**, 1503–1506 and 1510?. Oil on wood, 30 × 21 in (77 × 53 cm). Musée du Louvre, Paris. According to recent theories, this painting is not a likeness of the merchant's wife, Lisa del Giacondo, but of Pacifica Brandani of Urbino, mistress of the pope's brother, Giuliano de' Medici.

and can therefore be expressed through painting. Thus, in his portrait of Ginevra de' Benci, he banished the laurel wreath and palm leaf, testaments to her virtue, to the reverse side of the panel. In his portrait of *La Gioconda* (or according to the most recent interpretations, of Pacifica Brandani), he did away with such symbols completely. The spiritual virtue of this woman who died at a young age—the mother of the illegitimately born Ippolito de' Medici, who later became a cardinal—was considered clearly evident from her beauty.

In as early a painting as his Milan mural, *The Last Supper*, Leonardo had already dispensed with conventional attributes such as haloes, concentrating instead on the expressions and gestures of individual figures. The contrast between the figures' lively interaction and the strict geometric form of the room was a device which Leonardo deliberately chose in order to express the "movements of the soul".

◁ ◁ Donatello, *David*, ca. 1445. Bronze, 6 ft 1 in (154 cm) high. Museo Nazionale del Bargello, Florence

◁ Michelangelo, *David*, 1501–1504. Marble, 13 ft 6 in (410 cm), with pedestal 16 ft 10 in (516 cm) high. Galleria dell'Accademia, Florence. David's victory over Goliath is the Old Testament parallel to Christ's triumph over Satan. David is the embodiment of courage and justice.

◁ ◁ ◁ Michelangelo, *Dying Captive*, ca. 1513–1516. Marble, 7 ft 6 in (229 cm) high. Musée du Louvre, Paris

◁ ◁ Michelangelo, *Rebellious Slave*, ca. 1513–1516. Marble, 7 ft (215 cm) high. Musée du Louvre, Paris

◁ Michelangelo, *Bacchus*, 1496–1497. Marble, 58 in (148 cm) high. Museo Nazionale del Bargello, Florence

Michelangelo and Antiquity

Michelangelo Buonarroti's first visit to Rome in 1496 would also have marked his first conscious encounter with the monumental sculpture of the ancient world as an artistic ideal. In any case, the drunken Bacchus he completed there was so classical in appearance that its new owner placed it in his garden amid his other antique statues. As late as 1572, the sculpture was displayed in the classical section of the Uffizi gallery. As with the athletic nude figure of David, the classical influence is evident above all in the contrapposto—the contrast between the standing and the moving leg, the precisely observed anatomical interplay of tension and relaxation, of weighted and unburdened bodily axes. Originally intended for placement on a buttress of Florence Cathedral, Michelangelo converted his David to a freestanding figure in classical style. Its final placement in front of the Palazzo Vecchio, the town hall, imbued it with a political meaning as well. The slave statues, originally intended for the tomb of Pope Julius II, seem to have been inspired more by Hellenistic examples.

Michelangelo's Doubts

In the nineteenth century, sculptors studying Michelangelo's torsi along with those of antiquity discovered unfinished work as an art form itself. Even Michelangelo's contemporaries criticized the fact that he left many works incomplete (although some patrons accepted the works nonetheless). In many of his poems, Michelangelo admitted doubts as to whether he would truly be able to execute the work of art he envisioned when looking at a raw piece of stone. Vasari was also well aware that the artist's "great and terrible conceptions" often exceeded the limits of even his craftsmanship.

The dismembered arm in the unfinished *Pietà Rondanini* reveals that Michelangelo rejected an early idea he found unsatisfactory.

▷ *The Slave Atlas*, ca. 1520–1530.
Marble, 9 ft 3 in (282 cm) high.
Galleria dell'Accademia, Florence

◁ *Pietà Rondanini*, 1552/53–1564.
Marble, 6 ft 5 in (195 cm) high.
Castello Sforzesco, Milan

◁ Michelangelo, **Sistine Chapel ceiling**, 1508–1512. Fresco, 132 × 44 ft (4023 × 1330 cm). Sistine Chapel, Vatican, Rome. Center panels from bottom to top: (God Separates Light and Darkness), The Creation of the Stars, God Divides the Earth from the Oceans, The Creation of Adam, The Creation of Eve, The Fall, Noah's Sacrifice, The Flood, (Noah's Drunkenness).

▷ Michelangelo, **The Last Judgement**, 1536–1541. Fresco, 56 ft × 51 ft (1700 × 1550 cm). Sistine Chapel, Vatican, Rome

Creation and a Final Flourish

The papal chapel of the Apostolic Palace was built between 1473 and 1484 on the orders of Pope Sixtus IV. The unadorned, hall-like space was always intended to be painted. Pope Julius II commissioned Michelangelo to paint the ceiling—which was originally decorated with a simple starry sky—in a more complicated design. The center panels depict the creation of the world and the

first human couple as well as the story of Noah; these scenes are accompanied in the pendentives by sibyls, prophets and other scenes from the Old Testament. Limited to just a few colors and a restrained, rhythmic composition, Michelangelo placed particular emphasis on the figures' physical presence, revealing his great skill as a sculptor even in his paintings.

By contrast, *The Last Judgment*, which Michelangelo painted on the altar wall just two decades later, is almost Baroque in the opulence of its dynamic movement and drama. At the painting's center, Christ directs the ascent of the blessed and the descent of the damned into Hell in a fateful circular movement which pervades the entire composition.

Pure Faith and Lavish Churches

◁ Raphael, *Madonna and Child* (Tempi Madonna), ca. 1507. Oil on wood, 29½ × 20 in (75 × 51 cm). Alte Pinakothek, Munich

△ Raphael, *The School of Athens*, 1510–1511. Fresco, wall area approx. 34 ft 7 in (10.55 m) wide. Stanza della Segnatura, Vatican, Rome. Raphael inserted a portrait of his artistic rival, Michelangelo in the figure of Heraclitus, seated and writing in the center foreground.

For centuries, artists glorified the queen of heaven and the Savior of the world in varying degrees of magnificence in images of the Virgin Mary and the Christ child; the pictures are accordingly enhanced with symbols of sovereignty and allusions to the Passion. Raphael was the first painter who, after creating countless images of the Madonna, was able (or perhaps permitted by the painting's commissioner) to simply portray a loving mother with her child. Here Jesus is truly a baby and not a miniature adult. He seems to be the only thing in existence for his mother,

and there is nothing in the picture to distract viewers from this perspective. The figures are recognizable only from their implied haloes, Mary from her traditional red garment and blue cloak, and Christ from the scrap of loincloth, a reference to the Crucifixion.

In 1508, Pope Julius II commissioned Raphael to paint some rooms in his Vatican residence. *The School of Athens* depicts a gathering of ancient philosophers. In the center are Plato and Aristotle, whose teachings Raphael summed up in their gestures: Plato is pointing toward the heavens, Aristotle toward the world around him.

Painters and the Inquisition

In the Year of Our Lord 1573, Paolo Veronese was called before a tribunal of the Inquisition because of a painting he had made of the Last Supper. When asked why he had depicted "buffoons, drunkards, Germans, dwarves, and other like fooleries," the painter answered:

PV: "We painters take the same licence as do poets and madmen. . . for ornament, as one does."

Who did he think had been present at the Last Supper?

PV: "I believe that there was only Christ and His Apostles; but when I have some space left over in a picture I adorn it with figures of my own invention. . ."

Had anyone given him orders to paint Germans, buffoons and similar figures in this picture?

PV: "No, but I was commissioned to adorn it as I thought proper; now it is very large and can contain many figures."

Should the ornaments in the picture not be suitable to the subject?. . . or had he put them there only to suit his fancy, without any discretion or reason?

PV: "I paint my pictures with all the considerations which are natural to my intelligence, and according as my intelligence understands them."

Did he not know that in countries that were besieged by heresy—particularly in Germany—many such pictures full of foolishness had been painted in order to ridicule the Catholic church?

PV: "I agree that it is wrong, but I repeat what I have said, that it is my

duty to follow the examples given me by my masters."

What had his masters painted?

PV: "In Rome, in the Pope's Chapel, Michelangelo has represented Our Lord, His Mother, St. John, St. Peter, and the celestial court; and he has represented all these personages nude, including the Virgin Mary, and in various attitudes not inspired by the most profound religious feeling."

Veronese was advised that clothing was not necessary at the Last Judgment, but no foolishness was present there either:

PV: "I do not pretend to (defend) it, but I had not thought that I was doing wrong; I had never taken so many things into consideration."

A solution was reached whereby Veronese agreed to correct the picture according to the requests of the tribunal and at his own cost. Veronese simply changed the title of the painting—and the Inquisition was satisfied.

△ Paolo Veronese, *The Feast in the House of Levi*, 1573. Oil on canvas, 18 ft 2 in × 42 ft (555 × 1280 cm). Galleria dell' Accademia, Venice. This painting, commissioned for the refectory of the Convent of San Giovanni e Paolo, was originally entitled *The Last Supper*. After his appearance before the Inquisition, Veronese changed the title to the one it is known by today.

△ Giorgione (Zorzi or Giorgio da Castelfranco), *La Tempestà* (*The Storm*), ca. 1510. Oil on canvas, 32 × 29 in (82 × 73 cm). Galleria dell' Accademia, Venice

◁ Titian (Tiziano Vecellio), *Fête Champêtre* (*Pastoral Concert*), ca. 1509. Oil on canvas, 41 × 54 in (105 × 137 cm). Musée du Louvre, Paris

Enigmatic Country Outings

Giorgione and Titian had a teacher-student relationship, and as a result, a number of their paintings are subject to persistent art historical debate over their true authorship. Whereas *La Tempestà* is undoubtedly the work of Giorgione, attribution of *Fête Champêtre* oscillates between the two. The interpretation of the paintings is also unclear. In the master's painting, *La Tempestà*, the landscape has increased importance. Rather than simply serving as a backdrop for the figures' actions, it has clearly become a subject of the painting and thus the focus of many attempted interpretations.

Starting with the legend that Apelles, the most famous of ancient Greek painters, was particularly admired for his depiction of lightning bolts, and thanks to the identification of the mysterious monument with its stumps of columns as the ancient tomb of Apelles, scholars have interpreted the painting as Giorgione's promotion of his own virtuosity, understandable only to educated customers. Every possible female and male virtue, allegory, and mythological family has been suggested as an interpretation of the figures—but no firm conclusions have been reached. The elegant gentleman musicians and uninhibited ladies in *La Fête Champêtre* have frequently been interpreted as an allegory for music. For centuries, the scandalous combination of clothed men and nude women—which still shocked nineteenth-century viewers of Manet's *Luncheon on the Grass* (a painting inspired by Giorgione's, see p. 354)—was easier for viewers to accept if the latter could be interpreted as classical muses.

Architecture

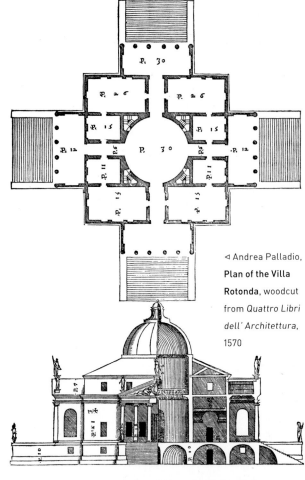

◁ Andrea Palladio, **Il Redentore**, Venice, 1576–1577. On September 4, 1576, in reaction to an outbreak of the Black Plague, the Venetian senate voted to build a church bearing the name *Redentor Nostro* ("Our Redeemer").

Leon Battista Alberti, who outlined the fundamentals of perspective for the painters of his generation in his treatise, *Della Pittura* (*On Painting*, 1435/36), was the ultimate "Renaissance man": he was an architect, sculptor, poet and musician, but also a jurist, mathematician and scientist. His treatise on architecture, *De re aedifiatoria* (*Ten Books on Architecture*), written in Latin and printed in 1485, was based on Vitruvius's classical theories. With its holistic, almost organic concepts of planned cities and their architecture, the work seems surprisingly modern, even today.

Following in the footsteps of Vitruvius and Alberti, Andrea Palladio revived the architecture of classical antiquity, not just for his own age, but for many centuries to come. Palladianism, the architectural style that evolved from his ideas, was influential as far away in time and space as the White House in Washington, D.C. His

◁ Andrea Palladio, **Plan of the Villa Rotonda**, woodcut from *Quattro Libri dell' Architettura*, 1570

▽ Leon Battista Alberti, **Façade of the Basilica of Santa Maria Novella**, Florence, ca. 1458–1470

most famous work is the villa La
Rotonda, a secular building whose
major elements originated in sacred
architecture: a domed rotunda with a
pronaos—the atrium of a temple—
with columns and gables. In the case
of the Teatro Olimpico in Vicenza, the
first freestanding theatre building
constructed since antiquity, it was
only logical that Palladio incorporated
elements of classical Roman theatre
architecture. The *scaenae frons* (back
stage wall) was designed in the spirit
of his humanistically educated spon-
sors, the Olympic Academy of Vicenza,
and combined with trompe-l'oeil
stage scenery designed using layered
perspective.

△ Andrea Palladio,
**Villa Almerico, La
Rotonda,** Vicenza,
1566–1567. Built for
the prelate Paolo
Almerico, this villa
is Palladio's most
famous work and
epitomizes his
architectural style.

◁ Andrea Palladio,
Teatro Olimpico,
Vicenza, 1580,
Palladio's final
architectural work

Art in Black and White

Since ancient times, books had been precious, one-of-a-kind objects. Repeatedly copied by hand onto papyrus or animal skins, they were available only to a small minority. In China, beginning around 175 CE, texts were carved into stone slabs and used to make negative copies (colorless letters on a black background). Later, people wrote mirror-inverted texts on slabs of wood, carved away the surrounding wood, laid paper on top and applied pressure (relief printing). With these one-page woodcuts, which were also common in medieval Europe, a relatively large number of copies could be produced. Although the Chinese had attempted reproduc-

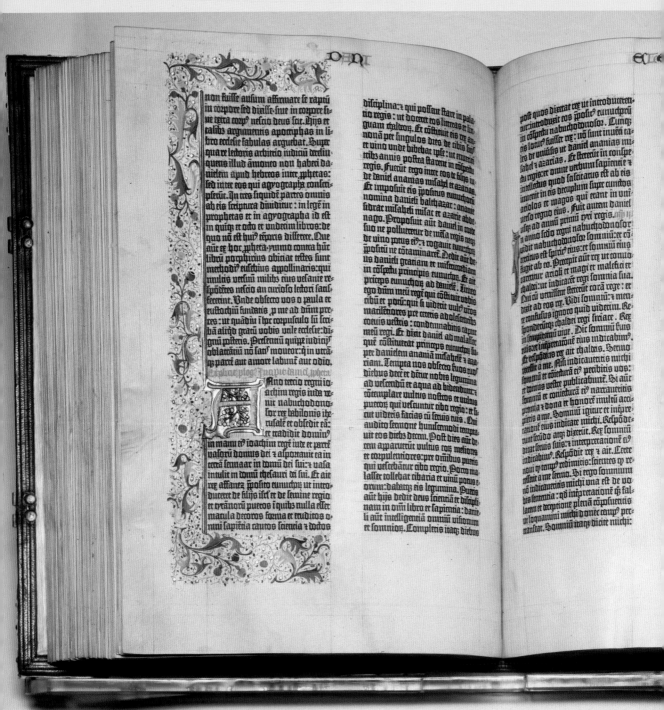

tion using individual character stamps, it is Johannes Gensfleisch (called Gutenberg, 1400–1468) who is credited with "inventing" book printing in 1445, when he developed a cast typography machine for twenty-

six individual letters and punctuation marks that could be combined to form words, lines, and pages from which printed copies could be produced. Using steel letter stamps pressed into soft (usually copper)

stencils, the casting forms were used to produce letters that could be reused as often as necessary. The step from printing single pages through rubbings or a screw press to the printing press was a relatively small one. An important prerequisite for this process was the invention of the paper mill around 1390—since such printing methods would hardly have been possible without paper.

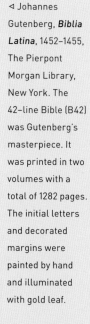

◁ Johannes Gutenberg, *Biblia Latina*, 1452–1455, The Pierpont Morgan Library, New York. The 42–line Bible (B42) was Gutenberg's masterpiece. It was printed in two volumes with a total of 1282 pages. The initial letters and decorated margins were painted by hand and illuminated with gold leaf.

▷ From the book *Ars Moriendi* (or *Ars Bene Moriendi*; "The Art of Dying Well"), single-page woodcut, Germany, 15th century

▷ André Thevet, **Johannes Gutenberg**, 1584, copperplate engraving; the earliest known portrait of Gutenberg. In his left hand he holds a stamp, in the right a stencil.

Draft, Plan, Concept

"Draw, Antonio, draw Antonio, draw, and do not waste time." Michelangelo reportedly wrote this on a page in one of his pupils' sketchbooks. *Disegno*, a key word of the Italian Renaissance, is more than simply "the art of drawing": it includes draft, plan or even concept.

In Leonardo's studies, *disegno* became a means of understanding. Michelangelo, Signorelli (ca. 1450–1523), and Raphael used it to create drafts for frescoes in the form of cartoons that could be transferred directly onto a wall. Pontormo (1494–1556), Dürer, and Baldung Grien (1484/85–1545) drew figure studies for paintings; Cambiaso (1527–1585) sketched geometrical studies of movement. Drawing became an art form in itself: even in the Renaissance, sketches such as the one by Bruegel shown here became collectors' items.

△ Raphael, **Composition study for the lower left corner of the Disputà**, ca. 1509. Pen over stylus marks, wash and highlights on paper, 9¾ × 15¾ in (24.7 × 40.1 cm). The British Museum, London. *Disputà* (The Disputation of the Sacrament) is a fresco in the Stanza della Segnatura in the Vatican (see p. 251).

▷ Michelangelo, **Study for the Lybian Sibyl**, ca. 1511. Red chalk and pen on paper, 11½ × 8½ in (28.9 × 21.4 cm). The Metropolitan Museum of Art, New York

▽ Albrecht Dürer, **Adam and Eve**, 1504. Pen and brown ink, wash, 9½ × 8 in (24.3 × 20 cm). The Pierpont Morgan Library, New York

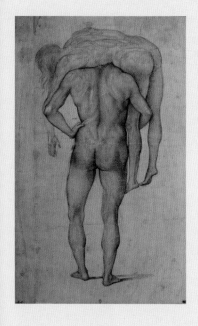

△ Luca Signorelli, **Nude man with a corpse on his shoulders,** no date. Watercolor drawing on paper, 14 × 10 in (35.5 × 25.5 cm). Musée du Louvre, Paris

△ Luca Cambiaso, **Cubically simplified figures,** ca. 1560/65. Pen and wash on paper, 13¼ × 9½ in (34 × 24 cm). Galleria degli Uffizi, Florence

△ Pontormo, study for *The Three Graces*, 1540–1549. Red chalk on paper, 11½ × 8¼ in (29.5 × 21.2 cm). Galleria degli Uffizi, Florence

▽ Pieter Bruegel the Elder, *Ira*, 1557. Pen and brown ink on paper, 9 × 11¾ in (23 × 30 cm). Galleria degli Uffizi, Florence

▽ Hans Baldung Grien (?), *Three Witches.* Pen and ink with white highlights, brown ground on paper, 12¼ × 8¼ in (30.9 × 20.9 cm). Albertina, Vienna

Everyday Farm Life and Visions of Hell

Although the ideas of Renaissance art spread rapidly throughout Europe, they were not immediately incorporated in the same way everywhere. Thus, for example, the works of the Dutch painter Hieronymus Bosch are completely different from those of Leonardo da Vinci, which were produced during the same time period. Bosch, who was financially independent and familiar with contemporary movements and sects critical of the church, created triptychs containing a fantastical world filled with dis-

turbing details; they were completely unsuitable as altar paintings. Rather than presenting illusions of people in their putative strengths and ideal beauty, he displayed human beings with all their weaknesses. His paintings are convincing as nightmares—not as visions of Paradise.

Pieter Bruegel the Elder revealed the extent of human folly in a painting of six blind men that illustrates one of Christ's well-known parables: "(I)f a blind man leads a blind man, both will fall into a pit." (Matthew 15:14). So how, in our world, can we put our trust in leaders who are spiritually blind and without faith? Even the presence of the church in the background is not enough to prevent the ultimate occurrence of the calamity which is hinted at in the downward sloping diagonal on the right. The conspicuously reserved color palette serves to further emphasize the tragic inevitability of the event.

Bruegel's predilection for subjects drawn from everyday farm life, frequently seasoned with satirical notes and hidden moralistic refrences, earned the painter the nickname "the Peasant Breugel". Like Bosch, he worked primarily for wealthy and discriminating collectors.

△ Pieter Bruegel the Elder, *The Blind Leading the Blind*, 1568. Tempera on canvas, 34 × 61 in (86 × 156 cm). Museo Nazionale di Capodimonte, Naples

▽ Pieter Bruegel the Elder, *The Peasant Wedding*, 1567/68. Oil on wood, 45 × 64 in (114 × 163 cm). Kunsthistorisches Museum, Vienna

972.

Albrecht Dürer

The calm face of this young, cosmopolitan artist reveals his great self-confidence. His clothing is elegant yet slightly casual; his shirt billowing as if by chance. Nevertheless, each detail has been carefully considered and executed with the greatest of technical precision.

This portrait shows Albrecht Dürer, a native of Nuremberg, at the beginning of his career. He had already completed his first journey to Italy in 1495; a second journey in 1505–1506 took him to Venice for a longer period as well. Upon his return, he devoted himself to studying the proportions of the human body as he had learned them from his Italian colleagues. He completed his *Four Books on Human Proportions* in 1528. Seen from this perspective, Dürer's depiction of the first human beings—created in the image of God, despite their fall from grace—was motivated by more than religion. In his later works, Dürer (who, like Lucas Cranach, shared the viewpoints of Martin Luther) concentrated on the central themes of the Christian faith.

With his extraordinary artistic skill, Dürer developed every medium of his art to perfection: not only painting, but drawing, watercolors, woodcuts and etching, which he refined far beyond the level of his time. His wife Agnes wrote that she sold her husband's woodcuts at fair stands.

▽ Albrecht Dürer, *Dead Roller*, 1512. Watercolor and pigment on parchment, white and gold highlights, 10¾ × 7¾ in (27.4 × 19.8 cm). Albertina, Vienna

△+◁ Albrecht Dürer, *Adam and Eve*, 1507. Mixed media on wood, 82 × 33 in (209 × 83 cm) each. Museo del Prado, Madrid. The inscription on the tablet reads: "Albertus Dürer alemanus faciebat post virginis partum 1507," monogram.

◁ Albrecht Dürer, *Self-portrait*, 1498. Mixed media on wood, 20 × 16 in (52 × 41 cm). Museo del Prado, Madrid

Devotional Images and Landscape Painting

Matthias Grünewald painted a series of altar panels for the abbey hospital in Isenheim, Alsace. The monks hoped that the saints depicted there would miraculously heal their patients before they began their treatment. On weekdays, an image of the crucified Christ was intended to provide comfort to the sick visitors: through their suffering, they would ultimately overcome death, and the more they suffered, the more certain they were to experience salvation in emulation of Christ.

In the darkening sky of the sixth hour, the location of the crucifixion was deliberately left undefined: it is not important. In contrast, in *Alexander's Victory at Issus*, Albrecht Altdorfer created a grandiose, heroic landscape as the idealized topographical setting for the victory of the Western World over the Orient. The viewer must work his or her way patiently into the ant-sized turmoil of battle depicted here: it is as if the painter had reduced human wars to the scale of their true significance.

△ Matthias Grünewald, *The Crucifixion*, center panel of the Isenheim Altarpiece, ca. 1512–1516. Oil on wood, 8 ft 10 in × 10 ft 1 in (269 × 307 cm). Musée d'Unterlinden, Colmar. The focus of the painting is the depiction of suffering.

▷ Albrecht Altdorfer, *Alexander's Victory at Issus*, 1529. Oil on wood, 5 ft 2¼ in × 3 ft 11½ in (158.4 × 120.3 cm). Alte Pinakothek, Munich. Alexander the Great is shown defeating King Darius of Persia (fleeing in his chariot) in the Battle of Issus in 333.

ALTDORFER (CA. 1480–1538) · GRÜNEWALD (CA. 1470/80–1528)   267

Portrait Painting

His appointment as court painter to the Electors of Saxony in Wittenberg in 1505 required Lucas Cranach the Elder to establish a large workshop, at the same time providing him with the opportunity to include the painting of female nudes in his repertoire. His highly-prized Venus figures combined the s-curve of late Gothic sculpture with an erotic charisma that was (quite insufficiently) disguised under the pretext of a mythological setting. A friend of Martin Luther and supporter of the Reformation, he placed his art and the full capacity of his workshop in the service of the movement and painted portraits of Luther.

◁ Hans Holbein
the Younger,
*Erasmus of
Rotterdam*, ca.
1523. Oil on wood,
16½ × 12½ in (42 ×
32 cm). Musée du
Louvre, Paris

Hans Holbein the Younger's portrait of Desiderius Erasmus of Rotterdam, a humanist who was initially receptive to the Reformation, already reveals the artist, who became court painter to King Henry VIII in London in 1536, as one of the greatest portrait painters of his time. His most ambitious group portrait is that of the two French ambassadors to the English court.

They are surrounded by objects which represent the arts and sciences as well as wealth and fame. A calendar displays the exact date; the subjects' attributes depict their ages. But on the floor, with its mosaic pattern from Westminster Abbey, the anamorphosis of a skull in a metal basin is discernable only from one distinct vantage point: even this glorious existence is finite.

△ Hans Holbein the
Younger, *The Am-
bassadors* (Double
portrait of Jean de
Dinteville and
Georges de Selve),
1533. Oil on wood, 6 ft
9 in × 6 ft 10 in (206 ×
209 cm). National
Gallery, London

Patrons and Mistresses

King Francis I of France (ruled 1515–1547), a great patron of the arts and fervent admirer of the Italian Renaissance, not only ordered the purchase of works by Michelangelo and Raphael, he also summoned artists such as Leonardo da Vinci to France. Shortly before his death, da Vinci even sold the king his *Mona Lisa*.

In 1528, Francis I commissioned a new palace to be built on the foundation walls of a twelfth-century hunting lodge in Fontainebleau. Under his successor, Henry II, the palace became a center of court life (*la vie seigneurial*) and lent its name to a new artistic genre, the School of Fontainebleau.

Italian artists worked on the building of the chateau, whose curving outdoor staircase is the most striking achievement of its architecture. However, Henry II soon ceased to visit Fontainebleau; he was drawn instead to Anet, the palace of Diane de Poitiers, probably the woman shown here in this portrait.

△ Philibert Delorme, **Palace of Fontainebleau**, Cour du Cheval Blanc with horseshoe-shaped staircase, construction begun in 1528

◁ François Clouet, *Lady in Her Bath*, ca. 1570. Oil on wood, 36¼ × 32 in (92.1 × 81.3 cm). National Gallery of Art, Washington, D.C. The lady in the picture is thought to be Diane de Poitiers (1499–1566), mistress of King Henry II of France (reigned 1547–1559).

▷ *Scène de la vie seigneurial: The Bath*, ca. 1500. Tapestry (No. 3 of 6), 9 ft 5 in × 8 ft 6–8 in (287 × 261/6 cm). Musée National du Moyen Age, Paris

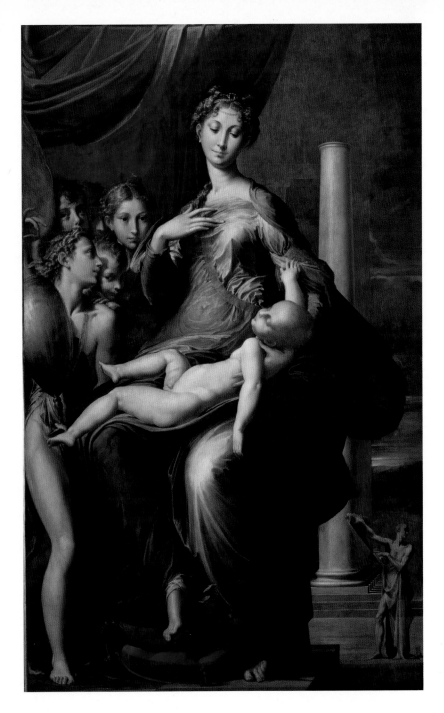

Mannerism

From a historical standpoint, mannerism is regarded as the stylistic transition between the Renaissance and Baroque periods. In a countermovement to a strict formal canon based on classical antiquity and nature, mannerist compositions became increasingly contrived, filled with elongated figures with twisted, artistically moving bodies topped with artificially small heads. The image field no longer determined a picture's perspective; a fractured, turbulent color palette took precedence over adherence to the object being portrayed: *maniera* was an idiosyncratic genre in Renaissance painting.

Ever since 1900, critics debating the legitimacy of modern art have repeatedly referred to mannerism as an example of distortion, of manner as mania, even as degenerate art, a viewpoint with all-too-familiar consequences. Exponents of the avant-garde see mannerists as artists who were able to free themselves from rigid constraints and achieved a great degree of autonomy in the age of court artists. They celebrate El Greco as a prophet of the Modern era.

△ Parmigianino, **Madonna with the Long Neck**, 1534–1540. Oil on wood, 7 ft 1½ in × 4 ft 5 in (219 × 135 cm). Galleria degli Uffizi, Florence. Vasari praised this example of twisted and elongated figure painting as "a highly commendable work... full of grace and beauty."

▷ Giuseppe Arcimboldo, **The Vegetable Gardener**, ca. 1590. Oil on wood, 14 × 9½ in (35 × 24 cm). Museo Civico Ala Ponzone, Cremona. Arcimboldo's heads, composed of realistically depicted everyday objects, anticipated the surrealists' experiments with reality in the 20th century.

△ El Greco, *Laocoön*, ca. 1610–1614. Oil on canvas, 4 ft 6 in × 6 ft 8 in (137.5 × 172.5 cm). National Gallery of Art, Washington, D.C. El Greco used Toledo as the setting for the story of Laocoön, who was punished for warning his people not to accept the Trojan horse.

◁ *The Door of Hell* in the Garden of Bomarzo, ca. 1552–1585. For over 30 years, Vicino Orsini, owner of Bomarzo in the province of Viterbo, allowed various artists to place their creations in this bizarre and mysterious sculpture park, the Sacro Bosco.

The Image of the World

From time immemorial, people have attempted to record and map important points in their landscape. In the Bible, Joshua sends men out to travel the land and describe it (Joshua 18). Ancient geographers such as Strabo (ca. 63 BCE–23 CE) and Ptolemy (ca. 100–175 CE) shaped the image of the world in their time. The Roman *Tabula Peutingeriana* depicts a directory of military settlements and the distances between them. The first maps of the Christian Western World served no practical purpose. T and O maps documented the three known continents and were oriented toward the east—whence the sun rises, where Paradise was believed to be,

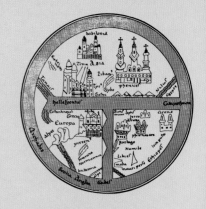

and from which Christ was expected to return to earth. World maps such as the Anglo-Saxon or Cottonian map or the Erbstorf map—with Jerusalem at their centers—were intended to illustrate the works of God on the (flat) earth. As new discoveries were made and the concept of the world changed during the Renaissance, a new image of the spherical world as a readable projection formed, based on the earlier work of Ptolemy. The early globes and atlases by Gerhard Mercator (1512–1594) or Abraham Ortelius bear witness to this.

△ **T and O map**, 11th crentrury; Asia is at the top, Europe and Africa below; the T and the border around the continents represent the oceans.

▽ **Tabula Peutingeriana**, segment V (Dalmatia, Pannonia, Moesia, Campania, Apulia, Africa), Österreichische National-bibliothek, Vienna; 12th-century copy of a map from the 4th century illustrating the road network of the late Roman Empire. The medieval copy is divided into 12 segments; its total length is 22 ft 4 in (682 cm).

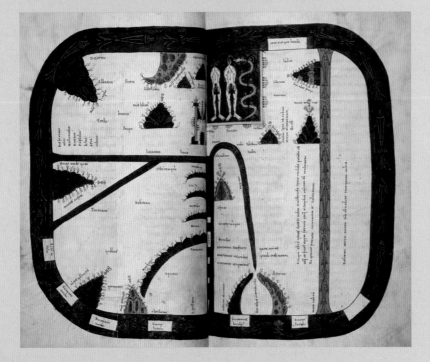

◁ World map from the *Commentary on the Apocalypse* by Beatus of Liébana, Abbey of Santo Domingo de Silas, Spain, 1106. British Library, London; Eden is pictured at the top of the map in the center.

△ **Cottonian world map**, from an English manuscript on geography, 11th century. British Library, London

▽ Rumold Mercator, **Map of the world**, 1587, 1595, reproduced in the Atlas by Gerhard Mercator. British Library, London

△ **Ebstorf world map**, ca. 1235, Erbstorf Abbey, Lüneburg; original destroyed in 1943; copy, British Library, London

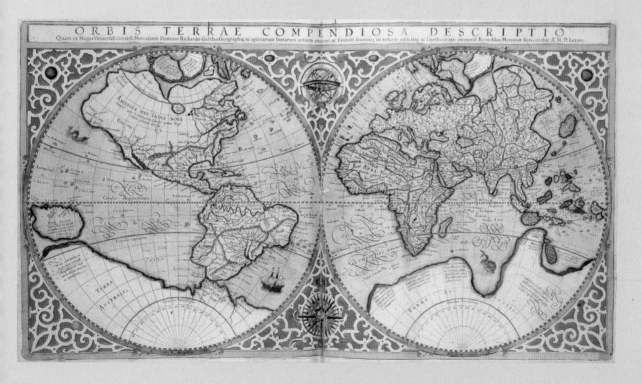

BAROQUE & ROCOCO

Absolute Art

Baroque literally means "irregular" and, figuratively speaking, "against the rules." The art of this period has been referred to in this way since the end of the eighteenth century. However it is primarily a Catholic art form in fact it is rigorously "controlled". It belongs to the strategy of the Counter Reformation, the Pope's response to Luther. The strategy was to re-Catholicize Protestants, by force if need be, and to strengthen Catholics in the true faith. The Jesuit Order, founded by Ignatius of Loyola in 1534, was the

Chronology

1581 Under William of Orange, the northern Netherlands breaks with Spain.
1588 The Spanish Armada is defeated in battle by the English fleet.
1600 In Rome, Giordano Bruno is publicly burned as a heretic.

Map labels: NORTH SEA, BALTIC SEA, The Hague, Delft, Brussels, Brühl, Kassel, Dresden, Paris, Würzburg, Versailles, Karlsruhe, Bruchsal, Vienna, Munich, Admont, ATLANTIC OCEAN, Santiago de Compostela, Stra, Escorial, Madrid, Aranjuez, Rome, Naples, MEDITERRANEAN, SICILY

Legend:
† Church/abbey
● Palace
▣ Painting
⚲ Sculpture

Caravaggio, *David and Goliath*, ca. 1605–1610

Rembrandt, *Self-Portrait in a Cap, with Eyes wide Open*, 1630

Giovanni Lorenzo Bernini, *The Rape of Proserpina*, 1621–1622

Diego Velázquez, *Las Men (The Maids of Honor)*, 1656–

| 1575 | 1600 | 1625 | 1650 | 1675 |

Baroque & Rococo (ca. 1575–1770)

elite force lined up to convert heathens and heretics. After Luther criticized Gothic cathedrals as "gigantic and impractical," and favored more simplicity in church structures and decoration, Ignatius of Loyola supported the expressive power of dramatic settings, statues and images to an even greater extent. Jesuit architects were schooled in the writings of their great Renaissance predecessors, Alberti and Palladio, and, like all other architects, in the teachings of the ancient classicist Vitruvius. On these bases, they created buildings that were intended to make absolute claims to power apparent, namely those of the Roman Catholic Church and of Catholic prince bishops. Like architecture, sculpture, painting and, shortly thereafter, horticulture supported these claims. After attaining independence, the northern Netherlands provided an island in the Catholic-absolutist commissioned artwork of Europe. There, genre painting developed in a free art market which included, in addition to portraits, various kinds of landscape, still life and genre paintings.

Cultural History

1605/15 *El ingenioso hidalgo Don Quixote de la Mancha* is written by Miguel de Cervantes (1547–1616).
1609 Kepler (1571–1630) publishes his laws of planetary motion.
1628 English physician William Harvey (1578–1657) discovers the blood circulatory system.
1666 Isaac Newton (1643–1717) deduces the law of gravity (and the three laws of motion).
1710 Augustus the Strong founds the Meissen porcelain manufactory.
from 1740 Johann Sebastian Bach (1685–1750), *The Art of the Fugue*.

1618–1648 Thirty Years' War
1624 Cardinal Richelieu becomes chief minister to Louis XIII and fosters absolutism.
1633 In his second trial before the Inquisition, Galileo Galilei recants Copernican principles.
1638 Abolition of torture in England
1643–1715 Louis XIV, known as the Sun King, rules France.
1683 Second Siege of Vienna by the Turks
1685 Louis XIV revokes the Edict of Nantes (freedom of religion).
1689–1725 Peter the Great rules Russia.
1740–1786 Frederick the Great rules Prussia.
1756–1763 Seven Years' War involves all the major European powers in conflict.
1776 Thirteen North American colonies declare independence from Great Britain.
1789 The storming of the Bastille and the beginning of the French Revolution

Jean-Antoine Watteau, *Pilgrimage to Cythera*, 1717

Johann Bernhard Fischer von Erlach, Vienna, St. Charles, 1716–1737

Giovanni Battista Tiepolo, *Apotheosis of the Pisani Family*, 1761–1762

1700   1725   1750   1775

At a Glance

Light and Shadow

In baroque painting, light was not only used for modelling of volume but in the main to heighten the expression of a painting.

Georges de La Tour, *The Magdalen with the Smoking Flame*, ca. 1640–1645, 50 × 37 in (128 × 94 cm). Musée du Louvre, Paris

Movement and Rest

Representation of movement, but also release and rest through the use of light, diagonal composition, and gesture was highly important in the baroque.

Giovanni Lorenzo Bernini, *The Ecstasy of St. Theresa*, 1645–52

Rocaille

Asymmetrical, shell-shaped, decorative motif of the rococo (*rocaille*, a style that may well be the source of the term, rococo).

Strapwork

Decorative motif and surface ornament of particular importance in the eighteenth century that consisted of symmetrically arranged, curved straplike bands, rather than forms from nature, such as tendrils. These were sometimes adorned with figurative motifs, especially on stucco ceilings and walls.

Total Work of Art

To a greater extent than in previous eras, the art of the baroque was characterized by the interplay of individual genres. The unified appearance of royal residences and churches, in particular, laid claim to the idea of *Gesamtkunstwerk* (total work of art), a term that did not actually become popular until the nineteenth century.

Beletage

The French term *beletage* (beautiful story; also *piano nobile*) refers to the main floor of a building. In baroque and rococo palace architecture, it was the floor on which the ruler resided and entertained guests.

Stucco

Malleable, fast hardening mixture of plaster, lime, sand and water used to decorate interior spaces, but also as raw material for sculptures and reliefs. Colored, painted with marble veins, and accented with lumps of stone, it became the ideal imitation marble.

Stucco decoration in the White Hall of the Würzburg Residence, 1744–45

Baroque & Rococo (ca. 1575–1770)

Johann Georg Hinz, *Curio Cabinet*, 1666. Oil on canvas, 45 × 36½ (114.5 × 93.3 cm). Kunsthalle, Hamburg

Iconology

Cesare Ripa's 1593 manual, *Iconologia*, is made up of mythological and allegorical figures in highly significant, detailed garb. It was first illustrated in 1603, translated into the major European languages, and went through countless printings. In contrast to iconography, i.e. pictorial representation, iconology interprets the content, the entire meaning of a work of art or artistic complex.

Cesare Ripa, *Deception*, page from *Iconologia*

Art Chamber and Cabinet of Curiosities

Collections of objets d'art, natural history objects and curiosities found in German patrician and aristocratic homes, above all in the sixteenth and seventeenth centuries, were the precursors of today's museums. Art chamber painting from real or fictitious collections emerged as a genre lying somewhere between interior paintings and still lifes, and can also convey allegorical content, such as impermanence.

Pathos and Opulence

The art of the baroque reached its zenith during the Age of Absolutism, a period in which rulers exercised absolute power. Giving expression to this unlimited power was not limited to architecture. The visual arts also exploited opulence and lofty formulas of power to represent this divinely authorized omnipotence.

Hyacinthe Rigaud, *Louis XIV*, 1701. Oil on canvas, 9 ft × 6 ft 2 in (279 × 190 cm). Musée du Louvre, Paris

Jean-Honoré Fragonard, *Happy Lovers*, ca. 1760, private collection

Eroticism and Sensual Pleasure

The rococo countered baroque heaviness and exuberance with lightness, delicacy and grace. Contemporary taste found particular expression in *galant* themes that showed worldly, tangible sensuousness unmitigated by mythological content. Poetry paired with frivolity made painters like Watteau, Boucher or Fragonard into delineators of contemporary manners and creators of cliché.

Key Terms

◁ **Il Gesù**, Rome: view of the main altar towards the east. Constructed between 1568 and 1584 to plans by Giacomo Vignola. Frescoes (1668–1683) by Giovanni Battista Gaulli, called Baciccio. In the apse *The Adoration of the Lamb*.

▷ **Il Gesù**, Rome: façade by Giacomo della Porta. The horizontal division of the two-story façade is balanced by a layout that emphasizes the vertical through increasing plasticity from the sides to the middle.

◁ **Il Gesù**, Rome: floor plan

▷▷ Baciccio, ***Triumph of the Name of Jesus***, 1679, vault fresco in the nave of Il Gesù, Rome. The apotheosis of the Monogram of Christ on the illusionistically painted "open" ceiling requires observers to think in abstract terms.

Il Gesù, the House of God

In the mother church of their order, the Jesuits needed an appropriate place for their mission. As in Early Christian basilicas, the hall form with open choir made room for pastoral care and homilies and created an ideal sense of community. For acoustic reasons, the flat ceiling was best. Based on a new papal resolution, houses of God were not to exhibit anything profane. Rather, they were to appropriately reflect the sacredness of the place and lead believers from darkness into the light. This was not new, but the available means offered leeway for contemporary tastes and new technologies. The financial problems of the young order made benefactors essential. Cardinal Alessandro Farnese stood out in particular in his patronage of Il Gesù. He wanted a noble tomb as a personal and fitting memorial. Therefore, he interpreted "nothing profane" as a barrel vault and crossing dome, which satisfied the Jesuits. In the course of their mission, they spread this type of churcharchitecture throughout the world.

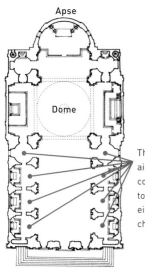

Apse

Dome

The side aisles contain a total of eight chapels.

Allegory and Apotheosis

Figures in baroque paintings and sculptures that fly or plunge, are enthroned or recline lasciviously, do not represent real human beings. They are allegorical, abstract ideas and images illustrated in the form of persons.

This was not an invention of the baroque period: genius figures were already known in antiquity. In the Middle Ages, these were virtues and vices and the seven liberal arts. But baroque, multi-figured compositions on ceilings and walls were the first to unite saints, mythological figures and sensual pleasures, and to make them emotionally accessible to observers.

Books, such as Cesare Ripa's *Iconologia* were important tools for artists, patrons and viewers alike. Ripa's manual is a compilation of mythological and allegorical figures depicted in highly significant, detailed garb.

◁ Francesco Solimena, *Faith, Hope and Charity*, 1689–1690. Fresco, San Paolo Maggiore Naples. An anchor for stability and flowers that hold the prospect of fruit represent hope (left). Hope looks at the divine light (communion cup, center), for all hope comes from God. Charity (right) is unambiguous.

◁ Pierre Le Gros the Younger, *Religion Overthrowing Heresy and Hatred*, 1695–1698. Marble, Il Gesù, Rome, altar with the grave of St. Ignatius: the representation of religion with cross and putto is clear, whereas heresy is more fascinating. Heresy is old, because old age is the last stage of human life, just as heresy is the last stage of perversion. She is ugly, because she has lost faith and truth. Lacking virtue, she is nearly naked. Unkempt hair and snakes symbolize heresy's ruinous ideas.

▷ Giovanni Battista Tiepolo, *Apotheosis of the Pisani Family*, 1761–1762. Fresco, Villa Pisani, Stra. A special aspect of the allegory is the apotheosis. Accompanied by properly arranged, allegorical "personnel," even mortals can apotheosize.

◁ Giovanni Lorenzo Bernini, *The Ecstasy of St. Theresa*, 1645–1652. Marble and gold bronze, life-sized figures, Cornaro Chapel, Santa Maria della Vittoria, Rome. Theresa of Avila (1515–1582): an angel is said to have repeatedly thrust a glowing arrow into her heart. She was canonized in 1622.

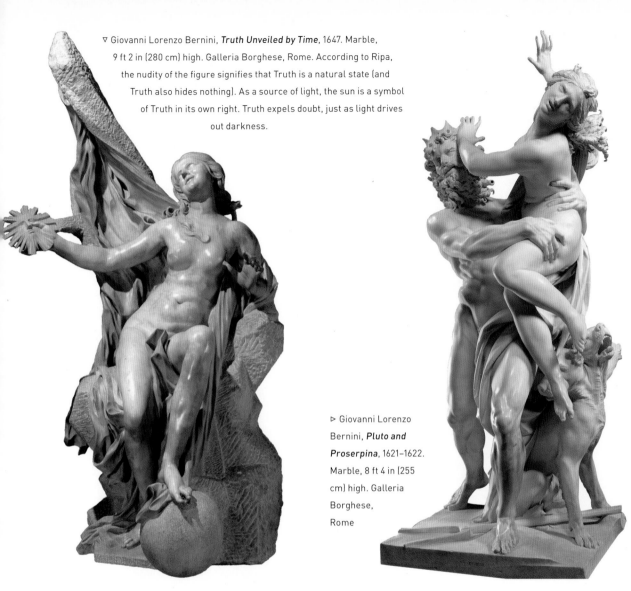

▽ Giovanni Lorenzo Bernini, *Truth Unveiled by Time*, 1647. Marble, 9 ft 2 in (280 cm) high. Galleria Borghese, Rome. According to Ripa, the nudity of the figure signifies that Truth is a natural state (and Truth also hides nothing). As a source of light, the sun is a symbol of Truth in its own right. Truth expels doubt, just as light drives out darkness.

▷ Giovanni Lorenzo Bernini, *Pluto and Proserpina*, 1621–1622. Marble, 8 ft 4 in (255 cm) high. Galleria Borghese, Rome

Bernini's Truth

Giovanni Lorenzo Bernini set up the colonnaded St. Peter's Square in Rome like a stage with optical illusions. For *The Ecstasy of St. Theresa*, he transformed the entire Cornaro Chapel in Santa Maria della Vittoria into a theater with an audience of benefactors' busts in the box seats. So that Theresa can yield to her ecstasy as chastely as possible under the gaze of her audience, however, the much too opulent, massive fabric of her habit takes on a passionately stirring life of its own as the expression of her inner excitement.

This degree of restraint is certainly not desirable for mythological themes. When Pluto abducts the wildly struggling Proserpina to the Underworld, holding her firmly in his grasp, the group all around Cerberus may be considerable. In contrast to the mannerist *figura serpentinata*, which emerges artificially from sheer delight in the spiral form, Bernini's figures seem to have a substantial reason for their spiraled positions.

Truth (Unveiled) also reveals an essential characteristic of baroque sculpture: it operates on a grand scale, the movement is directed outward, the contour of the work is no longer closed. With movement came a heightened interplay of light and shadow.

Versailles, Palace of Kings

Louis XIV was impressed with the papal sculptor and architect Bernini. A king of France must always build larger and more magnificently than any rulers of the past. The Italian addressed the young Louis with flattering remarks and spoke to him from the heart. Even though Bernini's exact plans for the Louvre were never executed, the Sun King began the expansion of his father's hunting lodge near Versailles in the same spirit. First, the palace received a new exterior by Louis Le Vau. Jules Hardouin Mansart built the south wing from 1878–1880.

◁ Hall of Mirrors, 246 × 33 ft (75 × 10 m), begun in 1679, designed by Jules Hardouin Mansart and decorated by Charles Le Brun

▷ The king at a distance: the baroque palace is no longer a fortified, enclosed rectangle, but a three-winged, open structure with a deliberately long drive to the entrance.

△ Giovanni Lorenzo Bernini, **Bust of Louis XIV**, 1665. Marble, 31½ in (80 cm) high. Palace of Versailles. At the request of the 27-year-old king, Bernini came to Paris to revise his designs for the new construction of the Louvre's east façade. The bust took shape during his 14-week sojourn.

◁ The total length of the garden façade is 2200 ft (670 m). Personified French rivers surround the pool.

With the relocation of the permanent royal residence from Paris to Versailles in 1682, work was begun on the north wing, because room had to be found for the court and offices of state. While the two-tone brick and sandstone façade of the old hunting lodge remained formally binding on the town side, the garden façade was built in sandstone of a single color. The markedly horizontal arrangement is offset vertically by means of a few symmetrically arranged blocks that protrude through the entire height of the building. On the garden side, a parapet hides the Mansard roofs.

The park, however, is what makes a baroque palace complex complete. The king's rooms not only lie at the center of the structure, but also at the intersection of perfectly straight roads between the town and park sides. As a result, they stand at the symbolic center of the realm. Put another way, the center is where the king resides. As a result of his work on the Park of Versailles, André Le Nôtre became one of the most important landscape architects of the baroque. His *Allée du Roi* stretches from the palace to the far horizon as the principal sight line of the structure. A palace with a park like that of Versailles became the vision of every baroque ruler.

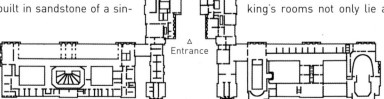

▽ Garden façade

△ Entrance

Nature Under Sovereign Control

An absolute monarch felt unassailable in his great power, which is why his palace needed no defensive enclosures and his parks needed no walls. A landscape design that merged from parterres via hedged trees into a naturally evolving forest was an expression of boundless power. Open strips of forest stretched into the countryside like *allees*. Enriched by ideologically suitable sculptures, pools filled with water and the highest, most powerful fountains, the park became walk-through propaganda. Upon reaching the formally organized promenade, every official state guest understood just who he was dealing with. Water came into Versailles from the banks of the Seine five miles (8 km)

away. It had to overcome a 525 ft (160m) change in elevation, a job undertaken by the expensive, not terribly efficient Machine de Marly (1681–1684), which was nonetheless celebrated as an engineering marvel. But even it could only cause those fountains to jet skyward that were directly within view of the monarch. When Margrave Karl-Wilhelm of Baden-Durlach placed the design of his new Karlsruhe Residence on the drawing board, he had a clear idea of what he wanted. An octagonal tower rises in the center of a circular forest area, around which the *Kavaliershäuser* of the princely household were arranged. Thirty-two lanes radiate from the tower and through the forest. Within nine of these

△ Étienne Allegrain, **Louis XIV's promenade with a view of the Parterre du Nord in front of the garden façade of the north wing**, 1688. Oil on canvas, 7 ft 6½ in × 9 ft 6 in (230 × 290 cm). Musée du Château, Versailles

▷ Johann Jacob Baumeister and Michael Rößler, **Map of Karlsruhe**, 1737–1739. Copperplate engraving, colorized, 7½ × 12½ in (19 × 32 cm): unlike more sweeping baroque town plans, such as St. Petersburg, Karlsruhe was actually built this way.

lanes, the three-winged, fan-shaped palace, complete with French park, stretches out within the circle like a great slice of cake. The city stands outside the circle, sectionalized in accordance with the radiating lanes. But here it is the tower, rather than the ruler, that stands at the center as an emblem of the state.

▷ Giovanni Francesco Guerniero, **Wilhelmshöhe**, Kassel, Hercules Monument, 1701–1711. The hilly terrain above the palace culminates in an octagon with an embossed copper reproduction of the Farnese Hercules. From there, a cascade pours down which, according to the architect's plans, was indended to flow all the way down to the palace.

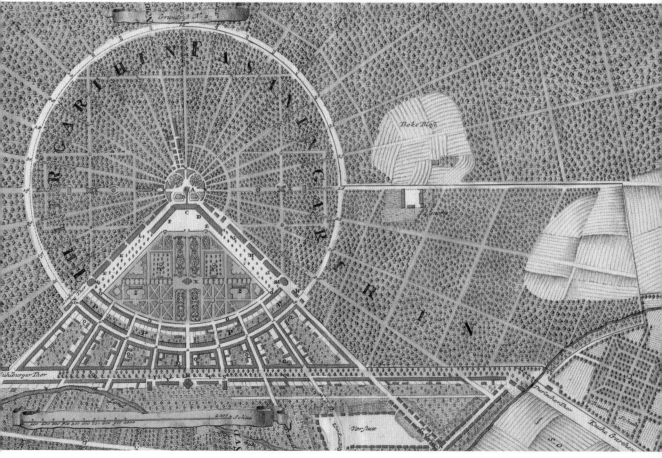

Baroque Architecture

Johann Balthasar Neumann's residence of the prince bishops in Würzburg is among the few large-scale projects of the baroque that was completely realized according to a consistent plan. The Zwinger Palace in Dresden, by contrast, originally an orangery, is only a modest portion of a new palace complex for Prince Elector August the Strong. Absolutist building projects, apparently, were often more expensive than planned.

The interiors of German baroque palaces and royal residences boast stairwells that function as prestigious

△ **Würzburg Residence**, stairwell (1735–1753) with Giovanni Battista Tiepolo's ceiling fresco, *The Four Continents* (1753)

◁ **Augustusburg Palace**, Brühl, stairwell (1741–1744): design by Johann Balthasar Neumann, who also built in Würzburg

ceremonial spaces. Neumann's stairwells in Würzburg, Brühl and Bruchsal begin as a single staircase, then part and reach the upper floor via two sets of stairs leading in the opposite direction. By contrast, exterior steps were the standard form in baroque sacred buildings because they led visitors up to the house of God. Unusual sections could also be integrated into buildings, as long as the patron was an emperor and the architecture expressed an unconventional idea. In Vienna's St. Charles Borromeo, church and state were to become a structural unity, whereby the state dated back to the Roman Empire, as could be seen in the temple façade and Trajan's column.

▽+△ Johann Bernhard Fischer von Erlach, Vienna, **Church of St. Charles Borromeo**, 1716–1738. In the 18th century, Vienna "had as much right to be called New Rome as Constantinople formerly." Similarities to mosques that Fischer von Erlach had visited in Constantinople may well have been entirely deliberate.

△ **Zwinger Palace**, Dresden, 1697–1716. Gallery and Rampart Pavilion, design by Matthäus Daniel Pöppelmann, decoration of the pavilion by Balthasar Permoser

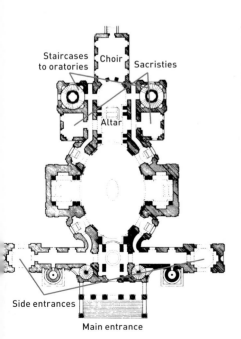

Staircases to oratories · Choir · Sacristies

Altar

Side entrances

Main entrance

Court and Monastery Libraries

◁ Austrian National Library (former Court Library), Vienna, State Hall (1723-1726). Design by Johann Bernhard Fischer von Erlach, frescoes by Daniel Gran: War and Peace are in the wings, the apotheosis of Charles VI in the oval.

▽ Benedictine Monastery Library, Admont (1764–1773). Design by Josef Hueber, frescoes by Bartolomeo Altomonte: in the main cupola, Divine Wisdom. The south vault shows the Arts and Technology, Medicine and the Natural Sciences, Theology and Religion. To the north are Jurisprudence, History and the Awakening of the Spirit.

The enlargement of the Viennese Court Library and its State Hall, which is divided into a central oval and two wings at the longer sides, was based on Johann Bernhard Fischer von Erlach's designs. The three-way division was originally less obvious; only at a later stage did engineering require the arches and supports at the transition from the oval to the wings. The collection was continuously expanded in the second half of the fourteenth century. Like all court libraries, it served a prestigious purpose, yet the spaces offered welcome opportunities to exalt each ruler as a patron of scholarship and learning. Monasteries, on the other hand, were traditional centers of learning under the protection of the Church, where knowledge was preserved, but not as a rule imparted. In 1773, when the monks in Admont treated themselves to Denis Diderot's *Encyclopédie* (1751–1772, twenty-eight volumes), a work that had been on the papal index since 1759, in celebration of their new library, this was less as a result of open-mindedness and more because they wanted to learn how "The Enemy" reasoned.

When monasteries were closed down after the French Revolution, court libraries were the beneficiaries. They took charge of the valuable holdings of cloister libraries.

▽ **San Lorenzo de El Escorial** (1563–1584), designed by Juan Bautista de Toledo and Juan de Herrera. The joining of cloister and royal residence symbolized the unity of church and state. The royal couple's rooms were in the eastern part of the basilica and accessible from the choir. The façades were conservatively decorated, and most ornamentation was reserved for the sanctuary.

Spanish Architecture

About seventy years had passed since the complete emancipation of Catholic Spaniards from Moorish rule when Philip II ordered the building of El Escorial. The residence that is also a monastery testifies to how unimaginable Reformational criticism of the Church must have been within his realm. Rather than placing a chapel somewhere on the edge of the residence, there are "several rooms" for the king behind the central basilica. Absolutist, three-winged palace complexes with forecourts took hold later in Spain than elsewhere. Architects schooled in the austere image of El Escorial made sparing use of baroque decorative forms, such as wall mural art and window finishes. But they eventually overcame their reservations.

△ **Cathedral of Santiago de Compostela:** the baroque western façade of the Romanesque church (1738) extended around the north tower in accordance with a design by Fernando de Casas y Novoa.

△ **Cathedral of Santiago de Compostela,** high altar, ca. 1650. At the very top of the altar, St. James appears anachronistically in triplicate on horseback as a fighter of Moors.

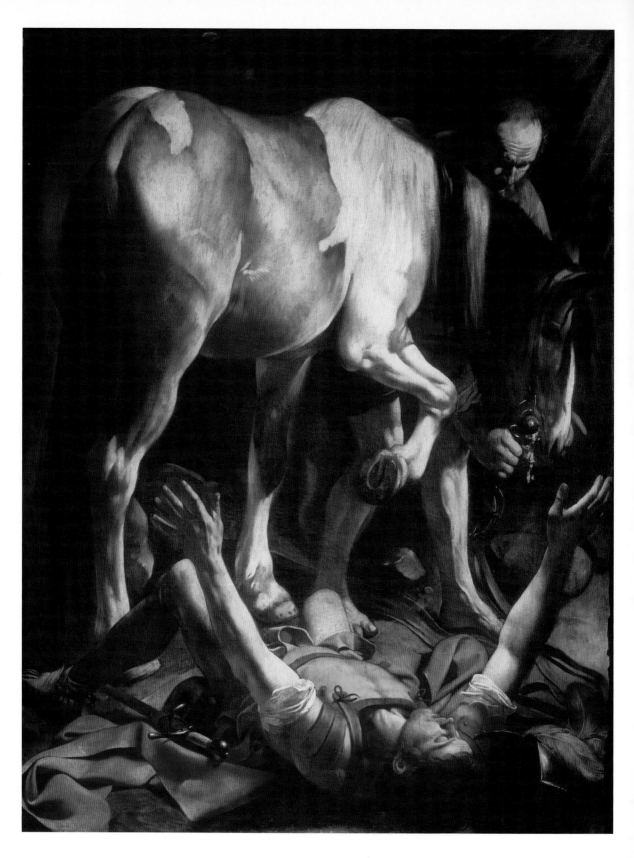

Caravaggio's Light

Potential patrons often rejected Caravaggio's work. People praying with dirty feet, saints who looked like peasants, and paintings with practically no background were just not what they expected from artists. But what overtaxed paying clients was precisely what his colleagues admired: Caravaggio's new handling of light, space, and figures. In *The Calling of St. Matthew*, Jesus is almost a peripheral character, practically concealed by Caravaggio's later addition of Peter. Whatever the unprepossessing man with the tired, outstretched arm may have said, people would have expected the call to discipleship to be more forceful and godlike since, according to the Bible, Matthew obeyed it immediately. Caravaggio taught that this was not required.

The next divine calling came posthumously and concerned Paul of Tarsus. The appearance of the Light, also illuminating his horse's belly, threw the zealous persecutor of Christians from his steed. His enlightenment takes place as he lies on the ground in an unholy mess of horses' hooves and men's legs. This, too, was not considered a suitable pose for the devotional image.

△ Caravaggio, *David and Goliath*, ca. 1605–1610. Oil on canvas, 4 ft 1 in × 4 ft 2 in (125 × 101 cm). Galleria Borghese, Rome

◁ Caravaggio, *Conversion of St. Paul*, 1601. Oil on canvas, Santa Maria del Popolo, Rome

▷ Caravaggio, *The Calling of St. Matthew*, ca. 1600. Oil on canvas, 10 ft 9 in × 11 ft 5 in (328 × 348 cm). Contarelli Chapel, S. Luigi dei Francesi, Rome

Observation and Perception

◁ Diego Velázquez, *Las Meninas* (*The Maids of Honor*), the family of Philip IV, 1656–1657. Oil on canvas, 127 × 108 in (318 × 276 cm). Museo del Prado, Madrid

Velázquez und Zurbarán, contemporaries and colleagues, represented Spain's two most prominent patrons: Velázquez the royal family, and Zurbarán the church. We know Velázquez made two visits to Italy and also met Rubens at the Spanish court. Zurbarán apparently never left Spain. Despite the many conventions, Velázquez tried to give court life a sense of vitality. Zurbarán painted saints like still lifes: collected, in repose, motionless even while active. His paintings of the Holy Family often reveal thorough knowledge of theological commentaries; there is much more to them than meets the eye, probably even in the case of a plate of bread.

While Zurbarán only discloses many things to cognoscenti, looking more closely at Velázquez is fruitful. In *Las Meninas* he presents a portrait of the Infanta Margarita and her retinue. We see him at work in his studio with palette and paintbrush by a canvas on which the child cannot be pictured, because she is standing in the wrong position. So who was his subject? A mirror behind him reveals what he sees before him: the royal couple, upon which nearly all eyes are turned. The couple is also in approximately the same position as we, the viewers. As a result, the highest-ranking persons in the painting are less conspicuous than the painter himself.

▽ Francisco de Zurbarán, *Pewter Plate with Bread*, oil on canvas. Private collection, Madrid

Peter Paul Rubens

▽ Peter Paul Rubens, *Abduction of the Daughters of Leucippus*, ca. 1617–1618. Oil on canvas, 7 ft 4 in x 6 ft 10 in (224 × 210.5 cm). Alte Pinakothek, Munich

At the height of his fame, Rubens was not only court painter to the Spanish governors in the Southern Netherlands; he also worked for the Jesuits, the King of France, the Prince of Wales, Wittelsbach prince

electors, Italian bankers and the Spanish nobility. He was active either secretly or openly as an envoy and ran his workshop enterprise almost like a factory. He himself organized the dissemination of his works in the

form of engraved reproductions. Like no other baroque painter, Rubens has been associated with the era's ideal of feminine beauty. And it is not the fullness of women's bodies that is remarkable, but the particularly fair, vibrant flesh tones. With the glazed application of yellow and blue, embedded in wafer-thin resin glaze, it attains a carnal quality that one would not expect in a painter of the Counter Reformation, and which has inspired artists right up to the present.

A painting such as the *Abduction of the Daughters of Leucippus* shows the other side of Rubens' fame: two horses attempting to diverge with four figures between them engaged in a furious dance of opposing movements, but connected by gaze in a tragic eternal triangle. If any action takes place, it can only occur in a matter of seconds and, to the continuing pleasure of willing viewers, is caught at the most unlikely moment. On the other hand, *The Honeysuckle Bower*, a portrait of Rubens' own marriage, exudes proper bourgeois refinement.

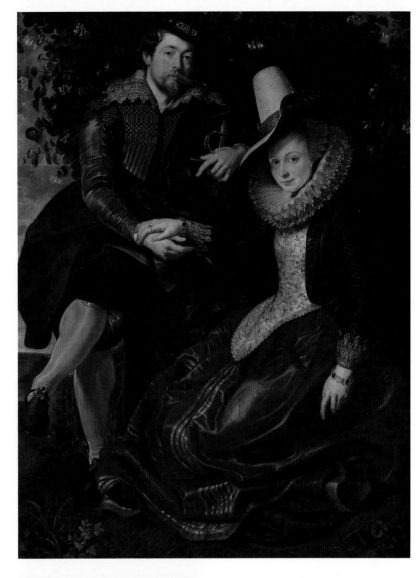

△ Peter Paul Rubens, *The Honeysuckle Bower* (Rubens with his wife, Isabella Brandt), ca. 1609–1610. Oil on canvas and wood, 5 ft 10 in × 4 ft 6 in (178 × 136.5 cm). Alte Pinakothek, Munich

◁ Peter Paul Rubens, *Head of Medusa*, ca. 1617–18. Oil on canvas, 25 × 46 in (68.5 × 118 cm). Kunsthistorisches Museum, Vienna. The moment after the severed, bloody head has fallen to the ground, the blood turns into snakes. What we do not see is the winged Pegasus and the warrior Chrysaor springing forth from her body.

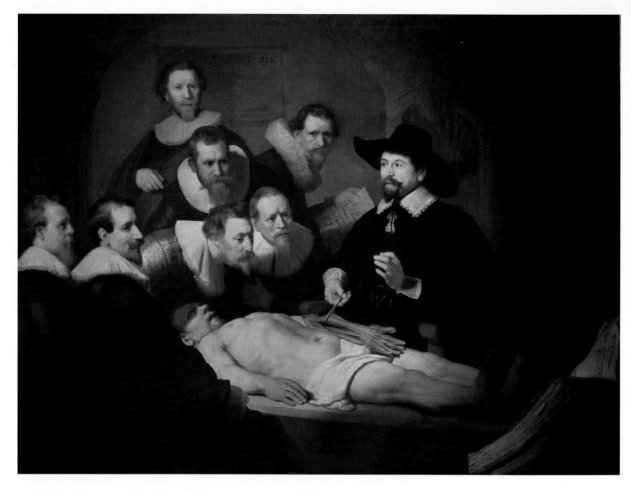

Rembrandt Harmenszoon van Rijn

Even more clearly than Velázquez and Zurbarán, the Protestant Dutchman Rembrandt employed light, brightness and a similarly limited palette to that of Caravaggio. As a painter of historical subjects, Rembrandt mostly chose biblical and mythological themes in which he, like Caravaggio, no longer presented nature as it should be, but as it was. He did not try to express the entire story in a single painting but confined himself to a point in time that he considered important. In this way he came up with paintings that caught his public by surprise. Rembrandt's version of Danae, who was visited

by Zeus in the form of a shower of gold, dispensed with the misleading portrayal of the power of money and showed a rather contented king's daughter, naked and virginal, bathed in golden light. The fettered Eros at the head of the bed is a sign that she safeguards her chastity despite the seduction.

Needless to say, the light on a cadaver is different. Rembrandt owed his financial success to his newly conceived (group) portraits and to drawing which, thanks to his subject matter, was finally promoted to the level of an independent, saleable genre.

△ Rembrandt, *The Anatomy Lesson of Dr. Nicolaes Tulp*, 1632. Oil on canvas, 5 ft 6 in × 7 ft 1 in (169.5 × 216.5 cm). Mauritshuis, The Hague. With a composition that tells a story according to the example of history painting, Rembrandt transformed the previously conventional, wooden presentation of group portraits into authentic events.

▷ Rembrandt, *Danae*, 1636. Oil on canvas, 6 ft × 8 ft 8 in (185 × 203 cm). State Hermitage Museum, St. Petersburg

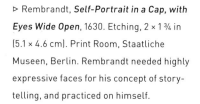

◁ Rembrandt, *Self-portrait with Open Mouth*, 1630. Etching (Bartsch 13), 2¾ × 2½ in (7.3 × 6.2 cm). Print Room, Staatliche Museen, Berlin

▷ Rembrandt, *Self-Portrait in a Cap, with Eyes Wide Open*, 1630. Etching, 2 × 1¾ in (5.1 × 4.6 cm). Print Room, Staatliche Museen, Berlin. Rembrandt needed highly expressive faces for his concept of story-telling, and practiced on himself.

Genre Painting

Genre painting became highly fashionable in Protestant Holland, and examples of it were displayed in countless middle-class households. Despite the moralizing undertone, many of these paintings winked at life congenially with a touch of irony. Thus, the religious efforts of the devout couple in the middleground of *Topsy Turvy World* are hardly helpful in the generally mismanaged chaos. While the lady of the house falls asleep from exhaustion, children, animals and husband show how best to bring themselves and the family to ruin. We may never be able to decipher what else the painting contains in terms of allusions to literature, plays, and wise sayings

of that era. On the other hand, things were a little strange in Vermeer's atelier. Really? The painter is too big; his canvas too small and most of what he has laid out on it doesn't fit. Since Vermeer never sold the painting, people see it as a showpiece for patrons. Clio, the Muse of History, as Cesare Ripa described her, stands with her trumpet in front an actual surviving map of the Seventeen Provinces of the Low Countries, both Spanish and free. She looks directly at a view of the Hague court, and the red ball of the incorrectly held maulstick points to the Brabant court. So is this painting as harmless as it seems, or does it contain a hidden political statement?

▷ Jan Vermeer van Delft, *The Art of Painting*, ca. 1666–1668. Oil on canvas, 47¼ × 39¼ in (120 × 100 cm). Kunsthistorisches Museum, Vienna. The title seems to hint at how one can manipulate viewers with virtuosity and craftsmanship.

▽ Jan Steen, *Topsy Turvy World*, 1663. Oil on canvas, 41¼ × 57 in (105 × 145 cm). Kunsthistorisches Museum, Vienna. On a panel in the painting at the lower right is written: *In weelde Siet Toe* ("Beware of riches").

Near and Far

An ironic wink even animates many paintings of typically Dutch church interior scenes. In a pleasingly simple sacred space, it can happen that a dog piddles unchecked on a pillar without the painter being brought before the Inquisition.

The supply of affordable art that was made to stock, as well as on commission, comprised still lifes and landscapes as well as interiors. Buyers could choose between coastal, river, meadow, winter and lunar landscapes. Dutch Italianists even offered mountain landscapes under the Italian sun. Many views could be localized, but they were still ideal-

◁ Emmanuel de Witte, *Interior of the Oude Kerk*, Delft, 1650–1652. Oil on wood, 19 × 13½ in (48.3 × 34.6 cm). The Metropolitan Museum of Art, New York
▽ Jacob van Ruisdael, *View of Haarlem with Bleaching Fields*, ca. 1670–1675. Oil

on canvas, 21¾ × 24¼ in (55.5 × 62 cm). Mauritshuis, The Hague

△ Willem Claeszoon Heda, *Dessert*, 1637. Oil on wood, 17¼ × 21½ in (44 × 55 cm). Musée du Louvre, Paris

ized landscapes, and topographical precision was not their goal. To a greater or lesser degree, all of them clearly served to instruct. Thus, sun bleaching was also a familiar metaphor for the purification of the soul in God. Landscapes with rainbows were reminiscent of the new covenant between God and man. Uprooted trees conjure up the impermanence of all earthly things. As "natural" as many of these landscapes may appear, none of them are entirely neutral.

The same is true of still lifes. No sooner does a glass or cup lie overturned than one has to exercise caution. Cracked nuts, fruit that has been broken open, perhaps an insect somewhere on a tablecloth that has been cleared away, a half-empty carafe. . .every contemporary observer seeing such things thinks, "memento mori." Even if all that glitters is gold, earthly joys are still finite.

▷ Nicolas Poussin, *Self-portrait*, 1650. Canvas, 35 × 29 in (89 × 74 cm). Musée du Louvre, Paris

▽ Nicolas Poussin, *Et in Arcadia ego II* (*The Arcadian Shepherds*), ca. 1638. Canvas, 33½ × 47½ in (85 × 121 cm). Musée du Louvre, Paris. The memento mori is even more clearly recognizable in his first version on this theme (ca. 1627), a painting in portrait format with an oblique view of events. One of the shepherds observes a skull lying on the sarcophagus.

Bright Arcadia

Poussin's shepherds and young woman, all classically robed, stand before a sarcophagus in an idyllic landscape. Two of them are trying to decipher the inscription. Another looks worriedly at the woman, who places a reassuring hand on his shoulder because she seems to understand. Arcadia refers to a pastoral landscape that was idealized in classical literature as a mythological place of carefree living in a Golden Age. *Et in Arcadia ego* appears in Virgil's fifth eclogue and acknowledges the omnipresence of death.

Like Poussin, Lorrain worked in Rome and studied classical antiquity there. Both were active at the time when baroque style made the tran-

sition to the austerity of French Classicism.

While the settings in Poussin's landscapes remained dramatically and heroically extravagant, Lorrain's scenes became places of lyrically nurtured yearning. Behind superficially classical and Christian themes, he lent them a special, bright ambience that deeply influenced eighteenth and nineteenth century landscape painting. His harbor and coastal landscapes with imaginary paragons of classically oriented architecture received early recognition. Both artists were also famous illustrators. Lorrain was especially known for his studies that stemmed from his expeditions to Italy.

△ Claude Lorrain, *Odysseus Returns Chrysseis to her Father*, ca. 1644. Canvas, 4 × 5 ft (119 × 150 cm). Musée du Louvre, Paris: the Homeric motif merely plays a minor role in the fanciful harbor with noble villas on the River Mole.

◁ Claude Lorrain, *John the Baptist in a Landscape*, 1670. Pen and brown ink on paper, 8½ × 8 in (22 × 20.1 cm). Yale University Art Gallery, New Haven

Fluid Transitions: The Rococo

There are also shades of yearning for Arcadia in the paintings of Jean-Antoine Watteau. The designation "rococo" comes from the decorative, shell-like motifs (*rocaille*) found in architecture. In keeping with the derivation of the term, Watteau's Arcadia looks more cheerful and natural than Poussin's version. The ideal of the worry-free Arcadian life, coupled with the gallant escapades of shepherds and the world of actors, is present in Watteau. The colors become brighter, and rather than being weighed down by baroque pathos, rococo painting dances with graceful buoyancy, for the most part full of musicality. This brightening is manifest in the preference for pastels, which the Venetian portraitist Rosalba Carriera successfully bestowed on her birthplace. When she visited Watteau, she also made pastels fashionable in Paris.

Chardin, who was known for his delicately colored still lifes that focused on a few simple objects, was an absolute master of the art of pastels. He portrayed himself as an old, unadorned, tired man, who nevertheless pointedly holds a red chalk pastel in his hand, making art until his last breath!

In a similarly uncompromising manner, the German sculptor Franz Xaver Messerschmidt looked at his own physiognomy under extreme conditions to create mask-like, grimacing character heads based on his observations. His portrait busts of Maria Theresia brought him to prominence. With shocking radicality, he ignored classical ideals of beauty, stated his rejection of sanctioned "fraudulent art," and decided in favor of grueling artistic self-discovery and autonomy.

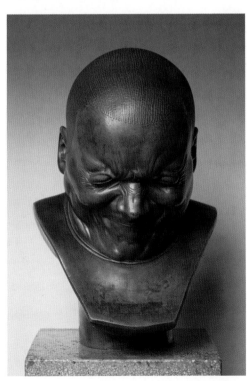 

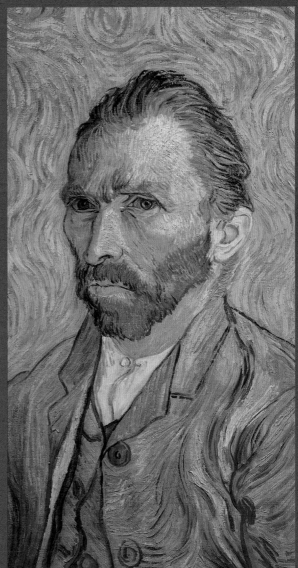

Historicism
& Revolution

Chronology

1755 The Lisbon earthquake shocks Enlightenment Europe.
1776 The American Declaration of Independence
1789–1795 The French Revolution; political birth of the modern
1799/1804–1814 Age of Napoleon
from 1810 Latin American states gain independence.

1814/15–1848 The Congress of Vienna signals the start of the reactionary Metternich era.
1830 July Revolution in France
1837–1901 The Victorian era in Great Britain
1848/49 Democratic revolutions take place throughout Europe.
1848–1916 The reign of Emperor Franz-Josef I in Austria-Hungary

1853–1856 The Crimean War
1857 The British occupy India.
1861/70 Italian unification
1861–1865 The Civil War rages in the United States.
1871 The German Empire is founded.
1884/85 The Congo Conference in Berlin; the apex of colonialism
1900 The Boxer Rebellion in China

Joseph Wright of Derby, *An Experiment on a Bird in the Air Pump*, 1768

Jacques-Louis David, *Napoleon at the Saint-Bernhard Pass*, 1801/02

Antonio Canova, *Venus*, 1804–1812

Jean-François-Thérèse Chalgrin, *Arc de Triomphe de l'Étoile*, Paris, 1806–1836

1755   1780   1800   1820

Historicism & Revolution (1755–1900)

New Perceptions

Until the mid-eighteenth century, Western art can essentially be understood as a succession of styles, albeit with some overlapping. In this period, however, the visual arts began to grow more varied, and more and more tendencies—often in opposition to one another—developed concurrently.

External factors aiding this process were the radical societal changes brought about by the Industrial Revolution and the French Revolution of 1789. Suddenly, courtly and ecclesiastical patronage faced strong competition from the state and its citizenry.

One factor influencing art in the nineteenth century was a growing appreciation of the value of Roman antiquity. This change was largely triggered by the writings of Johann J. Winckelmann (from 1755), and by the first semi-official excavations at Pompeii (from 1760). Another factor was the invention of photography. At first threatening to displace portrait painting, photography's greater visual objectivity nevertheless afforded artists new perceptions of their environment. From the beginning, the concern of art was conjuration and glorification—of gods, rulers, ideals—whereby artists were confined by composition and content. In the nineteenth century, artists were suddenly faced with a new choice: they could paint idealized pictures based on their own convictions, or they could make themselves advocates of the visible, topographic and social environment by painting pictures of real, everyday life. And they could decide if an illusory imitation of the natural world was among their priorities. At least theoretically...

Cultural History

1769 James Watt invents the steam engine, signifying the birth of the machine age.
1784 Edmund Cartwright invents the power loom.
1825 The first railroad is built in England, and the age of rail travel begins.
from 1830 Industrialization is widespread in Europe and the USA, resulting in rapid urbanization and social upheaval.
1848 Karl Marx and Friedrich Engels publish *The Communist Manifesto*.
1851 The Great Exhibition in London
from 1860 Workers throughout Europe form unions and socialist organizations.

from 1861 Development of the telephone
1869 Opening of the Suez Canal
1880 Thomas Alva Edison receives a patent for the electric light bulb.
1886 Carl Benz develops his motorcar, ushering in the age of automobiles.
1891 Otto Lilienthal makes the first flights with his glider.

Eugène Delacroix, *Liberty Leading the People*, 1830

Édouard Manet, *Boating*, 1874

Edgar Degas, *Little Dancer of Fourteen Years*, ca. 1880

Vincent van Gogh, *The Café Terrace on the Place du Forum, Arles*, September 1888

1830   1860   1880   1900

At a Glance

Neoclassicism

In reaction to the baroque and rococo, neoclassicism harkened back to the clean, straight-lined forms of classical antiquity. Classicizing and historicizing styles of this orientation typified the art of the nineteenth century, until they were stifled by rigid academic norms.

Claude-Nicolas Ledoux, Royal Saltworks at Chaux/Arc-et-Senans

Death of a Hero

Toward the end of the eighteenth century, the mytho-religious motif of the hero's death, like Hector before Troy or Christ on the cross, met earthly competition from a secular, contemporary figure: Marat, the modern hero of the Revolution, shown dying in a mundane setting. Having hoped to ease the symptoms of his skin disease with a bath, he is depicted in the tub, almost prosaically stabbed, holding a letter from his murderer.

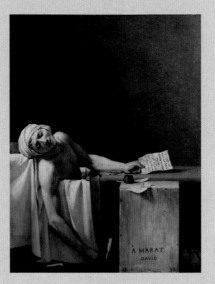

Jacques-Louis David, *The Death of Marat*, 1793. Oil on canvas, 5 ft 4 in x 4 ft 2 in (168 x 128 cm). Royal Museums of Fine Arts of Belgium, Brussels

Revolutions and "-isms"

The nineteenth century was marked by revolutions. Beginning at the time of the French Revolution, a succession of avant-garde "-isms" that reflected forward-looking social aims while remaining bound by traditional, classical norms, followed each other or existed side by side. By exploiting this tension, the artist could now reveal his political views through his work.

Enlightenment

Paving the way for the revolutionary developments that would overcome absolutism was the Enlightenment of the late eighteenth century. Through the use of reason, humankind was to free itself from its "self-incurred immaturity" (Kant). It was the "dawn of reason" (Voltaire) that would determine the image of Enlightenment in the arts, be it personified in the form of a luminary or represented concretely by a rising sun, illuminating the harmony between man and nature that Enlightenment thinkers hoped to achieve.

Daniel Chodowiecki, *Enlightenment*, 1791, etching

Secularization

In the territories conquered by Napoleon's armies, the church's possessions were seized and broken up (1803 in Germany). As the state assumed control of the former church lands, valuable works of art disappeared. Many were rescued by artistically minded citizens, often forming the basis of large private collections, and later coming to museums.

Historicism & Revolution (1755–1900)

The Dream of Reason

As Goya wrote in a comment about his *Capricho 43*, art arises from the conflict between reason and fantasy. When reason sleeps (*sueño* = sleep, dream), the monsters of fantasy, the mother of art, awake. Contrary to his expectations, it was not the longed-for reason of the Enlightenment that accompanied Napoleon's troops on their invasion of absolutist Spain, but rather terror and counterterror. This

sobering realization made Goya an accusatory chronicler of his country's suffering. His etchings mark the genesis of a critical graphic ethos that would peak in the mid-nineteenth century with Daumier's lithographs and continue through Otto Dix's war-themed etchings into the present.

△ Honoré Daumier, *Rue Transnonain*, 1834. Lithograph, 11¼ x 17⅜ in (28.6 x 44.2 cm). Yale University Art Gallery, New Haven

◁ Francisco de Goya, *Desastres de la Guerra*, 15, "*And it cannot be helped*," 1810–1820. Etching, 5¾ x 6½ in (14.5 x 16.5 cm). The Metropolitan Museum of Art, New York

▽ Francisco de Goya, *Capricho 43, The Sleep of Reason Produces Monsters*, 1797/78. Etching and aquatint, 8⅜ in x 5⅞ in (21.5 x 15 cm). The Metropolitan Museum of Art, New York

Romanticism

Romanticism arose as a reaction against neoclassicism. In terms of style, this movement did not develop its own visual language, for example in ornamentation or architecture. Rather, its primary mode of expression in the visual arts was painting. It is especially in German landscape painting that the "romantic ideal" finds substance and form. Artists depicted man and nature in relationships that exemplify feelings and moods. Christian symbolism was revived, while fairy tales and legends were collected and treasured.

Caspar David Friedrich, *Two Men Contemplating the Moon*, ca. 1830. Oil on canvas, 13¾ x 17⅜ in (34.9 x 43.8 cm). The Metropolitan Museum of Art, New York

Bohème

Those artists who did not fulfill the expectations of the general public were ridiculed as *bohème* (French for "Bohemian," denoting in this case "Gypsy"). The "long-haired and scruffy" artists welcomed the ostracism, and fed the cliché of Bohemianism as a byword for creativity. The Bohemians represented a liberated art—*l'art pour l'art* ("art for art's sake")—that could not be compromised, and which alone was capable of fulfilling its own expectations.

Key Terms

Iron Architecture

With the beginning of the Industrial Revolution toward the end of the eighteenth century, an ideal building material—mass-produced cast-iron, and from 1850, sections of rolled steel—became available, minimizing the need for columns, buttresses, and other architectural support structures. Engineers first combined it with glass to make greenhouses, then for exhibition buildings (such as the Crystal Palace in London), market halls and train stations. When combined with traditional stone buildings, this new building technique provided transparent roofing for courtyards and arcades. Even the naves of churches were vaulted with supporting iron constructions. The great exhibition hall of steel and glass was not

the only structure built for Paris' *Exposition Universelle* of 1889—the "300-Meter Tower" was assembled from 12,000 prefabricated iron segments, resting on four concrete and stone foundations, and covering an area of 125 square meters. Forward-looking architects had conceived the idea for what would become the world's tallest building as early as the first half of the nineteenth century. But it was due to the engineer Gustave Eiffel's experience building bridges and pillar-and-breast work that it was possible to complete the project in sixteen months, a feat documented step by step in photographs. Paris, the "capital of the nineteenth century," had a new landmark.

Gustave Eiffel, Eiffel Tower, 1887–1889, stages of progress in June and August 1888 [Photos H. Blanchard]

Realism

Depicting reality on canvas has been a central goal of art for centuries. In realism, "reality" also refers to an inner, emotional truth, for example the difficulty of the stonebreakers' work. The painterly modeling of visual appearance must do justice to the compositional qualities of the particular moment depicted.

Gustave Courbet, *The Stonebreakers*, 1849 (destroyed 1945)

Naturalism

Like realism, the objective of naturalism was to imitate reality as closely as possible. But in this case, the realm of raw, "unvarnished" outer appearances moved into focus, as did mastery of the required artistic techniques. Corot's discovery of the atmospheric feel for nature afforded by painting *en plein air* was this movement's achievement.

Jean-Baptiste-Camille Corot, *A Woman Reading*, 1869/70. Oil on canvas, 21⅓ x 14¾ in (54.3 x 37.5 cm). The Metropolitan Museum of Art, New York

Historicism & Revolution (1755–1900)

Salon Painting

Named for the exhibition space in the Louvre called the "Salon," paintings executed in this style followed the precepts of the art academies and conformed to public tastes. Hidden behind subjects with irreproachable classical pedigrees, the sensual fantasies of all levels of society were exhibited and indulged (see pp. 336/37).

Alexandre Cabanel, *The Birth of Venus*, Salon of 1863. Oil on canvas, 4 ft 3 in x 7 ft 5 in (130 x 225 cm). Musée d'Orsay, Paris

Color Theories

Using Newton's physical investigations of color as their basis, Johann Wolfgang von Goethe and his contemporary, the painter Runge, developed theories of color and their effects. The three primary colors yellow, red and blue (which cannot be produced by mixing other colors) can be combined to form the secondary colors orange, violet, and green as well as all other "intermediate colors." Arranged in a circle or on a sphere, the relationships and tensions between the colors become apparent, and can be utilized in painting. Impressionists and especially pointillists expertly manipulated these tensions and their effects on—and in—the eye of the beholder.

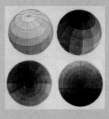

Philipp Otto Runge, *Perspectives and Sections of the Color Sphere*, 1810. Copperplate engraving/water-color, 8¾ x 7½ in (22.5 x 18.9 cm). Kunsthalle, Hamburg

Impressionism

This movement, which developed in France during the second half of the nineteenth century, introduced a new way of painting, utilizing sensory "impressions"—that is, capturing moments of visual perception on canvas. In contrast to conventional academic practice, these artists worked primarily *en plein air*, painting in the many moods of natural light. With their new aesthetic of light and color, the impressionists became revolutionaries of the avant-garde, paving the way for modern painting.

Claude Monet, *Impression, Sunrise*, 1873

Idealism

The opposite of realism, idealism was concerned with neither inner nor outer reality. Rather, its aim was to depict glorified, often ideologically motivated ideal conditions that did not exist in reality. In representative terms, idealism used the stylistic devices of naturalism.

Fathers of the Modern

Modern art of the twentieth century is rooted in the late nineteenth century. Four artists in particular can be considered the "fathers" of modern art. Seurat attempted to construct his paintings according to scientific principles, allowing the colors on his canvases to acquire a certain self-determinism (later to be invoked by abstract and Constructivist painting). The formal simplifications of Gauguin, who was the first to utilize "primitive" art forms, made him the discoverer of this modern formal potential. Van Gogh's impassioned explosions and spirals of color, with which he expressed his inner, psychic condition, served as a point of departure for fauvism

Paul Cézanne, *Foliage*, ca. 1900. Watercolor/pencil/paper, 19¼ ×22⅓ in (48.8×56.8 cm). The Metropolitan Museum of Art, New York

and expressionism. Compared to the work of the Impressionists, Cézanne's textural color structures are solid and crystalline. They provided inspiration for the cubists.

Key Terms

The Enlightenment in England

In the 1720s, landscape architects began to transform the "unnatural," architectonically constructed and trimmed gardens of the baroque into idealized natural landscapes. In 1771, Joseph Priestley discovered oxygen. In the meantime, enlightened artists began to relax the rigid themes and poses of their predecessors. It is no coincidence that a painting such as *An Experiment on a Bird in the Air Pump* (1768), which depicts the creation of a vacuum, makes use of familiar Christian visual codes. These include the experimenter, whose hair recalls portraitistic depictions of God; the cockatoo, reminiscent of the dove (symbol of the Holy Spirit); and the dramatic

lighting derived from scenes of religious adoration. At any moment, the natural scientist could, like God, bring the apparently dead bird back to life by opening the jar, thus allowing air to rush in. The provocative nature of this composition is hidden within these similarities, which were immediately recognizable to the artist's contemporaries. William Hogarth, on the other hand, made his point less subtly, be it condemnation of growing alcohol abuse among the lower classes or the immorality of marriage solely for financial gain. Hogarth's genre paintings usually contain biting commentary, hardly ever at peace with their subjects.

△ Joseph Wright of Derby, *An Experiment on a Bird in the Air Pump*, 1768. Oil on canvas, 6 ft x 8 ft (183 x 244 cm). National Gallery, London

△ William Hogarth, *Marriage à-la-mode, Part 1 (of 6): The Marriage Settlement*, ca. 1743. Oil on canvas, 27¼ x 32 in (69 x 81 cm). National Gallery, London

▷ Thomas Gainsborough, *Conversation in the Park*, 1746. Oil on canvas, 28¾ x 26¾ in (73 x 68 cm). Musée du Louvre, Paris. The England so sharply criticized by Hogarth appears in the works of artists like Gainsborough as a romantic realm peopled by well-dressed nobles—it was nobles, after all, who paid the commissions.

◁ William Hogarth, *Gin Lane*, 1751. Etching, 14 x 12 in (35.7 x 30.2 cm). Guildhall Library & Art Gallery, London

Giovanni Battista Piranesi (1720–1778)

Even as a ruin, it is powerful: the Colosseum, where the Roman emperors decided between life and death. The signs of Christian conversion (the Stations of the Cross along the edge and a crucifix in the middle of the arena) seem lost in the expanse. Before the viewer realizes that the perspective "folds out," thus distorting the proportions, or even that there is no location in Rome from which this view was (or is) possible, he or she has intuitively grasped the dimensions of the building. Piranesi's 135 large-format views of Rome (*Vedute di Roma*), available as individual works, were conceived with tourists in mind. With their dramatic interplays of light and dark, as well as their vigorous sense of line, these works depict antiquities not as relics of the past, but as great works that ennoble the present. The four-volume *Roman Antiquities* (*Antichità Romane*), on the other hand, presents an exhaustive visual inventory of archaeological finds, including floor plans, vertical sections, details and groups of fragments. In this work, Piranesi makes the invisible visible, not least of all in order to—in contrast to Winckelmann—elevate Roman art over that of the Greeks. With his suggestive, meticulous and fantastic images, Piranesi continues to influence perceptions of ancient Rome in the arts and in literature.

◁ Giovanni Battista Piranesi, **The Paving of the Via Appia Antica**, from *Antichità Romane*, vol. 3 fig. 7, 1756. Etching, 12²/₃ x 9 in (31.5 x 23.2 cm)

◁◁ Giovanni Battista Piranesi, **The Great Wheel, Carceri IX**, from *Imaginary Prisons (Carceri d'invenzione)*, 1st state, ca. 1749. Etching, 21²/₃ x 16 in (55 x 40.5 cm)

▽ Giovanni Battista Piranesi, **View of the Colosseum**, from *Views of Rome (Vedute di Roma)*, ca. 1745. Etching, 19¹/₃ x 28¹/₈ in (49.1 x 71.5 cm)

All three: Staatliche Museen, Museum of Prints and Drawings, Berlin

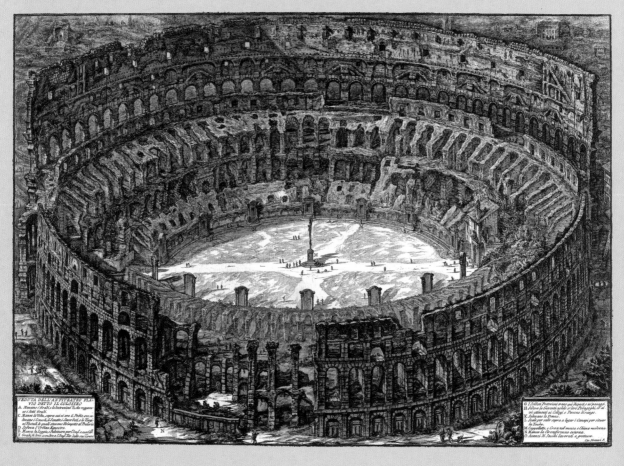

Imitation Recommended?

Johann Joachim Winckelmann (1717–1768), Prefect of Antiquities at the Vatican, inspired German classicism through his idealization of Greek art. In addition, his method of comparative visual analysis formed the basis for the academic disciplines of archaeology and art history. But even as he extolled the pure statues of white marble as the ultimate works of art, he was unaware of several facts. The "Greek" statues he saw were actually Roman copies, and the temples he praised were also not in their original condition. Not only did the "ancients" prefer their temples brightly, even garishly painted, but they also painted hair, eyes and clothes onto their statues. "The only way for us to become great, yes, inimitable, if it is possible, is the imitation of the ancients..." (Winckelmann, 1755). As it turns out, Winckelmann was suggesting the imitation of imitation...

Johann Joachim Winckelmann, engraving after Angelika Kauffmann, 1764

Veduta dell'antica Via Appia, che passa sotto le mura già descritte nelle passate tavole dell'Ustrino, oggi ricoperta nelle rovine del medesimo. A. Lato del terreno ben spianato e battuto con rulli, prima di stendere la grossa rempitura alta palmo uno a sinaloleza di lastrico con rigetti di colta percolana, e sashe di tolli; sino di lastricato a spesso i che B. basfalti nel riccesso e punta il dominato C. Allorché però posa a guisa di lastrico nel lastricato la Via già detta, fra quali sono so palmi cui-ove uno D. più continente e superiori degli altri di tal forma, quali doveva servire forse a quelli che montavano, e fin intorno da cavallo e di riposo a Piantavati. Chiesto e cli altri inferiori sone piantati sopra un grosso muro di remparo, di simili lastre di teduno pesanti, delle montagne d'Ispi.

Dream of the Classicists: Rome

From the 1750s on, Piranesi and Winckelmann's enthusiasm for antiquity contributed to Rome's becoming the center of the European art scene. Any self-respecting artist, collector, man of letters, connoisseur —or counterfeiter—had to go to Rome, where he could profit from the art of the Greeks and Romans. Close by Winckelmann's side was Anton Raphael Mengs, who would take over artistic direction in Rome. He dismissed the illusionist ceiling paintings of the baroque, whose often less than flattering low angle views compromised the elegance of Greek-inspired idealized bodies. Regardless of its future position, Mengs composed all his images from a perspective parallel to the viewer. The figures in his mythologically inspired works emanate a peaceful composure that later generations would consider stilted. Mengs, who influenced Angelika Kauffmann, Jacques-Louis David, Francisco de Goya, Gavin Hamilton and many others, remained famous thanks largely to the kindness of those who commissioned portraits from him.

▷ Anton Raphael Mengs, *The Judgment of Paris*, 1757–1759. Oil on canvas, 7 ft 5 in x 9 ft 8 in (226 x 295.5 cm). The Hermitage, St. Petersburg

◁ Angelika Kauffmann, *Self-Portrait*, ca. 1787. Oil on canvas, 50⅓ x 36¾ in (128 x 93.5 cm). Galleria degli Uffizi, Florence. With this portrait, Kauffmann herself determined the image viewers would form of her: that of the melancholy artist.

◁ Johann Heinrich Wilhelm Tischbein, *Goethe in the Roman Campagna*, 1787. Oil on canvas, 5 ft 5 in x 6 ft 9 in (164 x 206 cm). Stadel Museum, Frankfurt/Main. The epitome of neoclassicist portraiture: Goethe, in a flowing, classicizing garment, reclines on the blocks of a toppled obelisk. The fragments of Greco-Roman relief and ornament behind him direct the meditative eye of the viewer to ruins in the distance. The accuracy of anatomy (Goethe's left leg!), archaeology, and geography are of secondary importance.

▷ Gavin Hamilton, *The Rape of Helen*, 1784. Oil on canvas, 10 ft x 12 ft (306 x 367 cm). Galleria Borghese, Rome

△ Jacques-Germain Soufflot, **Panthéon** (formerly Ste.-Geneviève), Paris, 1757–1790

▽ Karl Friedrich Schinkel, **Altes Museum**, Berlin, 1823–1830

△ Jean-François-Thérèse Chalgrin, **Arc de Triomphe de l'Étoile**, Paris, 1806–1836

Neoclassical Architecture

The agitated architectural forms of the baroque and rococo were spent. As in the Renaissance, the reaction was a revival of the austerity of classical architecture. Buildings inspired by ancient Rome's example evince monumental tranquility, clarity of organization, and harmony of proportion. Decor is used sparingly, and the classically ordered colonnades actually bear the weight of the entablature, as opposed to simply providing ornamentation. The prototypes were sometimes imitated faithfully, as in the Arc de Triomphe in Paris, and sometimes less so, such as Schinkel's Altes Museum in Berlin. This somewhat freer interpretation of classical models blends a traditional four-winged structure with a rotunda in the style of Rome's Pantheon with such non-traditional elements as its colossal columned gallery and broad exterior staircase.

Ancient Roman architecture offers abundant designs. Because of changing political conditions in ancient Rome, its buildings served as symbols of majesty for modern monarchies, republics and empires alike. Even a single structure could be used by different governments to different ends: in Paris, Ste-Geneviève was repeatedly transformed into the Pantheon—burial place for the earthly remains of "great men"—and back.

Revolutionary Architecture

They represent a special phenomenon at the edges of neoclassical architecture, those designs and plans from the time of (although not necessarily in honor of) the French Revolution, which remain utopian ideals on paper. Among the main proponents of "revolutionary architecture" were Étienne-Louis Boullée, Claude-Nicolas Ledoux and Jean-Jacques Lequeu. Enthralled by the ideas of the Enlightenment, they sought to formulate its ideal architectonic representation. The defining characteristics included the simplest geometric forms on a monumental scale, clear structural boundaries, a renunciation of animated modeling on the structural shell, and an absence of décor. Their goal was to achieve a "speaking architecture" whose symbolic forms would indicate the appropriate functions.

Étienne-Louis Boullée, *Temple of Reason*, ca. 1793. Wash, 19 x 36 in (48 x 91 cm). Galleria degli Uffizi, Florence

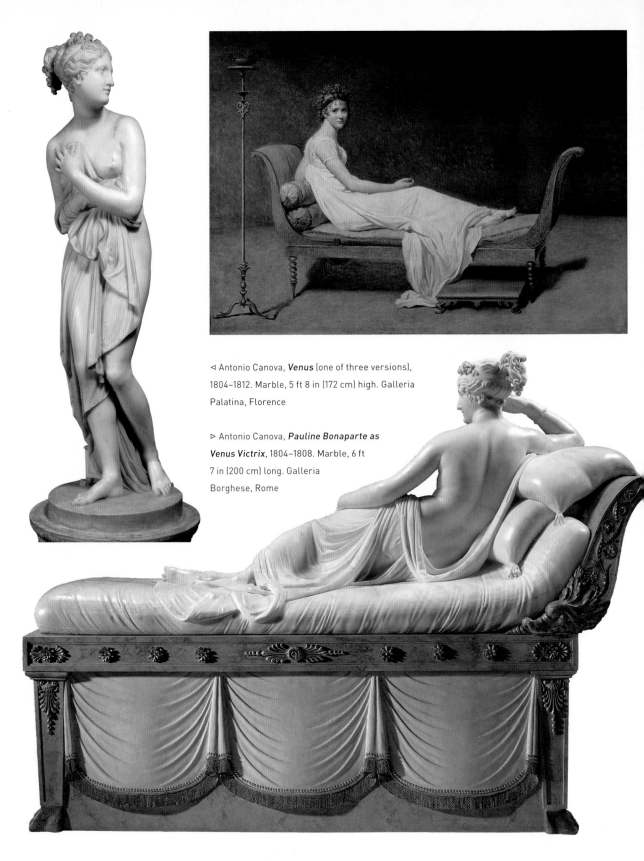

◁ Antonio Canova, **Venus** (one of three versions), 1804–1812. Marble, 5 ft 8 in (172 cm) high. Galleria Palatina, Florence

▷ Antonio Canova, **Pauline Bonaparte as Venus Victrix**, 1804–1808. Marble, 6 ft 7 in (200 cm) long. Galleria Borghese, Rome

◁ Jacques-Louis David, *Madame Récamier*, 1800. Oil on canvas, 5 ft 9 in x 8 ft (174 x 244 cm). Musée du Louvre, Paris

▷ Jacques-Louis David, *Napoleon at the Saint-Bernhard Pass* (one of five versions), 1801/02. Oil on canvas, 8 ft 1 in x 7 ft 7 in (246 x 231 cm). Kunsthistorisches Museum, Vienna

Superficially Ancient Roman

Jacques-Louis David painted in the employ of Louis XVI, for leaders of the Revolution, and for Napoleon. While his employers' goals differed, all exploited his talent and ancient Roman ideology for propaganda, culminating in Napoleon's cult of personality. David fulfilled all expectations; by painting the heroicizing *Napoleon at the Saint-Bernhard Pass* almost simultaneously with his portrait of Madame Récamier, in whose famous salon opponents of the First Consul met, perhaps he even exceeded expectations.

The twenty-three-year-old Madame Récamier exudes an air of antiquity, but it is not her own likeness that makes this impression. Rather, the portrait represents with almost documentary precision the prevailing fashion in terms of clothing and hairstyle.

In contrast, the posture of Napoleon's sister Pauline, depicted as a semi-nude Venus by Canova, evokes classical mythology.

Goya and the Horrors of Reality

Francisco José de Goya y Lucientes was named court painter to the Spanish Crown in 1798. His portraits of courtiers reveal a painter fascinated by sumptuous costume, but also one who is an alert observer with a psychologically penetrating gaze. Considering his portraits of the royal family, however, the openness with which Goya exposes Charles IV and his relatives is astonishing. Greed, lust for power, inanity and darkness are apparent in these countenances, and the viewer might risk mistaking these portraits for caricatures. In official commissions, however, any exaggeration would have been unthinkable. The faces had to be authentic, because the artist (or the fool) was allowed to show a queen as she was, even if she looked like a drab from the local market. This truthfulness makes Goya, who sympathized with the ideals of the French Revolution, a modern painter. With this honesty, he seared the gruesome savagery of the French occupiers and the Spanish insurgents onto paper in his *Horrors of War*. And in spite of its total sympathy with the victims, the painting of the execution of insurgents that occurred on May 3, 1808, does not attempt to ignore the fact that the executioners, mere instruments in this case, have no choice but to carry out the sentence. Toward the end of his life, Goya covered the walls of his house with his *"Pinturas negras,"* enigmatic, dark pictures that express the artist's isolation and fear.

△ Francisco de Goya, **The Third of May 1808**, 1814. Oil on canvas, 8 ft 9½ in x 11 ft 4½ in (268 x 347 cm). Museo del Prado, Madrid

◁ Francisco de Goya, **Charles IV of Spain and His Family**, 1800/01. Oil on canvas, 9 ft 6²⁄₃ in x 11 ft (280 x 336 cm). Museo del Prado, Madrid

▷ Francisco de Goya, **The Countess del Carpio, Marquesa de La Solana**, 1794/95. Oil on canvas, 5 ft 11 in x 4 ft (181 x 122 cm). Musée du Louvre, Paris

▷▷ Francisco de Goya, **The Dog**, 1820–1823. Oil mural transferred to canvas, 4 ft 4 in x 2 ft 7 in (131.5 x 79 cm). Museo del Prado, Madrid

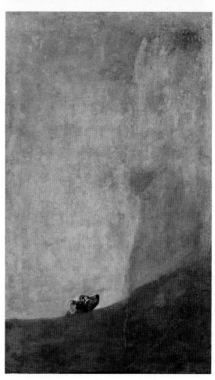

△ Théodore Géricault, *The Raft of the Medusa*, 1819. Oil on canvas, 16 ft x 23 ft 6 in (491 x 716 cm). Musée du Louvre, Paris

◁ Eugène Delacroix, *Liberty Leading the People (July 28, 1830)*, 1830. Oil on canvas, 8 ft 6 in x 10 ft 8 in (260 x 325 cm). Musée du Louvre, Paris

◁ Eugène Delacroix, *The Barque of Dante* (Dante and Virgil in Hell; Dante Alighieri, The Divine Comedy, Inferno, Canto VIII), 1822. Oil on canvas, 6 ft 2 in x 7 ft 11 in (189 x 242 cm). Musée du Louvre, Paris

Hell on Earth

In 1816, the *Medusa* capsized off the coast of West Africa. The captain and crew in their lifeboats left 149 people on a hastily built raft to their fate; only ten survived. When this became public knowledge, the French government faced a crisis. The storm had hardly passed when Géricault confronted the nation with the scandal in an appropriately large format and with dramatic exaggeration. The genre of history painting customarily depicted only the heroic events of antiquity, not the bestial happenings of the present. It took time for the public to get used to the idea of normal people in extreme situations engaging in cannibalism. Delacroix, who visited Géricault as he worked on this canvas, replied with *The Barque of Dante*. In this case, the damned are represented in hell, where they selfishly and desperately grasp for the raft they think will save them. The painting's audacious composition and red-green contrast are notable markers of Delacroix's renunciation of neoclassicism; even the impressionists marveled at his use of color. His revolutionary painting *Liberty Leading the People* is an allegory of the July Revolution of 1830 (which collapsed long before the painting was first displayed). The historic event is presented as the fruit of a victorious alliance between the intellectual Jacobins and the Parisian bourgeoisie, the bearers of the revolution. Like a contemporary Joan of Arc, Liberty personified storms over the casualties of the fights at the barricades. Surprisingly, the artist makes a stand: the revolutionary with the top hat and musket bears Delacroix's features.

The Masculine Gaze—and the Feminine

With the advent of the orientalism fad in nineteenth-century art, the painted nude became human; previously, goddesses and personifications of antiquity had served as pretexts for depicting the female nude. Now the erotically charged mental images of harems and hamams were justification for offering up dozens of voluptuous odalisques for voyeuristic pleasure—with or without eye contact, according to the patrons'

desires. The density of figures in such compositions offset any anatomical and architectural shortcomings. In the nineteenth century, such canvases disappeared into private collections as soon as the paint was dry, the satisfied patron gazing alone or in like-minded company. For honest pictures that

leave nothing to the imagination, like Courbet's *Origin of the World*, private display was the only possibility; this canvas was hidden from the public eye until its addition to the collection of the Musée d'Orsay in 1995. When Benoist unveiled her dignified portrait of a half-naked but proud African woman, in contrast, the painting caused a stir at the Paris Salon, and critics used the occasion to write polemics on the ugliness of Africans.

◁ Jean-Auguste-Dominique Ingres, *The Turkish Bath*, 1862. Oil on canvas, 42½ in (108 cm) diameter. Musée du Louvre, Paris

▷ Marie-Guilhelmine Benoist,
Portrait of a Negress, 1800. Oil on
canvas, 32 x 25½ in (81 x 65 cm).
Musée du Louvre, Paris

△ Jean-Auguste-Dominique Ingres, *The Source*, 1820–1856. Oil on canvas, 5 ft 4 in x 32⅓ in (162 x 82 cm). Musée d'Orsay, Paris. "Never has chaste nudity revealed itself so soft, so young, so permeated by light, so full of life. Here, the ideal has become illusion." (Théophile Gautier)

▷ Jean-Léon Gérôme, *Moorish Bath*,
1870. Oil on canvas, 20 x 16 in (51 x 41 cm).
Museum of Fine Arts, Boston

Romantic Painting or Painting of Romanticism?

They are pictorial riddles that make varying demands. The Swiss artist Johann Heinrich Füssli spent enough time in England to build an English pun into his successful composition: hence "nightmare" literally becomes "Nighthorse." The incubus on the woman's breast is there to carry out the deed for which he is notorious. This picture could have served as an illustration in English gothic novels, popular since 1764, and it reveals its basis through hallucination: rather than being the victim of a crime, the woman is sleeping, even if it is not pleasant sleep. The nature of the gruesome images in her mind must be determined and imagined by the spectator for him- or herself.

The visual world of the German romantics follows this precept, but more profoundly. In the paintings of Caspar David Friedrich, vistas that could be considered simple land-scapes are careful, complete con-structions designed with one purpose in mind: to depict in nature the sub-limity of God. As Friedrich wrote, "The noble man (painter) sees God in everything, the common man (also painter) sees only the form, not the spirit." Rome and antiquity remained for him insignificant. In 1803, he ex-perienced the dissolution of German monasteries and churches under Napoleon. With his idealized portraits of nature, he attempted to open up other holy spaces. his innovative, cen-tral *Rückenfiguren* ("back figures"), invited the viewer to join them as they marvelled at nature. Through his "naturalization" of God, however, he exposed himself to fierce criticism, his detractors seeing the "landscape creeping inadmissibly onto the altar."

In *The Sea of Ice*, the symbolic power of nature reaches its apex: caught amid the sheets of ice, the ship cannot right itself. Confronted with the overpowering nature of God, man must submit. Without the certainty of eternal life, he would be lost. But the idea is too powerful, the promise of consolation too obscure —Friedrich found no buyer for his painting.

△ Caspar David Friedrich, *The Wanderer above the Sea of Fog*, ca. 1818. Oil on canvas, 38¾ x 29⅜ in (98.4 x 74.8 cm). Kunsthalle, Hamburg

◁ Caspar David Friedrich, *The Sea of Ice (The Wreck of Hope)*, 1823/24. Oil on canvas, 38 x 50 in (96.7 x 126.9 cm). Kunsthalle, Hamburg

▷ Johann Heinrich Füssli, *The Nightmare* (2nd version), 1790/91. Oil on canvas, 30 x 25 in (76.5 x 63.5 cm). Freies Deutsches Hochstift, Goethe-Museum, Frankfurt/Main

△ John Constable, *Salisbury Cathedral from the Bishop's Grounds*, 1826 (1st version 1820/23). Oil on canvas, 34½ x 44 in (88 x 111.8 cm). The Metropolitan Museum of Art, New York

▷ John Constable, *Stoke-by Nayland*, 1811. Oil on canvas, 11 x 14¼ in (28.3 x 36.2 cm). The Metropolitan Museum of Art, New York

Landscape as Drama

For John Constable, it was not always easy to satisfy his patrons. The bishop of Salisbury, for example, criticized the depiction of weather in Constable's painting of Salisbury Cathedral to such an extent that Constable finally gave up and executed a sunnier version for him (there are three versions in total, one of them unfinished). Constable's completed landscapes appear natural, free from the weight of sublime import. Especially appealing are his "unfinished" works: lively, authentic oil sketches, watercolors, and drawings on paper or canvas, composed outdoors in all types of weather. For Constable, they served as tools for work, later used as models in the studio as needed for oil paintings.

William Turner went even further. In his landscapes, he gradually probed the atmosphere, the very air, until he could allow his scenes to dissolve into color and light, freeing them from form and contour. Acclaim was not the only reaction to his work: "Has any accident befallen Mr. Turner's eyes? Have they been put out by the glare of his own colours?" Or: "To refer to these works as 'paintings' would constitute an insult to the language."

△+▽ William Turner, *Valley of Aosta: Snow-storm, Avalanche, and Thunderstorm*, 1836/37. Oil on canvas, 36⅓ x 48⅜ in (92.2 x 123 cm). Art Institute of Chicago

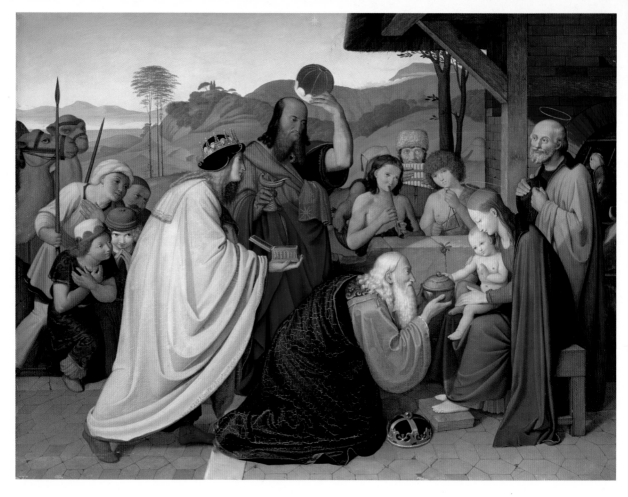

Nazarenes and Pre-Raphaelites

In 1809, mission-conscious students in the circle around Franz Pforr and Friedrich Overbeck founded the Brotherhood of St. Luke in Vienna. Rejecting academic training as too technical, they argued that pictures need content instead. They strove for a Christian regeneration in art that would be based stylistically not on ancient models, but rather on the graceful piety of medieval German painting. For this reason they abstained from cheap effects like artificial distribution of light, seeking instead to guide the viewer to salvation by limiting themselves to clear proportions, temperate colors and pensive, fully clothed figures. In Rome, like-minded artists joined their ranks. The group's name —the Nazarenes—was inspired by the hairstyle of its members. Apart from religious themes, its adherents devoted their art to patriotic depictions of German history.

Seven English artists likewise reacted to conventional academic art, forming the "PRB" (Pre-Raphaelite Brotherhood") in 1848. Desiring a return to the purity of medieval Italian art, no master was permitted apart from the artist's own intellectual ability and observation of nature. Critics accused them of assaulting beauty and good taste.

△ Friedrich Overbeck, *Adoration of the Magi*, 1813. Oil on canvas, 19½ x 26 in (49.7 x 66 cm). Kunsthalle, Hamburg

Nazarenes: Franz Pforr, Friedrich Overbeck, Ludwig Vogel, Joseph Wintergerst, Joseph Sutter, Johann Konrad Hottinger, Peter Cornelius, Ludwig Schnorr von Carolsfeld, Joseph Anton Koch, Wilhelm von Schadow, Carl Philipp Fohr (among others)

Pre-Raphaelites: Dante Gabriel Rossetti, William Holman Hunt, John Everett Millais, Thomas Woolner, James Collinson, Frederic George Stephens, William Michael Rossetti (and others)

◁ Edward Burne-Jones, *The Love Song*, 1868–1873. Oil on canvas, 45 x 61½ in (114.3 x 155.9 cm). The Metropolitan Museum of Art, New York

▽ John Everett Millais, *Ophelia*, 1851/52. Oil on canvas, 30 x 44 in (76.2 x 111.8 cm). Tate Britain, London. The blossoms floating in the river embody, like Ophelia, both beauty and mortality. Millais translates Shakespeare's *Hamlet* with buttercups, nettles and daisies into the Victorian language of flowers; the poppy stands for sleep and death.

◁ Pierre-Paul Prud'hon, **Study of a Boy**, no date. Pencil on paper, 23¾ x 17⅓ in (60.5 x 44 cm). Musée Condé, Chantilly

▷ Jacques-Louis David, **Study of a Male Nude**, 1764. Charcoal on paper, 24 x 18½ in (61 x 47 cm). Fitzwilliam Museum, Cambridge

Academy and Salon

Since the Middle Ages, a young artist's training had begun in the studio of a master, where the apprentice would learn through observation and imitation. The masters banded together in guilds (of St. Luke) whose regulations insured a high level of technical proficiency. As art slowly rose in regard from the status of handiwork to that of a science, academies began to take over the role of training young artists. In these schools, painting and sculpture were instructed not only practically, but also theoretically, and the academy's patron determined the norms taught. In the case of the *Académie royale de peinture et de sculpture*, this was the king of France, so the *Académie* became the place of instruction for state artists trained to glorify the monarchy. The practical training was limited to copying ancient sculpture. Advanced students refined their technique on live models—at first only males—beginning with drawing, then moving on to painting. The types of painting were strictly ranked. At the top was history painting, including not only historical themes but also mythology and religion. Whoever wanted to attempt this type first had to master all those ranked below it:

△ **Visitors at the Salon of 1880**, lithograph, Bibliothèque Nationale, Paris

(in descending order) portraiture, genre painting, animals, still life and landscape. After the French Revolution, the renamed *Académie des Beaux-Arts* maintained its control over "true" art (as did the other academies based on the French model), which now had other objectives. The *Académie* organized exhibitions at regular intervals. At first, only members of the *Académie* were allowed to show their work at these exhibitions, but they were later opened to outsiders who could convince a jury of the merit of their work. This most hallowed event of academic art—called the "Salon" after its exhibition space in the Louvre—soon met with criticism for its visitor-unfriendly presentation. During the nineteenth century, more and more artists began to reject academic art as irrelevant, and rivals opened private academies and salons. In the twentieth century, the Bauhaus would introduce a further development in artistic training.

△ Jean-François Millet, *Nude Study*, no date. Oil on canvas, 32 x 25½ in (81 x 65 cm). Musée d'art Thomas-Henry, Cherbourg

△ Théodore Géricault, *Study of a Man*, no date. Oil on canvas, Musée Ingres, Montauban

▷ François Joseph Heim, *Charles X Bestowing Honors on the Artists of the Salon of 1824* (detail). Oil on canvas, 5 ft 8 in x 8 ft 5 in (173 x 256 cm). Musée du Louvre, Paris

French Landscape Painting

Even as landscapes were painted in idealized form, intended to illustrate lofty emotions, and filled with clichés, artists made drawings or watercolors in the open air to use in their studios as mnemonic aids. From the beginning of the nineteenth century, they started to attach more and more worth to meteorological conditions and their effects on the character of light. Such studies had to be in color, quickly executed, and easily transported. Although this practice arose in accord with academic norms, young artists soon began to transfer these banal views of nature with brush or palette knife to the canvas, considering such works—"too unfinished even for sketches"—to be the actual finished product. The village of Barbizon in the forests of Fontainebleau gave its name to a loose group of French artists around Rousseau and Daubigny, who had been frustrated up with the academies' teachings and instructive pictures since the 1830s. Supported by a sense of nature that was blossoming in the literature of the day, they recognized the beauty of transitory effects and coincidence in the landscape's topography, thus becoming forerunners of the impressionists.

△ Théodore Rousseau, *An Avenue in the Forest of the Isle Adam*, 1849. Oil on canvas, 39¾ x 32⅓ in (101 x 82 cm). Musée d'Orsay, Paris

◁ Charles-François Daubigny, *Harvest*, 1851. Oil on canvas, 4 ft 5 in x 6 ft 5 in (135 x 196 cm). Musée d'Orsay, Paris

▷ Jean-Baptiste-Camille Corot, *Fontainebleau: Oak Trees at Bas-Bréau*, 1832. Oil on board, 15½ x 19½ in (39.7 x 49.5 cm). The Metropolitan Museum of Art, New York

▷ Jean-François Millet, *Haystacks, Autumn*, 1868–1874. Oil on canvas, 33½ x 43⅓ in (85 x 110 cm). The Metropolitan Museum of Art, New York

"Réalisme. G. Courbet"

When the jury for the *Exposition Universelle* of 1855 rejected his programmatic painting *The Artist's Studio* (unlike his *Stonebreakers*), Courbet financed his own pavilion, which he called *"Réalisme. G. Courbet."* Describing his work, he claimed to have studied the old and the modern objectively, so that he would be able to create from familiarity with tradition. "To know in order to be capable, [...]; to be in the position to represent the customs, the ideas, the face of my epoch according to my estimation."

Realism therefore stands in opposition to (academic) idealism. It is focused on the present, its concern is inner truth rather than outer exactness (naturalism). Idealism and realism reflect content-based demands as an expression of intellectual attitude. Naturalism's concerns are formal problems, a search for the artistic means needed to produce a true-to-nature representation of the material world.

Courbet did not create snapshot paintings, but rather status reports. He fetched the stonebreakers in his painting into his studio as they were. They do not show pride in their work; they are tired and oppressed. Courbet painted them as examples of the quotidian. He painted them life-size, in the format of history painting, thereby making the Parisian art critics very aware of a subject they would have found unworthy. His *The Young Ladies on the Banks of the Seine* also caused an uproar, as the public—with unusual facility—recognized and condemned the women blithely

▷ Gustave Courbet, *The Artist's Studio*, 1855. Oil on canvas, 11 ft 9 in x 19 ft 7 in (359 x 598 cm). Musée du Louvre, Paris

◁ Gustave Courbet, *The Young Ladies on the Banks of the Seine*, 1856. Oil on canvas, 68½ x 79 in (174 x 200 cm), Musee du Petit Palais, Paris

▷ Gustave Courbet, *The Stonebreakers*, 1849. Oil on canvas, 5 ft 3 in x 8 ft 6 in (159 x 259 cm). Gemäldegalerie, Dresden (destroyed 1945)

lounging on the grass as prostitutes. In *The Artist's Studio*, an imaginary meeting takes place: on the right are friends and patrons, and on the left are "exploiters and exploited" (Courbet), therefore potential artistic subjects—provided they are observed through the eyes of (naked) truth.

Adolph Menzel

The work of Adolph Menzel, who came from a liberal bourgeois background, bears a strong connection to the aristocratic, rococo Prussia of Frederick the Great. This association brought him fame and a title. But Menzel was also a realist with an unflinching eye who bound himself to the present and to the truth. His realism, according to Menzel's contemporary Theodor Fontane, demands the truth, not simply the palpable, and is the reflection of all of life's reality. A picture showing the workings of a Silesian steel mill provides a glimpse into this reality. In this scene, Menzel glorifies neither industrial progress nor the trade of producing segments of railroad. He shows people as cogs in the machine of factory labor. Everything is subservient to the optical and

△ Adolph Menzel, *Studio Wall*, 1872. Oil on canvas, 43¾ x 31⅓ in (111 x 79.5 cm). Kunsthalle, Hamburg

the content-related dominance of the rhythm-giving machine, even the workers' mealtimes. And one senses that about forty minutely observed people are working in the hot, loud, dirty machine hall. In his *Studio Wall*, Menzel unveils the attributes of academic painting—he himself had skipped the course in plaster casting. It is no coincidence

that his arrangement of death masks and other casts, symbols of transience and hollow pathos recalls a museum.

△ Adolph Menzel, *The Iron-Rolling Mill (Modern Cyclops)*, 1872–1875. Oil on canvas, 5 ft 2 in x 8 ft 4 in (158 x 254 cm). Nationalgalerie, Berlin

Art of the New World: Not So Different from the Old

With the Declaration of Independence in 1776, the new United States of America attempted to sever its ties, including cultural ones. But in the nineteenth century, most practitioners of the visual arts in America had either emigrated from the Old World or had been schooled there. Homer and Eakins also studied painting in Europe, but they soon transmitted value judgments of the evolving American society and culture through their depictions of real-life situations. In contrast to French impressionists, who transformed littoral or aquatic scenes into a painterly carpet of colors, their open-air compositions remained closer to reality. Sargent and Whistler aligned themselves much more closely with the artistic standards of Europe, where both would spend much of their lives.

Although their earlier works show the influence of Velázquez's dark coloring,

△ Thomas Eakins, *Starting Out after Rail*, 1874. Oil on canvas mounted on Masonite, 24¼ x 19⅞ inches (61.6 x 50.5 cm). Museum of Fine Arts, Boston

△ John Singer Sargent, *Madame X (Madame Pierre Gautreau)*, 1884. Oil on canvas, 6 ft 10 in x 3 ft 7 in (208.6 x 109.9 cm). The Metropolitan Museum of Art, New York

△ James Abbott McNeill Whistler, *Arrangement in Grey and Black, No. 1: Portrait of the Artist's Mother*, 1871. Oil on canvas, 4 ft 9 in x 5 ft 4 in (144 x 162 cm). Musée d'Orsay, Paris

▷ Winslow Homer, *Eagle Head, Manchester, Massachusetts (High Tide)*, 1870. Oil on canvas, 26 x 38 in (66 x 96.5 cm). The Metropolitan Museum of Art, New York

during the course of their development they found a more luminous, impressionistic palette. Both are famous for their portraits that are at once empathetic and elegant, which seize on the subject's essence.

Manet and the Obvious

Everyday situations and leisure activities, and these not even painted "correctly?" Although they were prized by his colleagues, Manet's paintings often met with disdain from the general public. His *Luncheon on the Grass* illustrates how he could transplant a traditional motif from the past into the present. The abandonment of perfect spatial illusion, exaggerated attention to detail, and narrative composition was sufficient to irritate the visual expectations of his contemporaries. Although usually capable of recognizing mythological themes, they reacted to many manifestations of the obvious with uncertainty.

Unlike the impressionists who revered him, he did not search for the incidental moment. His gaze is more matter-of-fact. It often appears as if his figures are pausing from their activities. The young woman behind the *Bar at the Folies-Bergère* is depicted in the midst of her turbulent workday, but she seems somehow withdrawn from her surroundings. To an extent, Manet achieves this effect with an evenly brightened palette, but primarily through introducing an additional level to the composition. Behind the "real" bar maid, who is depicted frontally and in the middle of the composition, a *Rückenfigur* version of this primary figure is visible in reflection (as are the bar and the entire scene of action). The woman's reflection, which should not be visible from this angle, leads an intriguing life of its own; the reflection serves a customer; the viewer, who actually stands before the "original," taking the place of the reflected customer, is invisible to the bar maid. She is therefore not simply dreaming, she is metaphorically outside of herself.

△ Édouard Manet, *A Bar at the Folies-Bergère*, 1882. Oil on canvas, 37¾ x 51¼ in (96 x 130 cm). Courtauld Gallery, London
▷ Édouard Manet, *Boating*, 1874, oil on canvas, 38⅓ x 51⅓ in (97.2 x 130.2 cm). The Metropolitan Museum of Art, New York
◁ Édouard Manet, *The Luncheon on the Grass*, 1863. Oil on canvas, 6 ft 10 in x 8 ft 8 in (208 x 264 cm). Musée d'Orsay, Paris. This work combines elements from Titian's *Pastoral Concert* and M. Raimondi's engraving after Raphael's *Judgment of Paris*, detail, 1514/18.

First Impressions

In the 1860s increasing numbers of artists, influenced by the Barbizon School, took their paints and canvases out into the French countryside. Painters including the Dutchman Jongkind and Boudin from Honfleur set up their easels on the popular beaches of Normandy. The slightest hint of a brushstroke and confluences of colors created atmospheric impressions. Boudin varied his beach scenes with distinct moods arising from the morning or evening sun. Above all, the ever-changing effects of light and color on the water became a challenge that was eagerly met. Boudin's student Monet titled an 1874 view of the harbor at Le Havre *Impression, Sunrise*. Henceforth, one critic began to mock the group of artists with whom Monet exhibited—and who, like Monet, were excluded from the Salon—as "impressionists." While the painters who were part of the Salon judged a picture's value by its motif,

△ Johan Barthold Jongkind, *Honfleur*, 1865. Oil on canvas, 20½ x 32 in (52.1 x 81.6 cm). The Metropolitan Museum of Art, New York

for the impressionists, the picture's colors and their relationship to each other were of supreme importance. The color of objects can thus lose significance and fall victim to the general atmospheric impression. The application of color in recog-

nizable brushstrokes shatters the outlines of objects, allowing them to melt into their surroundings, as if illuminated by a shimmering light. Shadows are no longer simply darkness, but rather patches of blended color.

▷ Eugène Boudin, *On the Beach, Sunset*, 1865. Oil on wood, 15 x 23 in (38.1 x 58.4 cm). The Metropolitan Museum of Art, New York

△ Claude Monet, *La Grenouillère*, 1869.
Oil on canvas, 29½ x 39⅜ in (75 x 100 cm).
The Metropolitan Museum of Art, New York

▷ Claude Monet, *Impression, Sunrise*,
1873. Oil on canvas, 19 x 24¾ in (48 x 63 cm).
Musée Marmottan, Paris

Pissarro and Cézanne

Camille Pissarro, one of the organizers of and participants in the first "Impressionists" exhibition of 1874, was a co-founder and tireless spokesman for the impressionist program. "The eye should not be fixed on a particular point but should take in everything, while simultaneously observing the reflections that the colors produce on their surroundings. Work at the same time on sky, water, branches, ground... for it is best not to lose the first impression." At first, he preferred to paint landscapes from the areas surrounding Paris. After 1895, however, an eye disease made it necessary for him to work indoors. The result was many urban landscapes, which Pissarro painted while looking from his studio window. Graded with the finest color variations, these cityscapes capture many moods. In these works, Pissarro attempted to record differences in light, atmosphere, movement and time.

In 1877, Paul Cézanne studied at Pontoise with Pissarro, who taught him to study nature without bias. *The Hanged Man's House*, with its almost sculptural brushwork, is the major work of his first year of impressionist activity, and found a buyer at the exhibition of 1874. But whereas Pissarro could not do without the intellectual stimulation of the other artists in the city, Parisian artists' gossip irritated Cézanne. He isolated himself from the impressionists

△ Camille Pissarro, *Montmartre Boulevard on a Winter Morning*, 1897. Oil on canvas, 25½ x 32 in (64.8 x 81.3 cm). The Metropolitan Museum of Art, New York

△ Paul Cézanne, *Bay of l'Estaque*, 1879–1883. Oil on canvas, 23½ x 28¾ in (59.7 x 73 cm). Philadelphia Museum of Art, Philadelphia

▷ Paul Cézanne, *The House of the Hanged Man at Auvers*, ca. 1873. Oil on canvas, 21¾ x 26 in (55 x 66 cm). Musée d'Orsay, Paris

when he returned to his hometown of Aix-en-Provence. Back in the South of France, he determined to "make out of impressionism something just as solid and long-lasting as the art in the museums."

△ Pierre-Auguste Renoir, *Dance at Le Moulin de la Galette*, 1876. Oil on canvas, 4 ft 3½ in x 5 ft 9 in (131 x 175 cm). Musée d'Orsay, Paris

▷ Edgar Degas, *The Tub*, 1886. Pastel on card, 23½ x 32¾ in (60 x 83 cm). Musée d'Orsay, Paris

Renoir and Degas

In terms of representing the effects of light on figures and objects, Renoir was perhaps the most consistent of the impressionists. Among his favorite subjects were people in the outdoors underneath canopies of leaves permeated by light. Hanging above the Sunday crowd at a popular dance venue in Montmartre, vegetation filters the sun's rays, seemingly creating a transparent net of delicately brushed color. Upon closer inspection, this web of light appears to take on a pulsing life of its own, reflecting the dancing couples. Through this illusory movement, the proximal and the distant, substance and color, shadow and light all melt together. When taking up the classical subject of the nude, the chance to depict the color and softness of normally covered skin in warm sunlight was sufficient justification.

Edgar Degas—when he was not painting scenes from the ballet or horse races—used mundane acts of personal hygiene as occasion for the representation of the nude. From these intimate situations, new and surprising compositions arise, thanks not least to his preoccupation with photography. Degas photographed himself and worked from those images, preferring to use pastels, with their vividness and powdery consistency. Contours allow themselves to be blurred, whereby the integration of figures and objects with light becomes more evident.

◁ Pierre-Auguste Renoir, *Nude in the Sun*, 1876. Oil on canvas, 32 x 25½ in (81 x 65 cm). Musée d'Orsay, Paris

▷ Edgar Degas, *The Star*, ca. 1876. Pastel on paper, 22¾ x 16½ in (58 x 42 cm). Musée d'Orsay, Paris

Seurat

Georges Seurat took impressionism a step further when he developed pointillism, or as he called it, divisionism. For the most part, he applied pure colors to the canvas. Due to an optical process perceived by the viewer, these "pixels" melt together into mixed colors, provided he stands far enough away from the canvas. This painstaking technique is best recognized when observing shadows; from close up, the viewer can see that an aquamarine tint results not from a mixture of blue and green on the palette, but from blue points positioned over and next to green points. Whereas the impressionists tried to capture transitory images of ever-changing interactions between light and atmosphere with ephemeral brushstrokes, Seurat's pictures represent the logical conclusion of a formal process in which everything that is coincidental is reworked, and all correlations are carefully balanced. Like the impressionists, he made outdoor studies of scenery, light and color, but he finished his larger canvases in the studio.

◁ Georges Seurat, *A Sunday Afternoon on the Island of La Grande Jatte*, 1884–1886. Oil on canvas, 6 ft 10 in x 10 ft 1 in (207.5 x 308 cm). Art Institute of Chicago

△ Kikugawa Eizan
(1787-1867), *Sitting
Woman*, 1800/30. Color
woodcut, 15 x 10½ in
(38.4 x 26.7 cm)

▷ Claude Monet, *La
Japonaise (Camille
Monet in Japanese
Costume)*, 1876. Oil on
canvas, 7 ft 7 in x 4 ft
8 in (231.5 x 142 cm).
Museum of Fine Arts,
Boston

Japonism

Inspired by the Japanese Pavilion at the *Exhibition Universelle* of 1867, kimonos and fans soon became a must in the elegant boudoirs of fashionable Parisiennes. As a result of the political and economic opening of Japan, traditional Japanese woodcuts (*ukiyo-e*) had already reached Paris, where they impressed printers such as Félix Bracquemond and artists including Monet, Renoir and the impressionists, who on their search for the "appearance" of nature had already succeeded in overcoming naturalistic (objective) means of representation through the dismantling and atmospheric interweaving of color, realized that it was only a matter of time before impressionism and even Seurat's pointillism would be artistically exhausted. As in the case of Gauguin, many painters were beginning to demonstrate increasing readiness to seek inspiration in non-European cultures. The Japanese woodcuts represented one potential source: artists marveled at the decorative, sometimes rhythmic ordering of pictorial elements, the linear strength, the clearly separated fields of color, and the tension of the often unshadowed surfaces. These are characteristic representative traits of the printmaker's art, and thereby served profited the nascent art of lithography and thus graphic design.

△ Ando Hiroshige (1797–1858), *The Teahouse with the View of Mt. Fuji at Zoshigaya* (from the series *36 Views of Mt. Fuji*), 1858. Color woodcut, 13 x 8¾ in (33 x 22 cm)

▷ Henri de Toulouse-Lautrec, *Divan Japonais*, 1893. Color lithograph, 31½ x 24 in (80.3 x 60.7 cm). Museum of Fine Arts, Boston. Toulouse-Lautrec was deeply involved with the development of art lithography and its application in graphic design.

Van Gogh in the South of France

By the mid-1880s, more and more artists were deciding to trade the rush of Parisian life for a more peaceful existence in the countryside, where the immediacy of nature and culture had been preserved, and where life was much less expensive than in the metropolis. Along with Brittany, southern France had always attracted poets and painters who hoped to gain inspiration from its unique atmosphere. Vincent van Gogh dreamed of founding an artists' colony in Arles with Paul Gauguin. During this period, van Gogh created landscape paintings in which his expressive, turbulently brushed representations of nature (having replaced the fleeting moment of impressionism) reflected his personal feelings.

The color combination of blue and yellow, its primal manifestation appearing as the sun in the sky, was

◁ Vincent van Gogh, *Café Terrace on the Place du Forum, Arles,* September 1888. Oil on canvas, 32 x 25¾ in (81 x 65.6 cm). Kröller-Müller Museum, Otterlo

▷ Vincent van Gogh, *Wheat Field with Cypresses,* Saint-Rémy, late June 1889. Oil on canvas, 28¾ x 36¾ in (73 x 93.5 cm). The Metropolitan Museum of Art, New York

▷ Vincent van Gogh, *Almond Blossom,* Saint-Rémy, February 1890. Oil on canvas, 29 x 36¼in (73.5 x 92 cm). Rijkmuseum Vincent van Gogh, Amsterdam

crucial for van Gogh's palette, and is everywhere to be seen in his paintings from this period. As if overcome by powerful surges of emotion, van Gogh's passionate brushwork swirls through the spectrum in massive rings and eddies.

In addition, blossoming almond branches recollect the Japanese woodcuts that had recently become fashionable in Paris. The south of France thus became not simply a place of refuge, but was also possessed of exotic appeal, and could itself provide the inspiration for van Gogh's Japanese experiments.

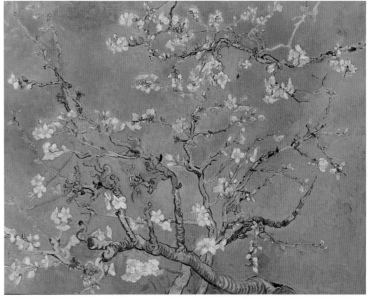

Gauguin in a Lost Paradise

When Paul Gauguin first sailed to Tahiti in 1891, he had put more than just a large geographic distance between himself and France. Since 1880, when he first exhibited with the impressionists, he had undertaken a step-by-step reworking of his opinions about light, color and form. He reacted to the increasingly scientific theories of the impressionists and their followers (especially the pointillists) with an emphatic turn to the "primitive." He achieved this by abandoning perspective, sculptural modeling and conventional coloring. Beginning in 1886, he assembled a group of followers called the "Pont-Aven School." In 1888, the shared a studio with van Gogh until their friendship came to a bloody end. On the island of Tahiti, discovered 125 years previously, hardly anything of the indigenous culture and way of life had survived French colonial domination. Many of the pictures executed by Gauguin in the South Pacific hearken back to a lost harmony between man and nature. Gauguin could only realize his dream of a primitive life with the help of an artistic device: the lining up of figures with few overlaps, the juxtaposition of frontal and profile views, the immobile faces and "talking" hands of the women all recollect Egyptian and Javanese art.

By superimposing the forms of a seemingly foreign and mysterious culture on the sober and mundane reality of the island, he was able to give expression to his exotic, primitive vision. He created for the viewer (and for himself) a simulated world full of mystery and wonder.

◁ Paul Gauguin, *Idol with a Shell*, 1892. Ironwood, mother-of-pearl, bone (teeth), 10⅝ in (27 cm) high. Musée d'Orsay, Paris. As the first European artist to engage aesthetically with "primitive" art, Gauguin appropriated an already extant visual language for his South Pacific sculptures.

△ Paul Gauguin, *Where Do We Come From? What Are We? Where Are We Going?*, 1897. Oil on canvas, 4 ft 7 in x 12 ft 3½ in (139.1 x 374.6 cm). Museum of Fine Arts, Boston

Monet: Water Lilies and Other Series

Rouen, 81 Rue du Grand Pont, at a third-story window: during the winter of 1892/93, Claude Monet painted the façade of the cathedral visible from this viewpoint, not once, but many times, and at all hours of the day. He always had multiple canvases in progress, and would work on each for just a short time every day before moving on to the next, on the geometric surfaces of the façade, the architecture of which did not interest him in the slightest, he was able to document visually the colorful play of shadows and light, the blurring atmosphere of fog and mist, the overall constantly changing appearance of the building.

In 1893, Monet acquired a house in Giverny with a garden that sloped gently down to the river. Here he laid out a flower garden and a pond with water lilies and a Japanese bridge. These became his favorite subjects to paint, as the interplay of water, sunlight and plants never ceased to create new impressions. The seemingly abstract swirls and strokes of his later paintings form a sort of contrived shorthand for gently flowing water, drifting leaves and glimmering reflections. Thanks to these devices, even sections of the lily pond depicted without a shoreline's helpful orientation preserve the spatial illusion of lateral views of the water's surface.

▷ Claude Monet, *Water Lilies (Nympheas)*, (left section of triptych), 1920. Oil on canvas, 6 ft 7 in x 13 ft 11 in (200 x 425 cm). Museum of Modern Art, New York

From left to right:
Claude Monet,
***Rouen Cathedral
(Early Morning)***,
1894. Oil on canvas,
41¾ x 29 in (106 x
74 cm). Museum of
Fine Arts, Boston

(Morning Effect),
1894. Oil on canvas,
41¾ x 28¾ in (106
x 73 cm). Musée
d'Orsay, Paris

(Sunlight), 1894.
Oil on canvas,
39 ³/₈ x 25 ⁵/₈ in
(100 x 65 cm).
The Metropolitan
Museum of Art,
New York

(At Noon), 1894. Oil
on canvas, 39 ³/₈ x
25 ⁵/₈ in (100 x 65 cm).
The Pushkin
Museum, Moscow

(Evening), 1894. Oil
on canvas, 39 ³/₈ x
25 ⁵/₈ in (100 x 65 cm).
The Pushkin
Museum, Moscow

Cézanne's Later Work

Paul Cézanne's works, most of which he painted in Aix-en-Provence, are dominated by figure compositions, landscapes and still lifes. In these paintings, he attempted not to imitate nature, but rather to construct a harmony parallel to nature.

Naturalistic modeling of the human body as taught at the academies, utilizing light and dark tones to represent brightness and shadow, represented for him a dead end. He developed his own color theory, which he described with the musical term "modulation." According to this system, colors follow one another based on the hue and luminance of similar but clearly distinct tones. Patches of color can therefore be arranged in a structure based on the modulation and repetition of tones.

With this system, Cézanne turned against the momentary nature of impressionism, whose practitioners sought to capture the most transitory effects of light and atmosphere. He also broke down classical perspective, which creates the illusion of space, by interweaving all the motifs of a composition—such as the mountain in the background or the twigs in the foreground—with equal emphasis. At the same time, the objects' boundaries are indicated such that the zones of transition can still be identified. In this way, the canvas starts to take on a practically autonomous structural significance, and abandons illusion.

△ Paul Cézanne, *Mont Sainte-Victoire Seen from Les Lauves*, 1902–1906. Oil on canvas, 25 x 32¾ in (63.5 x 83 cm). Kunsthaus Zurich, Zurich

▽ Paul Cézanne, *The Bathers*, 1906. Oil on canvas, 6 ft 10 in x 8 ft 2 in (208 x 249 cm). Philadelphia Museum of Art, Philadelphia. Throughout his life, Cézanne was preoccupied with the Arcadian motif of bathers. He was not interested in mythology or the human form; rather, it was the ordering of elements, limbs and parts, the unity of bodies with nature, as well as the reduction to and deformation through elementary forms that lend an Arcadian air to the painting's style and composition.

◁ Paul Cézanne, *Still Life with Onions*, 1895/1900. Oil on canvas, 26 x 32⅓ in (66 x 82 cm). Musée d'Orsay, Paris

Caillebotte and Liebermann

Gustave Caillebotte was a Parisian dandy and art collector, as well as a generous patron of the impressionists. He was also an unusual painter. The realism of his pictures of the working world, though frequently compared with the work of Courbet and Manet, is nowadays considered by many to be "vulgar." An unexpected perspective, popularly described as "bizarre," has become his trademark.

Caillebotte's urban subjects stroll about in steeply inclined streets and on iron bridges, with the thick steam of locomotives as their backdrop. And like the floor scrapers, they are not simply a part of their environment. Instead, they become teaching tools in a school of special perception in which the scene is viewed with not just the eye, but rather from several perspectives at once.

▷ Gustave Caillebotte, *Pont de l'Europe*, 1876. Oil on canvas, 4 ft 1 in x 5 ft 11 in (124.7 x 180.6 cm). Musée du Petit Palais, Geneva

▷▷ Max Liebermann, *Restaurant "De Oude Vink" in Leiden*, 1905. Oil on canvas, 28 x 34⅝ in (71 x 88 cm). Kunsthaus Zürich, Zurich

▽ Gustave Caillebotte, *The Floor Scrapers*, 1875. Oil on canvas, 3 ft 4 in x 4 ft 10 in (102 x 146.5 cm). Musée d'Orsay, Paris

Pissarro had stressed the importance of "the artist's own way of seeing" over painting meant to please the public. The German artist Max Liebermann is credited with rejuvenating the Old Masters of Dutch landscape painting with the palette of the Barbizon School. During his time in the Netherlands, he painted naturalistic but atmospheric canvases of a rural, pre-industrial world, visiting areas where life had remained much the same for hundreds of years. After 1890, Liebermann's technique became increasingly impressionistic, while the content of his pictures of everyday life became more realist. From a beer garden in Munich to the Oude Vink restaurant in Holland to his own garden by Berlin's Wannsee, his preferred subject was the play of light under canopies of leaves, where the corporeality of man and nature progressively transformed into colorful illusions of light.

△ Max Liebermann, *The Bleaching Ground*, 1883. Oil on canvas, 43 x 68 in (109 x 173 cm). Wallraf-Richartz-Museum, Cologne

Impressionist Sculpture

In the second half of the nineteenth century, the plastic arts struggled to free themselves from the neoclassicism that had been dominated by Canova (see p. 330). Carpeaux's sensually realized *Dance*, commissioned for the façade of Garnier's neo-baroque Opéra (1860–75), met with heavy criticism. That which was originally to represent an allegory of the dance—an Apollonian spirit surrounded by more or less revealing dancers—transmitted an impermissibly vivid physical and sensual naturalism,

cast as a spell in the lively movements of an obviously ecstatic Dionysian dance. The scrawny *Ratapoil* ("Ratskin") appeared as the embodiment of the Second Empire's Napoleonic propaganda, and thus as the gravedigger of the Republic. Daumier conceived the figure as a subversive caricature of dodginess made flesh. Degas, who admired and painted the ballet for most of his life, visualized bodily volume and movement with an ever-growing number of wax statuettes of ballerinas. Even his only large-scale

sculpture was first realized in wax, to which he later added real hair and clothing. This *Dancer* is therefore the first secular example of a mixed media sculpture in the modern era. Not until the early twentieth century would the pervasiveness of imitation and reality be the subject of experiment. The Italian artist Medardo Rosso worked only in wax, previously a medium used exclusively for preliminary studies, and his subjects seem to diffuse with the light and air surrounding them, hovering somewhere between

◁ Honoré Daumier, *Ratapoil*, ca. 1850–1891. Bronze, 17 in (43 cm) high. Musée d'Orsay, Paris

▷ Edgar Degas, *Little Dancer of Fourteen Years*, ca. 1880. Posthumous bronze cast, originally terracotta colored wax on wood framework, with hair, gauze, silk ribbon, cloth ballet shoes, 39 in (99 cm) high. The Metropolitan Museum of Art, New York

◁ Jean-Baptiste Carpeaux, *The Dance*, 1869. Stone, 13 ft 9 in x 9 ft 9 in (420 x 298 cm). Musée d' Orsay, Paris

formation and disintegration. Rodin also left the outer layers of his statues "open." They remain in a state of formation, thus allowing an impressionistic play of light and shadow that gives his primary themes—conditions of spiritual turmoil such as lust, passion, hopelessness—even more power of expression. In the heavy tread of the *Burghers of Calais*, who in 1347 had given their lives for their city, every limb, every gesture becomes an eloquent sign of despair.

◁ Medardo Rosso, *The Bookmaker*, 1894. Wax over plaster, 17⅓ in (44 cm) high. Museum of Modern Art, New York

▽ Auguste Rodin, *The Burghers of Calais*, cast from 1925 (original commission from the city of Calais 1885, dedication 1895). Bronze, 7 ft 3 in x 6 ft 6½ in x 5 ft 10 in (220 x 235 x 178 cm). Philadelphia Museum of Art, Philadelphia

Symbolism

Symbols of religious or ideological import, for millennia a primary component of the arts, must be familiar, such as white lilies as a representation of the purity of the Virgin Mary. But symbolist paintings are unfamiliar: "symbolism" means more than just the presence of symbols in painting.

During the nineteenth century, as artists could (or had to) start formulating their own conclusions about the meaning of their work, some began to "use" their art on a very personal level. Through mostly naturalistic means, they attempted to represent things and impressions that lay beyond visible reality. Their pictures arose from fantasies, daydreams, and fears. Their symbols were highly subjective, and it was significant for the essence of their art that their meanings were not readily apparent; a symbol might have a different meaning for the painter than for any of his observers. "Symbolism" was not a unified style, but rather resembled a sort of drug. In the end, symbolist painting remains enigmatic, but in reaction with a viewer's personal set of signs and symbols, it can lead to a fantastic revelation.

◁ Gustave Moreau, *Oedipus and the Sphinx*, 1864. Oil on canvas, 6 ft 9 in x 3 ft 5 in (206.4 x 104.7 cm). The Metropolitan Museum of Art, New York
◁ Arnold Böcklin, *The Isle of the Dead*, 1880. Oil on wood, 29 x 48 in (73.7 x 121.9 cm). The Metropolitan Museum of Art, New York
▷ Max Klinger, *Dead Mother (On Death, pt. 1)*, 1898. Etching, 15 x 11½ in (38 x 29 cm). Private collection
▷▷ Odilon Redon, *Germination (from In the Dream)*, 1879. Lithograph, 10¾ x 7¾ in (27.3 x 19.5 cm). Museum of Modern Art, NY

BÖCKLIN (1827–1901) · KLINGER (1857–1920) · MOREAU (1826–1898) · REDON (1840–1916)   379

◁ Hector Guimard, **Entrance to Métro Station Port Dauphine**, Paris, 1912

▽ Otto Wagner, *Kirche am Steinhof (Church of St. Leopold)*, Vienna, 1905–1907. Mosaic by Remigius Geyling and Leopold Forstner

◁ Henry van de Velde, **Poster for Tropon** (food product), 1899. Color lithograph, 44 x 30 3/8 in (111.8 x 77.2 cm). Museum of Modern Art, New York

▽ Thonet Bros., **Bentwood Rocking Chair**, design ca. 1880, Museum of Modern Art, New York

△ William Morris, **Wallpaper**, 1890. Hand-block-print, 27 x 21½ in (68.6 x 54.6 cm). The Metropolitan Museum of Art, New York

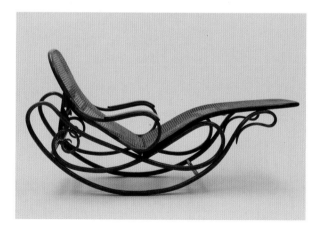

◁ Émile Gallé, **Bud Vase**, 1900, 3 in (7 cm) high. Museum of Modern Art, New York

Art Nouveau

William Morris and John Ruskin founded the "Arts and Crafts" movement in 1883. Their goal was to renew art and artisanry, at the same time bridging the gap between the two with high standards of workmanship. From this movement arose the Modern Style with centers in London and Glasgow.

"Jugendstil," as Art Nouveau is called in German-speaking regions, took its name from the magazine *Jugend* (published in Munich in 1896). As a long-overdue answer to fibrous amalgamations of historicizing flourishes, a new, elegantly fluid style burst forth from the vegetative base, establishing its hallmark motif of large vegetable forms that almost appear to have no depth or volume. Even when they are non-objective, these forms' generously curved and vibrantly animated lines give them a plant-like appearance. Suddenly, they were everywhere: on posters, wallpapers, fabrics, on cutlery and banisters, on furniture, they created dramatic new spatial possibilities. In architecture, Jugendstil also revealed a tendency to construct by means of ornamentation, as opposed to simply adding ornament to the construction. Centers of Jugendstil activity were Vienna, Munich and Darmstadt.

Art Nouveau was centered in Paris (jewelry by René Lalique), Brussels (architecture of Victor Horta), and Nancy, where the manufactories of Émile Gallé and the Daum Bros. (art glass—a distinctive feature of Art Nouveau) were located.

▷ Joseph Maria Olbrich, *Hochzeitsturm*, *Mathildenhöhe*, Darmstadt, 1908

△ Antoni Gaudí, **Palacio Güell**, Barcelona, chimney and ventilation shafts on the rooftop terrace, 1886–1889

▷ Antoni Gaudí, **Casa Batló**, Barcelona, façade, 1904–1906

▽ Antoni Gaudí, **Palacio Güell**, Barcelona, great hall, cupola, 1886–1889

Gaudí Enlivens Barcelona

Herbaceously exuberant curves and arches betray Gaudí's affinity for Art Nouveau. His earlier designs had shown neo-gothic and eclectic tendencies, but in Barcelona, he developed an innovative, fantastic architectural style that combines nature with geometry. Each of his buildings challenges the observer.

That which appears to be living growth comprises geometric figures such as parabolas and hyperbolas. Therefore, supporting columns could slant and list—they would still fulfill their structural purpose. Gaudí avoided symmetry and covered visible surfaces with color, often in the form of mosaics. Many of his all-embracing

works of art were designed for the textile manufacturer Güell. But his ambitious magnum opus is the as yet unfinished *La Sagrada Familia*, with its five naves. Gaudí took over the project from the diocesan architect Villar in 1883, but of the church's twelve projected towers, only four stand completed

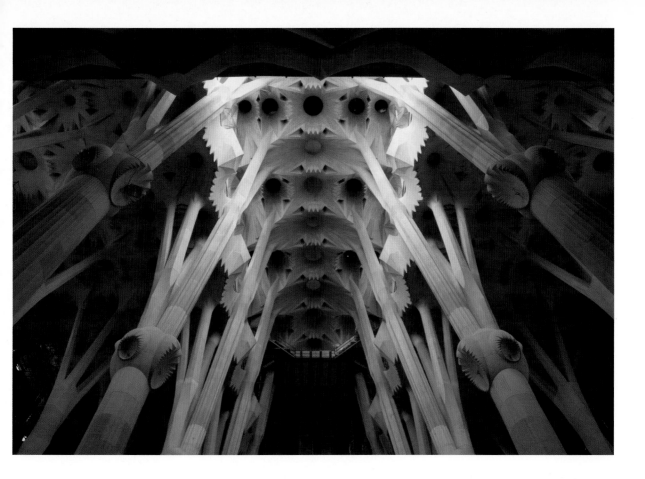

▽ Antoni Gaudí, **Sagrada Familia**, Barcelona, towers of the east façade, begun 1883

△ Antoni Gaudí, **Sagrada Familia**, Barcelona, interior begun 1883

▽ Antoni Gaudí, **Park Güell**, Barcelona, statues and fountains, staircase, 1900–1914

Hodler and Munch

Renouncing naturalism and impressionism, both Edvard Munch and Ferdinand Hodler granted their Jugendstil-influenced lines, which move and flow in rhythmic tension, a greater transmissive role in terms of expression. In doing so, both artists exposed human fear and entrapment that was inconsistent with Art Nouveau's *fin de siècle* ethos. With symmetry and "parallelism" of forms, the Swiss painter increased the intensity of his pictures' effect. In *The Night*, the repeated sleeping forms become a means of portraying the idea of night in all its shades. The sinister, black-clad apparition frightening the artist (in self-portrait) represents the phenomenology of the night in a general sense. The *Dance of Life* makes up the largest part of the *Frieze of Life*, in which the Norwegian painter Munch visualized a sweeping human narrative of birth and death, lust and fertility, melancholy and jealousy—in other words, an anthology of the modern person's emotional states. The three women in the foreground symbolize three stages of existence: the innocence of youth, the passion and jealousy of maturity, and the disappointment and bitterness of old age. *The Scream*, with its opposition between rhythmic, wave-like forms and straight lines, as well as its extreme perspectival skewness, is *the* expressive representation of humanity in the grip of fear.

▷ Edvard Munch, *The Dance of Life*, 1899–1902. Oil on canvas, 4 ft 2 in x 6 ft 3 in (126 x 191 cm). Nasjonalgalleriet, Oslo

◁ Edvard Munch, *The Scream*, 1893. Oil, tempera, and pastel on cardboard, 35¾ x 29 in (91 x 73.5 cm). Nasjonalgalleriet, Oslo

▽ Ferdinand Hodler, *The Night*, 1890. Oil on canvas, 3 ft 11 in x 9 ft 10 in (119 x 299 cm). Kunstmuseum, Bern. At the Geneva Salon of 1891, this canvas was so heavily criticized that it had to be removed from view. When the painting arrived in Paris, it was shown to great acclaim.

Awakening

Around 1900, those seeking to renew the visual arts through Art Nouveau, the Modern Style or Jugendstil were reacting against naturalism and realism. Why, they asked, should artists not try to make everything in their environment more beautiful, more poetic? At the same time, they saw no purpose in trying to compete with the art of photography which was advancing rapidly at the end of the nineteenth century. Many went their own way in search of a solution, while others joined artistic groups and movements.

One of these groups, calling itself *Les Nabis* ("the prophets"), developed around Maurice Denis. Its members drew from Gauguin and Japanese woodcuts to create

◁ Maurice Denis,
Die Musen, 1893.
Oil on canvas,
(171.5 x 137.5 cm).
Musée d' Orsay,
Paris

▷ Gustav Klimt,
The Kiss, 1907/08.
Oil, silver and gold
leaf on canvas,
5 ft 11 in x 5 ft 11
in (180 x 180 cm).
Österreichische
Galerie Belvedere,
Vienna

◁ Egon Schiele,
*Self-Portrait with
Spread Fingers*,
1911. Oil on wood,
(27.5 x 34 cm).
Historisches
Museum der Stadt
Wien, Vienna

an anti-naturalist, symbolist visual language using simplified shapes of color with dark contours.

Secessions splintered off from artistic movements: in Munich in 1892, in Vienna in 1897, and in Berlin in 1899. At the center of the Vienna Secession was Gustav Klimt, who combined non-objective ornament with representational, symbolic subjects. The theme of *The Kiss* became a symbol for the harmonic union of formal opposites.

Egon Schiele's bony portraits—especially his nudes, which at the time were widely considered im-moral—have a rather morbid effect. Leaving his impressionists beginnings behind him, he came under the influence of Klimt and Jugendstil, inventing through his nervous, aggressively draughtsman-like style a very personal form of expressionism.

On the Road to Genius: Picasso's Change of Color

Arriving in Paris from the Catalonian Art Nouveau of Barcelona, the young Pablo Picasso first became acquainted with the work of Toulouse-Lautrec, then mixed pointillist styles with those of the *Nabis*, painting contoured objects in powerful, shimmering colors.

During his "Blue Period" (1901–1904), Picasso developed his first individual style. As would happen later, a very personal experience led

to this artistic reorientation, namely the suicide of his friend, the artist Casagemas, in 1901. In addition to this event, Picasso rebelled against the influence of Toulouse-Lautrec, which can be seen in his sudden predilection for gently flowing contours. In terms of content, sentimental motifs corresponding to the theme of "the suffering and hopelessness of human existence" typify the increasingly monochrome blue pictures.

Upon joining the avant-garde in Paris, where Picasso finally settled for good in 1904, his outlook improved; the basic mood of his "Rose Period" (1904-06) is more balanced, and more cheerful. In the colorful world of jugglers and clowns, who act as symbols for the arts, Picasso's pictures (especially those from the Catalonian town of Gósol) began to show an increasingly sculptural approach to the depiction of corporeality.

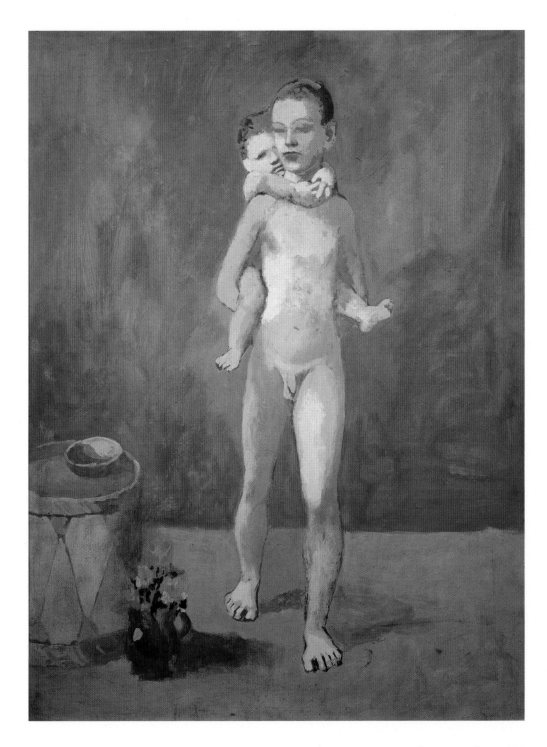

◁ Pablo
Picasso, *The
Wait (Margot)*,
Paris, Spring
1901. Oil on
board, 27 x
22 in (68.5 x
56 cm). Museu
Picasso,
Barcelona

◁◁ Pablo
Picasso, *Life*,
Barcelona,
spring-summer
1903. Oil on
canvas, 6 ft 5 in
x 4 ft 3 in (196.5
x 128.5 cm).
Cleveland
Museum of Art,
Cleveland

▷ Pablo
Picasso, *The
Two Brothers*,
Gósol, summer
1906. Gouache
on board, 31½
x 23¼ in (80 x
59 cm), Musée
Picasso, Paris

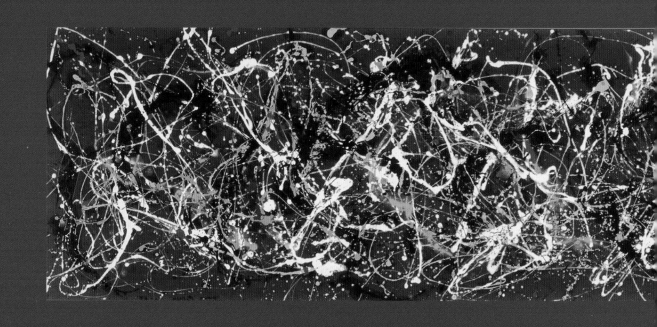

Jackson Pollock, *Number 2*, 1949. Oil, automotive lacquer and
aluminum paint, 3 ft 2 in x 15 ft 9 in (97 x 481 cm). Munson-Williams-
Proctor Arts Institute, Utica

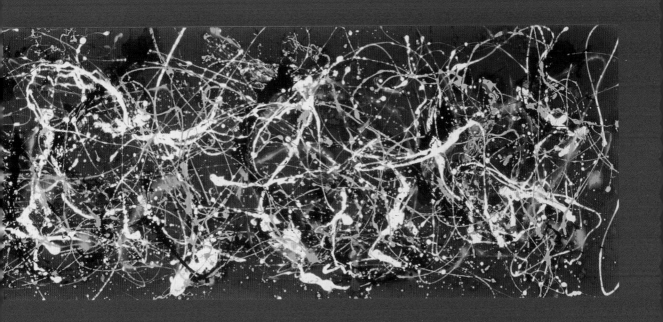

Twentieth Century

Centers of Modern Art

● Artist/style		
● Museum/exhibitions		

Amsterdam	CoBrA, Stedelijk Museum	**Copenhagen**	CoBrA
Barcelona	Picasso	**Leiden**	Abstraction
Berlin	Expressionism, Bauhaus	**London**	School of London, Pop Art, Tate Modern
Bilbao	Guggenheim Museum	**Los Angeles**	The J. Paul Getty Museum
Brussels	Surrealism, Symbolism, CoBrA	**Mexico City**	Muralism
Dessau/Weimar	Bauhaus	**Moscow**	Abstraction, Constructivism
Dresden	Expressionism	**Munich**	Expressionism
Kassel	Documenta	**New York**	Abstract Expressionism, Dada, Pop Art, Minimalism, Graffiti,
		Paris	Art Deco, Cubism, Fauvism, Centre Pompidou
		Rome	Arte Povera
		San Francisco	SF MoMA
		St. Petersburg	Suprematism
		Venice	Biennale
		Vienna	Secession
		Zurich	Dada
			MoMA, Whitney Museum, Guggenheim Museum

Cultural History

1900 Sigmund Freud publishes *The Interpretation of Dreams.*

1905 Albert Einstein develops the Theory of Relativity.

1913 Introduction of the assembly line in industrial manufacturing

1926 John Logie Baird invents the television.

1927 Charles Lindbergh makes the first non-stop transatlantic flight.

1941 Konrad Zuse develops the first digital computer.

1947 German authors start *Gruppe 47.*

1952 Samuel Beckett, *Waiting for Godot*

1957 *Sputnik* is the first man-made satellite to orbit the earth.

1969 Woodstock music festival

1979 Jean-François Lyotard publishes *The Postmodern Condition: A Report on Knowledge.*

1985 Discovery of the hole in the ozone layer over the South Pole

1989 Stephen Hawking writes *A Brief History of Time.*

1996 Birth of Daisy, a cloned sheep

Pablo Picasso,
Les Demoiselles d'Avignon, 1907

Marcel Duchamp,
Fountain, 1917

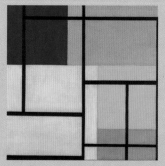

Theo van Doesburg,
Simultaneous Composition, 1929

René Magritte,
Not to be Reproduced, 1937

1900	1910	1920	1930	1940

Twentieth Century

Is Everything Art?

The expansion of form and content in the art of the twentieth century stemmed from developments and discoveries that radically changed humankind's perception of the world.

Two world wars destroyed the political and value systems that had long held sway in Europe. The industrialization begun in the nineteenth century took on unforeseen dimensions, causing social and ecological problems that have yet to be solved.

In its engagement with this transformed world, art became more open and diverse, but also more aggressive. Artists no longer wanted to imitate reality, but instead strove to create new and sometimes abstract realities. Their goal was not merely to show the visible, but rather to bring the invisible to light and make it visible. They wanted to dissolve the relationship between image and reality in favor of the independent reality of the artwork itself.

In terms of artistic experimentation, for which no technology or material was too great an obstacle, reality and existence itself were repeatedly called into question. Artists broke through boundaries, and the difference between art and non-art was dismantled according to the mottoes, "anything goes," and "everyone is an artist." In the end, it is up to the viewer: is art now a commodity for consumers and investors, or is it an indispensable expression of human identity?

Chronology

1914 Start of World War I (until 1918)
1917 Revolutions in Russia
1919 Treaty of Versailles
1929 "Black Friday" at the New York Stock Exchange
1933 Adolf Hitler becomes Reichs Chancellor of Germany.
1936 The Spanish Civil War begins.
1938 *Kristallnacht* pogroms
1939 Start of World War II (continues until 1945)

1945 Atomic bombs are dropped on Hiroshima and Nagasaki.
1957 The Treaties of Rome mark the beginning of European unification.
1961 Construction of the Berlin Wall
1963 Assassination of John F. Kennedy
1965 Escalation of the Vietnam War
1971 German chancellor Willy Brandt wins the Nobel Peace Prize.
1974 Watergate scandal

1977 Climax of the Baader-Meinhof group's terrorist activity during the "German Autumn"
1979 Ayatollah Khomeini founds the Islamic Republic of Iran.
1986 Chernobyl disaster
1989 Fall of the Berlin Wall
1991 Dissolution of the Warsaw Pact and the Soviet Union
1994 Nelson Mandela is elected president of South Africa.

Andy Warhol,
Marilyn, 1967

Bruce Nauman,
Human, Need, Desire, 1983

Andreas Gursky,
Schiphol, 1994

1960   1970   1980   1990   2000

At a Glance

Pluralism of Styles

Popular art encyclopedias list about seven prominent styles or movements between 1850 and 1900, but around eighty between 1900 and 1980. With the late nineteenth-century introduction of the term *avant-garde* (military "vanguard") in reference to new artistic directions (Arthur Rimbaud, 1873: "One must be absolutely modern"), artists—reinforced by critics and gallery-owners —shouldered the burden of creating constant novelty, seeking the new as soon as the shelf life of the old had passed.

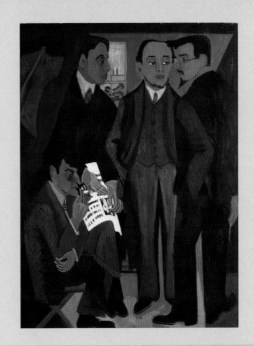

The Cult of the Artist

Artistic movements began to go in and out of vogue, and artists or groups no longer developed just one trademark style, but rather—like Picasso—kept an entire epoch breathlessly waiting for the next new means of expression. These were ideal conditions for the cult of the artist to blossom. Art was thus reduced to the artist, and this celebrity cult has retained its marketing power to this day.

Ernst Ludwig Kirchner, *A Group of Artists*, 1925. Oil on canvas, 5 ft 6 in x 4 ft 2 in (168 x 126 cm). Museum Ludwig, Cologne

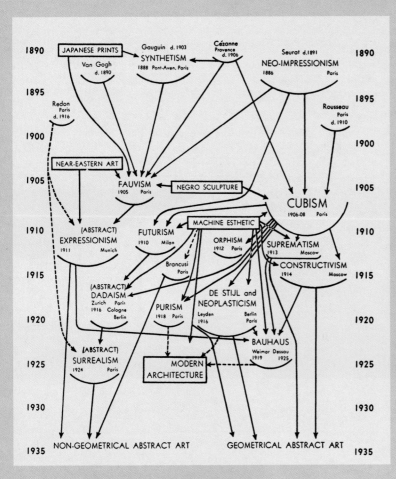

Family Tree of Avant-Garde

The field of art history arose in the early nineteenth century. Its objective was to describe the evolution of the visual arts as a succession of stylistic periods, viewed as a historical progression. But during that century, discrete artistic styles and movements began to run parallel to one another. In the twentieth century, the development of artistic trends grew increasingly complex: many styles mutually influencing each other progressed concurrently, with differing degrees of temporal overlap, or repeated themselves in variation. As a result, some artists and their work could not easily be classified. Art historians attempted to visualize the relationships and inter-dependencies of the diverse movements through diagrams. Artists also designed such diagrams to place themselves within a distinguished artistic lineage.

Alfred H. Barr, *Diagram of the Development of Styles, 1890–1935*. From the catalog of the exhibition *Cubism and Abstract Art*, Museum of Modern Art, New York, 1936

Twentieth Century

Pablo Picasso, *Les Demoiselles d'Avignon* (detail), 1906

Modern and "Primitive" Art

Following Gauguin's experiments with "primitive" formal language, Picasso engaged most notably with African sculpture in 1907. It was not the exotic that appealed to him: in the dissolution and deformation of volume, in the block-by-block construction of the picture's surface without regard for natural models, he found a solution to the formal problems accompanying his search for a newly rhythmized pictorial space. Almost simultaneously, painters of *Die Brücke* ("the Bridge") synthesized the arts of Australasia in their works.

Multiple Perspectives

With its multiple, simultaneous viewpoints—Picasso portrayed the violin's soundboard from the front, but the scroll from the side—modernism liberated itself from the classical, one-point perspective of the Renaissance. Now, as in medieval picture series, different levels and layers of reality could be depicted at the same time and in the same work.

Pablo Picasso, *Violin and Grapes*, 1912. Oil on canvas, 19⅞ x 24 in (50.6 x 61 cm). Museum of Modern Art, New York

Theo van Doesburg and Cornelis van Eesteren, *Contra-Construction Project*, 1923. Gouache on paper, 22½ x 22½ in (57.1 x 57.1 cm). Museum of Modern Art, New York

Art of Austerity

Constructivism in the nascent Soviet Union, Bauhaus in Weimar Germany, and *De Stijl* in the Netherlands—a group centered around Piet Mondrian and Theo van Doesburg, the editor of the journal of the same name—were connected by a common goal: an art that was strictly rational, that embraced all aspects of life, and that was committed to a utopian vision of social progress.

Poster for the Exhibition *KG Brücke*, 1910. Galerie Arnold, Dresden

Galleries, Art Journals and Artistic Literature

In the first decades of the twentieth century, gallery owners who joined forces with the avant-garde played a significant role in the promulgation and success of modern art. Also instrumental in publicizing the arts were political, cultural and artistic journals such as *Der Sturm* ("The Storm," 1910–1932) and *Die Aktion* ("Action," 1911–1932) in Germany, both of which helped expressionism to its breakthrough. Art dealers such as German expatriate Kahnweiler in Paris not only sold works by Picasso and the cubists, but also promoted them in historic exhibitions (see p. 412).

Daniel Henry Kahnweiler, *The Rise of Cubism* (cover). Munich, 1920

Key Terms

Gesturalism

Willem de Kooning, *Woman I*, 1950–1952. Oil on canvas, 75⅞ x 58 in (192.7 x 147.3 cm). Museum of Modern Art, New York

In the New York of the 1940s and 50s, young artists with bold visions and an innovative artistic vocabulary developed a new style marked by rebellion and freedom. De Kooning's gestures are—like Pollock's action painting and Rothko's strips of color—just one form of expression (see p. 460f).

Broadening of "Art"

The visual arts abandoned their traditional media: Duchamp elevated everyday objects to the status of art, practitioners of pop art augmented their pictures with consumer products and trash, happenings left behind all sorts of relics, artists made themselves into art (performance), new techniques and media were developed (e.g. light, video), graffiti artists incorporated urban architecture into their work, spaces were constructed (installation), landscapes were reshaped, and photography became a "legitimate" art form.

Harald Naegeli, Cologne *Dance of Death* on the walled-up portal of St. Cecilia, 1980/81

Postmodernism

After the repeatedly heralded "end of modernism," for which eulogists do not always choose the same date of death (abstract expressionism usually serves as the eschaton), every artistic work or movement that has declined to create its own style, instead quoting—often in ironic combination—previous styles, mythologies, and cultural history, has been considered postmodern.

Modernity and Popular Culture

One of pop art's primary feats was to remove much of the barrier separating "low" and "high" art. One way of doing this was to appropriate formal themes and techniques from comics and elevate them to canvas-worthy compositions.

Roy Lichtenstein, *Crying Girl*, 1964

Art Exhibition

The art exhibitions of the twentieth century, events inspired by France's nineteenth-century *salons*, fulfilled an essential role in the dissemination of modern art. One of the most significant outlets for European modernism before World War I was the 1912 exhibition of the *Sonderbund westdeutscher Kunstfreunde und Künstler* ("Separate League of West German Art Lovers and Artists") in Cologne. European modernism crossed the Atlantic in 1913 with the legendary Armory Show in New York, which provided the inspiration for American modernism. In 1955, Arnold Bode and Werner Haftmann organized the exhibition "documenta" in Kassel, re-establishing the German link with modern art that had been severed when the Nazis branded the works of many of Germany's most gifted artists as "degenerate." The exhibition, held every four years for 100 days, is now one of the most important international surveys of contemporary art.

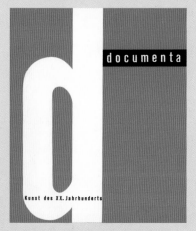

Catalogue for "documenta 1," 1955

Twentieth Century

The Poster: Art and Politics

In 1891, Toulouse-Lautrec elevated the poster to an art form. Ever since, this medium has drawn attention with its attempts at manipulating viewers. In other words, it advertises, even politically. During the Parisian student strikes of May 1968, students of the *École des Beaux-arts* and *École des Arts Décoratifs* printed and hung new posters daily. Their creative reaction to current events turned out to be an exact barometer of the prevailing mood.

La chienlit c'est lui!
Poster, Paris, 1968

Conceptual Art

In principle, every artistic endeavor is conceptual, since the process usually proceeds from idea to execution. Beginning in the mid-1960s, artists (especially in the USA) increasingly rejected the creation of individual pictorial worlds, searching instead for an ultimate objectivity, one that refers to nothing but itself. Traditional art forms were rejected, with textual or diagrammatic paraphrases of the artwork taking their place. According to another approach, paintings were created that only became real when set in a thought-associative process with the viewer. Kawara's pictures are not really pictures until the viewer knows that they only show the date of their creation.

Land Art

In land art, the natural landscape is transformed through large-scale concepts, becoming a medium for artists. Many of the works of art thus created are transitory, mutable by nature.

Robert Smithson, *Spiral Jetty*, Utah, 1970

Individual Mythologies

Max Beckmann owed his outsider role to the highly personalized iconography and mythology he developed in his painting. In the 1970s, this concept served primarily as an explanation for works of artists who did not fit any well-established classification. It became popular to attempt to establish a link between artistry and shamanism, including ritual costume and mythically loaded material (e.g. Beuys).

New Media

Television and manipulated video imagery have been established artistic media since their use in the Fluxus movement. Around 1970, a sculptural handling of video technology arose that led to increasingly sophisticated installations, as well as meticulously compiled sound and image sequences on monitors, a practice made even more prevalent by the advent of digital technology.

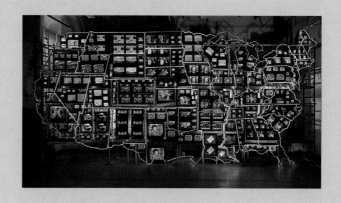

Nam June Paik, *Electric Superhighway*, 1995. Video installation.
Smithsonian American Art Museum, Washington, D.C.

Key Terms

▷ Henri Matisse, *Collioure*, 1905. Oil on canvas, 15¼ x 18⅜ in (38.8 x 46.6 cm). Museum of Modern Art, New York

▽ Henri Matisse, *Luxe, calme et volupté*, 1904. Oil on canvas, 38¾ x 46⅝ in (98.3 x 118.5 cm). Musée national d'art moderne, Centre Georges-Pompidou, Paris

Color Gone Wild

In 1905, a critic lambasted the artists around Matisse as *fauves*, or "wild beasts," thereby giving them not only a name, but also group status. This group had no explicitly formulated program, as that would have been too constrictive. But they did have influences: Seurat's unmixed points of color, van Gogh's pastose and vivid brushwork, and Gauguin's saturated, two-dimensional fields of color.

Whereas Matisse's engagement with Seurat's restrained "color pix-

els" can be recognized in his *Luxe, calme et volupté*, it is clear in the landscape of *Collioure* that the colors are no longer intended to depict the subject's hues literally, but rather to "represent" the subject with vehement brushstrokes on exposed, still visible canvas. Vlaminck and Derain unlearned natural coloration, allowing their use of pure, lush colors to convey their subjective interaction with the painted subject. Instead of creating an illusion of space, their use of light and color brought forth a new pictorial reality in which nature itself became the artistic impulse.

Henri Matisse

As a fauvist, Matisse used colors to convey emotions; they became his most important expressive tool. As soon as the "necessary relationship of colors" (Matisse) was achieved, and the figures with their surroundings were realized within this relationship, the composition was for him immutable.

His use of color is therefore best experienced, rather than explained. "I am incapable of making a slavish copy of nature. Instead I feel compelled to interpret it, and adapt it to the spirit of the picture. When I put colors together, they

△ Henri Matisse, *Still Life with 'La Danse'*, 1909. Oil on canvas, 35¼ x 46 in (89.5 x 117.5 cm). The Hermitage, St. Petersburg

◁ Henri Matisse, *Decorative Figure on an Ornamental Background*, 1925/26. Oil on canvas, 51⅛ x 38⅝ in (130 x 98 cm). Musée national d'art moderne, Paris

◁ Henri Matisse, *The Piano Lesson*, 1916. Oil on canvas, 96½ x 83¾ in (245.1 x 212.7 cm). Museum of Modern Art, New York

▷ Henri Matisse, *The Eskimo*, 1947. Gouache découpée, 16 x 33⅞ in (40.5 x 86 cm). Kunstindustrimuseet, Copenhagen

must join in a living chord or harmony of color, a harmony analogous to that of a musical composition" (Matisse).

Inspired by Islamic miniatures, Matisse abandoned any attempt at spatial depth, developing in its stead a flat and rhythmic essentialization. He was just as fascinated by Middle Eastern arabesques and other abstract decorative forms as he was by visual reality. Although he alternately favored one direction over the other in his developmental phases, his effort to unify both artistic approaches remained constant.

The brilliantly vivid, expansive decorative surfaces of his late paper cuts (*gouaches découpées*) achieve an almost independent ability to create expressive moods in color.

◁ Ernst Ludwig Kirchner, *Street, Berlin*, 1913. Oil on canvas, 47½ x 35⅞ in (120.6 x 91.1 cm). Museum of Modern Art, New York

Die Brücke (1905–1913)
Founding members:
E. L. Kirchner,
E. Heckel, K. Schmidt-Rottluff, F. Bleyl (until 1909)
1906: M. Pechstein (until 1912), E. Nolde (until 1907), C. Amiet, A. Gallén-Kallela
1908: F. Nölken, K. van Dongen
1910: O. Mueller
1911: B. Kubišta

Die Brücke ("The Bridge")

The members of the group known as *Die Brücke* also rejected salon painting as a sham, setting themselves in opposition to all the rules of academic art. They found the world of outer appearances banal; one's surroundings only became worthy of depiction after having submitted to visual synthesis, executed by a painter who had developed his own expressive language of form and color through personal experience. The founding members of *Die Brücke* were architecture students who first had to develop their powers of expression. In the process, they gave new life to the old technique of the woodcut. In relief printing, the raised sections of the woodblock tint the paper; sections to remain colorless must be cut out. Wood's natural resistance to cutting encouraged the formal simplification these artists sought, while their encounters with Australasian and African sculpture further sharpened their gaze. Their project was to attain the same honesty they perceived in the arts of indigenous peoples, and they vehemently rejected the taboos of bourgeois morality. With personal experience as the premise for their choice of subject, their primary motifs were studio, beach and street scenes.

△ Otto Mueller, *Two Women Seated In The Dunes*, ca. 1922. Distemper on burlap, 39⅜ x 54⅜ in (100 x 138 cm). Museo Thyssen-Bornemisza, Madrid

▽ Erich Heckel, *Fränzi Reclining*, 1910. Color woodcut, 8⅞ x 16½ in (22.6 x 42.1 cm). Museum of Modern Art, New York

Les Demoiselles d'Avignon

The painting was controversial even before it left the studio. Friends were appalled by the "ghastly composition," which looked like it had been "carved out with an axe." At first, Picasso himself kept the picture hidden, considering it "unfinished," even though it was the result of meticulous planning and sketching. Some sketches still show men entering the composition from the side, one even holding a skull. With the foreknowledge that the title refers to the street in Barcelona— *Carrer de Avinyo*—in which most of the city's bordellos were located, and that Picasso was terrified of the then devastating symptoms of syphilis, one might guess that "the wages of sin" was the picture's original theme.

But Picasso eventually abandoned this allegorical direction. The five female figures, their gaze focused on the viewer, remain isolated. Something else had become important.

In 1905, many artists were striving to "break" pictorial space and perspective as well as the rhythm of forms on the canvas, disregarding natural models or poetic ideas. Picasso compartmentalized the picture's layers, allowing its structure to grow forward rather than receding into the background. Interweaving frontal, side and rear views, he intentionally deformed the volumes of the objects. Around this time, many artists were inspired by the pristine nature of "primitive" art. In African and Australasian sculpture, copying nature is not as important as intuitive symbolism. One could say that this way of looking at things freed Western European artists from centuries-old academic blinders. But as Picasso would later claim, "African art? Never heard of it."

△ Frank Gelett Burgess, *Pablo Picasso in His Studio in the Bateau-Lavoir*, 1908, photograph. To the left are an African sculpture consisting of multiple figures from the Congo region (Yombe) and a musical instrument from Gabon (Fang?); to the right are two statues from New Caledonia.

◁ Pablo Picasso, *Les Demoiselles d'Avignon*, June 1907. Oil on canvas, 96 x 92 in (243.9 x 233.7 cm). Museum of Modern Art, New York

▷ Pablo Picasso, *Study for Nude with Drapery*, Summer 1907. Oil on canvas, 24¼ x 18¾ in (61.4 x 47.6 cm). Museum of Modern Art, New York

▽ Pablo Picasso, *Study for Les Demoiselles D'Avignon*, April 1907. Oil on canvas, 7½ x 8 in (18.5 x 20.3 cm). Museum of Modern Art, New York

More Than One Perspective

Braque, a Fauvist in Matisse's circle, visited Picasso in his studio in 1907 and was immediately fascinated by the shocking pictorial concept of *Les Demoiselles d'Avignon*. In the summer of 1908, the two artists worked together to develop a new manner of representing form and space. Both revered Cézanne's late work, in which he used short, parallel brushstrokes to distribute small patches of the same color, thus making foreground and background indistinguishable from each other. In 1908, the two engaged in serious debate concerning a theory of perception according to which one can develop a notion of an object only after viewing and feeling it from all sides. Therefore, instead of painting objects as one sees them, Braque and Picasso attempted to depict their surfaces from all sides at once.

They experimented with landscapes in unnatural lighting, with unforeshortened forms. This "reverse

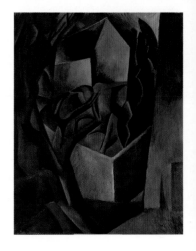

△ Pablo Picasso, *House and Trees*, August 1908. Oil on canvas, 36¼ x 28¾ in (92 x 73 cm). Pushkin Museum, Moscow

◁ Pablo Picasso, *Man with a Pipe*, 1911. Oil on canvas, 35¾ x 27⅞ in (90.7 x 71.0 cm). Kimbell Art Museum, Fort Worth

perspective" (Apollinaire) creates objects without the usual illusory depth, in which everything becomes smaller and brighter as it recedes into the background; the dimensions of the canvas provide the borders of the space represented, in which the forms appear to extend toward the viewer as if in relief. When two of Braque's pictures in the *Salon des Indépendants* of October 1908 led a critic to describe them as *"bizarreries cubiques,"* this type of painting was given a name. Since the visual experience of a landscape picture automatically implies depth, Picasso and Braque perfected their method from 1910 on with still lifes and portraits, thus avoiding this unwanted effect. They analyzed and deconstructed their subjects into faceted structures, allowing each facet to spring to the front until a unified, flat surface resulted.

△ Georges Braque, **Road near L'Estaque**, 1908. Oil on canvas, 23¾ x 19¾ in (60.3 x 50.2 cm). Museum of Modern Art, New York

▷ Georges Braque, **Candlestick and Playing Cards on a Table**, 1910. Oil on canvas, 25⅝ x 21⅜ in (65.1 x 54.3 cm). The Metropolitan Museum of Art, New York

Why Paint Collages?

Increasingly minute, monotone facets began to render the represented object unrecognizable, and the analytically motivated structure threatened to degenerate into an end in itself. Picasso and Braque therefore returned to a more representational concept. In the spring of 1912, Picasso first included real objects and references to those objects in his canvases. These cubist collages marked the beginning of synthetic cubism. By forgoing unity and deciding instead to include physical elements in pictures, the artists placed the relationships between objects next to the analysis of the visual world squarely in the foreground. An amusing side effect was the irritation of the viewer that resulted from using real and/or imitation objects. Letters simulated newspapers, spackled structures were wooden boards, printed oilcloth was a wicker chair... objects and patterns recalled nothing but other objects and patterns. An important step in the artwork's autonomy, freeing artists from their traditionally representative task, was thus taken.

Picasso as Sculptor and Graphic Artist

The cubists' formal project—the simultaneous, multiperspectival representation of a three-dimensional object spread out on a surface—translated into a three-dimensional form that can already be viewed from all sides? Picasso toyed with the idea of analytical cubism by constructing a bust of a woman out of more or less identically-sized pieces. He made synthetic cubism literally tangible in the form of a glass of absinthe: open and closed capacities, the sculpted plus the article of use. With an ironic regard, Picasso put found objects, unmodified, into new formal and representative contexts, exemplified by the bull's skull made of a bicycle saddle and handlebar. In his graphic work, Picasso made use of different techniques throughout all his stylistic phases, albeit with a predilection for etching and lithography. He combined ancient mythology with private biography, dedicated himself to Mediterranean themes like bullfighting, and to more traditional subjects such as "painter with model." But Picasso was also politically involved. In the series of etchings entitled *The Dream and Lie of Franco*, he laid Franco's political fantasies bare with surrealism and satire, using motifs that would later characterize his most important political work, *Guernica*.

▷▷ Pablo Picasso, **Head of a Woman (Fernande)**, Autumn 1909. Bronze, 16 in (40.5 cm) high. The Metropolitan Museum of Art, New York

▷ Pablo Picasso, **Bull's Head**, 1942. Bicycle saddle (leather) and handlebars (metal), 16½ in (42 cm) high. Musée Picasso, Paris

△ Pablo Picasso, **Glass of Absinthe**, 1914. Painted bronze with absinthe spoon, 8½ in (21.6 cm) high. Museum of Modern Art, New York. Six casts of this sculpture exist, each painted differently. One version with a white foot is covered with sand.

▷ Pablo Picasso, *Minotauromachy* March 23, 1935. Etching (seventh and last version) and engraving, 19½ x 27⅜ in (49.8 x 69.3 cm). Picasso's most important graphic work confronts the viewer with a complex, practically indecipherable private mythology or allegory.

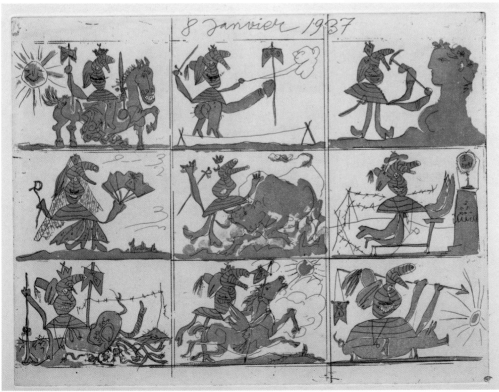

◁ Pablo Picasso, *The Dream and Lie of Franco I*, January 8, 1937. Etching and aquatint, 12¼ x 16½ in (31 x 42 cm). Musée Picasso, Paris. Created as a protest against Franco's coup d'état, the pages were intended to be separated and the individual scenes sold as "postcards" to benefit a relief fund for the Spanish republic.

Other Cubists

Beginning in 1911, cubism evolved into an artistic style that went beyond the work of Picasso and Braque. The art dealer Daniel Henry Kahnweiler acknowledged their role in its creation in his "The Way to Cubism" of 1920 (see p. 395). Gris, like Picasso from Spain, was at first an adherent of analytic cubism, but he soon developed an individual cubist style that is strictly geometrical, but in which objects are still recognizable. Léger's heavily formalized cubist compositions are dominated by cylindrical elements, a trait that earned him the nickname "tubist." Tube forms alternating with planar surfaces generate a rather nonrepresentational texture. Delaunay combined the impressionist model of serial representation of the same motif in varying grades of light with cubist stylistic devices and a tendency to abstraction. Apollinaire, poet and friend to the cubists, regarded Delaunay's *Window* series especially as a further development of cubism. Since they primarily were concerned with light effects, he described them as "orphism." Constructed on a lattice-like structure, these pictures show prismatic spectral effects that reflect no natural, object-bound colors, but which thematize color in and of itself. This recognition of color's autonomy would prove to be decisive for the artists of *Der Blaue Reiter*.

▷ Fernand Léger, **Contrast of Forms**, 1913. Oil on canvas, 39½ x 32 in (100.3 x 81.1 cm). Museum of Modern Art, New York

▷ Robert Delaunay, **A Window (Study for Three Windows)**, 1912. Oil on canvas, 43¾ x 35⅜ in (111 x 90 cm). Musée national d'art moderne, Paris

▽ Juan Gris, **Dish of Fruit**, 1916. Oil on panel, 16 x 9½ in (40.6 x 24.1 cm). Philadelphia Museum of Art, Philadelphia

LÉGER (1881–1955) · DELAUNAY (1885–1941) · GRIS (1887–1927)   413

Futurism

With a firm belief in the all-changing present and future, the Italian poet Marinetti propagated in his 1909 *Futurist Manifesto* a radical break with all tradition. In 1910, visual artists also aligned themselves with him, among them Boccioni, Balla and Carrà. They revolted against "academic formalism" and the "tyranny of words, harmony and good taste," calling instead for "dynamization." In the noise and tumult of the cities, sensing the restlessness of their inhabitants, the futurists thematized the changes in modern society. For them, a single, unified moment was insufficient, so they combined multiple temporal conditions sequentially in one composition.

Their aggression, as well as the pleasure they took in a militant pathos, eventually brought the futurists dangerously close to fascism. Al-

though futurism's sway was by far most pronounced in Italy, its influence on other significant artists of European modernism is unmistakable. Duchamp thematized the problem of simultaneous states of motion in his *Nude Descending a Staircase*: "The general appearance and brownish hue are clearly cubist, but the handling of movement contains a few undertones of futurism" (Duchamp).

△ Umberto Boccioni, *Unique Forms of Continuity in Space*, 1913. Bronze, 43½ in (110.5 cm) high. Civico Museo d'Arte Contemporanea, Milan. "We will give life to the static muscular line," wrote Boccioni in his manifesto of futurist sculpture.

◁ Carlo Carrà, *Funeral of the Anarchist Galli*, 1910/11. Oil on canvas, 78¼ x 102 in (198.7 x 259.1 cm). Museum of Modern Art, New York. Fragmented, interlaced, individual vignettes of a single event give a pictorial evocation of anarchic power.

▷ Marcel Duchamp, *Nude Desending a Staircase No. 2*, 1912. Oil on canvas, 57½ x 35 in (146 x 89 cm). Philadelphia Museum of Art, Philadelphia. The final version unifies several of Duchamp's different ideas, including the still-young art of film.

◁ Giacomo Balla, *Dynamism of a Dog on a Leash*, 1912. Oil on canvas, 35⅜ x 43⅜ in (90 x 110 cm). Albright-Knox Art Gallery, Buffalo

▷ Alexej von
Jawlensky, *The
Thinking Woman*,
1912. Oil on board,
21¼ x 19 in (54 x
48.5 cm). Museo
Thyssen-Borne-
misza, Madrid.
Jawlensky sought
the representation-
al archetype of his
motifs.

▷▷ August Macke,
*Lady in a Green
Jacket*, 1913. Oil on
canvas, 17⅜ x 17⅛ in
(44 x 43.5 cm).
Museum Ludwig,
Cologne. Macke
experimented with
the "space-forming
fluctuation" of cool
(background) and
warm (foreground)
colors.

▷ Franz Marc,
*The Trees Showed
Their Rings, the
Animals Their
Arteries (The Fate
of the Animals)*,
1913. Oil on canvas,
6 ft 4 in x 8 ft 9 in
(196 x 266 cm).
Öffentliche Kunst-
sammlung, Basel.
Right section
ruined, repainted in
1919 by Paul Klee.
Marc developed
distinct colors and
shapes for animals
and landscape, all
crystallized into a
natural unity.

The Mission of *Der Blaue Reiter*

△ Wassily
Kandinsky,
*Improvisation 20
(Two Horses)*, 1911.
Oil on canvas, 3
ft 1 in x 3 ft 6 in
(94.5 x 108 cm).
Pushkin Museum,
Moscow. Kandinsky
withdrew—for
many tastes too
far—from the
world of everyday
representation.

The almanac *Der Blaue Reiter* appeared in 1912: Kandinsky's and Marc's answer to censorship in the *Neue Künstlervereinigung München*. The articles in it were written by artists who were already busy extending the boundaries of artistic expression. Kandinsky himself wrote important contributions, establishing connections to music and the stage. Its 141 illustrations included a woodcarving by Gauguin next to an archaic Greek relief, El Greco next to Delaunay, medieval next to African sculpture—arranged so that the "inner resonance" of the first would be answered by the "counter-resonance" of the other. Apart from editing the almanac, Marc and Kandinsky organized two exhibitions (one of painting and one of graphic design) under this sign, in order to give an overview of the contemporary European artistic scene. Many artists in Munich saw the woodcuts of the *Brücke* artists for the first time; many Germans first became acquainted with Delaunay's work with color. More successful than the exhibitions, however, was the almanac: 1500 copies of the first edition were quickly snatched up, and 6000 more were printed in 1914. This would most likely have continued, but *Der Blaue Reiter* died along with Marc and Macke in the World War I.

Sculptural Architecture

◁ Erich
Mendelsohn,
Einstein Tower,
Potsdam, 1920–
1922. Mendelsohn
began planning
the observatory
in 1917 with Albert
Einstein, whose
theories and
predictions were
to be tested there.
Today it is used for
solar research.

The Jugendstil conception of statuary and organic structural forms heavily influenced the avant-garde architecture of the early twentieth century. Buildings were designed according to a readily apparent desire for expressive "physiognomy" and emotional response, allowing the building's function to occupy a position secondary to its form. As can be seen in his sketches for the Einstein Tower, Mendelsohn, a friend of *Der Blaue Reiter*, first conceived his designs in sculptural terms, without wasting so much as a thought on

practical matters of construction. After World War I, a growing preference for sharp angles and heavily accented verticals became apparent. Höger, who through his many office buildings in Hamburg brought about a renaissance in North German brick construction, achieved with his *Chilehaus* a masterpiece of this expressionist style of architecture. The east corner of this dynamic, crystalline building resembles the bow of a ship, its silhouette accentuated by a stacked-story design.

▽ Fritz (Johann
Friedrich) Höger,
Chilehaus,
Hambug, 1922/23.
This building's
name refers to
the activities
of its owner,
Henry Brarens
Sloman, who
made most of his
money trading in
Chilean saltpeter.
The design
earned Höger
the nickname
Klinkersticker
(the "brick
embroiderer"),
since the façade is
only clad in brick
slip—the inner
structure is a
precast concrete
skeleton.

Kandinsky "Tunes" Lines

Art can be found everywhere, as long as the "purely artistic" aspect of every object finds expression and asserts itself in the face of the *Zeitgeist* and the artist's personality. For Kandinsky, timeless, pure art was best expressed in the harmony of composition. The composition should place form, color and line in relationships in which an apple can in principle fit together just as well with a bottle as a circle can with a pointed, upright triangle. In the process of searching for such relationships, Kandinsky freed himself from the bonds of objectivity; he is credited with painting the first completely abstract watercolor (1910).

Critics who decried compositions full of blotches of color and scrawled lines as meaningless overlooked the fact that Kandinsky assigned colors, surfaces, and lines such attributes as hard, velvety, piercing and smooth, or that he ascribed to them inward or outward movement—and even the tones of specific musical instruments.

Viewed in this light, nonfigurative expression provides artistic enrichment, since the representational possibilities of an apple with a bottle of wine are not nearly as numerous as those of a circle with a triangle.

▽ Wassily Kandinsky, *Church at Murnau*, 1909. Oil on board, 19⅛ x 27½ in (48.6 x 69.8 cm). Museum of Modern Art, New York

▷ Wassily Kandinsky, *Yellow, Red, Blue*, 1925. Oil on canvas. 50 x 78¾ in (127 x 200 cm). Musée national d'art moderne, Centre Georges-Pompidou, Paris

△ Wassily Kandinsky, *Lyrical* (plate, folio 9) from *Klänge (Sounds)*, 1911. Woodcut, 5¾ x 8½ in (14.8 x 21.7 cm). Museum of Modern Art, New York

▷ Wassily Kandinsky, *Black Relationship*, 1924. Watercolor and ink on paper, 14½ x 14¼ in (36.9 x 36.2 cm). Museum of Modern Art, New York

Kandinsky was well aware of his resources when he layered geometric or free colored forms with straight or curved black lines: blue for example exercising an inward attraction, while yellow shines outward. The orientation of line and form determines their tonal temperature. Even the empty space of a canvas is defined by two pairs of lines: their tones are neutral when united in the form of a square, but they are cold when horizontal and warm when vertical, all of which must be taken in consideration by the composer.

Paul Klee

Like Kandinsky, Klee taught at the Bauhaus, an occupation which forced him, too, to engage intensively with his means of expression. But while Kandinsky elevated questions of form to an ideology, such matters remained tools of the trade for Klee—indispensable, but in the service of his artistic invention, which could be liberatingly frivolous (especially when seen against the backdrop of Weimar Germany and Hitler's seizure of power). For example, it is quite possible that the green "R" in his *Villa R*, isolated in a sparse milieu of architectonic forms, is following in a tradition of picture puzzles, and can be interpreted as a challenge to the vegetation: the pronunciation of *R grün* ("R green") is the same as *Ergrün!* ("Become verdant!"). Allowing oneself to be deceived by the apparent simplicity of Klee's pictures can ruin their sense of fun. Klee was always working on at least two levels. To demonstrate how so little substance can contain so much meaning, he connected "outer appearance" with "looking within," "architectonic" with "poetic painting." In *Ad Parnassum*, he showed how ten lines in varying colors—two vertical, one curved, and seven slanted—under and in a mosaic structure, and with a rich orange circle, create the impression of a landscape. The facial expression in *Senecio* takes form with corners, edges and asymmetry. "Art does not reproduce the visible, it makes visible" (Klee).

▽ Paul Klee, *Virgin in the Tree*, 1903, version 2. Etching, 9¼ x 11¾ in (23.7 x 29.7 cm). Museum of Modern Art, New York

◁ Paul Klee, *Villa R*, 1919, 153. Oil on board, 10⅜ x 8⅝ in (26.5 x 22 cm). Öffentliche Kunstsammlung, Basel

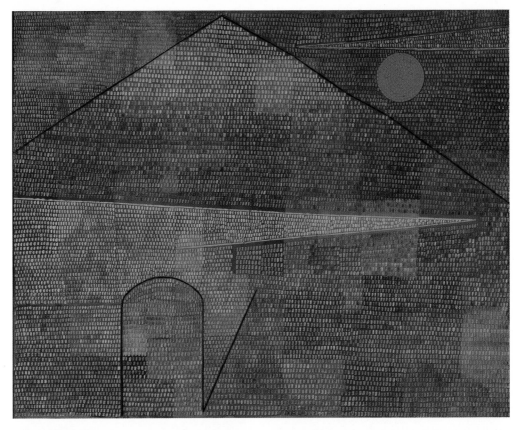

▷ Paul Klee, *Ad Parnassum*, 1932, 274. Oil on canvas, 39⅜ x 49⅝ in (100 x 126 cm). Kunstmuseum, Bern

▽ Paul Klee, *Senecio*, 1922, 181. Oil and gauze on board, 16 x 15⅛ in (40.5 x 38.4 cm). Öffentliche Kunstsammlung, Basel

◁ Paul Klee, *Handbill for Comedians*, 1938, 42. Colored paste and newsprint on board, 19⅛ x 12⅝ in (48.6 x 32.1 cm). Museum of Modern Art, New York

△ Lyonel Feininger, *Cathedral*, for *Program of the State Bauhaus* in Weimar, 1919. Woodcut, 16⅛ x 12¼ in (41 x 31 cm). Museum of Modern Art, New York

The State Bauhaus

Upon its founding in 1919 in Weimar, the goal of the Bauhaus School was proclaimed to be the unification of art and handicraft, to design buildings that were *Gesamtkunstwerke* ("total works of art"). Each student took an introductory class before choosing one of the following workshops: sculpture, pottery, theater, typography, bookbinding, joinery, weaving, stained-glass painting, mural painting, metalwork (in 1926, pottery, bookbinding and stained-glass painting were replaced by architecture, city planning and free painting). Every workshop was headed by an artist (Klee, Kandinsky, Feininger et al.) and a master craftsman. In practice, the latter had no say in important matters, and interdisciplinary projects between workshops were rare. In 1923 Germany was paralyzed by hyperinflation, and a shortage of funds forced the school to collaborate with the industries that needed (and paid for) functional, easily reproduced designs. Johannes Itten, who had developed the preparatory course, saw this as a compromise of his ideals and resigned in 1923. The craftsmen also criticized such close involvement with mass industry: the preparatory course now emphasized suitability of material and economy of production. In 1925, the Bauhaus Co. was founded to regulate the sale of (students') designs. From 1926 on, Bauhaus alumni oversaw most workshops.

Since the Bauhaus style represented such a radical departure from "traditional German" aesthetics, the Nazis forced the school to close in 1933. The first Bauhaus exhibition in New York opened in 1938.

◁ Marcel Breuer, *Armchair*, 1922/24. Oak, hand-woven wool. Museum of Modern Art, New York

▷ Marcel Breuer, *Chair B32*, 1928. Chrome-plated tubular steel, wood and cane. Museum of Modern Art, New York

◁ Joost Schmidt, **Exhibition Poster**, 1923

▷ Gunta Stölzl, *Tapestry* (section), 1924. Wool, silk, mercerized cotton and metal thread, 69½ x 45 in (176.5 x 114.3 cm). Museum of Modern Art, New York

◮ Marcel Breuer, *Club Chair B3 ("Wassily")*, Chrome-plated tubular steel and canvas. Museum of Modern Art, New York. The goal of the Bauhaus' carpentry workshop was to create affordable furniture with smaller dimensions.

▽ Marcel Breuer, *Lounge Chair B25*, 1929. Chrome-plated tubular steel, rattan and wood. Museum of Modern Art, New York

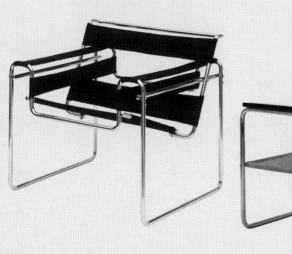

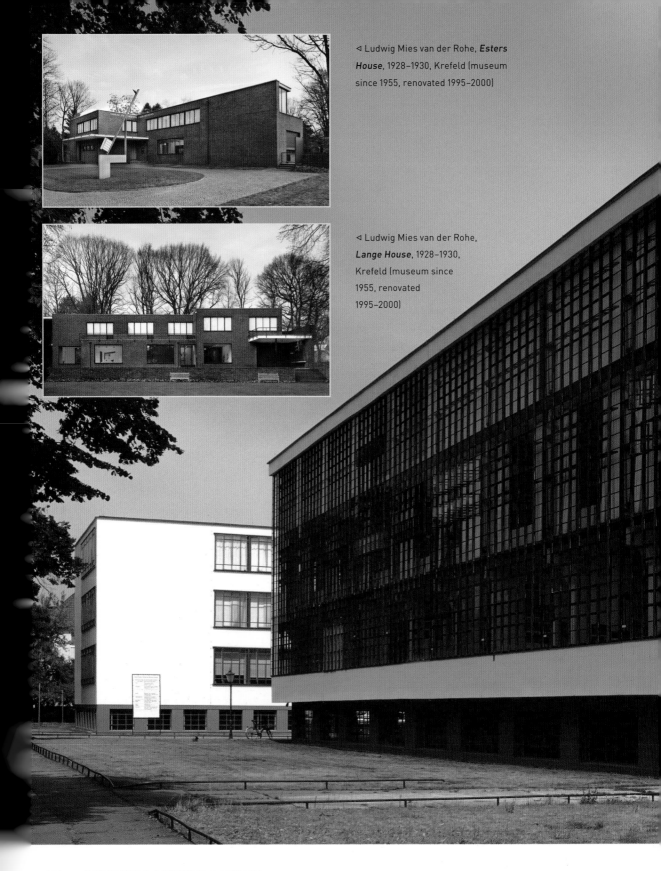

◁ Ludwig Mies van der Rohe, *Esters House*, 1928–1930, Krefeld (museum since 1955, renovated 1995–2000)

◁ Ludwig Mies van der Rohe, *Lange House*, 1928–1930, Krefeld (museum since 1955, renovated 1995–2000)

Bauhaus Architecture

In 1924, right-leaning parties in the Thuringian *Landtag* succeeded in having the Weimar Bauhaus closed. The school then moved to Dessau, where the new building designed by Gropius was ready for use in 1926. The Bauhaus's first classes in architecture followed in 1927, even though Gropius had designated the teaching of architecture as the school's most important task in its founding manifesto of 1919. Many alumni of the Bauhaus architecture workshop immigrated to Israel, which explains why the largest number of extant Bauhaus structures can be found in Tel Aviv.

With its strict objectivity, clear cubic elements, and white surfaces, Gropius's building in Dessau is the ultimate embodiment of Bauhaus architecture's ideals. The long "glass curtain" extending around the corner is the most striking characteristic of the workshop wing, and its interpenetration of exterior and interior space gives the building its transparence.

Mies van der Rohe, who from 1930 to 1933 served as the last Bauhaus director, had as early as 1919 designed a glass-exterior skyscraper for Berlin's Friedrichstraße. Using a clear, geometric formal language, he built villas in Krefeld for two silk manufacturers. As their story shows, Mies van der Rohe's conception of architecture withstood even their change of function.

◁ Walter Gropius, *Bauhaus (Workshop Wing)*, 1925/26, Dessau (rebuilt 1976)

Proportion

Beginning with the Bauhaus, architectural rationalism—the rational exploitation of land and low-cost design with partially prefabricated parts—led to a reduced formal language, with clear surfaces and right angles, that would determine the course of building in the twentieth century.

Even though the fanciful integration of the natural setting lends Frank Lloyd Wright's *Fallingwater* a dramatic effect, the multilayered house is cleanly ordered in block-shaped terraces and broad glass surfaces.

In the early 1940s, Le Corbusier devised his *Modulor*, a system of proportions inspired by the golden mean and based on the human body, and began to design residential blocks based on this system.

△ Frank Lloyd Wright, **Fallingwater**, 1936/37, Mill Run, Pennsylvania

▷ Le Corbusier, **Unité d'Habitation**, 1953–1955, Marseilles

▽ Le Corbusier, **Modulor**, published 1948. Theoretical scale of proportions

The intimacy of the private apartment was to fuse with a "vertical city" containing all the necessary establishments, so that its residents would only need to leave their homes to go to work. Le Corbusier never put this concept into practice, and it has failed miserably in many tower blocks built since.

Mies van der Rohe immigrated to the United States in 1938, where his work enjoyed considerable influence. In his post-Bauhaus architecture, he championed an architecture of severe, pure forms and balanced proportions.

The American Philip Johnson also propagated European rationalism. In the catalogue for an exhibition at the Museum of Modern Art, he christened it the "International Style."

Striking Structures

While the idea of high-rises with skeleton structures and maximal use of building space had been based on rational principles, the outer shells of these structures became ever more modeled, like the art deco Chrysler Building. Architects distanced themselves increasingly from the rationalism that, although dominant throughout the twentieth century, was perceived as too cold and emotionless. They embraced instead a notion already formulated by the expressionists: architecture as sculpture.

Wright achieved a sculpturally tangible architecture with the Guggenheim Museum. Its spindle-shaped, upwardly broadening

ramp, on which viewers pass by the museum's collection without using stairs, provides the central motif of the design. Even more systematically, Le Corbusier conceived the small pilgrimage church at Ronchamp, near Belfort, as a monumental, freestanding sculpture. Its exterior is dominated by the contorted surfaces of the roof, which rises on the southeast corner like a ship's bow. The effect of the interior is supported by the colored light falling through irregular windows that appear to have been chiseled into the church walls.

Finally, the legendary opera house designed by the Danish architect Utzon arches upwards like mussel shells, or swelling sails in Sydney's harbor.

Mondrian and *De Stijl*

In 1917, Mondrian, van Doesburg, Vantongerloo and others founded the artists' group and journal *De Stijl*. In their painting, they sought the universal principles of pictorial language. With the cubists' approach —no longer attempting the illusion of volume on a surface, but rather fragmenting it—as their starting point, Mondrian and his comrades took the Latin word *abstrahere* quite literally. By "pulling away" ever more

of the coincidental and unique in a picture, they reduced it to a rhythmic grid of horizontal and vertical lines that sometimes touch one another and sometimes even intersect. These lines join (completely or almost) to form primarily rectangular fields. Just as the few curves and diagonals in these grids are straightened, every field is assigned ever more distinctly one color. In the end, the only irreducible elements available for

this pictorial language are horizontal and vertical lines, right angles, and (for Mondrian) the primary colors red, yellow and blue, along with black for lines and white for the background. Every form, every color can in principle be produced from these elements.

The primary concern of *De Stijl* artists was to reduce the complexities of nature to pure and concretely formulated relationships. For

◁ Georges Vantongerloo, *Composition II, Indigo Violet Derived from Equilateral Triangle*, 1921. Oil on canvas mounted on cardboard, 13 x 14¾ in (33 x 37.5 cm). Museum of Modern Art, New York

▷ Theo van Doesburg, *Simultaneous Composition XXIV*, 1929. Oil on canvas, 19¾ x 19⅞ in (50.2 x 50.4 cm). Yale University Art Gallery, New Haven

Mondrian, this process consisted of three steps: the reduction of all the hues of nature to the primary colors, the deconstruction of color to surface, and the sectioning off of all colors from one another and into rectangular fields. Through this "abstract-real painting," as they called it, color and shape became an exact means of expression, and the most abstract of art ultimately became concrete.

◁ George Platt Lynes, *Artists in Exile, Exhibition at the Pierre Matisse Gallery, New York*, 1942. First row, l to r: Matta, Zadkine, Tanguy, Ernst, Chagall, Léger Second row, l to r: Breton, Mondrian, Masson, Ozenfant, Lipchitz, Tchelitchew, Seeligmann, Berman. Museum of Modern Art, New York

▷ Vladimir Tatlin, **Sailor (Self-Portrait)**, 1911. Tempera on canvas, 28⅛ x 21⅛ in (71.5 x 71.5 cm). Russian Museum, St. Petersburg. Even before he sought out Picasso in Paris in 1914, Tatlin's flat, ordered painting with its geometrization of form showed hints of cubist tendencies.

▷ Vladimir Tatlin, **Model for the Monument to the Third International**, 1919/20. Wood, iron, glass. Photo 1920. Never constructed, the 1300-ft (400-m) tower of steel and glass with its double helix was intended to symbolize the ascent of revolutionary ideas, only made possible by the constructive work of supports.

The Russian Avant-Garde

The Parisian avant-garde had been present in Moscow since 1910. Muscovite businessmen acquired works by Picasso and Matisse and opened their collections to the public. Influenced by cubism, Tatlin devised constructivism in accord with Malevich's suprematism. He added simple geometric figures with no figurative intent to distinct, emotionless constructions—in his opinion, the only appropriate means of expression for a new, technically rational world. With Popova at its center, a group of younger, like-minded artists found inspiration in the October Revolution of 1917, its early spirit of optimism still encouraging artistic utopias.

In addition to his constructivist painting, Rodchenko also explored photography and typography, since, as he put it, "One has to work for life, not for palaces, churches, cemeteries and museums." El Lissitzky began his *Proun* projects in 1919—"Proun" is an abbreviation of "Project for the Confirmation of the New" (*proekt utverzhdenya novogo*). With their cool precision, these works recollect engineering designs, and Lissitzky himself described them as "stations on the way to constructing a new form." Lissitzky was responsible for the close contact between Russian constructivism and the German Bauhaus, as well as with Mondrian and the Dutch artists of *De Stijl*.

▷ Lyubov Popova, *Painterly Architectonic*, 1917. Oil on canvas, 31½ x 38⅝ in (80 x 98 cm). Museum of Modern Art, New York

▽ Alexander Rodchenko, *Composition*, 1920. Oil on canvas, 28 x 14½ in (71 x 37 cm). Rodchenko Archive, Moscow. A popular component in Rodchenko's work consists of a circle with two straight lines that intersect at a sharp angle (like scissors, or a compass).

▽ El Lissitzky, *Proun 99*, 1923–1925. Oil on canvas, 4 ft 3 in x 6 ft 6 in (129 x 199 cm). Yale University Art Gallery, New Haven

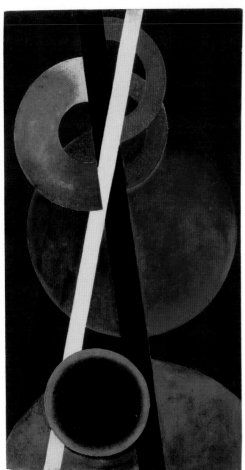

△ Kazimir Malevich, *Black Square*, 1924 (1915). Oil on canvas, 41¾ x 41¾ in (106 x 106 cm). Russian Museum, St. Petersburg

▽ Kazimir Malevich, *Suprematism (Supremus No. 58: Yellow and Black)*, 1916. Oil on canvas, 31¼ x 27¾ in (79.5 x 70.5 cm). Russian Museum, St. Petersburg

△ Kazimir Malevich, *Black Circle*, 1924 (1915). Oil on canvas, 41½ x 41½ in (106 x 106 cm). Russian Museum, St. Petersburg

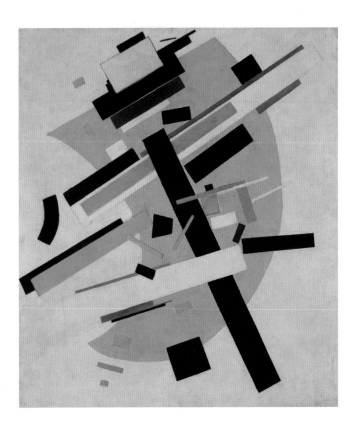

Nonobjective Sensation

Like other members of the Russian avant-garde, Malevich drew inspiration from cubism and futurism, which he tried to combine to form a sort of "cubo-futurism." In 1915 (he claimed 1913), he first used the term "suprematism," referring to the precedence (supremacy) "of pure feeling in creative art," a condition reached by completely liberating art from the ballast of figurative representation. His *Black Square*, first seen by the public at the end of 1915, was "the first form in which nonobjective feeling came to be expressed. The square = feeling, the white field = the void beyond this feeling" (Malevich).

The primal reality, the essence behind all visible objects, is the liber-

△ Kazimir Malevich, **Black Cross**, 1924
(1915). Oil on canvas, 41¾ x 41¾ in (106 x
106 cm). Russian Museum, St. Petersburg

△ Kazimir Malevich, **Red Square**, 1916/1917.
Oil on canvas, 20⅞ x 20⅞ in (53 x 53 cm).
Russian Museum, St. Petersburg

ated, nonobjective void, which leads
to the "essence sought by humanity."
In this way, painting becomes a purely
intellectual construction, beyond expression—and beyond description.
Elementary forms develop in variations and arrangements that evince
their unique, elementary harmonies.
Through his paintings and writings,
Malevich would also influence Western European geometric abstraction.

At first, Malevich's suprematism
was—like Tatlin's constructivism—
feted as the art of revolution. In the
1920s, however, it was supplanted
by the state doctrine of socialist
realism.

▷ Kazimir Malevich,
Head of a Peasant,
1928–1932. Oil on
plywood, 28¼ x
21⅛ in (71.7 x 53.8 cm).
Russian Museum,
St. Petersburg

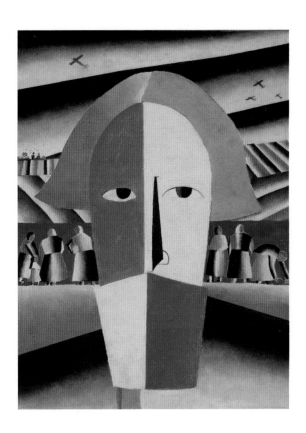

"Take Dada Seriously"

But Dada was nonsensical. Dada was absurd, often political, and always provocative. Dada was the systematic rejection of all contemporary bourgeois values. In 1915, young artists and writers, shocked and appalled by World War I, began using linguistic and pictorial devices in revolt against their fathers, their teachers, and the art and literature of the establishment. Dada was anti-art, exercising its influence into the 1920s and across national boundaries.

The preferred medium of Dada artists was the collage, incorporating different materials such as trash. With this "cheap art" made out of objects found by chance (*objets trouvés*), the Dadaists attacked the value that was too readily attached to art. In response to the uniqueness traditionally expected of the individual artwork, Marcel Duchamp released his "readymades," mass-produced objects he proclaimed to be art. "Art is useless and impossible to justify" (Francis Picabia), but the Dadaists availed themselves of every liberty in order to practice it.

△ Hans Arp, *Birds in an Aquarium*, ca. 1920. Painted wood relief, 9⅞ in (25 cm) high. Museum of Modern Art, New York

△ *First International Dada Fair*, July 30, 1920, Berlin. From left to right: Haussmann, Höch, Burchard, Baader, Herzfelde and his wife, Schmalhausen, Grosz, Heartfield

▷ Man Ray, *Gift*, 1958 (1921). Painted flatiron and tacks. Museum of Modern Art, New York

▷ Marcel Duchamp, *Fountain*, 1950 (1917), Readymade. Philadelphia Museum of Art, Philadelphia

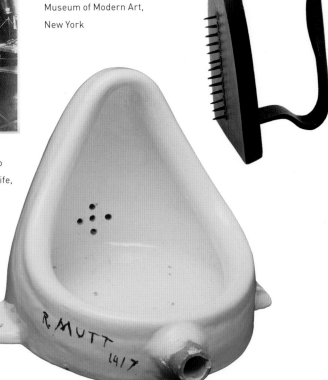

◁ Kurt Schwitters, *Merz Picture 32A. The Cherry Picture*, 1921. Collage, 36⅛ x 27¾ in (91.8 x 70.5 cm). Museum of Modern Art, New York

On the Border

What so impressed Paris's bohemian artists about the painting of Henri Rousseau, a customs officer and transitional figure of the modern, was the self-evident timelessness expressed in his art—making manifest long-past, magical dream worlds, and executing them with lapidary intensity. On the occasion of the 1908 banquet organized by Picasso in Rousseau's honor, the latter exclaimed, "We are the two greatest painters of this era: you in the Egyptian style and I (Rousseau) in the modern style!"

Marc Chagall's canvases, evoking the experiences of Jewish and peasant life in Russia, evince a mindset that reveals itself only reluctantly to the viewer, as the magic of

△ Henri Rousseau, *The Sleeping Gypsy*, 1897. Oil on canvas, 4 ft 3 in x 6 ft 6 in (129.5 x 200.7 cm). Museum of Modern Art, New York

▽ Marc Chagall, *Loneliness*, 1933. Oil on canvas, 3 ft 4 in x 5 ft 6 in (102 x 169 cm). Tel Aviv Museum of Art, Tel Aviv. Over the exiled Jew with his Torah and the cow with its fiddle hovers a redeeming angel.

fantasy often obscures any definitive explanation of individual motifs and their contexts.

Moving in the visionary sphere between surrealism and a willful, magically psychologizing realism that frequently crosses into the realm of the erotic, Balthus's logic of pictorial composition shows the influence of Renaissance role models like Piero della Francesca. He disdained human beings, whom he reviled for "constantly changing stations in the most idiotic way," and marveled instead at the inertia of a pebble. Miró's apparently cheerful paintings often conceal a magical, uncanny element. The "primitive" or "naïve" artists like Rousseau created their own individual universes of signs, in which humanity vegetation, and the cosmos intermingle.

△ Balthus (Balthazar Klossowski de Rola), *The Mountain (Summer)*, 1936/37. Oil on canvas, 8 ft 2 in x 12 ft (248.9 x 365.8 cm). The Metropolitan Museum of Art, New York

▽ Joan Miró, *Animated Landscape*, 1927. Oil on canvas, 4 ft 3 in x 6 ft 4 in (129.5 x 195 cm). The Metropolitan Museum of Art, New York

The Marvelous

In order to see the marvelous, surrealists advocated the abandonment
of reason, education, morality and
aesthetics. This state can be achieved
in dreams, hallucinations, under the
influence of drugs, or through "auto-
matic" processes in which several
people work on a story or drawing
that remains hidden. Pictures resulting from this process arise from the
(collective) unconscious (which at the
time was being investigated by the
young discipline of psychoanalysis)
and, for the surrealists, were more
authentic than any consciously executed artwork. Surrealism, founded in
1924, was not simply a style of writing
or painting. It was a way of life.

   Some surrealists had already discovered the absurd through Dadaism.

They had used the absurd to provoke the bourgeoisie, which, with its ideology of honor and patriotism, they held responsible for World War I. In surrealist compositions, they were reacting to the mendacity of consciousness. They considered themselves successors to the fantastic visions of Hieronymus Bosch, Johann Heinrich Füssli and Francisco de Goya, and most recently of Giorgio de Chirico, whose "metaphysical" painting was a direct influence for many.

The marvelous took many forms. Almost secretively, Max Ernst animated organic and inorganic objects. Playing with the unexpected, Magritte differentiated between the invisible and the unseen. Dalí interlaced multiple compositions in one painting, where they make themselves visible to the viewer as if in sequence.

◁ Giorgio de Chirico, *The Song of Love*, 1914. Oil on canvas, 28¾ x 23⅜ in (73 x 59.1 cm). Museum of Modern Art, New York

◁ Salvador Dalí, *Invisible Afghan with the Apparition on the Beach of the Face of García Lorca in the Form of a Fruit Dish with Three Figs*, 1938. Oil on wood, 7½ x 9½ in (19.2 x 24.1 cm). Private collection

Postwar is Prewar

Deeply shaken by the horrors of World War I, many German artists watched as ever more basic ethical values disappeared in the whirl of the Golden Twenties, and they saw the old social order falling apart. With technique recalling the Old Masters, they revealed a sobering reality. Artists were chroniclers, accusers, satirists—this was no time for paintings meant merely as décor. In 1925, an exhibition in Mannheim displayed their *Neue Sachlichkeit* ("New Objectivity").

In his paintings, Grosz unmasked the intrigues of the rich and the hollowness of nationalist pathos. In so doing, he pilloried war profiteers as well as mendacious, phrasemongering politicians and militarists.

Schad, apparently the most objective of these committed artists, dissected reality with a cool detachment and unsettling sensibility.

Dix was more of an admonisher than an accuser. Although like Goya, he depicted people in his painted and graphic works about the war as both victims and perpetrators, he portrayed the gruesome aftermath of the war as states of being. As early as 1933, he was dismissed from his post as a professor in Dresden. In his *Seven Deadly Sins*, disgusted and clairvoyant, he augured the coming disaster.

▷ Otto Dix, *The Seven Deadly Sins*, 1933. Oil and tempera on wood, 5 ft 9 in x 3 ft 11 in (179 x 120 cm). Staatliche Kunsthalle, Karlsruhe

▷ George Grosz, *The Pillars of Society*, 1926. Oil on canvas, 6 ft 6 in x 3 ft 5 in (200 x 108 cm). Nationalgalerie, Berlin. With drastic exaggeration of clichés regarding social elites, Grosz laid bare the powers controlling the Weimar Republic.

▽ Christian Schad, *Operation*, 1929. Oil on canvas, 4 ft 1 in x 3 ft 1 in (125 x 95 cm). Lenbachhaus, Munich

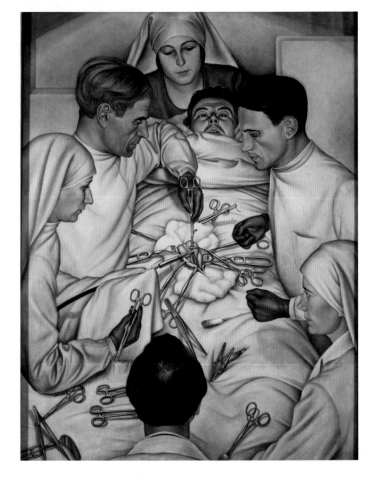

Max Beckmann

Beckmann presented himself as an indifferent observer, but the qualities that served his portraits so well make his large, figure-heavy compositions hard to tolerate. In *Night*, in which the brutal attack on a family becomes a metaphor for the bestiality of a human nature that neither victim nor perpetrator can escape, the viewer is spared nothing.

While his early style shows the influence of German impressionism, the experience of World War I hardened his graphic design, especially, in an expressionist manner. In the content of his pictures, he criticized social wrongs similar to those depicted by Grosz and Dix in the contexts of Dada and the *Neue Sachlichkeit*, but his images of a

▽ Max Beckmann, *Night* (Plate 7 of *Hell*), 1919. Lithograph (after the painting in the Kunstsammlung Nordrhein-Westfalen, Düsseldorf), 21⅞ x 27⅞ in (55.6 x 70.2 cm). Museum of Modern Art, New York

world completely out of balance are deeply coded.

Beginning with his works created in the 1920s, Beckmann's style is characterized by a distinct individualism and an expressive, contour-oriented framework. His primary theme is that of humanity threatened in an apocalyptic world. In the triptych *Departure*, martyred life, physical and spiritual suffering stand on the wings, contrasted with the comforting liberation from the torments of existence in the middle. The king and queen with their child—which according to Beckmann symbolizes freedom as the most valuable treasure—are transported by a masked ferryman to an unseen but certainly better world. The fish, the only object that appears in all three panels, is an important leitmotif. In Beckmann's personal symbolism, the fish represents the life force, occasionally

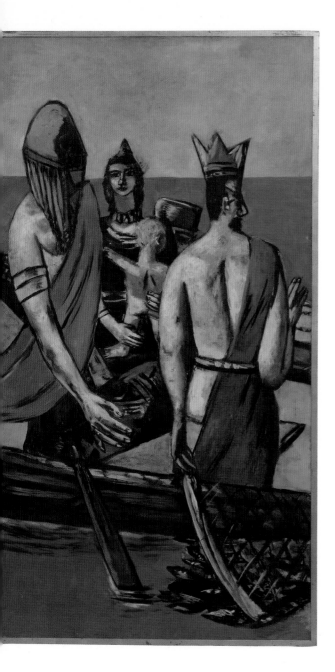

with sexual connotations. Captive fish in the wrong hands therefore present a serious warning.

Executed before and after the Nazis' seized power in Germany in 1933, the triptych may contain references to a dark future, but Beckmann always combined the personal with the universal. "Departure, yes departure, from the illusions of life toward the essential realities that lie hidden beyond. But in the end, this true of all my pictures" (Beckmann).

△ Max Beckmann, *Departure*, triptych, 1932, 1933–1935. Side panels 7 ft x 3 ft 3 in (215.3 x 99.7 cm), center panel 7 ft x 3 ft 9 in (215.3 x 115.2 cm). Museum of Modern Art, New York. To prevent their confiscation by the Nazis, Beckmann labeled the backs of the panels with innocuous references to Shakespeare.

Painted Horror: Guernica

On April 24, 1937, warplanes under German command bombed the Basque city of Guernica on the northern coast of Spain, taking no heed at all of the civilian population. The German planes were acting in support of Generalissimo Franco, the leader of the fascist revolt against the elected republican government. The attack prompted outrage worldwide.

In January 1937, the legitimate Spanish government had commissioned Picasso to execute a representative painting for the International Exposition in Paris. Inspired by newspaper photos, he decided—like Goya in his *Third of May 1808*—to commemorate this fateful event for Spain. Both artists, although using completely different formal and compositional means, succeeded in transcending the historical moment, creating timeless, universally valid representations of the horrors of meaningless, inhuman wars.

△ Pablo Picasso, *Guernica*, June 4, 1937. Oil on canvas, 137½ x 305¾ in (349.3 x 776.6 cm). Museo Nacional Centro de Arte Reina Sofia, Madrid

In his painting, Picasso united the formal fragmentation of cubism not only with the clearly contoured, almost classical aesthetic acquired on his 1917 journey to Italy, but also with the deformation that had evolved in his surrealism-influenced works. In occasionally interlocking, partial views of a building's interior and exterior, the picture—reduced to black, white, and gray—shows human beings and animals in pain and despair. The screaming mother with her dead child; those dying prostrate on the ground; the burning, falling woman —all represent the sufferings of the civilian population. The bull and the wounded, terrified horse remind the viewer that even animals cannot escape this insanity. The shattered statue of a warrior with a flower in its sword-bearing hand; the candle-carrying woman and the ceiling lamp, bringing the disaster to light; these provide perhaps a faint glimmer of hope.

△ John Heartfield, *The Spirit of Geneva*, Title page of the *Arbeiter-Illustrierte-Zeitung* (A-I-Z), Berlin, November 27, 1932

△ John Heartfield, *They twist and turn and call themselves German judges*, from the *Arbeiter-Illustrierte-Zeitung* (A-I-Z), Prague, October 19, 1933. The Dadaist Heartfield is considered the founder and main proponent of the satirical political photomontage.

△ Joan Miró, *Help Spain*, 1937. Poster design after stencil print, 9¾ x 7⅝ in (24.8 x 19.4 cm)

Foreboding and Resistance

After the German aerial attack on Guernica in 1937, there was no longer any doubt about the Nazis' real intentions. All those who had warned of the evil consequences to follow Hitler's rise to power in 1933 were now proved right. Artists too had openly foretold of the catastrophe looming on the horizon, or had engaged in resistance.

As early as 1932, John Heartfield (Helmut Herzfeld) had shown with his provocative, Dada-influenced photomontages that even keeping silent in the face of the Nazis would endanger peace in Europe. His work against militarism and fascism earned him forced exile from Germany in 1933.

Inspired by Otto Dix's craftsmanlike, precise brushwork, Richard Oelze created surreal, magical imagery in his paintings. His picture *Expectation* seems to anticipate the dismay of emigration and war as dark clouds shrouding the horizon.

Like his compatriot Picasso, Miró completed a painting for the Spanish Republic's pavilion at the 1937 International Exposition in Paris. He also designed posters for Republican Spain.

Kokoschka, an Austrian who fled to London after the 1938 *Anschluss* (the annexation of Austria into the German Reich) and lived through the aerial bombardment of his new home, did not merely paint a superficial indictment of the Nazi terror. Rather, his *Anschluss—Alice in Wonderland* is a cynical reckoning with the Western powers' earlier policy of appeasement toward Hitler's regime. Mimicking the gestures of the three monkeys, the "air raid wardens" refuse to involve themselves in the fate of the naïve Alice who, wearing the armband of a Red Cross worker, is depicted as a prisoner behind barbed wire.

△ Richard Oelze, *Expectation*, 1935–1936. Oil on canvas, 32⅛ x 39⅝ in (81.6 x 100.6 cm). Museum of Modern Art, New York

▷ Oskar Kokoschka, *Anschluss—Alice in Wonderland*, 1941–1942. Oil on canvas, 25 x 29 in (63.5 x 73.6 cm). Wiener Städtische Wechselseitige Versicherungsgesellschaft, Vienna

"Degenerate Art"

Beginning in 1933, diverse exhibitions with this title opened throughout Germany, culminating in the (in)famous 1937 show at the Munich Hofgarten that would later travel to other large German cities. The exhibition reviled any art that was not consistent with official Nazi propaganda. Highest on the list of targets were works by impressionists, expressionists, fauvists, cubists, Dadaists, and abstract artists; these were held up as degenerate and decadent, and therefore as inferior and damaging to the nation. The exhibition's defamatory arrangement of texts and pictures was calculated to create an impression of irredeemable chaos, connected to a sense of satisfaction in the well-earned proscription of this "art." In the accompanying guide to the exhibition, works by prominent artists were shown next to art produced by the mentally ill, and the works of Jewish artists were dismissed as "pathetic efforts." Consequences of the prohibition

of avant-garde art included the seizure of countless artworks, their removal from museums, and not uncommonly, their destruction. In 1939, 125 examples of "degenerate art" were spared obliteration so that they could be auctioned off for foreign currency at the Galerie Fischer in Lucerne—a revealing example of Nazi double standards. Sooner or later, all "degenerate" artists were forbidden to exhibit, and some even to paint.

Artists labeled "degenerate" include: Ernst Barlach, Willi Baumeister, Max Beckmann, Marc Chagall, Lovis Corinth, Otto Dix, Max Ernst, Lyonel Feininger, Otto Freundlich, George Grosz, Erich Heckel, Karl Hofer, Johannes Itten, Alexej von Jawlensky, Wassily Kandinsky, Ernst Ludwig Kirchner, Paul Klee, Oskar Kokoschka, Wilhelm Lehmbruck, El Lissitzky, Franz Marc, László Moholy-Nagy, Piet Mondrian, Otto Mueller, Emil Nolde, Max Pechstein, Oskar Schlemmer, Karl Schmidt-Rottluff, Kurt Schwitters, and many others.

△ Poster for the exhibition "Degenerate Art," Munich, 1936

▷ Cover of the guide to the exhibition "Degenerate Art," 1937. Photo: Otto Freundlich, *Der neue Mensch*, 1912

▽ North wall in the exhibition "Degenerate Art" (with the slogan of the "First International Dada Fair," 1920, Berlin). Archäologisches Institut, Munich 1937

◁+◁◁ Guide to the exhibition "Degenerate Art," 1937. Page 7, "Racial Cross-Section," and page 25, "Two 'Saints!'"

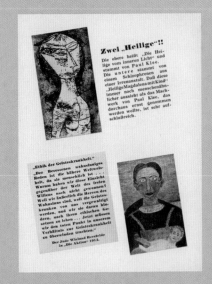

ENTARTETE

"KUNST"

Ausstellungsführer

PREIS 30 PFG.

Propaganda

Even before World War II, the totalitarian regimes of Europe measured their strength in the visual arts. In an excessive neoclassicism with a tendency toward the gigantic, their apparent objective was to impress through bulk alone. In 1934, after a brief period of creative freedom, socialist realism supplanted the Soviet avant-garde—always held in suspicion by Lenin—as the official state artistic style. Brodsky's almost private, naturalistic portrait of Lenin shows the recently deceased Soviet leader at work as the legitimate interpreter of party doctrine.

Mukhina's clearly more pathos-laden statue, created for the Paris Exposition of 1937, monumentalized the working class and peasantry,

△ Isaac Brodsky, *Lenin in Smolny*, 1930. Oil on canvas, 6 ft 3 in x 9 ft 5 in (190 x 287 cm). Tretyakov Gallery, Moscow

◁ Vera Mukhina, *Worker and Kolkhoz Woman*, 1936. Bronze, 5 ft 2 in (158.5 cm) high. Russian Museum, St. Petersburg. The version Mukhina created for the World's Fair in Paris was made of millimeter-thin, stainless aircraft steel and stood 78 ft (24 m) high.

with hammer and sickle held aloft, as pillars of the Soviet state.

Hitler's favorite sculptor Breker was responsible for the profane Pietà with muscular gesturing and hollow pathos. Even as a preliminary cast, it made a splash in the media, since positioning in the correct light imbued it with illusory size. (The drapery between the naked heroes was meant to smother any hint of tabooed homosexual love.)

In his *Judgment of Paris*, Saliger depicted the mortal Paris as a member of the Hitler Youth, granting the viewer (and the party officials who commissioned the work) a voyeuristic peek at the three naked goddesses, with a German landscape as the backdrop. In their classical (Aryan) beauty, they appear robust, healthy, available and fertile.

◁ Arno Breker, *Comrades*, 1940. Contemporary photograph of the plaster cast of a relief for a planned 394-ft (120-m) tall triumphal arch in Berlin.

▷ Ivo Saliger, *The Judgment of Paris*, 1939. Oil on canvas, 5 ft 3 in x 6 ft 6¾ in (160 x 200 cm). Oberfinanzdirektion, Munich

◁ **International Exposition, Paris, 1937.** View of the German and Soviet pavilions at the edge of the Trocadéro exposition grounds (contemporary photograph).

The American Scene

At the beginning of the 1920s, the Unitded States was largely cut off from the artistic developments taking place in Europe. By the end of the decade, the great stock market crash of 1929 and the Great Depression took their toll. For American artists of this period, being "modern" did not necessarily involve being against tradition. Rather, they tried to modernize that which was customary. Thus arose the American Scene, a style of painting whose goal was the realistic portrayal of contemporary American life. Everyday objects and occurrences became worthy of depiction, from a bottle of Odol mouthwash to poetic allusions. According to Davis, "A picture should be as romantic as a streetcar conductor and nothing more."

An unnaturally sharp light illuminates Hopper's paintings, casting long shadows, and seeming to freeze the forms in the composition. With their few, solitary figures, his scenes of American cities appear to be extinct; they transmit a feeling of loneliness, silence and human isolation.

Shahn, who had grown up in an Armenian neighborhood in Brooklyn, represented a newer, more socially engaged American art. In 1933, he collaborated with Diego Rivera to create murals for the Rockefeller Center. The poor, ugly, petit-bourgeois/proletarian reality of backstreet New York was the central theme of this group of artists, mockingly referred to as the "Ash Can School." Bellows' forty-six paintings, drawings and prints of boxing are unflinchingly realistic.

▽ Stuart Davis, *Odol*, 1924. Oil on cardboard, 24 x 18 in (60.9 x 45.6 cm). Museum of Modern Art, New York. In his diary, Davis writes that a picture must consist of "an alphabet of letters, numbers, canned goods labels, tobacco labels."

▽ Charles Demuth, *The Figure 5 in Gold*, 1928. Oil on cardboard, 35½ x 30 in (90.2 x 76.2 cm). The Metropolitan Museum of Art, New York. This work, inspired by William Carlos Williams' poem about the figure 5 in gold on a fire engine driving through the night, would in turn provide inspiration for pop art.

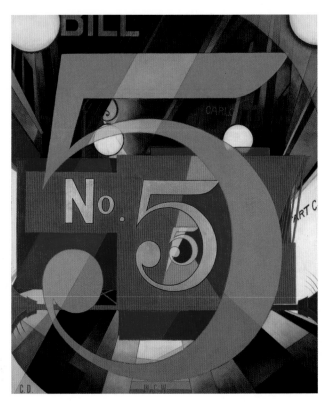

△ Edward Hopper, *Gas*, 1940. Oil on canvas, 26¼ x 40¼ in (66.7 x 102.2 cm). Museum of Modern Art, New York

▽ Ben Shahn, *Handball*, 1939. Gouache on paperboard, 22¾ x 31¼ in (57.8 x 79.4 cm). Museum of Modern Art, New York. This picture and another depicting a lonely boy playing in front of a dismal wall were acquired by the museum directly from a much-noticed exhibition at the Julian Levy Gallery in 1940.

▽ George Bellows, *Dempsey and Firpo*, 1923/24. Lithograph, 18⅛ x 22⅜ in (46 x 56.9 cm). Museum of Modern Art, New York. This image portrays the instant at which the Argentinean challenger Luis Firpo knocked the champion Jack Dempsey out of the ring. Dempsey went on to win the match.

Revolutionaries and Muralistas

The incorporation of the visual arts into the social renewal following the Mexican Revolution led to *muralismo*, a movement whose hallmark was the socio-politically committed mural. Upon receiving commissions for public buildings, the leading *muralistas* (Rivera, Orozco and Siqueiros) developed a powerful, sometimes symbolic pictorial language to represent their main theme of Mexican history, especially the *conquista* and its devastating effects on the native population. This human tragedy, ever-recurring in the historical context, inevitably led in their work to a new, better, fairer utopia filled with strong, chthonic, happy people. In the 1930s, the *muralistas* also carried out commissions for public buildings in the United States.

Frida Kahlo, the revolutionary wife of Rivera and passionate collector of pre-Columbian Mexican art, taught herself how to paint. Surviving a bus wreck in 1925, she was so seriously injured that she repeatedly had to take to her bed for months at a time; it was to pass the long hours in bed that she first began to paint. The consequences of her injuries were lifelong disability and childlessness, both of which she worked through in her autobiographical art. Most of her pictures are therefore self-portraits, and are often harrowing testaments to her will to survive.

▽ José Clemente Orozco, *Zapatistas*, 1931. Oil on canvas, 45 x 55 in (114.3 x 139.7 cm). Museum of Modern Art, New York. Apart from his major works for the university and government buildings in Guadalajara, Orozco also painted panels that grew increasingly abstract with time.

▷ Diego Rivera, *Sugar Cane*, 1930. Fresco, 57⅛ x 94⅛ in (145.1 x 239.1 cm). The Philadelphia Museum of Art, Philadelphia. While living in Paris (1911–1920), Rivera was impressed by Cézanne and the cubists. On a journey to Italy (1920–1921), he discovered Renaissance fresco painting.

△ David Alfaro Siqueiros, *Echo of a Scream*, 1937. Enamel on wood, 48 x 36 in (121.9 x 91.4 cm). Museum of Modern Art, New York. ▷▷ Frida Kahlo, *The Two Fridas*, 1939. Oil on canvas, 68¼ x 68 in (173.5 x 173 cm). Museo de Arte Moderno, Mexico City. This work shows Kahlo's essence as a combination of discrete Mexican and European selves.

Turmoil

European intellectuals and avant-garde artists, persecuted at home, had been arriving in the United States since the mid-1930s, and the outbreak of World War II only served to increase their numbers. The surrealists André Breton and Max Ernst especially left their mark while in exile with their "psychic automatism": with the aid of Sigmund Freud's notion of free association, the unconscious was to reveal itself in preferably "thoughtless" scrawlings, uncontrolled by reason, and thus become a source of free, creative work. Some American artists heard "uncontrolled," but understood "abstract."

The abstract expressionists (in spite of their name, they did not always create nonobjective art) transferred the actual creative process from the idea of content to the performance of the painting technique, which would come to be a free, dynamically flowing calligraphy. Pollock invented drip painting, in which he would pour, spray, and dribble his colors in a partially random action onto the canvas that he had laid out flat on the floor.

▷ Jackson Pollock, *One: Number 31, 1950*, 1950. Oil and enamel paint on canvas, 8 ft 10 in x 17 ft 5 in (269.5 x 530.8 cm). Museum of Modern Art, New York

▽ Arshile Gorky, *The Leaf of the Artichoke Is an Owl*, 1944. Oil on canvas, 28 x 36 in (71.1 x 91.2 cm). Museum of Modern Art, New York

◁ Hans Hofmann, *Spring*, 1944/45. Oil on wood, 11¼ x 14⅛ in (28.5 x 35.7 cm). Museum of Modern Art, New York

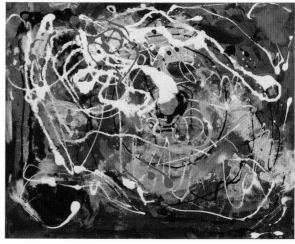

In "action painting," the canvas was no longer simply the carrier of the image; it was elevated to an apparently limitless space of action, on which a purely gestural event took place. The artist chose the type, tone and sequence of colors, and decided —in perhaps the last connection to traditional painting—on the ductus, or level of energy and intensity, with which the colors came into contact with (or left untouched) the canvas.

◁ Franz Kline, *Chief*, 1950. Oil on canvas, 58⅜ x 73½ in (148.3 x 186.7 cm). Museum of Modern Art, New York

▷ Barnett Newman, *Vir Heroicus Sublimis*, 1950–1951. Oil on canvas, 7 ft 11 in x 17 ft 8 in (242.2 x 541.7 cm). Museum of Modern Art, New York. Where no more myths and legends remain, according to Newman, the artist must create a sublime art that reveals humanity as heroic and noble.

The Sublime

While a number of the abstract expressionists were proponents of gestural abstraction ("action paint-ing"), others chose an abstraction primarily expressed in color. They applied colors in countless thin, flat layers, without the slightest hint of the formal structures that could be misunderstood as attempts at spatial illusion. In an expansive format, color field painting can virtually grow outside of itself. The intensity of the color suggests the expansion of the colored surface beyond the canvas's edge. For Newman, "sublime" meant the experience of exaltation made possible in the viewer by the per-ception of gigantic, vivid and luminous fields of color. Viewed up close, the narrow strips of color can no longer be overlooked; they act as fault lines, or as reinforcers of the separate experiential spaces. The goal of this art should, according to Newman, "be vision and inspiration."

Beginning around 1948, Rothko created characteristic, large-format compositions consisting of canvas-filling, vague fields of color with diffuse, sfumato borders. Thanks to a special glaze technique, these fields seem to hover before the colored background, achieving their suggestive power through the magic, meditative accords and finely tuned contrasts of color.

△ Mark Rothko, *No. 3/No. 13*, 1949. Oil on canvas, 85⅜ x 65 in (216.5 x 164.8 cm). Museum of Modern Art, New York

◁ Ad Reinhardt, *Red Abstract*, 1952. Oil on canvas, 5 ft x 3 ft 4 in (152.4 x 101.3 cm). Yale University Art Gallery, New Haven. In Reinhardt's compositions, scarcely perceptible nuances of one color cross each other in geometric forms. His later works show differences only through gradated light absorption.

With his numerous texts and statements, Reinhardt became one of the most significant inspirations for a theoretical redefinition of art. He answered the repeated complaint that abstract pictures do not represent anything with a biting caricature.

Abstraction after 1945

After the cultural devastation wrought by the Nazis and other totalitarian regimes, especially in Europe, the only possibility for the arts was a comprehensive new beginning. The victorious US troops brought with them more than just CARE Packages and the "economic miracle." They brought jazz (previously denounced as degenerate "negro music") and the art of the American avant-garde: abstract expressionism. Kandinsky, Malevich and Mondrian had indeed developed abstraction, but their art had not had sufficient time to establish itself in Europe. Abstract art's success in the USA, where New York succeeded Paris as the world's artistic capital, now spread back to Europe.

◁ Wols (Alfred Otto Wolfgang Schulze), *Mother of Pearl*, 1949. Oil on canvas, 25⅝ x 19⅝ in (65 x 50 cm). Private collection

▷ Jean Fautrier, *Variation on a Rectangle*, 1957. Oil and paper on canvas, 18⅛ x 21⅝ in (46 x 55 cm). Private collection

▷▷ Ben Nicholson, *1949*. Oil and pencil on paper, 9 x 11¾ in (23 x 30 cm). Private collection

◁ Lucio Fontana, *Spatial Concept: Expectations*, 1960. Slashed canvas and gauze, 39½ x 31⅝ in (100.3 x 80.3 cm). Museum of Modern Art, New York

▷ Willi Baumeister, *Kessiu (Scherzo)*, 1954. Oil with synthetic resin and sand on hard fiberboard, 21¼ x 25⅝ in (54 x 65 cm). Galleria Nazionale d'Arte Moderna, Rome. In his *Kessiu* or "black rock pictures," Baumeister varied the motif of the black monolith with differently colored surfaces as well as colorful or monotone cheerful symbols.

Now abstract art became the universal language, at least in the Western world; the Cold War was also being fought in the galleries. Every manifestation of realism aroused bad memories of socialist realism and the art of the Nazis, and thus fell flat.

Once it had started, abstract art in Europe went in gratifyingly different directions. Wols' lyrical-surreal tachism (*tache* = "stain") and Baumeister's informal (formless) painting availed themselves of seemingly prehistoric but invented signs. Fautrier's pastel-colored entities, spackled onto fissured backgrounds, coexist with Fontana's slashed, space-opening canvases. The English scene found expression in Nicholson's geometrically constructed compositions. One characteristic of post-war abstract painting is its reluctance to let itself be hemmed in by traditionally distinct media classifications, for example combining painting with relief.

▷ Wilhelm Lehmbruck, *Kneeling Woman*, 1911. Cast stone, 69½ in (176.5 cm) high. Museum of Modern Art, New York. Seeing a cast of this statue, which had first been shown in 1911 at Paris's Grand Palais, the Nazis found it too emaciated and deformed to suit their feminine ideal. In 1937–1938, it was, along with other works by Lehmbruck, pronounced "degenerate," confiscated, and seriously damaged.

The Human Form

In the plastic arts, the human form has always been a central motif. Narrative was reduced to a minimum, individual characteristics were deemphasized in favor of universality and harmonious proportion, as in classical antiquity. The school-determining classicisms of the nineteenth century led to formulaic rigidity, and impressionistic surfaces led to no new clarification of form. Sculptors inspired by the breakthroughs in painting at the start of the twentieth century thus sought a new sculptural language. After classicizing beginnings, Lehmbruck devised an expressive style with extended, expansive forms in which the corporeal framework replaces bodily volume. Barlach also combined expressivity and occasionally the representation of passionate feelings with simple, monumental form.

Before World War II, the Swiss artist Giacometti created surrealistic,

▷ Ernst Barlach, *Singing Man*, 1928. Bronze, 19½ in (49.5 cm) high. Museum of Modern Art, New York. Denounced as "degenerate" in 1937, 381 of Barlach's works were confiscated by the Nazis.

spatial constructions that recollect dream images and hallucinations. In 1940, he began to mold his groups of extremely thin and overextended figures. It was not corporeality that interested him, but rather the balance of power between the figure and the space it occupied. His bodies convey a sense of the forsakenness of human existence in the void of space.

Starting with block-like figures showing the influence of Egyptian and pre-Columbian American art, the English sculptor Moore changed his style to create more extended bodies. His new style, combining objectivity and abstraction, deeply influenced European sculpture after 1945.

▷ Alberto Giacometti, **Three Men Walking (II)**, 1949. Bronze, 30⅛ in (72 cm) high. The Metropolitan Museum of Art, New York

◁ Henry Moore, **King and Queen**, 1952/53. Bronze, 5 ft 5 in (164 cm) high. The Henry Moore Foundation, Much Hadham. This pair, of which five casts exist, was originally created for a barren moor in Scotland.

△ Alexander Calder, **Untitled**, 1939. Painted sheet aluminum and steel wire, 14⅝ in (37.1 cm) high. Museum of Modern Art, New York

◁ Antoine Pevsner, **The Dancer**, 1927/28. Brass and celluloid, 31⅞ in (81 cm) high. Yale University Museum of Art, New Haven

◁◁ Constantin Brancusi, **Bird in Space**, 1923. Marble, 56¾ in (144.1 cm) high. The Metropolitan Museum of Art, New York

▷ Eduardo Chillida, *Anvil of Dreams XIII*,
1953/54. Iron and wood, 29⅛ in (74 cm) high.
Fundación Telefónica, Madrid

▽ Barbara Hepworth, *String Figure (Curlew)*,
1956. Brass, strings, and wood, 15 in (38.1 cm)
high. Private collection

The Essential Form

Painting, which creates an illusory two-dimensional world, "only" needs to abandon the object in order to be abstract. Sculpture, on the other hand, always consists of real, corporeally tangible form, and is therefore in and of itself fundamentally objective. If one reduces detail, as in archaic Greek or African sculpture, one approaches the essential form, its proportion, and its dialogue with the space it occupies. In a singularly extreme reduction and concentration of form, the Romanian sculptor Brancusi achieved self-containing but also symbolically laden basic forms. "Simplicity is not an objective in art, but one achieves simplicity despite one's self by entering into the real sense of things" (Brancusi).

Despite his commitment to constructivism, the Russian sculptor Pevsner often had an elementary natural form in mind as well. He made hollows and breaches—forms through which air can flow—the central elements of his works.

Through her use of tensile strings, the open, mostly nature-mimetic sculptures of the English artist Hepworth manifested a lively dynamization.

In his mobiles, the American Calder finally achieved "abstractions that are like nothing in life except in their manner of reacting" (Calder). A new sculptural medium—movement—was created.

The Basque sculptor Chillida was also more interested in space than in volume. Through the process of forging, he educed extensive, semiotically functioning abstract formal divisions out of a solid, uniform block of iron. He also frequently combined and contrasted raw steel with other materials such as wood or stone.

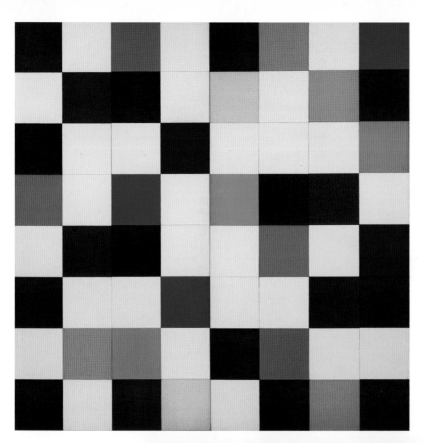

Geometry Meets Optics

In the 1950s, an emphatically geometric, "hard-edged" style of abstract painting developed in the USA alongside color field painting and in contradistinction to the gestural abstraction of action painting. Its means of representation was defined by sharply contrasting fields of color. Kelly, the leading exponent of hard-edge painting, painted in a style incorporating starkly monochrome, clear geometric forms. By combining individual panels—rectangles, squares, rhombuses—to make wall-sized installations, he removed the boundaries between painting, sculpture, and architecture.

With Stella's shaped canvases, the very shape of the artwork became the image-carrying object, thereby

△ Ellsworth Kelly, *Colors for a Large Wall*, 1951. Oil on canvas, mounted on 64 wood panels, 7 ft 11 in x 7 ft 11 in (240 x 240 cm). Museum of Modern Art, New York

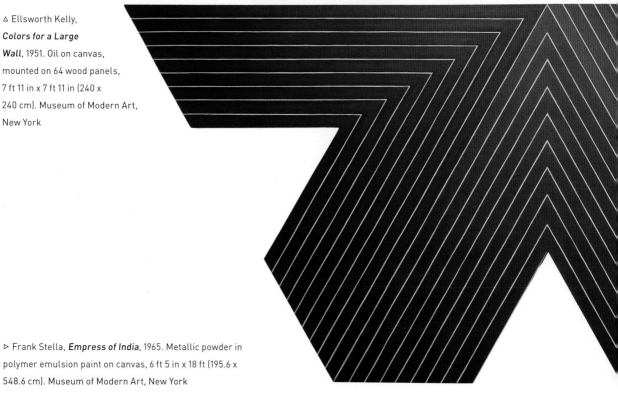

▷ Frank Stella, *Empress of India*, 1965. Metallic powder in polymer emulsion paint on canvas, 6 ft 5 in x 18 ft (195.6 x 548.6 cm). Museum of Modern Art, New York

assuming its matrices and structures in its outer shape and allowing a pure correlation between the work's form and content—and a protrusion into space.

Another form that evolved out of geometric abstraction in the 1960s was op art. In the work of the English artist Riley, purely geometric forms were transformed into optically shifting apparitions of color and light. Especially in op painting, an optical illusion is achieved on the canvas that exploits the lassitude of the human eye. In the eye, the regular and at the same time rhythmically distorted rows of dots or lines become an apparently three-dimensional pictorial space in motion.

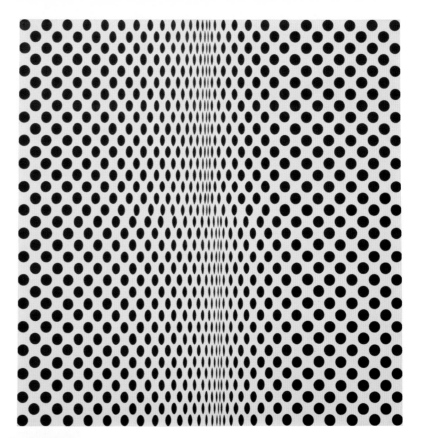

△ Bridget Riley, *Fission*, 1963. Tempera on composition board, 35 x 34 in (88.8 x 86.2 cm). Museum of Modern Art, New York

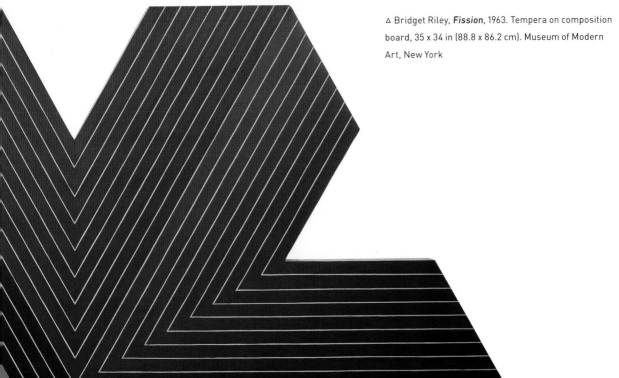

Everyday Life Becomes Pop

△ Robert Rauschenberg, *Rebus*, 1955. Oil, synthetic polymer paint, pencil, crayon, pastel, cut-and-pasted printed and painted papers and fabric on canvas mounted and stapled to fabric, three panels, 96 x 131⅛ in (243.8 x 333.1 cm). Museum of Modern Art, New York

In order to pull art down from its pedestal, to make it popular—but also as a reaction to abstract expressionism and the sublimity of color field painting—American and English artists in the 1950s turned to the pictorial heritage of consumer and mass culture. In England, the Independent Group at the Institute of Contemporary Arts (ICS) in London investigated everyday life and subcultures on the basis of pulp magazines, advertising design and science fiction illustrations.

The poster for the exhibition "This Is Tomorrow" (1956) was based on a collage by Hamilton that iron-

ically challenged modern life and living. Hamilton's medium of collage and *objets trouvés* using truly trivial items found in the trash and on the street, hearkened back to the anti-art of Dadaism. In 1949, Rauschenberg was already participating in happenings, which soon led to his "combine paintings." In these works, he added everyday consumer objects and garbage such as photos, printed material and scraps of cloth to painted canvases. The canvases thus extended into space, becoming objects themselves. In contrast, Johns' *Flag* paintings are rather an ironic reaction to abstract painting, and at

the same time a game of illusion and reality. Even more refined in terms of objectivity than Mondrian's work, the picture-object here is artfully aligned with the picture itself. "Is it a flag or is it a painting?" asked Johns, who never saw himself as a pop artist. In their first show, the artists referred to themselves as "new realists" in order to emphasize their confrontation with banal reality. But the designation "pop art," first adopted later, underlines more concretely their connection to big-city life and popular culture.

△ Jasper Johns, *Flag*, 1954/55. Encaustic, oil and collage on fabric mounted on plywood, three panels, 3 ft 6 in x 5 ft (107.3 x 153.8 cm). Museum of Modern Art, New York

◁ Richard Hamilton, *Just what is it that makes today's homes so different, so appealing?*, 1956. Collage, 10¼ x 9¾ in (26 x 23.5 cm). Kunsthalle Tübingen, Tübingen

Business Art Is the Best Art

△ Andy Warhol, *Campbell's Soup Cans*,
1962. Synthetic polymer paint on 32
canvases, each 20 x 16 in (50.8 x 40.6 cm).
Museum of Modern Art, New York

For Warhol, art and business were not only *not* opposites; he saw them as unified and interdependent. Having earned his living as a commercial artist for magazines, as a window dresser, and as an illustrator of books, he began in 1960 to paint his first pictures of comic book figures and consumer goods like soup cans and soda bottles, and the dollar bills with which to buy them. In his reproduction and proliferation of the picture-object, he mirrored the consumer world, even putting conventional ideas of originality and individual creativity in question. Thanks to the serial silkscreen prints that became his trademark, he gained substantial influence in the pop art world. He used Marilyn Monroe's death in 1962 as an occasion for numerous *Marilyn* portraits, using a still photograph from the film *Niagara*.

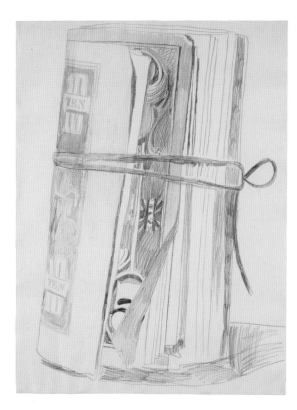

▷ Andy Warhol, *Roll of Bills*, 1962. Pencil, crayon and felt-tip pen on paper, 40 x 30 in (101.6 x 76.2 cm). Museum of Modern Art, New York

▽ Andy Warhol, *Marilyn*, 1967. Silkscreen on paper, 36 x 36 in (91.5 x 91.5 cm). Museum of Modern Art, New York. One page from a portfolio of ten screenprints in various colors.

Warhol turned his studio into a "Factory," opening it to young artists, dancers, dropouts, and his fans. He made films (such as *Sleep*) and used a Polaroid camera to make templates for his silkscreens. Among his most famous (and controversial) silkscreen series are those of suicides, automobile accidents, electric chairs, skulls, automotive logos, and hammer and sickle.

Art Gets Closer

In the 1960s, pop art defined the international art scene, although—or perhaps because—it never developed a program, and it gave artists a great deal of freedom. Pop was modern, irreverent, life-oriented, and the name suggested a connection to "pop culture" and "pop music," both of which were understood as expressions of youthful rebellion.

Hockney was one of the founders of English pop art. Since 1963, he has spent many years living and working in California. There he painted works with a brightened palette and a cool, artificial acrylic surface that conveys a sense of the unreal or surreal. Hockney's penchant for water gave him occasion to carry on the tradition-rich motif (in Western art) of bathers.

Lichtenstein preferred to seek out his subjects in popular mass media like comics, from which he transformed motifs from the trivial to the monumental. In doing so, he used the traditional comic-book technique of matrix dots, which he applied with stencils.

Swedish-born Claes Oldenburg modeled oversized food items in painted plaster and upholstered gigantic household implements in soft fabric, thus robbing consumer items of their consumer function.

Segal placed his life-sized, white plaster figures in walk-in installations (environments). He used plaster bandages to take casts of his figures directly from the models, giving them the appearance of being frozen in space. Segal combined these figures with real objects, creating a quotidian and—thanks to the neutral white of the plaster—simultaneously unreal situation.

◁ David Hockney, *Sunbather*, 1966.
Acrylic on canvas, 6 ft x 6 ft (183 x 183 cm).
Museum Ludwig, Cologne

▷ Roy Lichtenstein, *Crying Girl*, 1964. Enamel
on steel 46 x 46 in (116.8 x 116.8 cm). Milwaukee
Art Museum, Milwaukee

▷ George Segal, *The Bus Driver*, 1962. Plaster
over cheesecloth, steering wheel, driver's seat,
dashboard, 7 ft 5 in x 4 ft 4 in x 6 ft 5 in (226 x 131
x 195 cm). Museum of Modern Art, New York

▽ Claes Oldenburg, *Pastry Case I*, 1961/62.
Enamel paint on plaster sculptures in glass-
and-metal case, 20¾ x 30⅛ x 14¾ in (52.7 x 76.5 x
37.3 cm). Museum of Modern Art, New York

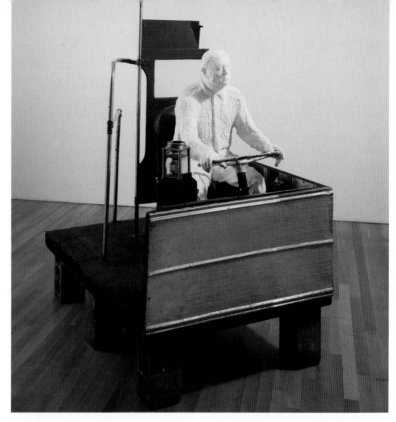

Images of Inner Truth

Abstraction and the attempts to broaden the range of traditional artistic techniques and media were a central concern of modern art. But at the same time, realist tendencies led in various directions. Even when not apparent at first glance, propo-nents of these tendencies were not committed to outer reality—their goal was not naturalistic—but rather to portraying the deeper connections and characteristics of inner reality.

Francis Bacon was not concerned with representing reality. His objec-tive was "to remake the violence of reality itself" (Bacon), and to give expression to humankind's vulner-ability and pain.

Freud emphasized balanced composition and—despite the un-compromising directness of a nude

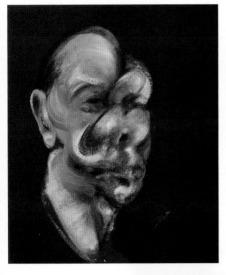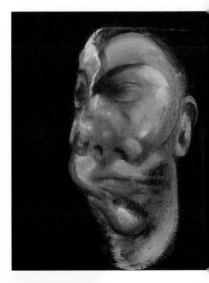

△ Francis Bacon, *Study for Three Heads*, 1962. Oil on canvas, three panels, each 14⅛ x 12⅛ in (35.9 x 30.8 cm). Museum of Modern Art, New York

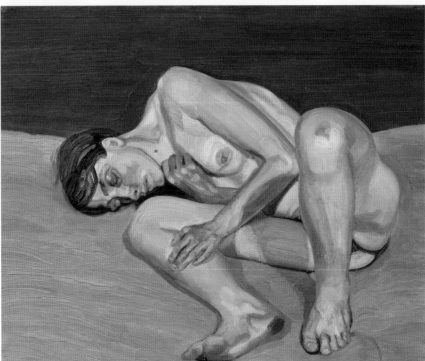

◁ Lucian Freud, *Small Naked Portrait*, 1973/74. Oil on canvas, 7⅞ x 8¾ in (20 x 22.2 cm). The Ashmolean Museum, Oxford

—a psychologically empathetic portrait of the revealed model.

Photorealists like the Swiss artist Franz Gertsch or the American Chuck Close engaged in a balancing act between realism and naturalism. Using oversized slides, they completed intricately detailed, "true to nature" images of reality-capturing photographs, paying special attention to distinct hues and light reflexes. Chance moments in time, camera, projector, format, brush, and the gaze of the viewer were to act as filters in the process of perception, a game of "image," "illusion," "truth," and "honesty."

△ Franz Gertsch, *Medici*, 1971. Dispersion on canvas, 13 ft 1½ in x 19 ft 8¼ in (400 x 600 cm). Ludwig Forum für Internationale Kunst, Aachen

◁ Chuck Close, *Keith*, 1972. Mezzotint, 50⅞ x 41¾ in (129.4 x 106.2 cm). Museum of Modern Art, New York

More and More Realists

The *Nouveaux Réalistes*, a group that formed around the French critic Restany in 1960, appeared at the same time as the "New Realists" (later called pop artists) in America. Their objective was to "record sociological reality without any controversial intention." Incorporating forms and objects from everyday life, they created assemblages of *objets trouvés* that recalled Dadaism's formal repertory (but without Dada's sometimes enigmatic humor).

Apart from sponges soaked in blue paint, Yves Klein did not assemble very much. Rather, he sought sensitization, liminal dissolution and liberation through art in monochrome form. To this end, he developed the patented color mixture IKB (International Klein Blue), a deeply radiant ultramarine that represented for him the incarnation of the cosmic. He covered objects and models with blue paint and used them to make impressions on paper in the context of special performances. In this way, he created his *Anthropometries*, works which are reminiscent of cave paintings and magical rituals.

Christo and Jeanne-Claude gave the art world huge assemblages of oil barrels in Cologne and Paris, "wrappings" of extant buildings (like the Pont Neuf in Paris or the Reichstag in Berlin), sculpted landscapes (*Surrounded Islands*), and the twenty-four mile-long *Running Fence* in California. They financed their "wrappings"—as expensive as they were temporary—by selling drawings. The wrapping actions themselves were carried out in precisely organized happenings.

▷ Daniel Spoerri, *Kichka's Breakfast I*, 1960. Assemblage, 14⅜ x 27⅜ x 25¾ in (36.6 x 69.5 x 65.4 cm). Museum of Modern Art, New York. Spoerri's "snare-pictures" remove the remains of a meal from their natural (horizontal) context to the vertical illusion of a panel painting.

▽ Yves Klein, *Untitled Anthropometry with Male and Female Figures (Ant 100)*, 1960. Synthetic resin and paper on canvas, 4 ft 9 in x 9 ft 9⅜ in (145 x 298 cm). Hirshhorn Museum and Sculpture Garden, Washington, D.C.

△ Arman (Armand Fernandez), *Accumulation*, 1973. Assemblage, 18½ x 12⅝ x 3¼ in (47 x 32 x 8.4 cm). Museum of Modern Art, New York. The basic principle behind Arman's work is the notion of repetition, accumulation and piling up of identical objects in Plexiglas containers.

◁ Christo and Jeanne-Claude, *Wall of Barrels Iron Curtain, Rue Visconti, Paris*, 1962. Environment of 240 oil barrels, 14 ft 2 in x 12 ft 6 in x 5 ft 6 in (430 x 380 x 170 cm). The environment *Iron Curtain* appeared in Paris in 1962, recollecting the construction of the Berlin Wall the previous year.

Art Happens

In Pollock's action painting, the artistic process itself had gained in meaning and importance, and painting became an event. By the end of the 1950s, Kaprow's New York happenings were evidence of a new type of action art whose roots lay primarily in Dadaism. It soon became obvious that the demand for the melding of art and life had brought with it an arrant broadening of the range of artistic media. Now, any object within a certain situation and any moment in the process of creation could be material for art. Dance, music, film and everyday noises were just as readily integrated as seemingly absurd acts. Closely related to the happening was the genre of Fluxus: heavily inspired by musical form, Fluxus works were conceived as composed collages of actions.

For both happenings and Fluxus, the element of free play with objects was essential. Without the action, however, the objects were mean-

ingless. But the art market found a solution to this dilemma: that which attacked bourgeois tastes could subsequently be acquired by one of the attacked as a valuable relic.

Toward the end of the 1960s, Beuys was the first to present the "relics" of his Fluxus events and installations as independent sculptures and inscribed panels. Now detached from any action but laden with autobiographical and mythical significance, he proclaimed these relics to be autonomous artworks. The artistry that, according to Beuys, everyone could perform was analogous to shamanism, in that it represented an attempt to restore the lost unity of nature and the mind. He formulated a theoretical "extended definition of art" in which the artwork was to be understood as "social sculpture," and thus as a combination of artistic and political action.

▷+△ Allan Kaprow, *Grandma's Boy*, 1957. Assemblage, 18½ x 28¼ x 1¾ in (47.1 x 71.8 x 4.8 cm). The Newark Museum, Newark

▷ Nam June Paik, *Zen for TV*, 1963 (replica 1976). Readymade, 19 x 22½ x 18 in (48.3 x 57.2 x 45.7 cm). Smithsonian American Art Museum, Washington, D.C. Paik reduced the televised image to a single horizontal line; in some versions, he turned the television on its side.

◁ Joseph Beuys, **EURASIA Siberian Symphony**, first performance Copenhagen 1963, assemblage 1966. 6 ft x 7 ft 6¾ in x 20 in (183 x 230 x 50 cm). Museum of Modern Art, New York. The divided cross symbolizes the split between East and West, between Europe and Asia, and the hare is a symbol for fleetingness. The rods, joined with wedges of felt and fat, delineate the space in which the action occurred.

▽ Joseph Beuys, **We Are the Revolution (La Rivoluzione siamo Noi)**, 1972. Diazotype and rubber stamp on polyester, 75⅜ x 39⅝ in (191.5 x 100.7 cm). Museum of Modern Art, New York

Métamatics + Nanas = Animated Water

In 1960, the Swiss sculptor Jean Tinguely began, along with Rauschenberg and others, to participate in international happenings, affiliating himself with the *Nouveaux Réalistes*. His delight in sound and movement (kinetics) can already be seen in his first constructions. He built *Métamatics*, machines with which one could produce works of art, or machines that intentionally went out of order while operating. The famous assemblage *Homage to New York* self-destructed at the Museum of Modern Art.

Tinguely's constructions, welded together out of objects found in junkyards, reflect the contemporary

▽ Niki de Saint-Phalle and Jean Tinguely, **Stravinsky Fountain, Firebird**, 1982/83. Place Igor Stravinsky (Centre Georges Pompidou), Paris

fascination with technology while simultaneously ironizing the modern industrial world as well as the art business itself, as the only purpose of their movements was purposelessness.

The French artist Niki de Saint-Phalle rose to prominence through her *Nanas*—colorful, plump female figures in painted polyester, one of which was accessible through a door between its legs. She collaborated with Tinguely to make the *Stravinsky Fountain* in Paris. The individual figures in this aquatic spectacle were inspired by the works of the composer Igor Stravinsky, for example Saint-Phalle's *Firebird*, which—thanks to Tinguely's machinery—moves, squirts, and sprays water.

△ Jean Tinguely,
**Carnival Fountain
(Theater Fountain)**,
1977. Theaterplatz,
Basel

▷ Jean Tinguely,
**Homage to
New York**, 1960.
Photograph
from the self-
destructive
performance on
March 17, 1960 in
New York

▷ Jean Tinguely,
**Fragment from
Homage to
New York**, 1960.
Assemblage,
6 ft 8 in x 29⅝ in x
7 ft 4 in (203.7 x
75.1 x 223.2 cm).
Museum of Modern
Art, New York

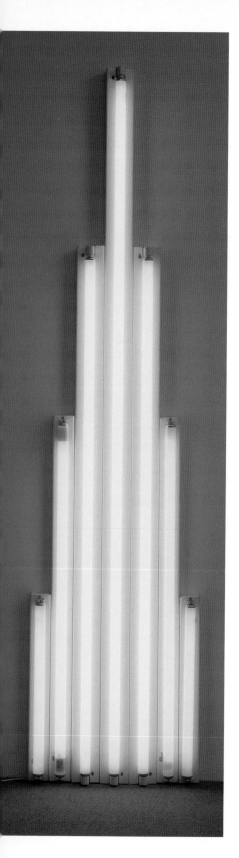

As Little Art As Possible

Faced with the "everyday" aspects of pop art, the minimalist object artists of the 1960s reduced their formal language to simple structures and elementary geometric forms. As in the abstraction of color field painting, references to images and meaning were eschewed to a large degree until a "minimal artistic content" in connection with serial assembly and industrial materials and means of production had been achieved. The minimalist object rid itself of all ornament, instead emphasizing its relationship to the surrounding space through specific light effects interacting with the material.

Flavin's works of art create additional "sculptures" of light through optical changes in the space, generated with the help of white or colored light.

Both LeWitt and Judd created art through the systematic performance of theme and variation, while the industrial production of numerous identical objects nullified the individuality of any single work.

When Serra propped enormous and massively heavy plates of steel or lead against one another, he was playing with gravity in a way that surely caused some spectators to become nervous as well. Although the plates were propped and balanced reciprocally and with great care, requiring no anchoring to the floor or to each other, the lightness of their assembly appears almost careless. Serra always conceives his monumental outdoor sculptures in an impressively close relationship to their surroundings.

◁ Dan Flavin,
"Monument" for V. Tatlin 1, 1964. Fluorescent lights and metal fixtures, 8 ft x 23⅛ in x 4½ in (243.8 x 58.7 x 10.8 cm). Museum of Modern Art, New York

▷ Sol LeWitt, *Cubic-Modular Wall Structure, Black*, 1966. Painted wood, 43½ x 43½ x 9⅜ in (110.3 x 110.2 x 23.7 cm). Museum of Modern Art, New York

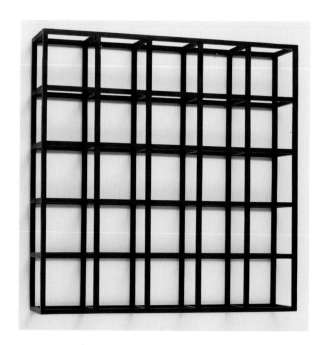

▷ Donald Judd, *Untitled*, 1968. Brass, 22 x 48¼ x 36 in (55.9 x 122.6 x 91.4 cm). Museum of Modern Art, New York

▽ Richard Serra, *One Ton Prop (House of Cards)*, 1969. Lead antimony, four plates, each 48 x 48 x 1 in (122 x 122 x 2.5 cm). Museum of Modern Art, New York

△ Richard Rogers
and Renzo Piano,
*Centre national
d'art et de
culture Georges-
Pompidou*,
1971–1977, Paris

◁ Günter Behnisch
and Frei Otto,
*Olympic Park with
Olympic Stadium*,
1972, Munich

▷ Frank O. Gehry,
*Guggenheim
Museum*, 1991–
1997, Bilbao

Open and Unexpected

In principle, every building is a technically organized structure, and therefore—especially considering the tendency in the visual arts to reject any surface illusion—it was not long before architects decided that they no longer wanted to hide this technical organization behind a façade. Rogers and Piano achieved this new ethos most consistently with the Centre Pompidou. In order to do justice to the concept of a flexible use of all levels of the cultural center, they removed all the building's "disruptive" functions—supporting framework, escalators, ventilation shafts—to the exterior, before the façade.

Starting with experiments with wire models dipped in soapy water that showed how optimally extended and contoured surfaces (membranes) should appear, Frei Otto devised the principle of supporting frameworks with lightly tensile surfaces, which he and Behnisch used in Munich's Olympic complex in 1972.

The goal of the deconstructivist architect Gehry was to load buildings with myth and meaning that went above and beyond their function, creating aesthetic distances between them and the everyday world. His structures seem to pile up haphazardly, or to collapse in disarray. Forms burst apart, creating an explosive impression. It is only with the help of special computer simulators that such unpredictable concatenations of spherical exterior forms can be combined with a plausible interior space.

The Upside Down German Art Scene

Despite being pronounced dead, despite artists' most imaginative attempts to get beyond the two-dimensional image, painting—specifically objective painting—never ceased to exist. Thanks to the *Neue Wilde* ("new wild ones"), in the 1970s and 80s Germany experienced the euphorically welcomed rebirth of a figurative, heavy painting style executed in expressive brushwork. Its themes consisted not simply of repeated or private myths, but also, time after time, of the artist's own existence.

Baselitz's gestural and distorted painting followed in the tradition of German expressionism. His upended, fragmentary compositions direct the observer's gaze from the motif to the technique.

Polke developed a subjective pictorial language that utilized contradiction and cliché to create humorous picture puzzles.

Kiefer's often monumental canvases address themes from German history and myth, including the long-taboo subject of the Third Reich.

Like Baselitz and Penck, Richter was originally from East Germany, where socialist realism was the standard. At first, he based his paintings on photographs that he had smudged and smeared. His later work is abstract, with enlarged traces of brushwork and spackling that represent nothing more than themselves.

Penck's psychogramatic figures recall prehistoric signs which, in extremely reductive representation, portray human mental states and primal fears.

Moderne Kunst

◁ Sigmar Polke, *Modern Art*, 1968. Synthetic resin and oil on canvas, 4 ft 11 in x 4 ft 1 in (150 x 125 cm). Hamburger Kunsthalle, Hamburg

▽ Georg Baselitz, *Woodmen*, 1967/68. Charcoal and synthetic resin on canvas, 8 ft 2 in x 6 ft 6 in (248.7 x 200 cm). Museum of Modern Art, New York

◁ Gerhard Richter, *Clouds*, 1982. Oil on canvas, 6 ft 7 in x 8 ft 6 in (200.7 x 260.7 cm). Museum of Modern Art, New York

▽ Anselm Kiefer, *Wooden Room*, 1972. Charcoal/oil/burlap, 9 ft 10 in x 7 ft 2 in (299.7 x 219.7 cm). Museum of Modern Art, New York

△ A.R. Penck (Ralf Winkler), *Night Vision*, from the series *First Concentration I*, 1982. Woodcut, 39¼ x 30¾ in (99.8 x 78.1 cm)

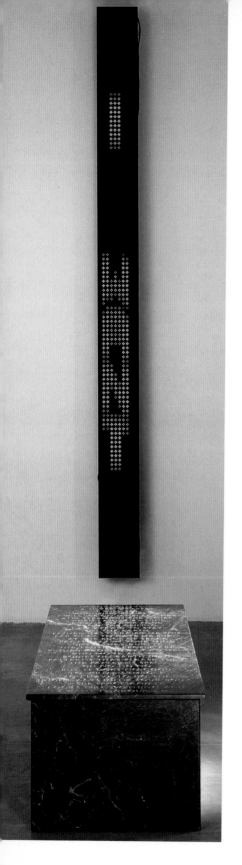

Inherent Art, Electrified

After the apparent exhaustion of abstraction and realism; after pop had elevated the banal to high art; after Fluxus and happenings had dismantled the definition of artwork; after minimalism had reduced everything to its most basic form; when only the concept of art was of periodic interest, the only obvious course remaining to the avant-garde was to concentrate on the bodies of artists themselves (body art, performance art), or on installations utilizing the newest communications technology.

The works of Viola, a leading proponent of video art, often include people submerged in water; they are shown diving in, breathing out, surfacing, inhaling, all the while sur-rounded by an interplay of currents and radiant bubbles. His concerns are the great questions of human existence: love, suffering, death and dying.

Rather than employing detached speech and sober presentation, Holzer uses an electronic marquee to further emphasize the often shocking content of her language installations.

Nauman makes use of the most diverse forms of media. Neon-light installations display self-ironic texts, or illuminate universal desires in intervals, while the flickering intentionally disturbs the viewer's perception so that no "art appreciation" can take place.

◁ Jenny Holzer, *Laments (I Want to Live...)*, 1989. Marble sarcophagus 18 x 54⅛ x 24⅛ in (45.7 x 137.3 x 61.3 cm), LED sign 10 ft 8 in (325.8 cm) high. Museum of Modern Art, New York

△ Bill Viola, *Quintet of the Silent*, 2000. Video installation, 15 min., 28½ x 47½ x 4 in (72.4 x 120.7 x 10.2 cm). Actors: T. Fitzpatrick, D. Gerrity, C. Grove, D. Hernandez, J. Malpede. Indianapolis Museum of Art

▷ Bruce Nauman, *Human, Need, Desire*, 1983. Installation with neon lights, 7 ft 10⅜ in x 5 ft 10½ in x 25¾ in (239.8 x 179 x 65.4 cm). Museum of Modern Art, New York

Art for the Market

Without success, an artist's work has no effect. This is banal. Andy Warhol already perfected the art of successfully and lucratively manipulating the banal and trivial.

In the 1980s, Haring's graffiti-inspired treatment of subculture themes ensured his meteoric success. His pictorial forms were so simple and catchy that they became a sort of international language of signs. And they conveniently allowed themselves to be marketed just as well on consumer objects as on canvas.

Basquiat's career also began in New York's graffiti scene. His repertory of motifs combined the magic of African art with wall scribblings, comics and traditional iconography.

△ Jean-Michel Basquiat, *Baptism*, 1982. Acrylic, oilstick and paper collage on canvas, 7 ft 8 in x 7 ft 8 in (233.5 x 233.5 cm). Private collection

◁ Jeff Koons, *Pink Panther*, 1988. Porcelain, 41 x 20½ x 19 in (104.1 x 52 x 48.2 cm). Museum of Modern Art, New York

Jeff Koons has his art made for him (sometimes commissioning craftsmen in Oberammergau or Ortisei). He delivers ideas, but they are not always so simple. The reproductions of trivial porcelain figurines or comic book figures in shiny stainless steel, glazed ceramic or tranquil woodcarvings move in an ironic-satirical limbo on the border between art and kitsch, where they embody the artist's fantasy in market value.

Hirst also belongs to the artists who have successfully marketed themselves as labels. Like Koons and Warhol, he has his artworks made for him. His projects, frequently dealing with taboo, death-related themes, usually require a large staff of workers to complete. The aquariums containing animal carcasses such as tiger sharks suspended in formaldehyde provide not only market-oriented publicity—one can even smell them.

Photography I

△ Joseph Nicéphore Niépce, *View from the Study Window at Maison du Gras*, 1827. Heliograph, 6½ x 8 in (16.5 x 20.3 cm)

Niépce was among the first to successfully capture the image of a camera obscura on light-sensitive material. Through the efforts of Daguerre and especially Nadar, the fast developing art of photography first began to assume the role previously occupied by the painted portrait, and soon those of architectural and landscape painting as well. Before long, it had mastered the traditional ideal of Western art—

△ Nadar (Gaspard-Félix Tournachon), *Pierrot Laughing*, 1855. 10¾ x 7¾ in (27.3 x 19.8 cm). Museum of Modern Art, New York

△ Eadweard J. Muybridge, *Sprinter*, 1890–1900. 6⅛ x 14⅝ in (15.4 x 37.2 cm). Museum of Modern Art, New York

▷ Karl Blossfeldt, *Adiantum pedatum. American Maidenhair Fern. Young rolled-up fronds enlarged 8 times*, from *Art Forms in Nature*, pub. 1928. 11⅝ x 9¼ in (29.5 x 23.6 cm)

the imitation of nature—so well that painters had to seek new ways of seeing.

Studies of motion like Muybridge's inspired futurism. At the same time, artists themselves began to experiment with photography, at first for templates, then as a medium in its own right. Dadaists like Man Ray ironized art history and toyed with different types of exposure. In his photographic studies, Blossfeldt analyzed and visualized the relationship between art and nature. Moholy-Nagy's sculptural light experiments with his light-space-modulator (1922–1930), which he developed while teaching at the Bauhaus, were essentially first made tangible in his photographs.

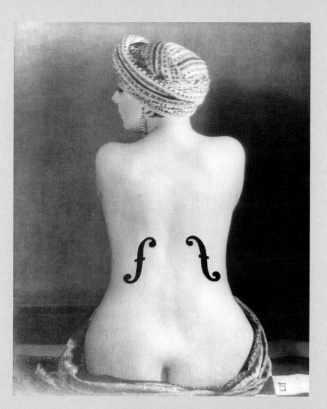

◁ Man Ray, *Violon d'Ingres*, 1924. 19 x 14¾ in (48.3 x 37.6 cm)

▽ László Moholy-Nagy, *Lightplay: Black/White/Gray*, ca. 1926. 14¾ x 10¾ in (37.4 x 27.4 cm). Museum of Modern Art, New York

Photography II

Photography has been used in the most diverse ways in advertising, and since the invention of the digital camera, it has become more personal an art than ever before. Benefitting from the evolving definition of what constitutes art, the photograph has developed into a self-reliant, self-evident artistic medium.

Following in the tradition of Blossfeldt's systematically documentary style, the Bechers have compiled a worldwide survey of industrial buildings. In so doing, they have transformed the structures' primarily functional forms into anonymous sculptures. These are prosaic views that simultaneously enable comparative ways of seeing.

The Blumes take a completely different approach to reproducing reality through the medium of photography. With bizarre, grotesque stagings, they create narratives of outlandish occurrences using the apparently normal world of material objects.

△ Bernd and Hilla Becher, *Typologies of Industrial Buildings*. Water towers: Krefeld 1970, Bebra 1980; Furnaces: Duisburg-Ruhrort 1970, Duisburg-Hamborn 1979. Each 15¾ x 11¾ in (40 x 30 cm)

◁ Andreas Gursky, *Schiphol*, 1994. 6 ft 2 in x 7 ft (188 x 216 cm). Hamburger Kunsthalle, Hamburg

▷ Cindy Sherman, *Untitled*, 1989. 5 ft 7 in x 4 ft 8 in (170 x 142 cm). Museum of Modern Art, New York

△ Anna and Bernhard Blume, *Kitchen Frenzy*, 1986. Each 66⅞ x 42½ in (170 x 108 cm). Museum of Modern Art, New York

The self-stagings of the American photographer Cindy Sherman, who plays (and plays with) diverse roles and stereotypes, are couched in a more precisely arranged world. Wall's seemingly coincidental every-day shots are also staged carefully, and as oversized slides set in light boxes, they convey a forceful, illuminative power.

In the large-format pictures of Andreas Gursky, a student of the Bechers, excerpts of the real world are presented without commentary, but with a comprehensive attention to detail. Truncated buildings, landscapes, cities devoid of people depict the isolation of modern life.

▽ Jeff Wall, *The Stumbling Block*, 1991. Back-lit photograph, 7 ft 6 in x 11 ft (229 x 335 cm)

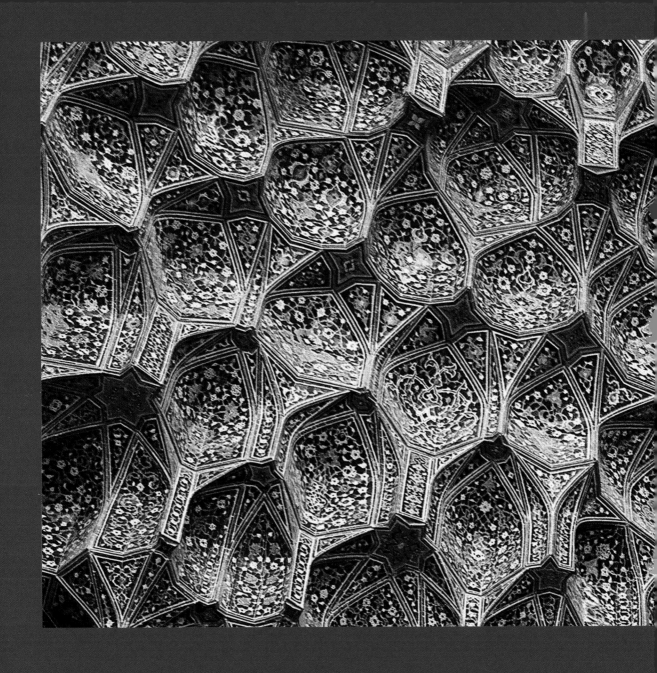

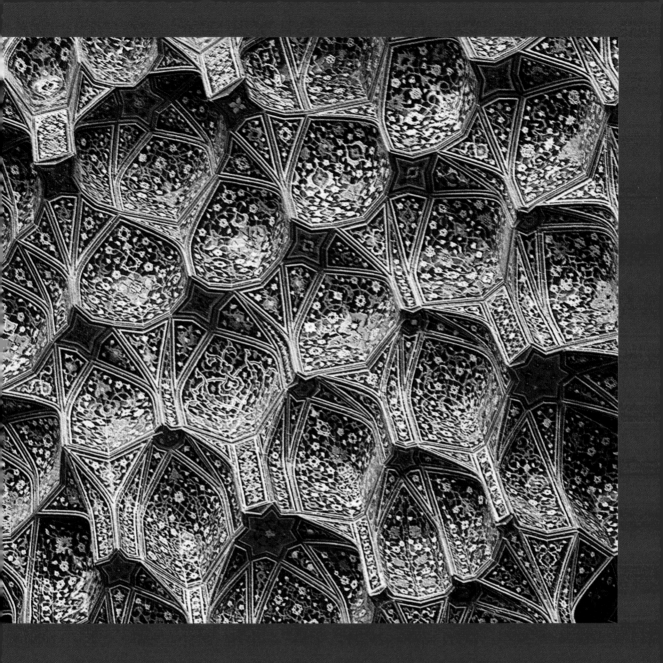

Islamic Art

Chronology

ca. 570–632 Life of Muhammad
661–750 Umayyad Caliphate in Damascus
711–1492 Islamic states in Spain
750–1258 Abbasid Caliphate in Baghdad
from 800 Emergence of regional Islamic states
909–1171 Shi'ah Counter-Caliphate of the Fatimids in Cairo
998–1030 Mahmud-e Gaznawi (Mahmud of Ghazni), conqueror of northern India, ruler of the Islamic East
1171–1193 Sultan Salah ad-Din (Saladin) conquers Egypt and Syria, then wrests the Holy Land from its crusader rulers.
1258 The Mongols take Baghdad, ending the rule of the Abbasid Caliphate.
1300–1922 Ottoman Empire
1370–1405 Timur Leng (Tamerlane) establishes a vast empire in Asia (Timurids in Samarkand).
1501–1722 Safavid dynasty in Persia
1526–1858 Mughal Empire in India
from 1920 Founding of most modern Islamic states
1932 'Abd al-'Aziz ibn Su'ud establishes the Kingdom of Saudi Arabia.
1954–1970 Gamal 'Abd an-Nasir (Nasser) is president of Egypt.
1979 Islamic Revolution in Iran

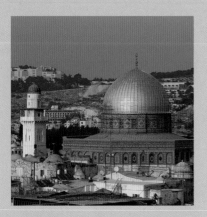

Dome of the Rock, Jerusalem, after 690

Mosaic in the baths of Hisham's Palace, Khirbat al-Mafjar, ca. 740

Great Mosque, Córdoba, 966

600   700   900   1050

Islamic Art from 600

What Is Allowed by Allah in Art?

Since Allah leaves this question unanswered, Muslims have followed the guidance of their religious leaders. The label "Islamic art," imposed by Western European art historians in the nineteenth century, is therefore just as unsatisfactory as "Christian art" would be. The same is true of "the art of Islamic countries," since the sudden religious unity provided by Islam in lands that had previously been in completely different cultural orbits does not automatically make art "Islamic." The question remains, what makes a work of art "Islamic?"

Islam is a religion "of the book," as are Judaism and Christianity. Books, even non-Islamic ones, have therefore been treasured cultural assets for centuries, and were from the beginning, reading and writing widespread abilities in the Islamic sphere of influence. The young religion's leaders were much more open to foreign learning than their Catholic counterparts. The caliphs of the Umayyad and Abbasid dynasties reputedly requested that books on philosophy, physics and medicine be sent from Byzantium in order to have them translated. In fact, many Greek texts only survived later Catholic book burnings because they had been rendered in Arabic. These earliest Arabic translations were copied with the original illustrations, even the anatomical sketches and charts in medical works.

This lively interest in the sciences went hand in hand with a conspicuous indifference to "art." Art was considered little more than handiwork, and was at first left to the capable local masters already living in the conquered territories. The earliest "Islamic art" is therefore Greek, Roman, or Byzantine in nature, its "only" significant individual development being in its content.

Cultural History

830 Founding of the "House of Wisdom" in Baghdad

9th century Hunain ibn 'Ishaq is the first in a long line of great Arab doctors.

973–1048 Al-Biruni, Persian scholar and polymath

980–1037 Ibn Sina (Avicenna), a major Persian philosopher and doctor

ca. 1010 Firdausi writes the *Sahnameh* (*Book of Kings*)

1126–1198 Ibn Rushd (Averroes) advances the teachings of Aristotle.

13th century Ibn an-Nafis, a Syrian polymath, discovers the circulatory system.

ca. 1350 Hafez composes the poems of his *Divan*.

19th century As-Salafiyah: Islamic cultural and political self-reflection

Bowl with Rider, Iran, ca. 1200

Taj Mahal, Agra, 1632–1643

Pavilion of Osman III, Topkapı Palace, Istanbul, 1755

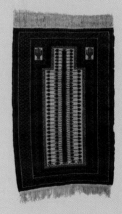

Prayer rug, Iran, ca. 1925

1200   1600   1700   1900

At a Glance

Muhammad

Muhammad was a caravan trader in Mecca when he received his first prophetic revelation at the age of forty. He began to proclaim unerringly the doctrine of "the one God, Allah," who rewards the faithful and punishes the unfaithful. In 622, he and his followers were forced to migrate to Medina, marking the beginning of the Islamic calendar (*Hijrah*). There Muhammad proved himself a capable statesman and leader of the fast-growing Muslim community; in 630, they gained his hometown of Mecca without bloodshed. In visual arts, the prophet's face is always veiled, or not represented at all.

Muhammad, detail of an illuminated book, 1594/95

Quran

The holy book of Islam is believed to have been transmitted directly by God to Muhammad. It is divided into 114 surahs (chapters). The first is *al-Fatihah*, a prayer; the second is the longest, followed by surahs of decreasing length.

Sahnameh

Firdausi (941–1020) composed the Persian national epic, the *Sahnameh* ("Book of Kings"), in 1010. In sixty-two legends and some 60,000 verses, it tells the heroic history of Persia, from the first kings to the Sassanids, who ruled before the Islamic conquest.

Five Pillars of Islam

The five pillars of Islam are the religious duties of every Muslim: the profession of faith (*Sahada*); prayers performed five times daily (*Salah*); giving of alms or "social tax" (*Zakat*); fasting (*Saum*), specifically during the month of Ramadan; and the pilgrimage to Mecca (*Hajj*).

Al-Hariri

The poet and grammarian al-Hariri (1054–1122) perfected the Arabic literary genre of the *maqama* ("assembly"), in which verbal duels and speeches in rhymed prose with verse insertions are preserved.

"Hand of Fatimah"

This good-luck charm, especially popular in the Maghreb, wards off the evil eye, as well as the attentions of wicked ghosts (*jinni*). Its name refers to Muhammad's daughter Fatimah, a pure, sinless virgin, and later mother of the prophet's descendants. It symbolizes not only a defensive attitude against evil, but also a beneficent and lucky helping hand.

Talisman, Hand of Fatimah, 18th century, Musée du Quai Branly, Paris

Friday Mosque

The central mosque of each city, in which an imam officiates over communal Friday prayer, is called the "Friday Mosque." Every mosque has a mihrab (prayer niche) in the qiblah (wall facing Mecca). The faithful always pray in this direction.

Carpet Art

The earliest surviving Islamic rugs were woven in thirteenth-century Anatolia. Under the Safavids (1501–1722), weaving experienced a golden age that carried this art form as far as India. Islamic rugs usually have a framed, geometric and ornamentally patterned center; Persian rugs also include a medallion in the middle. Plant and animal motifs are fancifully incorporated. Typical of prayer rugs is the niche-shaped form in the middle representing the mihrab (see pp. 518–519).

Iwan

The iwan is a hall with walls on three sides, the front side being completely open, and therefore creating a space that is not explicitly indoors or outdoors. These monumental niches distinguish Persian and Central Asian architecture. Rulers held audiences and pronounced judgment in them. Four iwans were often built in a cross formation around a mosque's inner courtyard, in which case the main iwan facing Mecca was crowned by two minarets (see p. 528).

Islamic Art from 600

Ka'bah

The cubic Ka'bah holds the black stone (a meteor), which Muslims believe to be the basis of the shrine Abraham (Ibrahim) built to commemorate the God whose relevance was restored by Muhammad. Nearby is the Well of Zamzam, caused by Allah to gush forth in the desert, thus saving Hagar (Hajar), Abraham's second wife, and their son Ishmael (Isma'il).

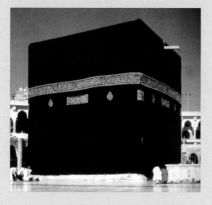

Ka'bah, Mecca, from 632 (rebuilt 1630)

Hajj

Every adult Muslim should make at least one pilgrimage to Mecca in their lifetime. People making the pilgrimage wear a white pilgrim's garment and are under special protection. Once in Mecca, pilgrims walk seven times around the Ka'bah (ritual prayer or *tawaf*) and then proceed to Mount 'Arafat, where they pray standing. Finally, pilgrims walk to Mina, where they symbolically stone the devil. The end of the pilgrimage, the most important religious holiday in Islam, is marked by a farewell *tawaf* and a sacrificial feast. Most pilgrims then go on to visit significant sites in Medina.

Muqarnas

Arab architecture uses ogival elements in the design of niches and cupolas whose concertina-like forms often resemble the stalactites of a dripstone cave. This architectural motif was most masterfully employed in Granada's Alhambra (al-Hamra').

Façade Design

The façades of Islamic buildings are usually very rich in ornament. Geometric designs were often artfully laid in brick or colored tile. In India, colored marble and stone inlays were also common. The outer ornament was designed as a frieze, or consisted of botanical, geometric or calligraphic pattern, and often covered the building's exterior (see p. 526).

△ Page from Firdausi, *Sahnameh*, ca. 1525

▷ Illustration from al-Hariri, *Maqama*, 1237

The Portrait in Islam

In spite of the Muslim tendency not to depict the human form in the arts, the painting and miniature workshops of the Ottoman sultans in Turkey, the Safavid shahs in Persia, and the Mughal emperors in India created numerous portraits and tableaux.

Key Terms

Word Becomes Writing

For the faithful, the Quran is literally the word of God. In the Night of Power (610 CE, at the end of the fasting month of Ramadan), Allah "deposited" the entire text of his book of books into Muhammad. In the twenty-two remaining years of the Prophet's life, the archangel Gabriel helped him gradually disseminate the 114 surahs in 6236 rhymed verses. Five times a day, Muslims worldwide feel the presence of Allah when they recite verses from the Quran in the original Arabic, because the true word of Allah is holy. Understanding the disclosure of that which pleases Allah—and that which does not—can be difficult even for native Arabic speakers, since the texts place serious demands on the typical worshipper, especially when one considers that the surahs are not arranged chronologically, but in order of decreasing length.

The complex, stylistically unique language of Allah can only be represented in an appropriate form, if it is possible at all, in calligraphy. That is one of the fundamental reasons that there are no illustrated versions of the Quran. At first, the word of Allah was written in the angular, linear form of Kufic calligraphy, which was considered especially ceremonial. Because this style lends itself to being worked in stone or wood, it remained a feature in architecture even after the eleventh century, while the flowing, cursive Naskh style took its place in manuscripts. Both forms developed local variations, whereby the curves and loops, can be incredibly complex and intricate, depending on the content of the document (and find secular use, for example, as a safeguard against forgery in decrees).

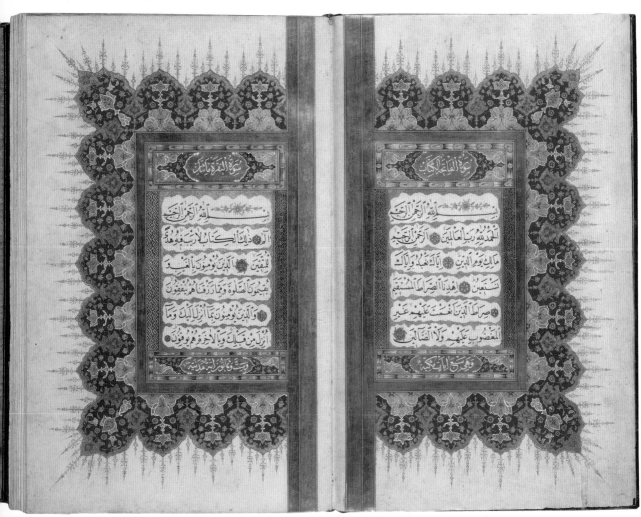

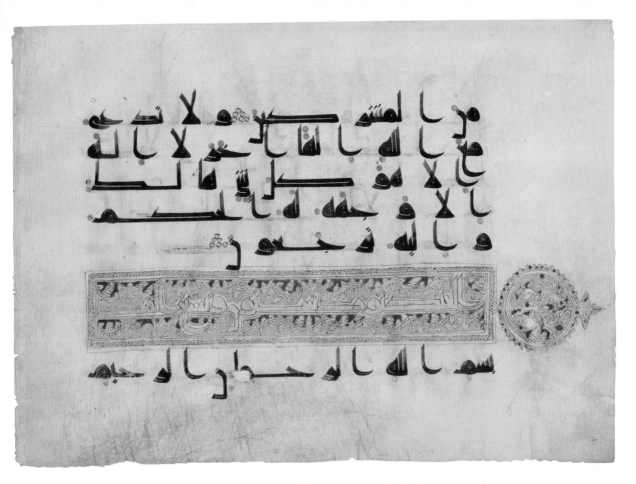

△ **Quran**, ca. 900 (?), Ms. 712, fol. 19v. Parchment, The Pierpont Morgan Library, New York. Early Kufic manuscripts focus completely on the text, with the occasional decorative element taking a subordinate role to the script-image. The red dots facilitate reading.

◁ **Quran**, 1867, parchment. The cursive Naskh style of writing can be elegantly inserted in the tendril borders. Acting as a frame for the text, the edge of the page becomes a stylistic device.

▷ **Basmala in the form of a bird**, calligraphy, 1816. Ink on paper, 9¼ x 14 in (23.5 x 35.5 cm). Musée du Quai Branly, Paris.

▷ **113 of the Quran's surahs** begin with the basmala (*bismillah*), the opening formula "In the name of Allah, the merciful, the compassionate." It has frequently been shaped with exceeding care and artistry.

▷+▽ **Dome of the Rock** (Temple Mount), Jerusalem. Built after 960 by Byzantine-educated craftsmen under Caliph Abd al-Malik

The Dome of the Rock and Desert Castles

For Muslims, Islam is the completion of Judaism and Christianity. Therefore, the site where Muhammad's night journey (al-Isra') ended is also considered sacred because it is where Abraham almost sacrificed his son, and because the Arc of the Covenant stood here. The Umayyads' first holy building, an octagonal structure surmounted by a round dome, was designed by masters of Byzantine training. Its interior double arcade allows a ritual procession that in uncertain times can take the place of a pilgrimage to Mecca. The décor of marble cladding and mosaics on the interior (and originally on the exterior as well—the geometrically patterned tiles are copies of the originals from 1554) betrays a Byzantine repertoire. Due to the site's holiness, they refrain from depictions of people and animals, but include familiar stylized vases full of exuberantly climbing grape and acanthus vines. In their desert castles, the caliphs or their governors showed themselves to be more open to representational art. Walls, ceilings, and floors are covered with women bathing, men engaged in gymnastics, or bears playing music (Qasr Amra, Jordan). These desert castles, varying in size but generally representative, aided their owners in more easily controlling extensive spheres of influence, but thanks to the frescoes depicting bathing and hunting, they have acquired the oversimplified reputation of being little more than private pleasure palaces.

△ **Qasr al-Karanah**, Jordan, ca. 710. This building boasts a typical half-tower-reinforced façade and a distinct, roundly protruding portal. The interior includes stables, living quarters, an audience hall and a bath, all surrounding a central courtyard.

◁ **Mosaic in bath**, HiSam's Palace (Kirbat al-Mafjar), Holy Land, ca. 740

▽ **Mounted archer from Qasr al-Hair al-Garbi**, Syria, floor fresco, ca. 740. National Museum, Damascus

△ **Great Mosque**, Damascus, Syria, built 705–725 under al-Walid I. View of the prayer hall with the broader and higher mihrab aisle. It follows the direction of prayer, oriented toward the mihrab in the middle of the qiblah, and crosses the subordinate aisles that run parallel to the qiblah.

◁ In the west colonnade of the courtyard, pieces of the original **Barada mosaic.** It depicts a number of different buildings separated by oversized trees, all on the banks of a stylized river. The buildings are portrayed in perspective, but not from the same point of view.

The Great Mosque of Damascus

In the seventh century, the Umayyads moved the capital of their empire from Medina to Damascus, because on the one hand there was much arable land in the vicinity, but also because the important Mediterranean coastline was within reach. Caliph al-Walid I had the Great Mosque built on what had been the site of the Roman Temple of Jupiter and the Christian Basilica of St. John. Like his father Abd al-Malik, al-Walid I commissioned Byzantine masters with the building's design. He also seems to have imported tons of mosaic tiles from Byzantium, presumably recycled from ruins, since no Islamic chronicler ever mentioned "domestic" tile production. Mosaics therefore did not become customary in Islamic ornamentation until later.

The Mosque of Damascus has a broad courtyard, and its prayer hall is almost as large. The courtyard recalls Muhammad's house in Medina, where the first Muslims prayed, but the prayer hall with its rectangular floor plan is a departure from the square plan of the house. As in many early mosques, the aisles in the Damascus Mosque run parallel to the important south (qiblah) wall of the hall (haram), probably because some buildings originally designed as Christian basilicas—whose naves always lead east to the choir (parallel to the south wall)—were rededicated for Muslim use.

A mosque's essential components are a prayer hall with mihrab and minbar at the qiblah wall, a fountain for ablutions in the courtyard—and since Damascus, the minaret (the tower from which the call to prayer is chanted). Its primary purpose is to house group prayer, but it is also well suited to be a place of assembly for the community. Unlike temples or churches, no ritualized services take place here. In principle, no distinctive, individual style of mosque architecture evolved, since these building always incorporated elements characteristic of the regions in which they were built.

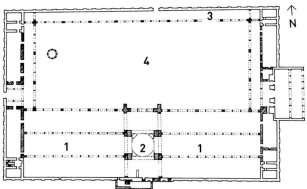

◁ Floor plan of the Great Mosque of Damascus, with its three-aisled prayer hall (haram, 1) broken by the mihrab aisle (2) and the three-sided colonnade (riwaq, 3) surrounding the courtyard (4).

Qiblah

(Arabic "direction"). In the Quran, God commanded Muslims to pray in the direction of the Ka'bah in Mecca. Emphasizing this orientation, a mosque's qiblah wall includes:
Mihrab, an empty niche signifying the presence of the Prophet and
Minbar, a raised seat similar to the one in the courtyard of Muhammad's house in Medina, from which the Prophet spoke. Like the caliphs who succeeded him, imams speak on Fridays from the steps of the minbar; no one can take the place of the Prophet.

△ **Mihrab** and **minbar** of the Sultan Hassan Mosque, ca. 1360, Cairo

Islamic Prohibition of Images?

"The most severely punished of people on the Day of Resurrection will be those who try to make the likeness of Allah's creation. Whoever has made pictures in this life will be commanded to breathe life into them, and he will not be able to do so." These are not the words of Allah, but of Muhammad. This passage therefore cannot be found in the Quran, but rather in the commentaries known as the Hadi, also an important source for Muslims. "Pictures" can be painted and sculpted, and the ban of "pictures that cast shadows" is an early amendment to the rule. This qualification refers to sculpted idols, which are not tolerated in Islam. Only Allah may receive prayers, and His form is unimaginable. As He created

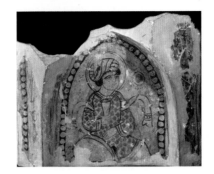

◁ *Boy Holding a Glass*, ca. 1050. Mural from a mansion in Fustat (Old Cairo). Museum of Islamic Art, Cairo. A well-drawn image showing stylized facial characteristics with no modeling through the representation of light and shadow is not considered insolent.

everything, it would be sacrilegious to create a form for Him.

In Islam, the painting of living beings such as animals and people is also unwelcome, and no one does it. Some follow Allah's command, creating only geometric or floral patterns. Others interpret the command: if "imitation of life" is forbidden, then it should not be done. First, painters simply placed drawn figures on bare surfaces. Then they would hint at the surroundings by painting a sort of vegetative cordon at the figures' feet that did not resemble Allah's creation. Painters included no light or shadow in their work, no unified perspective, and no natural color scheme.

The pictures obviously follow their own rules. "Inside," "outside," "in front of," and "behind" are suspended. The figures "float" through an unrealistic landscape. Almost nothing corresponds to observed reality, and everything is as improbable as comprehension allows. Whereas artists north of the Mediterranean considered a beguiling imitation of nature to be their greatest skill, Islamic artists developed a cunningly expressionistic way of seeing: as long as their work was sufficiently distant from nature, the ban on painting images did not apply.

△ **Bowl with rider**, Iran, ca. 1200, 8½ in (21.7 cm) diameter. The Metropolitan Museum of Art, New York. Woven into the ornamental background, this image is sufficiently distant from literal objectivity.
▷ Al-Hariri, *Maqama* (*Assemblies*), 1237. Ms. arabe 5847, fol. 101r, 5⅜ x 10¼ in (13.8 x 26 cm). Bibliothèque nationale, Paris. These camels graze with undifferentiated legs, seemingly floating. They appear without transition, in the middle of the text.

▷ *The Angel Surush Rescues Khusrau Parviz*, from Firdausi, **Sahnameh (Book of Kings)**, ca. 1525, fol. 708v. Colors, ink, silver, and gold on paper, 18½ x 12½ in (47.1 x 31.8 cm). The Metropolitan Museum of Art, New York. The colors, shapes, and representation of space make clear that this image is "autonomous"; it is not an imitation of the visible world of appearances. It remains color on a page, and it flows without care over the bottom of the frame.

How Does One Make an Image of Muhammad?

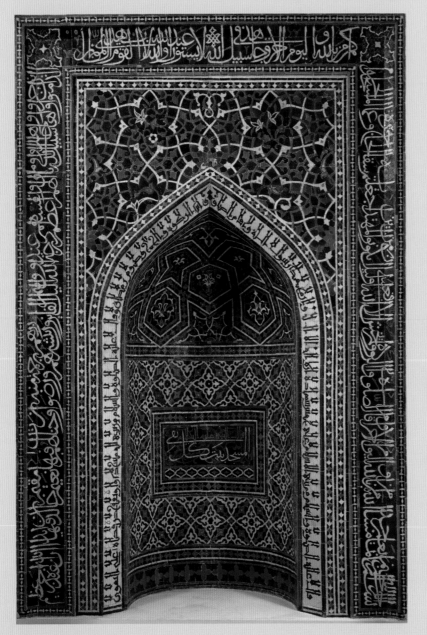

◁ **Mihrab**, Isfahan, Iran, 1354–1355. Tile, 11 ft 3 in x 9 ft 6 in (343.1 x 288.7 cm). The Metropolitan Museum of Art, New York. Scrolls run around the inner area, around the niche itself, and in the inner area; Naskh (Quranic verses) alternates with Kufic (Hadi).

At first, not at all. When Caliph al-Walid I had a magnificent mosque built on the site of Muhammad's house in Medina in 705, he knew that the new prayer hall would cover the very ground on which the Prophet had walked, where he had prayed and preached to the faithful. The pictorial or plastic depiction of a living being was unthinkable in the prayer hall, but at the same time, it was desired that the Prophet's historical presence in the mosque located at the site of his house should not be forgotten. An obvious solution was devised: the Byzantine masters knew that in other places, statues of dignitaries were further elevated in prestige by being placed in a niche, so they included in their design a niche rising from the floor, but remaining empty. In Medina, the empty niche marks the location of the first person to speak God's word, while the mihrab in every mosque built since symbolizes the presence of the Prophet, oriented to Mecca. The mihrab is therefore specially decorated, and the floor underneath is anointed. And therefore, no imam steps into the mihrab to pray, but rather bows before it like all other supplicants.

As Islam is a religion of the word, the Prophet is also honored in calligraphy. Since painters have found a way to observe the ban on images while still depicting living beings, Muhammad often appears surrounded by an aureole, colorless or behind a veil, unless this precautionary measure is also omitted.

△ **Triptych with calligraphic description of Muhammad**, Ottoman, 18th century. Museo nazionale d'arte orientale Giuseppe Tucci, Rome

◁ *The Archangel Gabriel Reveals the Eighth Surah of the Quran to Muhammad*, illumination, 1594–1595. Musée du Louvre, Paris

▷ *The Prophet Muhammad with His Daughter Fatimah, His Son-in-Law Ali, and Two Children*, illumination, 13th century. Bibliothèque nationale, Paris

◁ *Name of the Prophet*, written by al-Qandusi, 19th century, Morocco

△ Viewed from a certain perspective, the crossed ribs of the cupola before the mihrab form an octagonal star. This geometric motif, formed out of squares turned in a circle, is omnipresent in the arts of Islam.

△ Al-Hakam II expanded the eleven-aisled prayer hall (962–966); its stacked double arches with their bichrome voussoirs rest on the same antique capitals.

◁ The north wall of the prayer hall, facing the courtyard. The qiblah is on the other side, behind the nave of the Catholic church, built in 1523 in a west-east orientation.

The Great Mosque of Córdoba

After the Umayyads' defeat at the hands of the Abbasids, Abd ar-Rahman I was able to escape to the Damascene caliphate's Spanish "outpost." As in the Great Mosque of Damascus, the courtyard and prayer hall of the mosque that he began building in 785/86 in Córdoba are of equal size. Another similarity is apparent in the two-level arcades that traverse the prayer halls; this stacking of arches is characteristic of Umayyad sacred architecture, even if the arcatures differ in the details. Unlike in Damascus, the aisles of Córdoba's Great Mosque—there are eleven!—run perpendicular to the qiblah wall on the southern side. Over the next 200 years, the aisles were repeatedly extended southward, and supplemented by eight additional aisles on the eastern side. Since then, the magnificent mihrab is no longer in the center of the qiblah wall as was customary. The extension of the niche into a little room was unusual (and ineffective).

Refined "Pillars"

◁ **Prayer rug**
with colonnaded
mihrab, Bursa or
Istanbul, ca. 1590.
Wool, cotton and
silk, 4 ft 2 in x
5 ft 8 in (127 cm x
172.7 cm). The
Metropolitan
Museum of Art,
New York. The
floral ornament
of tulips and
carnations is
characteristic of
Ottoman weaving.

▽ **Prayer rug**
with mihrab and
spaces for hands,
Torbat-e Jam
(Iran), ca. 1925.
Cotton and wool,
66⅞ x 40½ in (170 x
103 cm). Musée du
Quai Branly, Paris

The Muslim faithful have five basic
duties, the "five pillars of Islam:" to
profess one's faith, to pray regularly,
to pay the "social tax" (alms for
the poor), to fast, and to undertake
at least once during one's life the
pilgrimage to Mecca.

Five times a day, every Muslim
bows in prayer toward Mecca. This
act of faith does not need to occur
in a mosque—it can be performed
anywhere. Thus, at prayer time,
all the world becomes a giant
haram (prayer hall), in which all the
faithful focus their belief toward the
same point. Otherwise, they need
nothing else apart from the word
of God and a "pure space." This
space is provided by a special form
of Oriental rug, the handy prayer
rug, which separates the praying
Muslim from the impurities of his
surroundings. Unlike other rugs,
its design is asymmetrical. This is
because the rug's central motif is
the mihrab, the prayer niche that in
mosques indicates the direction to
Mecca.

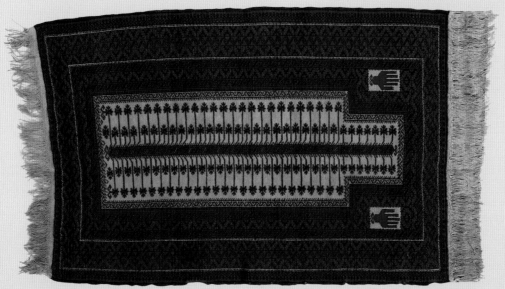

△ **Kilim**, Ladik
(Turkey), 1774.
Wool and metal
thread, 63 x 43 in
(160 x 109 cm).
The Metropolitan
Museum of Art,
New York. Prayer
rug with stepped
mihrab, after a
design created
around 1690 in
Gördes

Al-Azhar versus al-Qarawiyin

The Umayyad model of the courtyard-hall mosque proved itself to be crisis-proof. Even the Shi'ah Fatimids built their al-Azhar mosque (970–972) in Cairo after Damascus's example, dominated by its mihrab aisle, its other aisles running parallel to the qiblah. The theological seminary

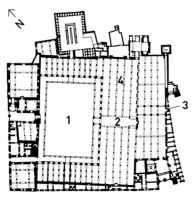

△ **Al-Azhar Mosque**, floor plan: 1 courtyard; 2 mihrab aisle; 3 mihrab; 4 prayer hall

(Shi'ah until 1171, Sunni since 1268) standing today has been expanded many times, but its exterior has been modified only slightly.

Tunisians who had fled Fatimid aggression built the unassuming al-Qarawiyin mosque and madrasah in the Moroccan city of Fès according to the Damascene model. By 1142, following the Almoravids' comprehensive expansion of the building, the number of aisles in the prayer hall had increased from four to six (large enough to accommodate 20,000 worshippers), but at the expense of the courtyard. The only slightly higher and broader mihrab aisle is accentuated on the interior by nine vaults of varying design. With their low horseshoe arches, the prayer hall and arcaded promenades give a solid and sturdy—if also somewhat squat—impression.

△ **Al-Azhar Mosque**, 970–972, Cairo, Egypt. View of the courtyard and prayer hall with its mihrab aisle. The compressed, pointed arches on very slim columns, the stucco decoration of blind niches and medallions, and the stepped crenellations are typical of Fatimid architecture.

▷ **Al-Qarawiyin Mosque**, founded 859, expanded 1142, Fès, Morocco. View of the entry area of the prayer hall

△ **Al-Qarawiyin Mosque**, founded 859, expanded 1142, Fès, Morocco. View of the courtyard and prayer hall with mihrab aisle. The two ablution pavilions with the fountain between them in the narrow courtyard's longitudinal axis date from 1620 and recollect the Alhambra's Court of the Lions.

▽ **Al-Qarawiyin Mosque**, floor plan: 1 courtyard; 2 mihrab; 3 fountain; 4 ablution pavilions; 5 prayer hall

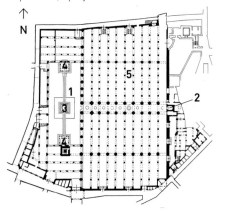

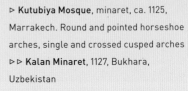

△ **Great Mosque**, ca. 850, Córdoba, Spain. Façade with blind cusped arches, a horseshoe arch and crossed horseshoe arches

▽ **Great Mosque**, minaret, 836, Kairouan, Tunisia

△ **Great Mosque**, courtyard, ca. 1120, Tlemcen, Algeria. Pointed horseshoe arch, cusped arch, round horseshoe arch, modified cusped arch

▽ **Great Mosque**, Malwiya Minaret, ca. 850, Samarra, Iraq

▷ **Kutubiya Mosque**, minaret, ca. 1125, Marrakech. Round and pointed horseshoe arches, single and crossed cusped arches
▷▷ **Kalan Minaret**, 1127, Bukhara, Uzbekistan
▽ **Ibn Tulun Mosque**, minaret, 1296 (rebuilt), Cairo

◁ **Bibi-Khanym Mosque**, ca. 1403 (rebuilt), Samarkand, Uzbekistan. Persian arch

▷ **Stucco decoration**, Museo Arqueológico Nacional, Madrid

▷▷ **Selimiye Mosque**, ca. 1570, Edirne, Turkey. "Needle minarets"

Minarets and Arches

The minaret has been an essential element of mosque architecture since 705. In its early stages, its form recalled church and watchtowers, which explains its usually square floor plan. But the spiral design of the Malwiya Minaret erased all debts, reinventing the form. If the minaret forms an axis with the mihrab, it reinforces the qiblah's Meccan orientation. The minaret allows the voice of the muezzin to be heard, and the number of minarets adorning a mosque is in direct correlation to the mosque's (or its patron's) importance. Cylindrical brick minarets are considered a Persian invention, but they found perfection under the Ottomans. That which had begun as a watchtower was now an architectural symbol for the call to prayer. Inspired by the Islamic devotion to ornament, arches transcended the bonds of necessity, instead becoming freely combinable decorative elements. Especially popular arch forms were the horseshoe, the cusped, and the Persian (also with an extended point to form a keel).

"The Red Fortress"

It is the oldest fully preserved Islamic palace complex. Remarkably, the Alhambra, begun in the fourteenth century, is built mostly of brick rather than stone. Its continued existence is largely due to the Catholic kings who took up residence there after the Reconquista, adding to it somewhat, but by and large preserving the original structure. As a palace complex, the Alhambra was the administrative seat of the sultanate, as well as the ceremonial and domestic residence of the sultan, or secular ruler. As in domestic architecture throughout the subtropical zones, the individual sections of the palace follow a time-honored principle: rooms with closed exterior walls open in the interior onto fountained courtyards.

▷ **Comares Palace of Yusuf I** (reigned 1333–1354), **Court of the Myrtles**, looking north; the Comares Tower (containing the throne room) is in the background. Alhambra, Granada

◁ **Palace of the Lions** (ca. 1375), muqarnas cupola of the **Hall of the Abencerrages** (a noble family), north of the Court of the Lions. Alhambra, Granada. The sculptural ornamental forms of (demi-) cupolas and arches spread from the 11th century with the expansion of Islam.

▷ **Palace of the Lions** (ca. 1375), view along the east-west axis of the Court of the Lions. Alhambra, Granada. The architects' manifest objective was to create an impression of hovering levity, and thus the tiles and intricately carved stucco that cover the walls hang in a lace-like finish. The water channels symbolize the rivers of paradise.

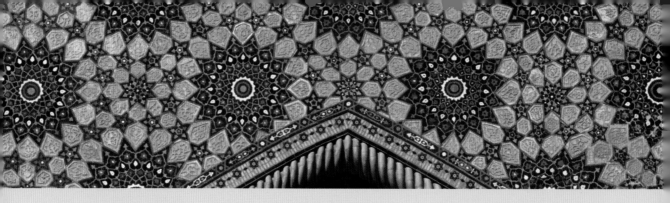

The Arabesque

Carved, chiseled, painted, woven, or burned onto surfaces—complex, polygonal stellar patterns ceaselessly cover walls, textiles and everyday objects. There is a good reason for this: in many Islamic lands, objects (including buildings) cannot be considered art until their surfaces are ornamented. To this end, elaborate strips of trim divide the surfaces into sections that are filled with symmetrical, infinite patterns (this also applies to the plant-inspired tendril patterns). Such a well-loved decorative scheme challenges the viewer to interpretations, one of which refers to the motif's constructive origins. The classic form of the polygonal star is the octagram, which is constructed from two superimposed squares, one turned forty-five degrees from the other. Both are inscribed in a circle (for the woven pattern, they are usually turned and their edges are lengthened). The four corners of the square offer an interpretation derived from Greek and Near Eastern numerology, in which an ever increasing number of squares produces a circle, thus representing infinity, eternity and the concept of divinity.

△ Ornamental tiles in the entrance iwan of the **Ulugh Beg Madrasah**, 1417–1420, Samarkand, Uzbekistan

◁ Endplate from a **Quran manuscript**, 1568, British Library, London. If one stares at the plaited stars long enough, the pattern appears to move.

▷ Ornamental ceramic tiles, **Alcázar, Seville**, Spain (copied from the Alhambra in Granada)

△ **Door panel**, ca. 1300, Cairo. Wood with ivory inlay, 5 ft 5 in (165 cm) high. The Metropolitan Museum of Art, New York

△ **Silk cloth** (detail), ca. 1350 (Nasridic), 40⅛ in (102 cm) high. The Metropolitan Museum of Art, New York

△ **Mamluk rug** (detail), ca. 1500. Wool, 11 ft 7 in (353 cm) high. The Metropolitan Museum of Art, New York

The Place of Blue Shimmering Paradise

A courtyard prayer hall mosque is centered on the mihrab and follows the qiblah's orientation toward Mecca. The same is true of a Persian four-iwan mosque (the mihrab-iwan replaces the mihrab aisle), but with its four oversized, axial gate halls, it has a clear center in the courtyard. The high, open, hall-like niche of the iwan (a hall with three closed sides, which is completely open in front, sometimes called "liwan") is formally linked to the pre-Islamic fire altar. Also pre-Islamic is the massive rectangular portal (*pishtaq*). The prayer hall's prominent opening, facing the qiblah elite school, should combine with the court's remaining sides to create a "focus of theological energy," making a strong visual im-

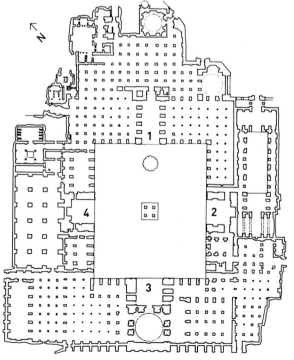

△ Jameh Mosque, north iwan of the madrasah (theological seminary), Isfahan, Iran

◁ Jameh Mosque, floor plan, Isfahan, Iran. The mosque's current condition shows the former oblong-rectangular four-iwan layout (1088–1089) built by the Seljuks and since expanded to the west, north, and east. 1–4 north, east, south, west iwan

pression through the shimmering, turquoise ornamental tile work that covers the brick substructure like an iridescent skin. The popularity of this magnificent ornamental technique spread east of Persia, whereas mosques to the west mostly retained severe exteriors that reflected their desert environments. In Samarkand, the capital of the Timurid Empire, Ulugh Beg (who ruled 1409–1449) erected a representative center at the Registan. Since 1660, this square has been surrounded on three sides by blue- and yellow-tiled four-iwan buildings with enormous entrance iwans, thus becoming an iwan installation itself.

▷ Identical structures of red sandstone and white marble flank the mausoleum; the building on the west side serves as a mosque, the one on the east as a guesthouse. The mausoleum's individual architectural elements are repeated in variations in their façade design.

Taj Mahal

◁ **Taj Mahal**, 1632–1643, Agra, India. Sah Jahan had this mausoleum for his wife built of white marble and set in an enclosed garden; its organization and intersecting pools of water symbolize paradise.

Under the Mughal emperors, who saw themselves as the heirs of Timur Leng, Persian stylistic elements finally arrived in India. Chief among these was the iwan, a graded keel arch carved into a high rectangular gate (pishtaq), and flanked by double rows of (blind) keel niches. In addition, the penchants for axial symmetry and mirroring were also realized in the reflecting pools laid out for precisely that purpose. The minarets are Persian in form, but the bulbous onion domes might be of Indian provenance. The carved red sandstone with decorative accents in white marble is certainly Indian in origin.

The Taj Mahal, constructed solely of white marble with a few black inlays, reveals a confident mastery of proportion. Despite its size, it gives an impression of lightness; it is open and gracious despite its central focus.

▷ Detail of the marble relief at the foot of the mausoleum. Different plants, executed with painstaking attention to nature, are each represented on their own mound of earth.

△ *Sah Jahan on Horseback*, ca. 1650. Ink and gold on paper, 14 1/8 x 9 3/4 in (35.9 x 24.8 cm). The Metropolitan Museum of Art, New York

Shah Jahan's Background

The Mughal ruler Akbar (reigned 1556–1695), famous for the religious tolerance he showed his Hindu subjects, did not consider the Islamic prohibition of images to apply to painting. His court, like that of his successors, therefore propounded a "Europeanization" of painting. The landscapes behind the figures populating these compositions appear more naturalistic, offering broad vistas with classical perspective. The human figures still had to wait a long time before painterly body modeling took hold, but with this development, the unique "Islamic" aspect of painting—the creation of autonomous pictorial spaces parallel but not equal to nature —underwent a slow disappearance.

Sinan's Süleymaniye

Sometime around 1550, Sultan Süleyman I (reigned 1520–1566), who had been busy founding Quranic and elementary schools, hospitals, public kitchens for the poor, public bathhouses and mausolea, undertook an ambitious project. The Ottoman capture of Constantinople lay almost a century in the past, and with the construction of his new mosque, Süleyman also wanted to create an ideological symbol. In this spirit, the Byzantine Hagia Sophia served as the model, because such a synthesis allowed the vanquished Christian past to become part of a legitimating, logical continuum into which the Ottomans' sovereignty was to fit naturally.

The court architect Sinan (ca. 1490–1588) borrowed Hagia Sophia's rectangular courtyard, its prayer hall (or former sanctuary), and its central dome, carried by crossing arches that rest on monumental supports. The structure, with its practically square floor plan, which in cross-section almost appears to be a central-plan building, boasts three aisles at ceiling level. Like a Christian basilica, the dome is expanded along the longitudinal axis of the central aisle by equally broad but shorter semidomes. Along the lateral axis, the crossing arches are sealed with masonry, albeit with windows. The side aisles carry an idiosyncratically designed ceiling that is topped with smaller domes. The spatial impression made by the prayer hall with its height, luminescence and colorful décor is overwhelming. The mihrab on the southeast qiblah wall—originally the only ornamented element in most mosques—is now part of a comprehensive decorative scheme (which, in its current condition, is only partially visible).

After completion of the Süleymaniye, this type of mosque would be built in other regions in the Ottoman sphere of influence, taking on something of the character of a victory monument.

◁+▷ **Sinan, Sultan Süleyman Mosque (Süleymaniye)**, 1550–1557, Istanbul. View of the southwest side of the prayer hall with the smaller domes of the side aisle, above it the windowed screen wall supporting a stepped barrel vault. Although not the front side of the mosque, the sight of pyramidally stacked domes is unmistakable.

From Soldier to Court Architect

Born around 1490 (perhaps in Austria) and baptized as a Christian, Sinan was swept up with his mother in the wave of Ottoman conquest while still a child. Around the age of twenty, converting to Islam and forcibly recruited in Anatolia, his path led him to Istanbul, where he was trained as a janissary. After twenty years of active duty, including as an engineer, he was named court architect in 1539, a post he held for fifty years. He died in 1588 and was buried near the Süleymaniye. Approximately 320 works are attributed to him, from Friday mosques to aqueducts.

◁ **Süleymaniye**, Istanbul, view through the center aisle to the mihrab

▷ **Süleymaniye**, floor plan

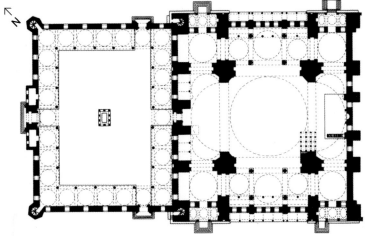

The Idea Behind It

Before designing the Süleymaniye, Sinan grappled with Hagia Sophia. For the Sehzade Mosque, he matched the two semi-domes along the church's main axis with two identical semi-domes on the lateral axis, extending the interior space in equal amounts in all four directions. One distinctive feature of Sinan's first monumental domed space is the low-lying central dome, which is no higher than any side of the square prayer hall is long. The prayer hall can thus be imagined as a cube, which is perhaps meant as a reference to the Ka'bah. But a centrally located prayer hall does have its disadvantages: in a traditional courtyard prayer hall mosque, the direction of Mecca is visually expressed through an emphasis on the mihrab aisle. Not only does a central prayer hall offer no space for this orientation, it also makes such a device impossible.

For the Selimiye, Sinan gave up the Hagia Sophia plan in favor of a central dome that rests on eight pillars, and whose arch thrust is transferred to the exterior through eight buttresses, as opposed to semi-domes. The mihrab is located in a qiblah-iwan outside of the inner octagon—an unsatisfactory solution, since it is hardly visible from the sides.

Sinan's high, pyramidally domed prayer halls, framed by towering "needle minarets," represent a break with a broader Islamic tradition. The Islamic prayer space was originally conceived in terms of a horizontal surface, with the faithful oriented through the qiblah toward Mecca. One Hadi even advises worshippers against elevating their gaze above the horizon. In Sinan's new Islamic space, which seemingly owes more to Christian influence, worshippers must maintain their connection to the earth, even though the heavens open up above them.

▷ Sinan, **Sehzade Mosque**, 1543–1548, Istanbul. Exterior view of the portal side of the courtyard, behind it the prayer hall's "cascade of cupolas"

◁ Mehmet Aga, **Sultan Ahmet Mosque (Blue Mosque)**, 1609–1616, Istanbul. Sinan's student Aga incorporated the forms of the Sehzade Mosque into his design.

▷ **Blue Mosque**, view of the central dome with its four flanking semi-domes

◁ Sinan, **Sultan Selim II Mosque (Selimiye)**, 1569–1575, Edirne, Turkey. View from the southwest

◁◁ **Selimiye**, view of the central domed crossing, to the right the minbar

Topkapı Sarayı

The ground plan of the sultans' palace in Istanbul is organized in a succession of four courtyards. The oldest building in the palace complex, Mehmet II Fatih's Cinili Kösk, dating from 1472, is found in the former first courtyard. The actual sarayı (palace) begins today in the second courtyard's pleasure ground. Even in this semi-public area, speaking was forbidden in the presence of the sultan. The palace kitchens, which could serve up to 6000 meals a day, are located on the east side of the second courtyard, while buildings on the west side housed the stables, bodyguard, treasury and privy council. In the middle of the third courtyard are the audience chamber, and in the north, the sultan's apartments. The palace complex, built and added on to over the centuries, was in use until 1853. It is generally typical of Ottoman residential buildings that the rooms are organized (and expanded according to necessity) around an inner courtyard, without following an underlying plan. Thus the Topkapı Sarayı possesses the most ostentatious apartments and pavilions, but no monumental façades.

▷ **Kiosk of Osman III**, 1754–1755, at the north curtain wall of the sarayı (harem, second/third courtyard)

▷ **Privy chamber of Murad III**, 1578 (harem, second/third courtyard)

▽ **Baghdad Kiosk**, built in 1638 by Murad IV in commemoration of the taking of Baghdad (fourth garden terrace, courtyard)

△ **Imperial Hall**, built 1583–1585, with décor from 1755

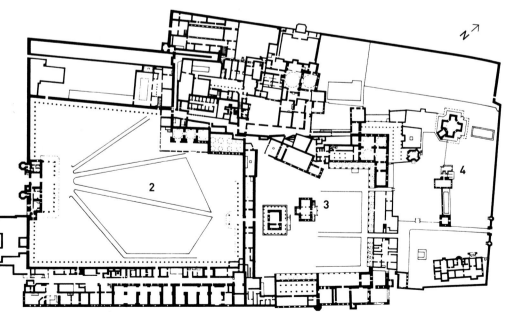

◁ **Topkapı Sarayı**, plan of courtyards 2–4 and of the harem (northwest); courtyard 2: to the south are the palace kitchens, to the north administrative buildings; courtyard 3: audience chamber, sultan's apartments, palace school; courtyard 4: gardens with the Baghdad Kiosk (cruciform structure)

India & Southeast Asia

1526–1857 CE Rule of the Mogul emperors

1857–1947 CE British occupation of India

1930 CE Mahatma Gandhi's Salt March and resistance

1947 CE Indian Independence

Cambodia

1st century BCE–550 CE Kingdom of Funan

802–1431 CE The Khmer people rule over Southeast Asia (Angkor Wat).

1431–1945 CE Foreign rule, French rule from 1863 onward

1945 CE Independence

Thailand

5th–10th centuries CE Mon kingdom (also includes Burma)

1258–1317 CE Mangrai the Great founds the Lanna empire in Thailand, Laos and Burma.

1351–1767 CE Kingdom of Ayutthaya

1782 CE onward Rule of the Chakri dynasty (Rama kings)

India

ca. 2800–1800 BCE Harrapan Culture or Indus Valley Civilization

ca. 1500–600 BCE Aryan invasions and settlement

550–350 BCE Magadha kingdom

321–180 BCE Maurya kingdom

272/68–232 BCE Reign of Emperor Ashoka, who fostered Buddhism.

50 BCE–230 CE Kushan Empire

centered in Gandhara

320–550 CE Gupta kingdom

606–647 CE King Harsha unites northern India.

ca. 700–1200 CE Divided kingdoms of medieval India, Chola kingdom in southern India

1206 CE Founding of the Islamic Delhi Sultanate

Priest-king, Mohenjo-daro, ca. 2100 BCE

Frescoes of Cloud Maidens, Sri Lanka, 5th century CE

The Buddha Vairocana in front of openwork stupas, Borobudur, Java, Indonesia, ca. 800 CE

2100 BCE

400 BCE

800

India & Southeast Asia

Hinduism

As a religion born of old myths and texts regarding sacrificial rituals, Hinduism had no single founder and no immutable canon or heaven with gods. There was no uniform creed, although it had numerous teachings and schools. Since the incursion of Indo-Aryan peoples into India from 1500–600 BCE, the priestly caste of Brahman scribes had written down spiritual knowledge and truths in Sanskrit in the four holy Vedas that still form the basis of Hindu life today. Common to all Hindus were belief in an absolute world order, the Dharma, to which all life conformed and the world was subject, and in the doctrine of the law of karma, the consequences of good and bad deeds that a person had committed in this or in a previous life. Karma determined a person's future incarnations in the realms of Samsara, the cycle of birth, life, death and rebirth. Hindus worshipped personal deities, the most important of which were Shiva and Vishnu.

Buddhism

The art of Southeast Asia was predominantly shaped by Buddhism. The historical Buddha, Siddhartha Gautama, was born in 563 BCE. In the face of suffering and death, he attempted to break the sorrowful cycle of birth and death. After meditating for a long time under the Bodhi tree in Bodhgaya, he attained enlightenment. Around two hundred years after the Buddha's death in 483 BCE, the Buddhist canon was laid down on the basis of the oral tradition. At first, Buddhism knew only the monastic ideal of withdrawing from the world to search for wisdom. This form was called Hinayana, meaning Small Vehicle. Later on, the need for redemption came to include lay people, and the broader path of Mahayana, the Great Vehicle, smoothed the way for Buddhism to become a religion of the people. The ethical ideal of compassion for all creatures now merged with the Perfection of Wisdom.

Vietnam

4th century–1312 CE Champa kingdom in South Vietnam
1009–1407 CE Dai Viet kingdom, Ly and Tran dynasties
1427–1789 CE Le dynasty
1802–1820 CE Emperor Gia Long, start of Nguyen dynasty (through 1945)
1883 CE French protectorate
1946–1954 CE Indochina War and partition of the country
1964–1975 CE Vietnam War

Burma (Myanmar)

ca. 240–1280 CE Pyu city-states and Bagan kingdom
825–1725 CE Mon kingdom at Bago
1885–1948 CE British occupation
1962 CE on Military dictatorships

Shiva as Lord of the Dance (Nataraja), 11th century CE

Angkor Wat, Cambodia, ca. 1150 CE

Young woman, Bikaner, Rajasthan, India, ca. 1800 CE

1000   1100   1800

At a Glance

The Bodhisattva Avalokiteshvara

S/he was the Bodhisattva (Enlightenment Being) of universal compassion, meaning "lord who gazes down at the world." As a protective deity and savior, s/he enjoyed great popularity. In Buddhist art, s/he was often depicted with multiple heads and the suggestion of 1000 arms and hands, the symbol of universal help.

Avalokiteshvara, Cambodia, mid-12th century CE. Sandstone, 6½ × 3¾ × 3 in (16.5 × 9.5 × 8 cm). Los Angeles County Museum of Art, Los Angeles

Mandalas

Buddhist, paradisiac images of the Pure Lands were portrayed in complex, circular or square-shaped geometric configurations. To this day, monks create artful, highly detailed images out of colored sand (see also p. 595).

Mahabharata

The greatest Indian epic poem originated between 400 BCE and 400 CE. In approximately 100,000 double verses, it relates the battle between two ruling families, and tells of the hero Arjuna's purification and attainment of wisdom. The epic also contains the sacred Hindu scripture the *Bhagavad Gita*, in which Lord Krishna teaches Arjuna about various Yogic and Vedantic philosophies.

Krishna

This Indian hero with messianic traits was considered the incarnation of the god Vishnu. In Indian mythology, he grew up among cattle herdsmen and was the symbol of religious piety, philosophical wisdom and valor. Radha was his spiritual companion. Krishna became the archetype of numerous teachings about devoutness, e.g., the Hare Krishna movement.

Krishna battles with the Horse Demon Keshi, India, 5th century CE

The Goddess Kali

Along with the Goddess Durga, Kali chiefly symbolizes the female aspects of divinity in its double meaning of fertility and destruction. The "black Kali" is terrifyingly depicted with sacrificial knife, a chain of skulls, and her tongue showing.

Ramayana

In seven books with around 24,000 verses (*shlokas*), the Epic of Ramayana told of the deeds of King Rama who, as an incarnation of the God Vishnu, embodied goodness. The epic also told of his fight against evil demons and his love for the princess Sita.

Stupas

In Buddhism, these hemispherical or pagoda-shaped burial mounds mainly served to store relics. Their interior and exterior construction followed strict rules that represented elements of Buddhist cosmology, such as the sacred Mount Meru or the "cosmic egg" from which all life hatched.

The Great Stupa at Sanchi, India, 2nd century BCE

India & Southeast Asia

Trimurti

The "Great Trinity" represented the three most important Hindu gods: Brahma (the creator), Vishnu (the preserver), and Shiva (the destroyer), symbol of Samsara or the Cycle of Existence. In many modern Hindu teachings, Vishnu and Shiva enjoy nearly monotheistic veneration.

Shiva Temple at Elephanta, relief, India

Apsara combing her hair, relief, Khmer, ca. 1000 CE.
Musée Guimet, Paris

Apsaras

In Hindu and Buddhist art and mythology, they were shown as half-human, half-godlike young women full of comeliness and grace. Most were portrayed in dancing pose and were comparable to Greek nymphs. Their presentation on the walls of Angkor Wat was particularly impressive.

Mantras

In Hinduism and Buddhism, the short formulae used in prayers and recited many times are a means of meditation and of serving god.

Mudras

The Sanskrit word for "seal" refers to specific, symbolic hand positions and gestures, such as blessing, protection or meditative contemplation. Buddhas and bodhisattvas are depicted in this way. In Indian dance, mudras are also stylistic modes of positioning the hands.

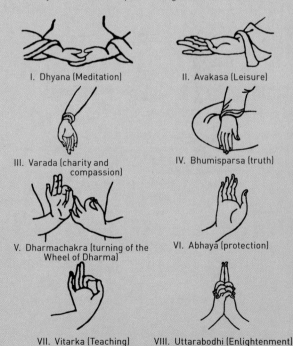

I. Dhyana (Meditation)

II. Avakasa (Leisure)

III. Varada (charity and compassion)

IV. Bhumisparsa (truth)

V. Dharmachakra (turning of the Wheel of Dharma)

VI. Abhaya (protection)

VII. Vitarka (Teaching)

VIII. Uttarabodhi (Enlightenment)

Key Terms

Dim, Distant Past in the Indus Valley?

◁ **Torso of a male figure (priest-king)**, Mohenjo-daro, ca. 2100 BCE. Limestone, 6¾ in (17.5 cm) high. National Museum of Pakistan, Karachi

▽ **Seal with animal figures**, Harappa, ca. 2500–2000 BCE. Steatite, 1½ in (3.8 cm) high. National Museum of Pakistan, Karachi

Along with Egypt and Mesopotamia, the Indus Valley Civilization in the area of today's Pakistan and bordering regions was the third of the early Bronze Age civilizations known to us so far. Also called the Harappa culture, it is named for the place where it was first discovered. From the eighth century onwards, Neolithic settlements were built in the northwestern part of the Indian subcontinent. The Harappa culture flourished along the Indus around 2600 BCE. Seals with the (not yet decoded) pictorial Indus script show motifs that seem to be related in subject matter to those from Mesopotamia, since they concern specific mythical creatures.

The ancient city of Mohenjo-daro is better preserved. Located approximately 373 miles (600 km) southwest of Harappa, it had a population of up to thirty-five thousand. The largest stone sculptures of human beings include the so-called priest-king, a

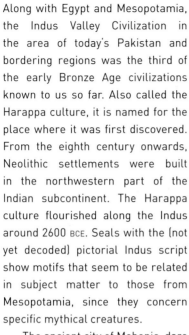

figure that had to be shown kneeling or squatting. The auspicious cloverleaf ornament on his mantle is conspicuous and, in Mesopotamia, was already known as a symbol of the divine. Like the settings on the head and arm bands, the cloverleaves were once filled with colored paste. The many female terracotta figures show women with conspicuous jewelry and often extravagant hairstyles. The material in itself may suggest that these figures had ritual significance as mother goddesses because according to many ancient creation myths, humans were created from earth or clay.

△ **Female figure (mother goddess)**, Mohenjo-daro, Pakistan, ca. 2500 BCE. Clay, National Museum of Pakistan, Karachi

Access to Stupas

The Mauryan emperor Ashoka (ca. 273–236 BCE) was able to unite almost all of India, which fostered the spread of Buddhism. He is credited with founding the first temple complex at Sanchi, site of one of the oldest ritualistic Buddhist stupas. Stupas are called *chörten* in Tibet, *chedi* in Thailand and Burma, and pagodas in China, Korea and Japan. They are usually memorials to the Buddha that evolved from burial mounds, and are often used for the safe storage of some kind of relic. Most importantly, stupas are esoteric symbols of the Buddha's enlightenment and the path to Buddhahood. The center is not accessible, as there is no interior, and a person can only reach it through meditation. In many stupas, the center consists of a smaller stupa, and each is a symbol of the Buddha. At the same time, the base represents the earth and its dome represents the heavenly regions. The smaller building at Sanchi lies beneath the present stupa and dates back to the time of Ashoka; like all stupas, it has been renovated time and again. Gates lead the faithful coming from the cardinal directions into circumambulation (▷) and instruct them with reliefs depicting the life of the Lord Buddha.

△ **Back view of the eastern portal of the Stupa at Sanchi**, India, 1st century BCE

△ **The Great Stupa of Sanchi**, seen from the south, Sanchi, India, 2nd century BCE

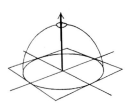 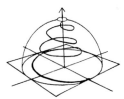 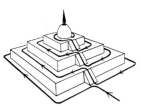

△ Just as every stupa is oriented towards the spire, the aspirations of the believer should be oriented towards achieving Nirvana. For this reason, the ascending movement during ritual circumambulation (Pradakshina) is an ascent from the edge to the center and from lower to higher levels. The individual merges with cosmic consciousness, resulting in the experience of spiritual enlightenment and the attainment of Buddhahood.

◁ The form of the stupa symbolizes the seated Buddha.

First Images of the Buddha

Siddhartha Gautama died in 483 BCE. In the first centuries after the Buddha achieved Nirvana, followers apparently refrained from portraying the religious founder in figural form, but his footprint and other symbols signaled his presence. The first images in human form come from the Kushan period (50 BCE–230 CE), especially from Mathura (southeast of Delhi). They show a fairly soft modeling of the enthroned Buddha in a translucent robe, his right hand raised in the gesture of protection (Abhaya mudra). He is flanked by disciples, and the lion throne shows him as universal ruler.

The Buddha figures from Gandhara (now in Pakistan) also belong to the Kushan period. As a result of Alexander the Great's conquests in India, Gandhara art shows the influence of Hellenistic culture. So it was that Greco-Buddhist artists presented the Buddha as an ancient philosopher among his pupils (opposite, top). The robe with lush folds is reminiscent of ancient togas and gives few clues as to the body underneath it. Only in Gandhara was the Buddha portrayed as an emaciated, fasting ascetic (opposite, bottom left). Not until after this test did he find the path to meditation under the Tree of Enlightenment.

◁ The Buddha teaching on a lion throne, Mathura, Uttar Pradesh, India, 1st–2nd century CE. Sandstone, 36½ in (93 cm) high. Kimbell Art Museum, Fort Worth. The typical bun or cranial dome on the Buddha's head beneath his hair, a symbol of Enlightenment and transcendent wisdom (ushnisha), has been lost. Compared to the elegant art of Gandhara, the Buddha from Mathura looks archaic.

△ **The Buddha's first sermon at Sarnath**, Gandhara, Pakistan, 2nd century CE. Slate, 11¼ in (28.6 cm) high. The Metropolitan Museum of Art, New York

▷ **The Shakyamuni Buddha**, Gandhara, Pakistan, 3rd century CE. Slate, 20 in (50.8 cm) high. The Metropolitan Museum of Art, New York

▽ **The Fasting Buddha**, Gandhara, Pakistan, 3rd–5th centuries CE. Slate, 11 in (27.8 cm) high. The Metropolitan Museum of Art, New York

The Bamiyan Buddha

In Central Asia, Buddhist art was mainly found in cave temples and monasteries in the valleys of Afghanistan, where caravans stopped to rest after crossing the Hindu Kush. Bamiyan had always been a Buddhist center with ties to India. That is why Hellenistic influences from Gandhara can be felt in works of art created there between 400 and 900 CE. The style was pure at first, but then incorporated elements from the neighboring Persian Sassanid Empire (224–642 CE).

The Buddha of Bamiyan, roughly hewn from the rock, was originally wrapped in a Gandhara-style folding robe and wore baggy trousers. Paintings in the rocky alcove above his head show a number of Buddhas with nimbi and halos.

Dome paintings from the temple ruins in the Kakrak Valley also show the Buddha with a nimbus surrounded by multicolored aureoles. He sits on a lotus cushion and performs the gesture of explanation or teaching (Vitarka mudra) with right hand raised, while the left one rests on his knee with fingers in motion. Pictures of stupas fill the spandrels of the vault.

◁ **Colossal statue of the Buddha**, Bamiyan, Afghanistan, 5th century CE. Rock, 174 ft (53 m) high. The Buddha figure, originally the tallest in the world, had already been damaged several times by Islamic iconoclasts before it was blown up by the Taliban in 2001.

▷ **Seated Buddha**, Kakrak near Bamiyan, Afghanistan, 6th century CE. Painting on clay, a fragment of a painted dome of the temple ruins of Kakrak, 19½ in (50 cm) high. Kabul Museum

Courtly Life

Important ancient Indian paintings have been preserved as murals in cave monasteries and residences. The twenty-nine caves surrounding the rocks at Ajanta were inhabited by Buddhists from the second to the fifth centuries. Along with scenes from the Buddha's earthly existence, there are revealing images of a courtly life that was filled with sensuality. Illustrations concerning the history of palace life give highly accurate information about clothing, musical instruments and everyday implements They frequently cover the walls of the caves without clear demarcation, so descriptions blend into one another, and the original context becomes blurred. In many of the faces, the treatment of the eyes keeps a fifth-century ideal of beauty alive. Extended lid lines accentuate the almond-shaped look of the eyes.

In Sri Lanka, the Sinhalese King Kasyapa I (478–96 CE) had a residence built atop the "Lion Rock" of Sigiriya. The ascent led beneath an over-hanging cliff that was decorated with half-length pictures of lithe girls emerging from clouds and welcoming visitors, the most important of whom was, of course, the godlike king himself. These are the Apsaras of Hindu epics like the *Ramayana*. After the ocean was stirred up, they rose out of the water and were celebrated as celestial nymphs on account of their grace and beauty.

△ **Lovers**, scene from the legend of Prince Visvantara, Ajanta, India, Cave 17, 5th century CE, wall painting

▷ **Two Women Praying**, Ajanta, India, Cave 1, 5th century CE, wall painting. These cave dwellings (Vihara) were decorated with scenes from the life of the Buddha.

▷ **Apsaras above the clouds** (cloud maidens), Sigiriya, Sri Lanka, 5th century CE, wall painting

◁ **Standing Buddha**, Mathura, Uttar Pradesh, India, 5th century CE. Sandstone, 33½ in (85.5 cm) high. The Metropolitan Museum of Art, New York

▽ **Buddha, Gal Vihara** (rock temple), Polonnaruwa, Sri Lanka, late 12th century CE. Granite, 46 ft 4 in (14.12 m) long. The figure shows the Buddha in transition between the world and Nirvana (parinirvana). The height of the standing Buddha on the left is 22 ft 8 in (6.93 m).

The Classic Image of the Buddha

In northern India, the golden age of classical Indian art took place under the Gupta (330–ca. 550 CE). Sutras on architecture, sculpture and painting attempted to lay down the inherent form and meaning of a work. In spite of many local variants, these art forms retained unifying elements that had a far-reaching spatial and temporal impact. There is no doubt that these Buddhist sculptures were in the tradition of the Mathura School and, especially in the case of Buddha images, held very firmly to the fron-tal, upright form. As with Gandhara sculptures, the Buddha was fully clothed, but the natural Hellenistic drapery had given way to a purely ornamental linear pattern The Buddha's right hand was originally and customarily raised in the gesture of protection. His head, covered with tightly curled locks, was framed by a richly decorated nimbus, the most impressive feature of the statue.

By sending his son and daughter there as ambassadors of the faith, Emperor Ashoka won the island of Sri Lanka for Buddhism in the third century BCE. In the centuries that followed, monasteries, stupas (Sinhalese dagobas), and Indian-influenced works of art were built on the island. Even much later on, both the hairstyle and clothing of the colossal reclining Buddha at Polonnaruwa retained traditional stylistic elements from the Gupta period.

Hindu Vitality

In contrast with the peaceful, almost incorporeal Buddhist sculptures of the Gupta period, the vitality exuding from concurrent Hindu sculptures is astonishing. Hindu gods are depicted primarily as youthful nobles in action. A style centered on supple, well-proportioned figures in characteristic tribhanga pose (triple bend, standing) would emerge and remain in force long after the Gupta period. Their faces look ethereal, the clothing of the figures smooth, almost unadorned, so that nothing diverts attention from their lithe bodies.

The ritual, erotic movements that typify the decorative figures on the Khajuraho temples suggests that physical unification was auspicious and enjoyed special divine approval. The fanciful forms of mating pay little consideration to what was anatomically possible and follow their own laws of dynamic motion.

△ **Krishna in battle with the horse demon Keshi**, 5th century CE. Fired clay, 21 in (53.3 cm) high. The Metropolitan Museum of Art, New York

◁ **Bas-relief with erotic scenes**, south wall of the Kandariya Mahadev Temple, Khajuraho, India, 11th century CE. Sandstone. The figures are almost life size.

▷ **Shiva as The Lord of Dance** (Nataraja), 11th century CE. Bronze, 27 in (68.3 cm) high. The Metropolitan Museum of Art, New York. Shiva performs the dance of wisdom within the flaming circle of cosmic forces, thereby crushing the demon of worldliness and ignorance. He holds the drum of creation in his upper right hand and the fire of destruction in the upper left one.

Java, the Sacred

Borobudur lies in the middle of Java, northwest of Yogyakarta, and is the most extensive example of Buddhist sacred architecture in Southeast Asia. Built ca. 800 CE, the structure is a monumental stupa in the shape of a 148-ft (45-m) high mountain on a square base whose sides are 371 ft (113 m) long. The base consists of five terraces, topped by three circular platforms that lie atop one another. These in turn are crowned by a central stupa reached by four axial staircases. In the imagery of pre-Buddhist Java, mountains were important religious symbols. The same is true for Buddhism, where they are symbols of the sacred Mount Sumeru (or Meru) at the center of the universe.

△ Statue of the Buddha Vairocana in front of open-work stupas, Borobudur, Java, Indonesia, ca. 800 CE. The Buddha shows the gesture of setting the Wheel of Dharma teaching in motion (Dharmachakra mudra).

▷ Plan of Borobudur

It is not known if a relic was stored in the central stupa. The ground plan of Borobudur, in the shape of a mandala, is intended to lead ritually to higher spiritual consciousness, hence pilgrims circumambulate the square terraces, one after another. The Buddhist cosmos unfolds in approximately 1500 reliefs on the walls of the terrace galleries. The life of Buddha is shown in 120 reliefs over the entire length of the first gallery. The reliefs illustrate the text of the Lalitavistara Sutra (The Unfolding of the Play), which arose from the idea that the Buddha's life was a kind of performance intended to enlighten humanity.

World Mountains

Every Hindu temple embodied the mythical Mount Meru, seat of the gods and navel of the universe. There was space in its cavernous interior for images and symbols of deities. Logically enough, early ritual locations were cut into natural rock. The ends of rocky promontories could be made into small, individual monolithic shrines whose shapes were probably derived from wooden ritual buildings that have not sur-vived. From about the ninth century, more and more temples were built as free-standing stone structures. Most temple ground plans were sacred geometric diagrams that took on the shape of a mandala. This concentric geometric figure, resting on repeatedly subdivided squares, was understood to represent the structure of the universe. Walls and towers symbolized mountaintops, forming a cosmic axis with the sacred relic within the temple. The tiered sequence of towers with sweeping contours was modeled on mountain summits. As in Khajuraho, the various components could also be merged into a single edifice that rose up to the temple tower. In contrast to Buddhist architectural sculpture, Hindu design followed a strictly prescribed, canonical plan with regard to a particular temple.

▷ Lakshmana
Temple,
Khajuraho, India,
954 CE (dated by
inscription)

▷ Monolithic
temples (rathas),
Mamallapuram,
India, ca. 620–
630 CE

▽ Base of the
Surya Temple,
Konark, India,
ca. 1250 CE. The
concept of the
temple as chariot
of a god (ratha) is
shown here.

The Smile of Angkor

At the beginning of the ninth century, classical Khmer art developed in the wake of Khmer unification under King Jayavarman II. This art was centered in the vast temple complex in the Cambodian jungle at Angkor. Although many of the buildings were erected to honor rulers rather than to glorify god, it remains the largest sacred edifice in the world when taken as a whole. Suryavarman II

(r. 1113–1150 CE), a staunch Hindu, commissioned Angkor Wat, meaning City Temple. Its structure and arrangement made it the largest, most harmonious edifice at Angkor.

Religion did not become important again until Jayavarman VII took the throne in 1181 CE and embraced Buddhism, which is expressed in the form known as "the smile of Angkor." The sculpture of this classic Khmer

period remained uncompromising in its frontality, and the contours of facial features, such as brows, eyes and mouth, were markedly horizontal. This art deliberately used simpler shapes in order to achieve an ideal full of clarity and suffused with inner peace. It was solely oriented towards a religious goal and created as a single cosmologically devout whole, the most important

◁ **Sanctuary of Angkor Wat**, Cambodia, ca. 1150 CE

▽ **Demons fight for the possession of Apsaras**, detail of a relief from Angkor, Cambodia, ca. 967 CE. Sandstone, total dimensions 6 ft 5 in × 8 ft 10 in (196 × 269 cm). Musée Guimet, Paris. The scene recalls an episode from the *Mahabharata* that portrays the triumph of virtue over vice. It is the second great Hindu epic, the other being the *Ramayana*.

◁ **Kneeling Prajnaparamita**, Angkor, Cambodia, ca. 1200 CE. Sandstone, 4 ft 3 in (130 cm) high. Musée Guimet, Paris. The goddess of transcendental wisdom and mother of all Buddhas probably has the features of Queen Jayarajadevi, the wife of Jayavarman VII.

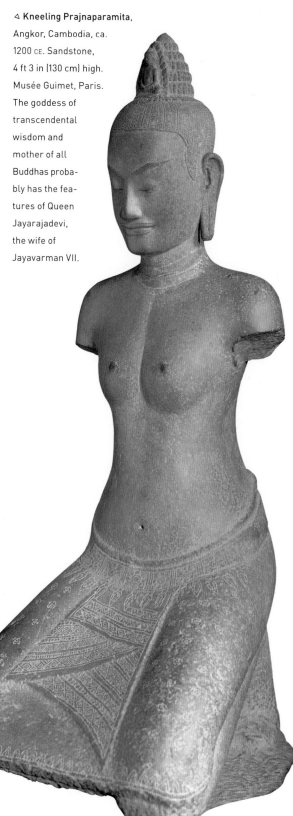

component of which was meditation. The sculptors already understood their work to be a sacred act. They performed no individual artistic feats, but considered themselves part of a religious event.

◁ **Buddha Kakusanda**, ca. 1100 CE. Painted and gilt wood, 31 ft (9.5 m) high. Ananda Temple, Bagan, Myanmar (Burma)

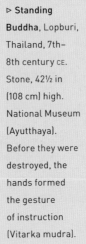

▷ **Standing Buddha**, Lopburi, Thailand, 7th–8th century CE. Stone, 42½ in (108 cm) high. National Museum (Ayutthaya). Before they were destroyed, the hands formed the gesture of instruction (Vitarka mudra).

Rest and Movement, Symmetry and Opposition

Buddhism had already reached Burma with the Indian Emperor Ashoka (ca. 273–236 BCE) and became firmly rooted at Bagan during the city's heyday in the mid-eleventh century. The most ancient temple in Bagan, the Ananda Temple, housed the four Buddhas that had appeared up to that time: Kakusanda, Konagamana, Kassapa

and Gautama. The unusual hand gestures (mudras) of these Buddhas have not yet been deciphered. Along with the legendary Dvaravati Kingdom (now in central Thailand), the Mon people of southern Burma also embraced Buddhism. The art of the Mon (seventh to eighth centuries) was based on Indian models and for the

most part, the Buddha appears in strictly symmetrical form in a standing position with frontal view. From approximately 1000 CE until the founding of the first independent Thai kingdom of Sukhothai in ca. 1236 CE, the country's ruling Khmer also influenced Thai art. With the development of an independent style, Sukhotai became the cradle of Thai culture and the nation. The sculpture reveals an effort to do anatomical justice to the frequently cited, supernatural physicality of the Buddha. The idealized shapes accord with the concept of transcendent beauty.

Laotian figures of the Buddha were inspired by Thai art and show a similar tendency toward stylization of the facial features. Among the most striking features are the sweeping, crescent-shaped eyebrows that merge into the sharp-edged bridge of the curved, beak-like nose.

Champa was an Indianized kingdom along the east coast of the Indochinese peninsula in what is known today as South Vietnam. The art of Champa, like that of the neighboring ancient Khmer civilization, contained both Hindu and Buddhist subject matter. Champan style was a blend of influences from Khmer and Indonesian art. An example of classical, tenth-century Champa art is known as the My Son A1 style, which was distinguished by the special dynamism and smoothness of the figures. It reached its zenith in the rhythmic movements of the temple dancers on the reliefs at Tra Kieu.

◁ **Head of a Buddha**, Sukhothai, Thailand, 14th–15th century CE. Bronze, 30 in (77 cm) high. National Museum, Bangkok

▷ **Female dancer**, Tra Kieu, Vietnam, 10th century. Stone, Cham Museum (Bao Tang), Da Nang

◁ **Seated Buddha**, Ho Phra Keo, Vientiane, Laos, bronze. The Buddha's hand position shows the Bhumisparsa (Touching the Earth) mudra. He touched the fingertips of his right hand to the earth, calling it as witness to the truth of his words.

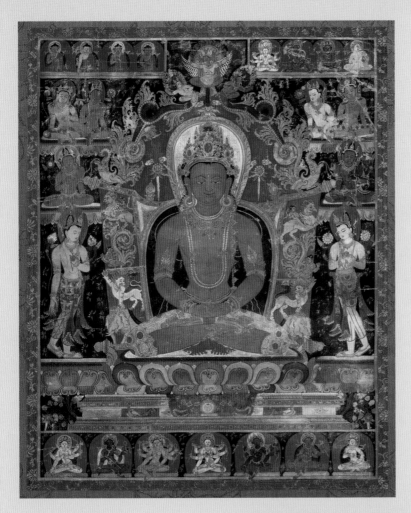

Portable Painting

Ancient Indian literary references testify to the fact that, in addition to wall paintings, there were small-scale, portable paintings. Miniature paintings give us an idea of what these were like and can be broken down into two genres: illustrations of religious texts, and courtly themes and portraits. Buddhist miniatures in the style of Indian Ajanta have been preserved only in Nepal and Tibet, where monks were able to save them from the Islamic invasion. With the spread of Islam to India after 1200 CE, Hindu art and architecture were neglected, having already been marginalized by Buddhist art and architecture. With the Moguls, a more tolerant dynasty came to power after 1516 CE, and Hindu themes, which had never quite been forgotten, became popular subjects for miniature paintings once again. Krishna's affair with the shepherd girl Radha, whose love ran the gamut from the physical and

△ **Buddha of the Eternal Life (Amitayus) and Eight Bodhisattvas**, Tibet or Nepal, 11th century CE. Distemper and fabric, 16¼ × 13 in (41.3 × 33 cm). Museum of Fine Arts, Boston. The crowned Buddha is shown with a halo and aureole surrounding his entire body. He is accompanied by eight Bodhisattvas above and seven deities below.

▷ **Krishna Battles the Armies of the Demon Naraka**, page from a dispersed *Bhagavata Purana* (Ancient Stories of Lord Vishnu), Delhi-Agra region, India, 1520–1530 CE. Ink and opaque watercolor on paper, 7 × 9 in (17.8 × 23.2 cm). The Metropolitan Museum of Art, New York. Krishna, whose name means black or dark blue, was the eighth incarnation of Vishnu, one of the main Hindu gods.

worldly to the divinely transcendent, was particularly in demand. Islamic-trained miniaturists were at pains not to expose themselves to charges of realistically mimicking God's creation. In their pictures, therefore, they deliberately invented a world with its own optical laws. There were no shadows or foreshortening, but the same image was seen from several perspectives, from above and below, inside and out. Their human and historical figures are serene, their faces in profile, making it immediately clear that they neither can nor should ever come to life.

△ **Young woman holding cup and flask**, Bikaner, Rajasthan, India, ca. 1800 CE. Opaque paint and gold on paper, 9½ × 6½ in (24 × 16.9 cm). Museum of Fine Arts, Boston

◁ **Krishna visiting Radha**, Bikaner, Rajasthan, India, 1694–1695 CE or earlier. Opaque paint, gold and silver on paper, 7¾ × 5½ in (19.8 × 13.8 cm). Museum of Fine Arts, Boston

▽ **Portrait of Darab Khan**, period of Mogul rule, 17th century CE. Ink and color on paper, 4¼ × 6¼ in (10.8 × 16 cm). Museum of Fine Arts, Boston

East Asia

Legend:
- Palace, mausoleum
- Pagoda, temple, monastery, shrine
- Buddha statue
- Garden
- School of painting
- Ceramics
- Silk Road
- Great Wall

Confucianism

Confucianism became China's ethical and philosophical system and spread from there to many countries in Asia. Confucius (K'ung-fu-tzu, 551–479 BCE) developed his theories during a spiritually fertile but politically unstable time. The first emperor Qin Shi Huang (221–210 BCE) used harsh laws to unite the kingdom, and this caused the teachings to fail initially. But they gained subsequent acceptance as the state philosophy in China and, from the sixth century onwards, in Japan as well. Confucianism called for strict, ethical living that was oriented towards *Ren* (the concept of humanness) and lifelong learning with a positive view of the arts.

China

ca. 7000–4000 BCE Hemudu culture
ca. 5000–3000 BCE Yangshao culture
ca. 3000–2000 BCE Longshan culture
ca. 2205–1766 BCE Xia dynasty
ca. 1600–1039 BCE Shang dynasty
ca. 1045–222 BCE Zhou dynasty
475–211 BCE Warring States period
221–206 BCE Qin dynasty
206 BCE–220 CE Han dynasty (Western Han until 8th century)
220–280 CE Three Kingdoms period
265–316 CE Western Jin dynasty
317–420 CE Eastern Jin dynasty

386–589 CE North and South dynasties (Wei, among others)
581–618 CE Sui dynasty
618–906 CE Tang dynasty
690–705 CE Second Zhou dynasty
907–960 CE Five dynasties in the north
902–979 CE Ten kingdoms in the south
907–1234 CE Foreign dynasties, including Jin (1115–1234) and Liao (907–1125)
960–1279 CE Song dynasty
1279–1368 CE Yuan dynasty (Mongols)
1368–1644 CE Ming dynasty
1644–1912 CE Qing dynasty (Manchus)

1912–1949 CE Republic of China
1949 CE–present People's Republic of China and Taiwan

Japan

ca. 10,000–300 BCE Jomon period
250 BCE–300 CE Yayoi period
300–700 CE Kofun or Yamato period
552–710 CE Asuka period

Storage vessel, Yangshao, ca. 2200 BCE

Kneeling archer, Qin, ca. 210 BCE

Yan Liben, Wu Ti, ruler of the Northern Chou, Tang (618–906 CE)

Daibutsu (Amida Buddha), Kamakura, 1252 CE

2000 BCE   200 BCE   900   1200

East Asia

Taoism

Taoism also goes back to the time of the Warring States. It has been attributed to the sage Lao Tse, who may have been a mythical figure, and to his work, the *Tao Te Ching* ("True Classic of the Way and the Power"). Taoism is a nature-loving philosophy of wisdom that soon took on features of popular religion and formed sects. The observance of *Tao* (universal law) is an ideal that harmoniously guides everything and is easier to grasp intuitively. In contrast to Confucianism, Taoism promotes the "live-and-let-live" of the Tao and the ideal of *wu-wei*, "without action" or "without striving."

Shintoism

Shinto (Way of the Gods) is Japan's indigenous spirituality, a set of practices whose holy places are mountains and springs. Early on, Shinto was linked to Japan's creation myths, whose supreme deity was the sun goddess Amaterasu. Shinto divine beings or souls are called *kami*. Kami were everything outstanding and exceptional, be it natural phenomena or important people, so their numbers grew constantly. Ancestral kami played a special role as guardian spirits of families.

Buddhism

Buddhism reached East Asia in the first centuries of the Common Era. After initial attacks, its inherent flexibility allowed it to combine with Confucianism and Taoism in China, and with Shintoism and Confucianism in Japan. Thus, many religious practices in these countries are hybrids. The predominant form in China is meditative Chan Buddhism. In Japan, it developed into Zen Buddhism, which significantly influences the Japanese way of life to this day. Zen masters practice sitting meditation with the help of anecdotes; they also place great value on manual labor.

710–1185 CE Nara period
794–1192 CE Heian period
1192–1333 CE Kamakura period
1333–1568 CE Muromachi period
1568–1603 CE Azuchi-Momoyama period
1603–1868 CE Edo period
1868–1912 CE Meiji period
1912–1926 CE Taisho period

1926–1989 CE Showa period
1989–present Heisei period

Korea

2333–108 BCE Gojoseon kingdom
108 BCE–668 CE Three Kingdoms
668–936 CE Unified (Later) Silla kingdom
936–1392 CE Goryeo kingdom

1392–1897 Joseon (Choson) dynasty
1897–1910 CE Greater Korean Empire
1910–1945 CE Japanese occupation
1948–present Partitioning of the country

Mandala of Jnanadakini, Tibet, 14th century CE

Palichuang Pagoda, Beijing, 1576 CE

Katsura Rikyu, interior view of the Imperial Villa, Kyoto, 1624 CE

Katsushika Hokusai, *The Great Wave off Kanagawa*, 1830–1832 CE

1500   1600   1800

At a Glance

Imperial Cults

In China and Japan, emperors had mainly ceremonial functions like drawing up calendars or tasting the first harvest. By means of complex rituals at court, they also ensured harmony between heaven and earth. These duties were gradually replaced with real power, especially in Japan. The first Japanese *tenno* (heavenly emperor) was Jimmu. Descended directly in an unbroken line from the sun goddess Amaterasu, he was a sacred "living god" or kami. On the other hand, the Chinese emperor could "lose the mandate of heaven." This is how dynasties were legitimately overthrown on many occasions.

Temple of Heaven, Beijing, Forbidden City, Ming, 1420 CE

The Family

The Confucian concept of the family is conservative and strictly hierarchical. Confucius and, to an even greater extent, the second great teacher of Confucianism, Meng-tzu or Mencius (ca. 370–290 BCE), formulated the deferential and obedient relationships of a wife to her husband, children to their parents, younger persons to their elders, and officials to the emperor. Those in stronger positions were, therefore, obliged to grant protection and guidance to those who were weaker.

Portrait of an ancestor, China, ca. 1800 CE. Silk painting, 64¾ × 39¾ in (165 × 101.5 cm). Private collection

Samurai

The knightly or warrior class in Japan was occasionally a kind of state within the state and followed its own strict *bushido* (code of honor). This loyalty to the *daimyo* (feudal lord), even to death, included willingness to sacrifice, toughness and resistance. The samurai were primarily archers and swordsmen. They adhered mostly to Zen Buddhist teachings and, in cases of shame or failure, were required to commit suicide by *seppuku* (disembowelment). It was not until Meiji Emperor Mutsuhito (1868–1912 CE) that the samurai were ousted in favor of modern, Western-style armed forces.

Seated figure of Minamoto no Yoritomo, the first shogun, Kamakura, 13th–14th century, National Museum, Tokyo

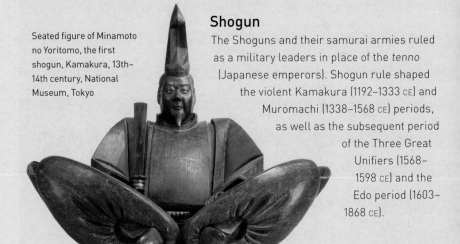

Shogun

The Shoguns and their samurai armies ruled as a military leaders in place of the *tenno* (Japanese emperors). Shogun rule shaped the violent Kamakura (1192–1333 CE) and Muromachi (1338–1568 CE) periods, as well as the subsequent period of the Three Great Unifiers (1568–1598 CE) and the Edo period (1603–1868 CE).

The Silk Road

This important caravan route between East Asia and the Mediterranean, whose control was often hotly contested, was an artery for important cultural exchange. The principal items transported between continents and cultures were silk, textiles, spices, herbs, perfumes, glass and porcelain, but so were books and manuscripts. Of course, the Silk Road also became a trading center for religions, philosophies and ideas that transcended borders.

East Asia

Writing and Calligraphy

Chinese characters, which also form the basis for writing in Japan, Korea and Vietnam, are a syllabic script in which each graphic symbol (Han character or logogram) represents both meaning and pronunciation. The writing is extremely complex and contains up to 87,000 different characters, only 3000–10,000 of which are commonly used. It developed out of simple symbols, called pictograms, that pictorially resemble what they signify. From time immemorial, brush calligraphy, mostly in black ink, has constituted high art in China and Japan.

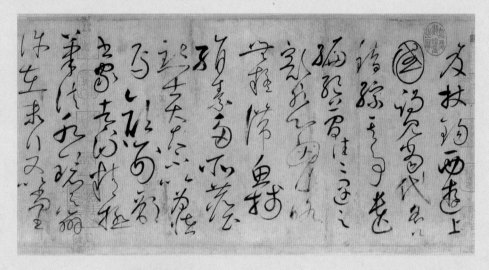

△ Huai-su, autobiographical calligraphy, Tang, National Museum, Taipei

◁ Seal script calligraphy

◁ Li Jinxne, modern calligraphy for the characters Mo, the Confucian philosopher Mozi (5th century BCE), and Zhuang, the Taoist philosopher Zhuangzi (4th century BCE), private collection, Sydney

△ Development of Chinese characters, using the symbols for sun (top row) and moon (lower row) as examples

Paper

Findings show that the Chinese already knew how to make paper in the second century BCE. In 105 CE, the scholar Tsai Lun (ca. 50–121 CE) was the first to describe the processing of plant fibers, which were crushed to a pulp, then formed into paper, pressed and dried. Before that, people in China wrote on discarded fragments of silk.

Printing

By 581 CE, woodblock printing was already known in China. This developed into printing with movable wooden type around 1040 CE. Printing with movable metal type, which is to say modern printing methods, originated in Korea around 1232 CE. The oldest surviving collection produced with the metal printing process was the Korean Buddhist Jikji from 1377 CE.

Key Terms

◁ Ding (vessel) with
taotie motif, Zhou, ca.
1050 BCE. Bronze, Museum of
East Asian Art, Bath

▷ Banshan ware, Yangshao, ca. 2200 BCE.
Clay storage container, 16 in (40.7 cm) high.
Kimbell Art Museum, Fort Worth

◁ Guang (ritual wine
vessel), Shang, ca.
1050 BCE. Bronze, 8½ in
(21.6 cm) high. The
Metropolitan Museum
of Art, New York

Early Works in Clay and Bronze

Ancestor worship was of central importance in Chinese art, and already appeared in the late-Neolithic Longshan and Yangshao cultures. In order to sacrifice to the ancestral spirits, people prepared food and heated wine in special containers that were placed in the grave with the deceased after burial. Simple geometric ornaments, some suggesting human faces, adorned clay pots that were thrown on potter's wheels as early as ca. 2000 BCE in the Middle Kingdom.

The artistic production of bronze ritual vessels came in with the Shang, one of the first historically documented dynasties. They were poured into clay molds that were taken from clay models (piece-mold casting). The decorations became increasingly elaborate, and a kind of zoomorphic symbolism developed that is only partly intelligible today. The *taotie* (wolverine) motif was an especially popular, eerily beautiful animal mask. Taotie apparently spread terror among alien tribes or clans and provided one's own with protection from evil spirits. In addition to decorative reliefs, other vessels also exhibited zoomorphic shapes.

Everyday motifs entered the repertoire toward the end of the Zhou period and in the subsequent Warring States Period.

▷ **Figure with candlesticks (Mongolian youth)**, late Zhou or Warring States, ca. 500 BCE. Bronze and jade, 11¾ in (30 cm) high. Museum of Fine Arts, Boston. The jade birds were a later addition.

Carrying Possessions into the Next Life

Death was considered the transition to another form of existence, so one took along whatever made life easier, even if it was an entire army. But how could one best accomplish this? This question was also of concern to Qin Shi Huang (r. 221–210 BCE), the first emperor of China and founder of the Qin Dynasty. Human sacrifice, the norm up until this point, became unacceptable. Even Confucius (ca. 551–479 BCE) condemned it in his moral philosophy. So the Emperor ultimately had a force of more than 7000 life-size terracotta warriors and horses in battle formations assembled in front of his mausoleum in Xi'an. This shows the high value accorded to such a portrayal since, from the Chinese point of view, it contained all the essentials.

These lifelike figures were made of mass-produced components, covered with fine clay, and modeled

△ **Kneeling archer**, 4 ft 2 in (122 cm) high

▷ **Armored officer**, ca. 210 BCE. Fired clay, traces of paint, 6 ft (184.5 cm) high. Museum of Qin Figures, Lintong. Both are Qin period figures from the tomb of Emperor Qin Shi Huang.

individually. After firing, they were painted and equipped with real weapons. The layout of the Qin burial site served as a model for many emperors of the Western Han dynasty; they simply changed the subject matter and dimensions. The Western Han figures are significantly smaller than life and less lifelike. Soft flowing lines and a rather schematic presentation show the playful world of courtly amusements and diversions, and even the figures on horseback seem doll-like.

▷ **Vase with two female acrobats,** Western Han. Painted clay, Musée Cernuschi, Paris

◁ **Female dancer,** Western Han. Painted clay, 21 in (53.3 cm) high. The Metropolitan Museum of Art, New York

▽ **Horse and rider,** Western Han. Painted clay, 22½ in (57.5 cm) high. Kimbell Art Museum, Fort Worth

Miniature High Art

Even after the end of the Han dynasty, the tradition of grave figures remained, and the images reached a new level of artistry in the Tang dynasty. Mainly delicate, but also surprisingly ample female figures in flowing robes with unconventional hairstyles and the very latest make-up offered the deceased an atmosphere of courtly life.

Dancers were frozen in elegant poses, their supple bodies in the midst of sweeping gestures. They showed a variety of facial features that seem highly individual. Plain and multi-colored glazed figures appeared alongside painted ones. The use of lead glazes, called *sancai*, was an innovation of the Tang dynasty. The colors were generally applied in clearly separated areas, but they could also flow decoratively into one another, as with demonic figures of animals.

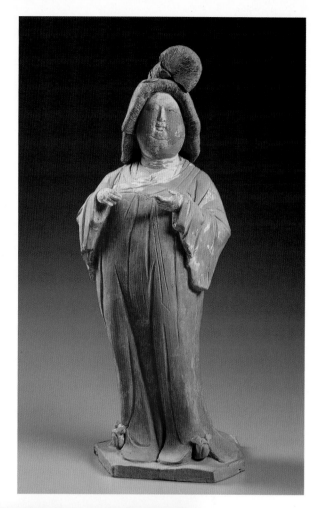

△ **Lady-in-waiting**, 618–906 CE. Painted clay, 17¾ in (45.5 cm) high. Kimbell Art Museum, Fort Worth

◁ **Horse and rider**, Tang, 618–906 CE. Clay with colored glaze, private collection

▷ Buddha,
Northern Wei,
385–557 CE.
Colored clay
and stucco wall
painting, Mogao
Cave 259, Dun
Huang, China

▽ Buddha,
Western Wei,
535–57 CE. Colored
clay and stucco
wall painting,
Mogao Cave 432,
Dun Huang, China

Buddhist Rock Sculptures

In the first century CE, the teachings of Siddhartha Gautama (563–483 BCE) and the Buddha's enlightenment reached China via the central Asian trade routes through Gandhara and Bamiyan. The Dunhuang Oasis lay at the place where the two branches of the Silk Road, surrounded by desert, came together. Here, from 366 CE, Buddhist monks received support from wealthy donors. They carved numerous grottos and caves into a 5248-ft (1600-m) high rock face for purposes of shelter and worship. In addition to wall paintings, the caves contained over 2000 sculptures of the Buddhist pantheon. Some were hewn from the rock, others modeled in clay and stucco over a wooden core. The Buddhas were always set frontally, shown with a nimbus, and performed specified symbolic *mudras* (hand gestures).

From Dunhuang, Buddhism reached eastward via the northern route to Yungang and via the southern route to Luoyang/Long-men. Between 460–525 CE, the Buddhist emperor of the Northern Wei had five large grottoes cut in the rock and furnished with sculptures at Yungang. Indian, Gupta-style sculptures, brought by wandering monks from Sri Lanka, served as models. Through the use of Indian models with strict orientation to religious and iconographic rules, the early Wei style that displayed figures statically and almost geometrically took form. Later Longmen and Tang period sculptures had softer shapes, and rapt facial expressions made them look more lifelike.

△ Buddha with bodhisattva, Northern Wei, ca. 460–480 CE. Rock, ca. 45 ft (13.7 m) high. Cave 20, Yungang, China

◁ Vairocana Buddha or great solar Buddha, Tang, 672–675 CE. Rock, ca. 56 ft (17 m) high. Longmen Grottoes, Luoyang, China

▷ Interior of Cave 12, Northern Wei, ca. 475–500 CE. Rock, Yungang, China

▷ **Standing Buddha**, Northern Wei, 477 or 486 CE. Gilt bronze, 4 ft 7 in (140.3 cm) high. The Metropolitan Museum of Art, New York. The inscription on the reverse side contains a date that can be read as either 477 or 486. The Buddha shows two different hand gestures. His right hand offers protection (Abhaya Mudra), while his left hand makes the gesture of blessing (Varada Mudra).

◁ **Altar shrine dedicated to Buddha Maitreya**, Northern Wei, dated 524 CE. Gilt bronze, 30¼ in (76.9 cm) high. The Metropolitan Museum of Art, New York

Buddhist Bronzework

The rock sculptures of Yungang have a slightly awkward appearance. Alongside them are bronze sculptures like that of the nearly life-sized Buddha Maitreya, the Buddha of the future and all-embracing love. The latter are more elegantly fashioned, although both types exhibit a similar stylization of the drapery folds. The broad shoulders of the Buddha Maitreya hark back to their Indian roots.

The relatively large, delicately carved altar shrine with nimbus and mandorla surrounding a decidedly slimmer Buddha are representative of the later Wei style. The Buddha is accompanied by bodhisattvas, figures paying homage, angels making music in tongues of fire and lions that are partially removable.

Dry lacquer figures were a special art form in which the artist modeled a clay figure that was then covered with multiple layers of hemp cloth dipped in a special lacquer. Each individual layer had to dry thoroughly. The artist worked on the head and hands separately and mounted them at a later time. He removed the clay core, covered the sculpture with additional layers of lacquer, and finally painted and gilded it. Only a few examples of these costly but not very durable artworks have survived.

After the period of the Tang dynasty, sculptured figures typically gestured out into space. The figures acquired a dynamism that made them look more natural and human. Unique to Buddhism was the fact that some forms of bodhisattvas turned into Kuan-yin, the goddess of mercy and protector of children.

△ **Seated Buddha**, Tang, ca. 650 CE. Dry lacquer with traces of gilt and polychrome pigments, ca. 38 in (95.5 cm) high. The Metropolitan Museum of Art, New York

▷ **Bodhisattva Guanyin**, Jin, dated 1168 CE. Polychromed wood with gilt, 5 ft 5 in (165.1 cm) high. Yale University Art Gallery, New Haven

The Concentrated Buddhist Energy of Pagodas

Even before the spread of Buddhism in China, people built watchtowers and signal towers. When carried over to the sacred realm, tower architecture rapidly assimilated Indian stupa design and developed into the pagoda. In contrast to stupas, pagodas are accessible. They have a square or even-numbered, polygonal ground plan and are usually multistoried. Cosmic numerology dictates that there must be an odd number of stories. Originally located in or near a temple area, pagodas preserved relics and Buddhist scriptures. The exteriors were furnished with images of the Buddha that radiated in the four cardinal directions, so that pagodas acted as energy regulators in the *feng shui* sense and as acupuncture needles in the earth's energy flow. When chinoiserie was all the rage, pagodas reached eighteenth-century European gardens in the form of secular ornaments.

Reliquary and burial pagodas (e.g., those of famous monks), such as the Four-Door Pagoda, came about in China under the influence of related images of graves, hills, reliquary shrines and pagodas. Tiered pagodas like the Giant Wild Goose Pagoda combined the model of the Indian stupa with tower construction. Pagodas with floors, such as the Palichuang Pagoda outside Beijing, usually had stories of nearly equal height that were only slightly recessed. Pagodas with galleries like the one at the Fogong Temple had covered balconies on various levels.

◁ **Stages of development** from the Indian stupa to the Chinese pagoda. From the Stupa of Sanchi, by extension to the Chinese form: reconstruction is partially based on the wall paintings in the Dunhuang Caves.

◁ **Simen (Four-Door) Pagoda**, Sui, 611 CE, Licheng, China. This is the oldest stone pagoda in China, as attested to by the date found on an inscription inside.

△ **Dayan Ta (Giant Wild Goose) Pagoda**, Tang, ca. 650 CE, Xi'an, China

△ **Pagoda of the Fogong Temple**, Liao, 1056 CE, Datong, China

△ **Palichuang Pagoda**, Ming, 1576 CE, Beijing, China

Access with Protection

The Great Wall is not only China's best-known construction, but also the most famous wall in the world. Its massive ramparts hug the landscape, winding their way to heights of up to 9840 ft (3000 m). The walls were equipped with watch towers which, along with an effective messaging system, warned of conquering hoards on horseback.

Classical Chinese architecture used timber or wood frame construction for private buildings, temples and palaces alike. There were columns or pillars on both the long and short sides of a building. These were connected at the top by crossbeams that supported the tiled roof. Owing to the perishability of materials like pine and precious nanmu wood, which was used solely for the most important buildings,

hardly any original structures have survived. So reconstructions are frequently based on ceramic models found in graves. Large halls often had several rows of columns to better support the roof. Since walls had no structural function, they could consist of wooden boards, wickerwork, clay or brick. At the entrance, these could easily be replaced by doors so that the building could be opened across the entire width.

△ The history of the **Great Wall** began around 656 BCE in the kingdom of the Zhou (ca. 1045–222 BCE). Under Qin Shi Huangdi (r. 221–210 BCE), it had already reached a length of 3105 miles (5000 km) and doubled during the Han period (206 BCE–220 CE). The partially ruined wall was rebuilt under the Ming (1368–1644) to a total length of 5500 miles (8850 km). On average, it is 33 ft (10 m) high and 33 ft (10 m) wide.

◁ Structure of a Chinese timber or wood frame building, a prime example being the Great Hall of the Temple of the Shining Buddha at Wutai Shan

As a result of combining pillars with beams that lay above them, an increasingly complex system of consoles with stacked and inter-twined support arms developed over time. These not only made the ceiling secure, but offered suitable support for the typical curved eaves found in traditional Chinese architectural style.

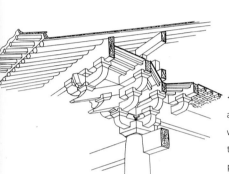

◁ Dougong construction, a system of timber and wood frame consoles that developed during the period of the Han Dynasty

△ Model of an estate (Zhuang Yuan), Han, 2nd century BCE. Clay with traces of paint, 35 ft (89 cm) high. Museum of Henan Province

▽ Hall of Supreme Harmony (Taihe Dian), Imperial Palace in the Forbidden City, Beijing, completed under the Ming in 1420 CE

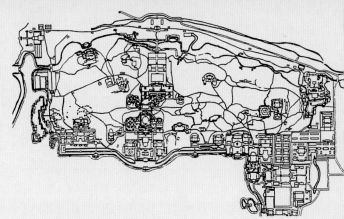

Gardens and Countryside Summer Resorts

As early as the Zhou period (ca. 1045–222 BCE), princes organized hunting parties in specially designed zoological gardens, and many a hunt resembled military maneuvers. The first emperor, Qin Shi Huang, brought plants and animals to his capital, Xianyang. As a further demonstration of his power, he also rebuilt ruined palaces of defeated nations in Shangli Park. Other emperors placed bizarrely shaped stones or rock islands in their gardens. These symbolized the islands of the immortals, and rulers gained confidence from looking at them.

Key elements in Chinese gardens were rocks or mountains and water, because they jointly stood for landscapes. In fact, *shan shui* (mountain-water) means landscape in Chinese. Mountains also embodied *yang*, firm masculine power, while water was considered the soft, feminine *yin* principle. According to Taoist ideas, the universe was made of a whole that could only exist when both principles united. Thus, mankind found a way to get in touch with the cosmos through nature.

At the Summer Palace in Beijing, numerous pavilions, palaces and pagodas were grouped around a lake against the backdrop of the Western Mountain. In addition to imperial gardens like these, it was primarily the private gardens of wealthy officials or merchants, as in Suzhou, that shaped the image of the Chinese garden. This is where they indulged in thinking, enjoyed poetry, painting, music and the comforts of old age. Landscape architects, painters and poets were often given free reign in the gardens to pursue their own association with other art forms.

△ Garden of the Master of the Nets (Wangshi Yuan), Suzhou, ca. 1140 CE

◁◁ The Humble Administrator's Garden (Zhouzheng Yuan), Suzhou, 16th century CE

◁ Plan for the Gardens of Nurtured Harmony (Yihe Yuan), the former imperial summer palace near Beijing, 1153–1764 CE

▷ Marble Boat (Shi Fang), Summer Palace in Beijing, 1750 CE

◁ **Dignitaries, fragment of a grave painting**, Western Han, 1st century BCE. Ink, paint and tile, 2 ft 5 in × 7 ft 11 in (73.8 × 240.7 cm). Museum of Fine Arts, Boston

Brush Strokes

From the third century BCE, Buddhist painting mainly took shape in cave monasteries like Dunhuang. In addition to Buddhist painting, secular painting existed in China as early as the Han dynasty (206 BCE–220 CE), and concerned images of man and his environment. Thus, we find tomb paintings on brick walls in stan-

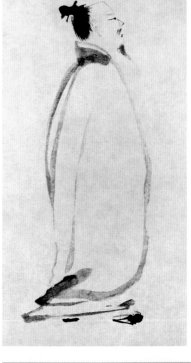

▷ Liang Kai, *Li Bai Reciting a Poem*, scene from a scroll, Southern Song. Ink on paper, 31¾ in (80.9 cm) high. National Museum, Tokyo. Paper was used for painting and calligraphy from around the 13th century.

▷ Yan Liben, *Wu-ti, ruler of the Northern Chou*, scene from the Thirteen Emperors Scroll, Tang, 7th century. Ink and color on silk, 20 × 208 in (51.3 × 531 cm). Museum of Fine Arts, Boston

dardized style that are filled with stories of apparently loyal and deserving civil servants of the Confucian state bureaucracy. During the Tang Dynasty, the favorite subjects of painters like Yan Liben were virtuoso, detailed portraits and the flourishing courtly life of emperors who patronized the arts. In the Song period (960–1279 CE), painters developed a monochrome style of figure painting with moving, dynamically modulated ink lines. Liang Kai's *Jianbi* (reduced brush stroke) style allowed the viewer to understand the painting process in terms of concentrated, flowing traces of movement.

The term *hua shanshui* was first used in the fifth century for landscape paintings of mountains and water. It described a specifically Taoist-influenced, Chinese view of nature that represented a quasi-religious way of looking at art. Reduced color palettes and brush strokes in graded tones gave rise to depth and dramatic effects that never allowed nature to appear threatening, and invited meditative contemplation of the lines instead.

△ Xia Gui, *Mountain Market, Clear with Rising Mist*, Southern Song, album leaf. Ink and silk, 9¾ × 8¼ in (24.8 × 21.3 cm). The Metropolitan Museum of Art, New York

▽ Dong Qichang, *Invitation to Reclusion at Jingxi*, Ming, 1611–1615 CE, handscroll. Ink on paper, 10¼ × 36¼ in (26 × 92.6 cm). The Metropolitan Museum of Art, New York

Fine Shards, Shimmering Lacquer

The Chinese had known about the production of ceramic objects since the Neolithic period. But they were not able to manufacture stoneware with high amounts of kaolin until the Shang Dynasty (ca. 1600–1039 BCE), when the potter's wheel and a firing technique at about 2012–2192 °F (1100–1200 °C) were both developed. The first ceramic glazes came into use in the Zhou Dynasty (ca. 1045–222 BCE). Only at temperatures this high or higher will they melt and adhere to the pottery. This enabled the production of thin-walled, compact vessels (proto-porcelain). During the Song Dynasty (960–1279 CE), green-glazed celadon was developed

△ **Plate with incised decoration**, Song, 12th century, celadon, Museum of East Asian Art, Bath

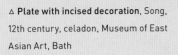

△ **Bowl with incised decoration**, Southern Song, 12th century. Qingbai ware (porcelain), 7¾ in (19.7 cm) diameter. Kimbell Art Museum, Fort Worth

▽ **Plate**, Ming, ca. 1550–1600, porcelain with blue underglaze, Museum of East Asian Art, Bath

▽▽ **Plate with mounted warriors**, Kangxi emperor, 1662–1722, porcelain with polychrome glaze, Museo degli Argenti, Florence

▷ **Amphora with dragon handles**, Tang, 7th–8th century CE. Stoneware with transparent glaze, 14¾ in (37.8 cm) high. Kimbell Art Museum, Fort Worth. Well-known Greek amphorae were imported and used as models here.

from the transparently glazed stoneware of the Tang dynasty (618–906 CE). In addition to celadon, transparent, white-glazed Xing ware came into its own during the Tang Dynasty. Xing ware was the direct precursor of genuine, bluish-white glazed Qingbai ware, which emerged in the Song Dynasty. With the ever-increasing popularity of porcelain, kaolin clay was glazed, and became almost pure white and partly transparent. Blue and white porcelain originally came from Persia. From the fourteenth century onwards, this type of underglaze color in cobalt blue gained importance, including for export. Copper color was used in addition to blue and, from the fifteenth century onwards, enamel paints made a wider range of colours possible. These were applied to the glaze and required a second firing.

Lacquerware

When you scratch the bark of native Chinese lacquer trees (Rhus vernicifera), a milky sap is released which dries brown and is impervious to moisture, acid and, largely, to scratches. Several thin layers of lacquer could thus be applied to wood, leather and fabric, among others things, and made into jars, trays or even furniture. The lacquer was stained with soot (black) or cinnabar (red), and one could eventually carve reliefs into 300 or more individually cured layers.

▷ **Plate with playing children**, Yuan, 14th century CE. Carved red lacquer, 21¾ in (55.6 cm) diameter. The Metropolitan Museum of Art, New York

△ **Mandala of Jnanadakini**, Tibet, 14th century CE. Distemper on cloth, 33¼ × 28¾ in (84.5 × 73.3 cm). The Metropolitan Museum of Art, New York. This mandala shows an imaginary palace from above. Enthroned in the center is the Buddha Jnanadakini, the female aspect of the Buddha Jnanadaka, a manifestation of the Buddha Vajrasattva (Diamond Being), which embodies the principle of purity and purification.

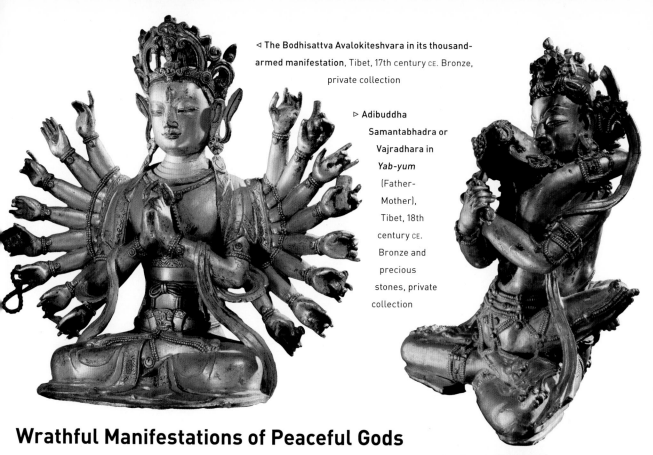

◁ The Bodhisattva Avalokiteshvara in its thousand-armed manifestation, Tibet, 17th century CE. Bronze, private collection

▷ Adibuddha Samantabhadra or Vajradhara in *Yab-yum* (Father-Mother), Tibet, 18th century CE. Bronze and precious stones, private collection

Wrathful Manifestations of Peaceful Gods

Tibet was converted to Buddhism between 600 and 842 CE. Tibetan Buddhist art is characterized by deep spirituality, a vision of enlightenment, wisdom, and compassion. New monasteries were established at the time of Tsongkhapa (1357–1419 CE), the eminent scholar and founder of the *Gelugpa* (Virtue) School or Yellow Hat sect. This finally led to the earthly manifestation of the Bodhisattva Avalokiteshvara in the person of the Dalai Lama and to Lamaism, the Tibetan form of Buddhism.

The ninth-century flight of Indian monks to the "roof of the world" left its mark on Tibetan Buddhism. Since that time, Tibetan art has shown a diverse pantheon of peaceful and wrathful female deities that were equal in stature to masculine gods. As a visual expression of the path to salvation and enlightenment, they are, in the broadest sense, part of the True Body of the Buddha. Through the union of male and female principles, they express both the polarity and the oneness of the universe.

Thangkas are the best known examples of Tibetan painting. These are silk-clad picture scrolls whose iconography is fixed with regard to expression, proportion and details. Thangkas also serve the visual realization of Buddhist doctrine. To merely paint a thangka is considered a religiously meritorious act. Mandalas fulfill the same purpose. As geometric and symbolic representations of cosmic powers, they facilitate meditation.

△ Guru Dorje Drolo, Conqueror of Demons, *thangka*, Tibetan, 18th century. Distemper on linen with brocade edging, 35¼ × 23½ in (90 × 60 cm). Private collection

◁ **Large footed bowl (offering bowl)**, Korea, 5th–6th century CE. Stoneware, 15¾ in (40 cm) high. Kimbell Art Museum, Fort Worth

▷ **Miruk sitting in thought** (Maitreya Bodhisattva), Korea, ca. 650 CE. Gold-plated bronze, 8¾ in (22.5 cm) high. The Metropolitan Museum of Art, New York

Transitions

Owing to its geographical location, Korea acted as an intermediary between the Chinese and Japanese cultures. China repeatedly tried to subjugate the Korean peninsula, and the island-studded waterway between Japan and Korea was never invincible. In 372 CE, the Chinese monk Shundao brought Buddhism to the court of the Goryeo Kingdom. Twenty years later, it became the state religion.

Artistic influences from China took some time to gain acceptance, but then took hold at a high technological level. In the seventh century, there was a particular preference for the type of thoughtful, meditating Bodhisattva Maitreya (Korean: Miruk) that was already known in India and Northern China, and finally reached Japan via Korea.

The predilection for decorative architectural styles was immense, particularly with the spread of wood frame construction from China to Japan. Ornate beams with dragon heads both decorated and protected against evil influences.

In addition to genre paintings, animal images have been particularly popular since the eighteenth century and were produced with exceedingly careful attention to detail.

△ Anonymous master, **Drawing of a Leopard**, Korea, 18th century. Ink on rice paper, 40 × 24¼ in (102 × 62 cm). Private collection

◁ **Rafter finial in the shape of a dragon's head**, Korea, 10th century CE. Gilt bronze, 11¾ in (29.8 cm) high. The Metropolitan Museum of Art, New York. A *pungtak* (wind chime) originally hung from the ring in the dragon's mouth.

◁ Sin Yun-bok, *Flirtation in the Moonlight*, Korea, 18th century. Ink on silk (detail), 11 × 10 in (28.3 × 25.2 cm). Gansong Art Museum, Seoul

Religious Figures

Molded clay idols were found as early as the Jomon period, the oldest era in the cultural history of Japan. In the Kofun period, idols were still being molded from the same materials. When Buddhism was introduced to Japan ca. 550 CE, Japanese sculpture acquired new contents, as well as other materials and designs. The musing, transfigured version of the Bodhisattva came over from Korea as the tender-limbed Miroku Bosatsu. Dedicated to compassion for mankind, this deity would become the most important religious figure in Japanese Buddhism.

Most Japanese sacred sculpture is Buddhist, because Buddhism is geared towards visible representations of holy figures. On the other hand, indigenous Japanese Shinto-ism worshipped the god-like power behind once inexplicable natural phenomena (kami). Because they often eluded pictorial representation, it is useful to give them a second identity and see them as incarnations of Buddhas and Bodhisattvas.

Like Daibutsu, giant statues of the Buddha that are found in Japan, the Buddha was readily depicted in the guise of a simple monk, the Amida Buddha (Amitabha Buddha, meaning "The Buddha of Infinite Light"), the embodiment of compassion and wisdom. The image of Shaka Buddha, the historical Buddha Gautama Shakyamuni, with the Gesture of Fearlessness (Sanskrit: Abhaya Mudra) is exceptional.

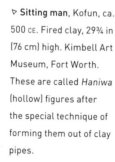

▷ **Sitting man**, Kofun, ca. 500 CE. Fired clay, 29¾ in (76 cm) high. Kimbell Art Museum, Fort Worth. These are called *Haniwa* (hollow) figures after the special technique of forming them out of clay pipes.

◁ **Female Figure**, Jomon, ca. 1000–200 BCE. Fired clay, 7¾ in (20.1 cm) high. Kimbell Art Museum, Fort Worth

▷ **Miroku Bosatsu (Maitreya)**, Asuka, ca. 650–700 CE. Wood, 35½ in (90.2 cm) high. Koryu-ji Temple, Kyoto

△ **Daibutsu (Amida Buddha)**,
Kamakura, 1252. Bronze,
37 ft 9 in (11.5 m) high. Temple,
Kotoku-in

◁ **Hachiman in the Guise of
a Buddhist priest**, Heian,
11th century. Wood with paint
fragments, 19¼ in (48.9 cm)
high. Kimbell Art Museum, Fort
Worth

▷ **Kaikei**, Standing Shaka
Buddha, Kamakura, ca. 1210. Gilt
and lacquered wood, 4 ft 8¼ in
(138.2 cm) high. Kimbell Art
Museum, Fort Worth

△ **Daibutsu (Great Buddha)**, 752. Bronze, 53 ft
(16.2 m) high; with base 98 ft 6 in (30 m) high.
Todai-ji Temple, Nara. The Buddha shows the
Gesture of Protection (Abhaya Mudra) with his
right hand, while the left shows the Gesture of
Leisure (Avakasha Mudra).

The Larger, the More Sun-Like

△ Todai-ji Temple, Daibutsu Hall (Hall of the Great Buddha), 744–757, Nara

Nara was the capital of Japan from 710–785. In the early years of Buddhism, it was the political and religious center of the country as well. This is the location of Japan's oldest, most extensively preserved temple complex, Horyu-ji (Temple of the Flourishing Law) and the vast area of Todai-ji (Eastern Great Temple). Emperor Shomu (701–756), who founded Todai-ji, was impressed by a monumental statue of the Buddha Vairocana (Great Solar Buddha), one of the Five Wisdom Buddhas, and decided to produce a statue of his own.

The manufacture of such large molds, as well as casting in general, presented enormous technical challenges. The Buddha's locks were cast as a separate piece and assembled afterwards. At the same time, the figures on either side of the Buddha had to be cast and the accompanying hall built. The hall is still the largest wooden structure in the world. The engravings on the lotus seat, which represent the paradise of Shakyamuni, were finished and the statue gilded.

The material body of the figure was finally ensouled at an eye-opening ceremony held in 752 that was the event of the Buddhist world and made Todai-ji into Japan's most important Buddhist center.

△ Todai-ji Temple, Daibutsu Hall (Hall of the Great Buddha), 744–757, Nara

▽ Figure of a gatekeeper, 711. Clay head, wooden body, probably restored in the 13th century, 10 ft 10 in (330 cm) high. Horyu-ji Temple, Nara

Imperial Architecture

The new capital of Heian-kyo (tranquility and peace capital), known today as Kyoto, was built in 794 CE and remained the imperial capital of Japan until 1868. It was probably also founded in order to escape the powerful influence of the Buddhist monasteries at Nara. A whole era, the Heian period (794–1192), bears the name of this residence. Along with the great temples, Kyoto's worldwide reputation was founded mainly on the timeless architecture of its palaces, mansions, and gardens.

In 1603, Shogun Tokugawa Ieyasu built the residential Nijo-jo Castle in the vicinity of the imperial palace. Estates like these had walls, watchtowers, and moats that were similar to European castle fortresses. The obligatory garden with tea house was never missing from the interior of the complex, which consisted of buildings placed one behind the other and connected by colonnades. The beams of the wood frame structures were magnificently decorated with ornate carvings and colorful painting.

The Katsura Imperial Villa (Katsura Rikyu) is a masterful example of a building perfectly integated with its garden. Unlike other official buildings, naturalness, subtle colors and restrained décor were in the forefront here. The grid of *tatami* (rice mats) was the unit of measurement for the ground plan. The inner and outer *fusama*, *shoji* (sliding doors) and painted folding screens had a special function: They allowed great variability within the rooms, made it possible to adapt them to seasonally

determined climatic and light conditions, and enabled optical unification of the interior and exterior with the gardens.

The Flying Fortress

During the sixteenth century, the homes of rich and powerful generals and feudal lords developed into magnificent, nearly impregnable fortresses. Himeji-jo is the most famous and best preserved castle in Japan. Located about sixty-two miles (100 km) west of Kyoto, it was built in 1581 by Shogun Toyotomi Hideyoshi. Its complicated layout (nawabari) served primarily as a strategic defense system. Over the centuries, however, the complex was converted from a fortress intended for siege warfare into a residential castle. Because of its white walls and curved roofs, it has also been called the White Heron Castle.

Growing Enlightenment

Japanese Zen Buddhism was already taking shape in the Kamakura period (1193–1333). This form of Buddhism came over from Song-dynasty China and referred mainly to the Buddha's own intensive practice of meditation. It helped people discover signs of the Buddha's actions in all of nature and within themselves, and taught them how to reach enlightenment through meditation rather than by means of rituals. Temples were placed on wooded hillsides. Even today, their landscaped gardens represent a microcosm of the eternal nature of water and mountains. Natural watercourses were always included and, wherever they were lacking, artificial ones were installed. Weathered, well-formed stones and rocks emulated mountains, and winding paths suggested spaciousness. Flowering trees and shrubs were exceptions; instead, arrangements centered on various shades of green and fall colors. In tea houses, the tea ceremony was elevated to the status of a spiritual Zen practice.

Dry gardens are a Japanese invention. They are gardens consisting entirely of rocks, with the pebbles raked into waves that symbolize a watercourse "flowing" between boldly set stones. They are not meant to be walked on, but to be experienced through meditative viewing (*kansho*) from a predetermined spot.

△ Bridge in the rock garden of Ryoan-ji Temple, ca. 1499, Kyoto

◁ Stepping stones in the garden of the Heian Shrine, Kyoto

▽ Ryoan-ji Temple rock garden, ca. 1499, Kyoto

◁ Garden of Ginkaku-ji Temple (Silver Pavilion), ca. 1500, Kyoto

Tea Ceramics

Zen monks in China already knew about tea, which was first used as medicine and as a stimulant during long meditations. Over time, the main interest shifted to ritual preparation involving strict rules that extended from the arrangement of the utensils to the temperature of the water.

The tea master Sen no Rikyu (1522–1591) elevated the ceremony to a spiritual practice called chado, meaning "the way of tea". In stark contrast to sumptuous, courtly tea gatherings, Rikyu attached particular importance to simplicity (wabi) and maturity (sabi) gained through practice. At his suggestion, the ceramic maker Chojiro (d. 1592) developed Raku tea bowls, which were deliberately formed from coarse clay into irregular shapes by hand and decorated with warm, earthy, sometimes black glaze, so that the individual vessels emphasized their own uniqueness as objects. The cracks in the glaze come from the special firing technique used in Raku ovens.

Another type of firing is named after the city of Karatsu on the north coast of the island of Kyushu in western Japan. Karatsu ware is made from dark brown clay and can be fired into very lightweight stoneware that is readily decorated with grass motifs or fluid glazes. In addition to tea bowls, Karatsu craftsmen also produced other vessels for everyday use.

◁ **Mizusashi (fresh water vessel)**, Edo, ca. 1700. Stoneware, Karatsu, 7¼ in (18.5 cm) high. Kimbell Art Museum, Fort Worth

△ **Tea bowl with bamboo leaf pattern**, Edo, ca. 1725. Stoneware with iron oxide underglaze and colorless glaze, 2½ in (6.2 cm) high. Kimbell Art Museum, Fort Worth

△ **Tea bowl with grass pattern**, Edo, ca. 1720. Stoneware with iron oxide underglaze and colorless glaze, 3¼ in (8.5 cm) high. Kimbell Art Museum, Fort Worth

△ **Bowl for side dishes (mukozuke)**, Edo, ca. 1650. Stoneware with iron oxide underglaze, Karatsu, 3½ in (8.9 cm) high. Kimbell Art Museum, Fort Worth

△ **Tea bowl (uzumibi)**, Edo, 19th century. Raku, 3½ in (9.2 cm) high. Freer Gallery of Art, Smithsonian Institution, Washington, D.C.

△ **Tea bowl (seppo)**, Momoyama, 17th century. Raku, 3¾ in (9.5 cm) high. Private collection

△ **Tea bowl with plum blossom**, Edo, 19th century. Raku, 3 in (7.7 cm) high. Freer Gallery of Art, Smithsonian Institution, Washington, D.C.

Panoramic Tales

With the painting of horizontal *emaki* (picture scrolls), Japanese art began to separate from Chinese and Korean models of sacred and, in particular, Buddhist subject matter. A courtly art form of the Heian period, they initially focused on aristocratic life in Kyoto and its vicinity, as did the courtly novel that emerged in at the same time.

The tales usually appeared in an uninterrupted series of pictures, proceeding from right to left. They illustrated war novels, biographies of priests and legends, to name a few. Emaki became the characteristic Japanese form of historical painting, but they also represented landscapes and folk life naturalistically.

Formally speaking, emaki influenced several characteristically

Japanese pictorial art forms. These included monumental and decorative paintings on the walls and sliding doors of palaces, particularly those on folding screens. On the other hand, they also influenced folding albums and woodcut-illustrated block books, including the series of the great woodblock masters and, ultimately, even mangas. Among screen-painters, it was mainly Ogata Korin who unified details of landscapes, flowers and grasses into an ornamental play of colors. His trademark was the gold-foil ground between stylized motifs, such as waves spraying foam, partly painted with relief-like effects.

◁ *Night Attack on the Sanjo Palace*, scene from the Heiji monogatari emaki, scroll 1, Kamakura, 1250–1300. Ink and color on paper, 16¼ in × 22 ft 11½ in (41.3 × 699.7 cm). Museum of Fine Arts, Boston. The pictorial scrolls tell of a revolt in the Heiji Era (1195 CE) and the transition from a courtly to a feudal-chivalrous era. Of the original 10–15 scrolls, only three have survived.

▽ Ogata Korin, *Waves at Matsushima*, Edo, 18th century. Folding screen, ink, color and gold on paper, 4 ft 11 in × 12 ft 1 in (150.2 × 367.8 cm). Museum of Fine Arts, Boston

Striking Woodcuts: Ukiyo-e

There were already genre scenes in emaki, although they were viewed more as burlesque additions to accounts of courtly events. The city of Edo, known as Tokyo today, became the capital of Japan in 1603. At the beginning of the Edo period (1603–1868), a school of painting came about that looked for clients among the urban middle class and was therefore oriented to their tastes. Ukiyo-e were contemporary "pictures of the floating world," e.g., entertainment districts and theaters. To meet the demand for affordable art, artists turned to woodcuts, which had been well known since the eighth century.

Around 1765, Harunobu was the first to produce multicolored prints from different kinds of plates with the help of registration marks (kento). In this two-dimensional art form, figures were defined by a line, and achieved their finished effect by well-defined areas of bold color. Sharaku was known for portraits of actors that bordered on the grotesque. Utamaro found his motifs in the brothels of Edo. Landscapes had previously served as mere backgrounds for the main subject matter, people. But Hokusai and Hiroshige, whose works influenced European artists like Toulouse-Lautrec and Van Gogh, made them the focus of attention.

△ Katsushika Hokusai, *The Great Wave off Kanagawa*, from the series "Thirty-six Views of Mount Fuji," 1830–1832. Color woodcut on paper, 10 × 15 in (25.7 × 37.9 cm). The Metropolitan Museum of Art, New York

▷ Toshusai Sharaku, *The Two Kabuki Actors Bando Zenji and Sawamura Yodogoro*, 1794. Color woodcut on paper, 15 × 10 in (38.3 × 25.2 cm). Museo Chiossone, Genoa

▷▷ Ando Hiroshige, *Ohashi Bridge in a Sudden Downpour*, from the series "One Hundred Views of Edo," 1857. Color woodcut on paper, 15½ × 10½ in (39.3 × 26.5 cm). Fuji Art Museum, Tokyo

◁ Suzuki Harunobu, ***Girl in Green Robe Playing with a Black Cat, Boy Peeping Over Shoulder***, 18th century. Woodcut on paper, 8 × 10¾ in (20.3 × 27.3 cm). The Newark Museum, Newark

▷ Kitagawa Utamaro, ***Pair with Screen***, ca. 1797. Color woodcut on paper, 15 × 9¾ in (38 × 25.1 cm). Museum of Fine Arts, Boston

Australia & Oceania

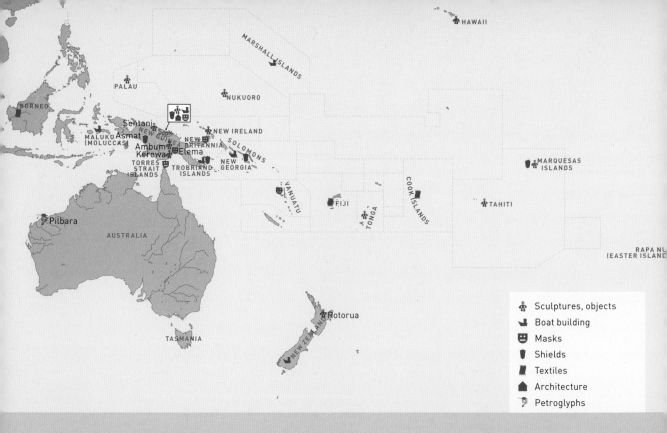

Australia & New Zealand

60,000–32,000 BCE First people settle Australia via a land bridge from New Guinea (today Indonesia).
800–1300 CE New Zealand is settled by people from Polynesia.
1606 The Dutch land in northern Australia.

1642 Abel Tasman discovers Tasmania and New Zealand.
1770 James Cook claims Australia for Great Britain.
from 1788 The British colonize Australia, chiefly as a penal colony.
from 1790 The British colonize New Zealand.

1843 Start of The New Zealand Wars between the British and the Maori
1867 The Maori receive the right to vote in New Zealand.
1931–1942 Australian Independence
1948 New Zealand Independence
from 1965 Australian aborigines receive the right to vote.

Petroglyphs, Pilbara, Western Australia, ca. 40,000 BCE

Moai, Rapa Nui (Easter Island), ca. 1100

Ki'i manu hula, Hawaii, 18th century

40,000 BCE — 1100 CE — 1750

Australia & Oceania

Australia

For a long time, the culture and art of Australian aborigines was not only suppressed but ignored. Since white settlers barely perceived the complex, aboriginal clan system, they regarded such people as "beneath" hierarchical tribal societies and as primitive Stone Age people with no artistic skills or cultural ambitions. Only interest in the Dreamtime and songlines, as well as the discovery of artistically impressive, colorful rock paintings of Dreamtime and ancestral beings opened people's eyes to aboriginal art. Their art consisted mainly of petroglyphs and rock carvings, bark paintings, wood sculptures, and ceremonial costumes in specially selected colors and patterns.

Ever since the first international exhibitions of these works of art in the 1920s, European artists have been influenced by the often "soft" outlines of aboriginal drawings and engravings.

Oceania

Beginning in the eighteenth century, Europeans identified most Polynesian peoples, including the Maori of New Zealand, with their ideal of the "noble savage." That is also why their art quickly garnered attention. Elaborate body decoration, known as tattooing, was just as widespread as ritual dancing, especially among the Maori, but also within other tribes. Even the jewelry—elaborate wreaths of floral sprays or shells—and finely woven textiles displayed "art on the body." Carvings, wooden figurines and stone sculptures had religious significance that was connected to ancestor worship. The stone *moai* of Easter Island are a particularly well known sculptural form. As seafaring peoples, Polynesian tribes also painted and decorated their boats and catamarans lavishly. Wooden towers at the bow that often portrayed entire scenes were very popular. Carvings and ornaments could also be found on houses, especially those of central male figures or chieftains.

Oceania

1500–1300 BCE Colonization of the Pacific islands, probably from Taiwan or the Philippines
400–1600 CE Polynesians colonize Rapa Nui, or Easter Island.
1521 Fernando Magellan discovers the Marianas.

1687 Europeans discover Easter Island.
from 1767 European vessels land on the Islands of Oceania. The idea of the "noble savage" of the South Seas emerges in Europe.
1768–1779 James Cook sails the Pacific.

1874–1885 Britain, France, Spain and Germany race to colonize the Pacific Islands.
1897 The United States annexes Hawaii.
1962 West Samoan Independence
1970–1980 Most island states declare their independence.

Ancestral figure (?), New Zealand, 1800–1840

Ceremonial shield, Salomon Islands, ca. 1850

Elema eharo mask, Papua New Guinea, ca. 1910

Irvala, Two male Mimi, Australia, 1963

1800   1850   1900   1960

At a Glance

The Ambum Stone

This stone statue of an unknown animal in crouching position with a long, trunk-like snout was found in the Ambum Valley of New Guinea in 1962. The statue is probably about 3000 years old and remains a mystery. Most scholars think it represented a tribal ancestor, which is to say a classic totem animal. But the stone has also prompted cryptozoologists to search for undiscovered or possibly extinct animal species.

The Ambum Stone, Ambum Valley, Papua New Guinea, ca. 1500 BCE. Zoomorphic figure, 7¾ × 35½ in (20 × 7.5 × 14 cm). National Museum of Australia, Canberra

Aboriginal Kinship and Marital Practices

Aboriginal clans were not hierarchically structured, but were organized according to the concept of extended family. All the father's brothers counted as fathers, all the mother's sisters as mothers, and their respective children as siblings. Uncles, aunts, male and female cousins were merely mother's brothers, father's sisters and their children. People could only marry into this group.

Oceania

The inhabitants of the islands of Polynesia, Melanesia and Micronesia lived in relatively similar, tightly organized, strictly hierarchical chieftain societies that were characteristically patriarchal. For the most part, each society was divided into free and unfree persons. The aristocratic caste played a special role in maintaining privilege, but was always ready to receive the very gifted into their ranks. The tribes led many bloody wars and raids on one another by boat, and some were also familiar with human sacrifice and ritual cannibalism. Other comparative similarities included their skills in agriculture, fishing, crafts and building houses.

Mana

Mana means "force" in Polynesian and refers to universal energy or the spiritual life force. It varies in strength and, although all beings actually have mana, it is mainly discernible in extraordinary natural phenomena, objects and persons, such as tribal chiefs, priests and "experts." This force was not seen as personal, yet was considered extremely powerful, for it connected this world with the hereafter. These two realms were never clearly separate in the minds of the Polynesians. European theologians held lengthy debates as to whether mana should be regarded as the primal religious experience.

The Maori

The original Polynesian inhabitants of New Zealand lived in relatively warlike, chieftain societies. They practiced headhunting and worshiped their ancestors as members of certain seafaring groups of which they felt a part. Even today, their facial and body tattoos are striking, and demonstrate social status and group affiliation.

Haka

This Maori ritual dance actually means "song and dance." It is a welcoming ceremony and an entertainment involving movement and sound. In earlier days, its purpose was also to give warriors courage before battle and to intimidate the enemy with a massive physical presence. Even today, many hakas appear martial and aggressive because snarling, threatening gestures, baring of teeth, eye rolling and protruding tongues are all part of the ritual.

Australia & Oceania

Moieties and Skin Groups

Each aboriginal clan or tribe consisted of two halves (*moieties*), and these halves were each divided into two to four subgroups (skin groups). The closest social interactions within the family extended to one's own skin group. There were strict rules for associations with other skin groups and moieties that indicated greater distance.

Feather Bonnets

In some Polynesian societies, chiefs and priests wore feather bonnets and feather-collared robes as status symbols. The former were narrow, high configurations that were tipped forward as a rule and fully covered in small, downy feathers.

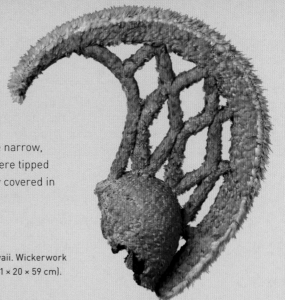

Chieftain's feather bonnet, Hawaii. Wickerwork with feathers, 28 × 7¾ × 23 in (71 × 20 × 59 cm). Musée du Quai Branly, Paris

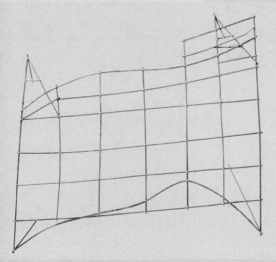

Boat Builders and Navigators

"Experts" played an important role in oceanic societies. Along with priests, boat builders and navigators consequently enjoyed special standing. They built and steered catamarans that were capable of covering great distances on the high seas. Experts navigated mostly by the stars and by means of orally transmitted knowledge.

Navigation Chart (*Rebbilib*), Marshall Islands, ca. 1900. Wickerwork, 35¼ × 43¼ × 1 in (89.5 × 109.9 × 2.5 cm). The Metropolitan Museum of Art, New York

Taboos

The word "taboo" comes from *tapu*, meaning sacred. In traditional societies of Oceania, certain places, objects or persons were either permanently or temporarily "outlawed." In that event, only particular persons could touch, approach or set foot on them. Certain groups were prohibited from eating specific foods. Violating a taboo resulted in ostracism by the community. Since many taboos applied only to ordinary people—and not to the nobility or officials—taboos were generally construed as observances of religious purity that were meant to strengthen hierarchical structures and compliance with social rules. The community assigned taboos mainly to events that were perceived as threatening, such as death, corpses and menses.

The Men's House

In Oceania, the men's or chieftain's house was where the leading men of the village lived, as did the ancestral spirits often depicted in wooden figures. They were usually built by skilled craftsmen, mainly as two-story structures in the center of the community, and richly decorated with bright colors and ornate carvings. Animals, especially sea creatures, and scenes of daily life were often painted on them. And they were usually decorated with money cowrie, which was intended to symbolize power and wealth.

Key Terms

△ Aboriginal petroglyph figures, Pilbara, Western Australia, ca. 40,000 BCE

◁ Irvala (Billy Yirawala), *Two Mimi Men*, 1963. Eucalyptus bark, natural pigments, 24¾ × 16½ in (63 × 42 cm). Musée du Quai Branly, Paris. In the minds of aborigines, mimi are delicate little nature spirits that are so light and frail as to be blown about by the wind. They are very shy and hide in rock crevices the minute they see humans. The figures are reminiscent of praying mantises and have the translucent appearance of an X-ray.

▷ Female figure painted with traditional patterns, wood, private collection. Her importance could vary from tribe to tribe, and she also served as "educational material."

△ **Whaling**, bark painting, Art Gallery of
New South Wales, Sydney

▷ Bob Bilinyara, *History of Ramingining*, ca.
1925. Bark painting, 35½ × 13¾ in (90 × 35 cm).
Art Gallery of New South Wales, Sydney

The Art of the Aborigines

About 40,000 years ago, when the earth was still flat and empty, there rose from the Australian soil gigantic mythical beings, half human, half animal, who wandered about and created the immovable landscape formations, as well as everything that moved. They then returned the soil they had given form to.

This Dreamtime creation myth explains the aborigines' relationship to nature and, perhaps, the dissemination of their most graphic images. Immobile and virtually indestructible, these images covered rocks and tree trunks, motionless and transitory soil and sand, flexible and transient skin and bark. And because they were not depictions, but incarnations, only the initiated may have been allowed to see them. Making graphic art constituted a religious act. Existing images also needed touching up at the right time, e.g., to set the seasons in motion. The motifs and patterns are so closely bound to tradition that aboriginal images have been preserved for thousands of years, which makes dating impossible, but also irrelevant.

Traditions began to slacken in the 1930s. Since the 1970s, the separation between art and worship has seemed to be complete. Because modern aboriginal artists remain very committed to their cultural heritage, traditionalists accuse them of giving away too much secret knowledge.

Maori Art

The Maori have always been conscious of ancestral protection. When they enter their houses, especially the great meeting house, they are enveloped by a particularly important ancestor: the roof is his spine, the rafters his ribs, and the gables his outspread arms and hands. The big mask at the top of the triangular gable was a catalyst for the idea of the house as a protective ancestral figure. The inner and outer support structures are liberally covered with characteristic Maori carvings that look plantlike, but are almost always figurative, with the exception of the spiral motif. Motifs on the faces and joints of human figures can be seen as tattoos, but can also symbolize movement. Gods reside in carved figures. When they are wrapped in a certain way with cords and decorated with tufts of feathers, spirals allow the god the necessary freedom of movement. Freely circling double spirals on a surface, often in the form of lace-like openwork, stand for "expansion." Spirals between the figures of the original pair, Earth Mother and Sky Father, denote the spread of light and knowledge.

The majority of the Maori carvings that survive date from what is known as the turning point after 1840, the period of the "new world." The "old world" covers the period from ca. 800–1840, that is, after their departure from their homeland in central Polynesian and their arrival in New Zealand. The old world is divided into three periods: Sowing (800–1200), Growth (1200–1500), and Flowering (1500–1840).

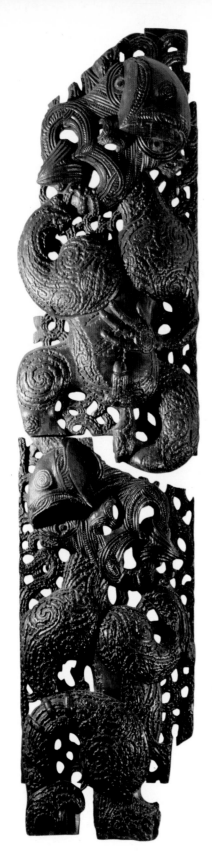

◁ Relief-carved wooden board from the side of a gable pitaka (storage space), Rotor, Bay of Plenty, 19th century. Wood, 4 ft 11 in (150 cm) high. Entwistle Gallery, London. The protruding tongue of the figure at the head is a gesture of courage and contempt.

▷ *Taumata atua* (godstick) with an image of Rongo, stone, Taranaki Museum, New Plymouth. Rongo helped to provide rich harvests. In this particular form, he is embedded in the field.

△ *Hei tiki*, chest ornament, New Zealand. Jade, 6½ in (16.5 cm) high. Entwistle Gallery, London. This kind of amulet probably represents Tiki, the first man.

◁ **Ancestral figure (?)**, 1800–1840. Wood, 17½ in (44.8 cm) high. Kimbell Art Museum, Fort Worth. The pattern tattooed on the face is incomplete.

△ **Head with tattooing**, wood and mother of pearl, Auckland Museum Institute, New Zealand. An ancestor who can be identified by his individual tattoos is shown here.

◁ Wiremu Kingi Te Rangitake, **bow board of a war canoe**, up to 131 ft (40 m) long, before 1882, Auckland Museum Institute, New Zealand

The Magic of Boats

Islanders lived by boats. They could build them. They understood how to navigate them. They knew the ocean, and experience had taught them they needed all the help they could get. Hence, the artistic decorations on their boats were more than just ornaments. They helped to keep the boats on course. When on trading voyages, for example, the Trobriand Islanders relied on the magical effects of the spiral shapes at the bow and stern of their boats. To a certain extent even against their will, the spirals were supposed to move their trading partners to offer better goods than intended. These spiral forms, called *doka*, seem to have been inspired by nautilus shells that symbolized natural perfection. Only master carvers were able to impart this almost hypnotic, spiraling effect to their sterns and bows. In addition, the lines had to be drawn in one continuous flow without tracing. Every single element of the bow or stern boards had a symbolic meaning that only master carvers could animate. The elongated slots (*weku*), for example, helped to sound the call of a rare bird that no one had ever seen.

The great war canoes could accommodate forty to eighty warriors. Magic had to help them not only on the water, but also on land when they were not in use. For that reason, they were stored in special boathouses with a view of the sea, and as long as they were depicted on the ornate door posts of the hut, guardian spirits protected them.

Boats even played an important role in death. In the views of various tribes, richly decorated canoes sheltered in sacred caves symbolically transported the spirit of a clan chief, as a corpse or even just as a skull, to the realm of the dead on the other side of the ocean.

△ **Bow decoration of a pirogue**, Sepik, New Guinea. Wood with painted trim, 21½ in (55 cm) high. Musée du Quai Branly, Paris

▷ **Bow board (hull board) of a canoe**, Maluku, Indonesia, 19th–20th century. Hard wood, 65 in (162.5 cm) high. Musée du Quai Branly, Paris

△ *Toto isu* (figurehead) from the prow of a war canoe, New Georgia, Solomon Islands. Wood and mother of pearl, 7 in (18 cm) high. Museum der Kulturen, Basel. Placed right at the water line, the figure was meant to protect the occupants from sea spirits (*kesoko*) and, with the addition of the bird, kept the boat on course.

◁ **Pirogue with hull board**, photo by Jacques Viot, 1933, Musée du Quai Branly, Paris

▽ **Prow board** as an extension of a canoe, Massim, Trobriand Islands, 1900–1940. Painted wood, 21 in (53.5 cm) long. Indianapolis Museum of Art, Indianapolis. The spirals, slots and asymmetry all have meaning. A decorated splash guard could also be mounted in the right-hand corner.

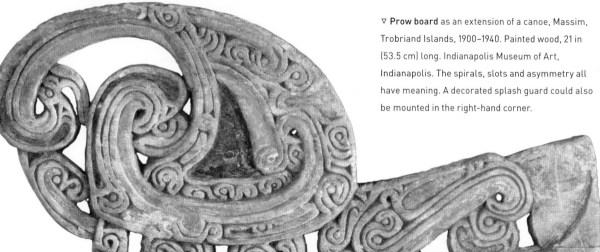

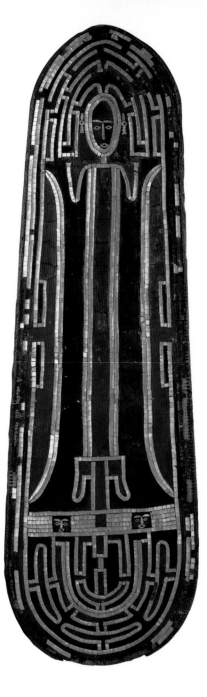

△ **Shield**, Bahinemo, Papua New Guinea, mid-20th century. Painted wood, 5 ft 5 in (166 cm) high. Musée du Quai Branly, Paris

△ **Ceremonial shield**, Salomon Islands, ca. 1850. Wickerwork, resin and mother of pearl, 33¼ in (84.5 cm) high. The Metropolitan Museum of Art, New York. 25 of these shields have been preserved, all from the same period. The central figure represents the bearer; the small heads at the bottom may refer to headhunting.

△ **Tattoo artist's signboard**, Marquesas Islands. Wood, 34¼ in (87 cm) high. Musée du Quai Branly, Paris. Symbols which provide protection on a sign will have the same effect on the skin, provided their power is not so great as to cause damage. As "mobile pattern books," tattoos contributed to the spread of certain motifs.

Shield and Protection

A shield that made a warrior feel secure enough to be brave offered protection both in battle and in everyday life. It could serve as a door, for instance, and when the occupant was away from home, could prevent unwanted people, as well as vengeful spirits, from forcing their way through the entrance to the hut. Shields are proudly displayed at ceremonial festivities and dances even today. But figures and patterns, such as those on the great war shields of the Asmat in southwest New Guinea, could supposedly do even more: if the shield was named after a sufficiently powerful ancestral spirit, then the shield embodied it, and the mere sight of it overcame all enemies. Consequently, enemies would drop their weapons and flee or remain spellbound. And more power accumulated with each additional shield that was set up in the village.

◁ **Shield**, Massim, Trobriand Islands, ca. 1890. Painted wood, 33 in (83.8 cm) high. Museum of Fine Arts, Boston. The few surviving shields of this type have an identical layout, but vary in the details of their motifs, which were most certainly arranged with the individual bearer in mind.

▷ **Shield**, Asmat, southwest New Guinea, mid-20th century. Carved and painted wood, 80 in (202.6 cm) high. Museum of Fine Arts, Houston. Stylized fruit bats and female praying mantises were popular motifs. Female mantises bite off the male's head, making them symbolic of head hunting.

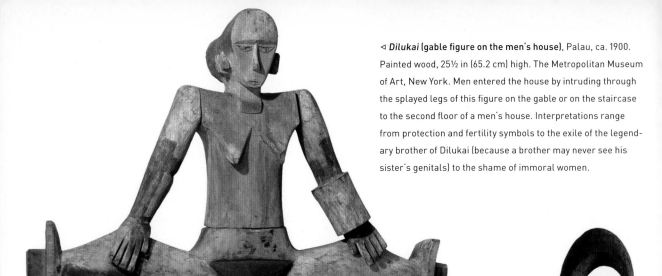

◁ *Dilukai* (gable figure on the men's house), Palau, ca. 1900. Painted wood, 25½ in (65.2 cm) high. The Metropolitan Museum of Art, New York. Men entered the house by intruding through the splayed legs of this figure on the gable or on the staircase to the second floor of a men's house. Interpretations range from protection and fertility symbols to the exile of the legendary brother of Dilukai (because a brother may never see his sister's genitals) to the shame of immoral women.

Male Cults

Adult men reserve certain areas for themselves, and these remain closed to women. An obvious example is the men's house, which constitutes the center of the political, social, and cultural life of a tribe. Women have no access to it. The furnishings include a skull shrine for every adult male. Once they contained the skulls of ancestors and, in head-hunting societies, the skulls of enemies as well. However, since the official ban on head-hunting in the early twentieth century, human skulls have been replaced by dummies or animal skulls, and no woman is ever allowed to view them. Like the skulls of ancestors, some skull trophies have been modeled over to create a new head. Courage and procreative power passed from the enemy to the man who killed him. They say that a man can only give life after he has taken it. These relics are inherited, and the creative power stored in them strengthens the whole clan.

◁ **Modeled-over skull**, Eastern Sepik, New Guinea, 11¾ in (30 cm) high. Musée du Quai Branly, Paris

▷ *Yipwon* figure (hook figure), Karawari, Middle Sepik, New Guinea. Painted wood and hide, Philip Goldman Collection, London. After a murder, the spirit beings hide in the men's house. Pressed flat against the wall, they are forever banished to that place as punishment. They help the men when they hunt and, on the eve of the hunt, are set on the prey to make it easier to kill. As a reward, meat or bones are attached to the ribs of the figure. If the hunt is a failure, the figure is replaced by a new one.

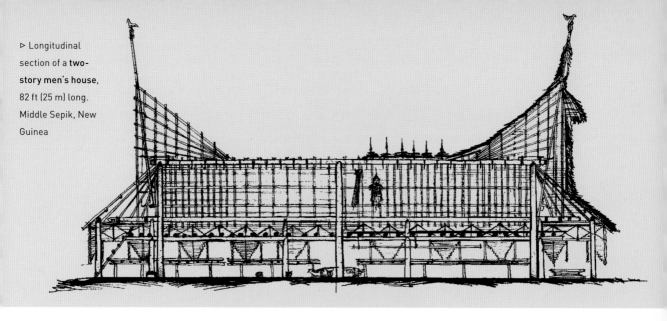

▷ Longitudinal section of a **two-story men's house**, 82 ft (25 m) long. Middle Sepik, New Guinea

▽ *Gope* board (detail of an ancestral table), Sepik, New Guinea, ca. 1900. Painted wood, private collection. Gope boards are made of canoe wood, often from an enemy's canoe, and are placed on skull shrines. The stylized, figurative representation is typical. Gope boards are bequeathed and thus increase the prestige of the owner.

▽ *Kerewa agiba* (skull hook), 19th–20th century, Gulf, Papua New Guinea. Painted wood, 56 in (142 cm) high. The Metropolitan Museum of Art, New York. Agiba inside the men's house were clan property. As the embodiment of ancestors, they were draped in skulls and great spiritual strength was attached to them. Only those who had captured an enemy head were allowed to carve them.

◁ **Tortoise shell mask**, Torres Strait Islands, 1860–1870. Mixed media, 17½ in (44.5 cm) high. The Metropolitan Museum of Art, New York. These masks, handed down since 1606, have been part of countless burial rituals and initiation ceremonies.

◁ *Elema eharo* mask, Gulf, Papua New Guinea, ca. 1910. Bark-cloth and cane, 38⅓ in (95.9 cm) high. The Metropolitan Museum of Art, New York. Young men wore these to enliven earnest entreaties to water spirits.

▷ *Chubwan* mask, Vanuatu, New Hebrides, ca. 1890. Wood, 14⅓ in (36.5 cm) high. Musée du Quai Branly, Paris. These hand masks were supposed to assist in growing yams.

Useful and Used Spirits

The varied appearance of masks was facilitated by the properties of the materials available in the oceanic island world at a given time.

The number of mask characters was immense, while the different purposes they served were not so many. The mask bearer temporarily set into motion the workings of a god or a spirit, whose apparent assistance offered hope for successful harvests, hunting, fishing and cam-paigns. Some masks were just for fun, others for an innocuous scare.

The making of many masks was kept secret from women. For this reason, they also served to exclude certain groups, especially when the masks were a feature of secret male societies. The best known of these secret societies was related to the Duk-Duk, a revered spirit on New Britain in Papua New Guinea. Male Duk-Duk masks were subordinate to female tubuan masks. The wealthy wearer of the latter also secured the extremely valuable right to keep most of the fines he collected while wearing the mask. In fact, this was a handy instrument of jurisdiction that could be used by the tubuan to indiscriminately terrorize and blackmail non-members, most of whom were women.

▽ **Romkun dance mask** (?), Breri or Igana, Lower Sepik, New Guinea, 19th century. Wood, 23½ in (60 cm) high. The Metropolitan Museum of Art, New York

▽ **Basket mask**, Papua New Guinea, Museo Missionario Etnologico, The Vatican

▷ **Tubuan mask** of the Duk-Duk secret society of the Tolai on New Britain, Horniman Museum, London. Leaf skirts cover the body of the wearer down to the thighs.

Textile Designs

Errors were not permitted in the making of ceremonial cloths. A spirit or god who felt diminished by inaccuracies in the pattern could punish the careless weaver woman with disease, miscarriages, blindness or death. For this reason, the most experienced women took charge of the riskiest sections. They had to offer sacrifices and then complete the work without interruption.

In *ikat* weaving style, the faithful repetition of a pattern was tricky, because it was neither woven in nor printed onto the fabric at a later time. With ikat, the warp and weft threads have to be partially dyed ahead of time in such a way that the pattern stands out properly in the weaving phase.

Not many women mastered the secret, magical patterns, the dyeing technique or the preparation of sometimes highly toxic or mordant dyes. The Iban of West Borneo therefore granted these women the same respect as head hunters. Whatever or whoever was wrapped in their cloths was reliably protected from evil influences. And only when a freshly captured skull trophy was wrapped in the most powerful of these cloths could a person be safe from the curses of his victims.

Weaving did not take hold in Oceania, because clothing and home textiles were produced from the peeled inner bark of particular trees. Women beat the bast fibers into a felt-like "cloth." The pieces were sewn together to form a wide strip, then painted or block printed. The ritual quality of the material most likely rested on the meditative manner in which it was produced and, in the case of gods and spirits, served as a path to mankind.

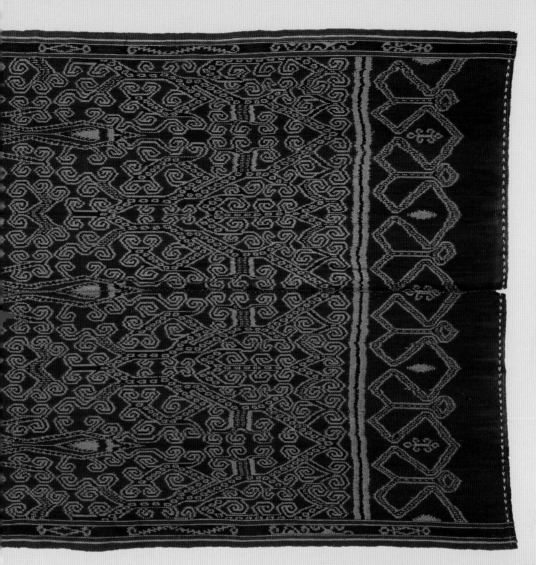

◁ *Iban pua kumbu*
(ceremonial cloth),
West Borneo,
ca. 1900. Ikat warp,
naturally dyed
cotton, 42½ × 81 in
(108 × 206 cm).
Musée du Quai
Branly, Paris

◁ *Tapa* (snippet of bark cloth), Fiji Islands.
Beaten dyed bark, 32¼ × 113¾ in (82 × 289 cm).
Musée du Quai Branly, Paris

▷ *Tapa* (snippet of bark cloth), Cook Islands.
Beaten dyed bark, 36 × 53 in (91 × 134.5 cm).
Musée du Quai Branly, Paris

Human and Divine Images

Christian missionaries saw Oceanic sculptures as idols that they were obligated to destroy. It was not the figures themselves that were worshipped, however, but the ancestral spirits and gods who temporarily resided in them. Tribal people summoned them with songs, dances and sacred materials such as red feathers, coconut fiber ropes and bark cloth.

The figure itself was insignificant, and its destruction was not a disaster as long as it was replaced by a similar one. Before the arrival of Europeans in Oceania, living persons were apparently never depicted, and historical figures only rarely. Representative, modeled-over skulls occupied a special place as relics filled with mythological creative power. Human figures not only served gods and spirits as "stopovers," but could also illustrate abstract concepts like fertility. Conversely, gods and spirits were found in door jambs, war shields, stones, and even in two seashells.

△ Uli, New Ireland, ca. 1890. Painted wood, 61 in (155 cm) high. Musée du Quai Branly, Paris. The hermaphrodite Uli probably symbolized the connection between paternal and maternal life energy in initiation ceremonies.

▷ Lono *Ki'i akua* (idol), Hawaii, ca. 1890. Wood, 35 in (89 cm) high. Musée du Quai Branly, Paris. Lono, one of the four main Hawaiian gods, was responsible for fertility, agriculture and peace. The helmet-like, extended backbone highlighted the importance of ancestry and, by extension, family. The priests' dances conjured up the posture. During the ritual, the deity was equipped with hair and a tapa "belt."

▷ *Dinonga eidu* (idol), Nukuoro, Caroline Islands, ca. 1800. Wood, 13¾ in (35 cm) high. Musée du Quai Branly, Paris. The initiated can distinguish between the masterfully stylized figures of male and female spirits and deities.

◁ *Ki'i hula manu* (image with feathers) of the war god Ku-Ka-ili-Moku, Hawaii, 18th century. Wickerwork, pearl, and dog teeth, 26⅓ in (67 cm) high. Musée du Quai Branly, Paris. To enhance the effect, the wickerwork was thickly decorated with red feathers that served as a medium.

▷ Tiki (human idol), Marquesas Islands. Volcanic rock, 6 in (15 cm) high. Musée du Quai Branly, Paris

◁ Double-figure depicting a mythical primal pair (?), Lake Sentani, New Guinea. Wood, 70 in (177.2 cm) high. National Gallery of Australia, Canberra

▽ **Handle of a fly whisk**, Tahiti. Wood, 7 in (18 cm) high. Musée du Quai Branly, Paris. The creative force Tane is depicted here.

▽ **Statuette of an ancestor or goddess** (Hikule'o or Sakaunu, responsible for death and posterity), Tonga, early 19th century. Whale bones, 5¼ in (13.3 cm) high. The Metropolitan Museum of Art, New York

▷ **To'o of the war god Oro** (god of the earth and air in times of peace), Tahiti. Wood, coconut wickerwork and feathers, 23¼ in (59 cm) high. Musée du Quai Branly, Paris. *To'o* was a man-made symbol or figurative image of a god, as opposed to *ata*, a natural object sought after by people. Prayers were "woven in" by the maker.

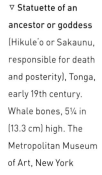

Moai

Currents and winds made it possible to drift from opposite directions and run aground on the same barren island just below the Tropic of Capricorn in the Pacific. In 1947, Thor Heyerdahl showed how it was done from South America. The colonization of Easter Island (Rapa Nui) has since been genetically proven from the Polynesian side, and from there alone.

But anyone who will not believe that a megalithic culture developed from the skills and scant knowledge brought there by the Polynesians might instead assume that the technical knowledge crossed over from South America, where cyclopean masonry was built from Mexico to Bolivia in the fifth century and enormously heavy stone sculptures were transported.

The legend, according to which the *mana* essence could release versatile, spiritual oceanic energy so that moai rose up and moved from quarry to coast on their own volition, practically paraphrases one of Heyerdahl's tested methods: by pulling and relaxing the ropes, one could "waddle" the giant statues, rocking them back and forth in a forward, pivoting motion.

Moai made from the wood of the toromiro tree have been known in Europe since 1775. Toromiro wood was unique to Easter Island.

▷ *Moai tangata* (human figure), ancestral idol (?), Rapa Nui, ca. 1810. Wood, 16 in (40.6 cm) high. The Metropolitan Museum of Art, New York

◁ *Moai Kavakava* (figure with ribs), Rapa Nui. Wood, 12 in (30 cm) high. Musée du Quai Branly, Paris. These gaunt figures are believed to be the dead or demons. They protected houses and were carried during ceremonies. Moai made after 1862 are tourist products. That was the year in which most of the men from Rapa Nui, including the wood carvers, were forcibly taken to Peru as slaves.

▷ **Ahu A Kivi**, five Moai, each about 13 ft (4 m) tall. Since the first settlement in 5th century, oversized stonemasonry for ancestor worship has existed on Easter Island. These unique *moai maea* (stone statues) as we know them today, reached their heyday as early as 1100. After a revolt in 1680, production was discontinued. Of the approximately one thousand surviving pieces, about 250 remain unfinished.

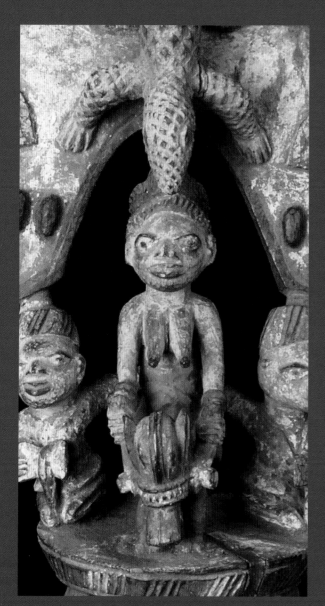

Africa

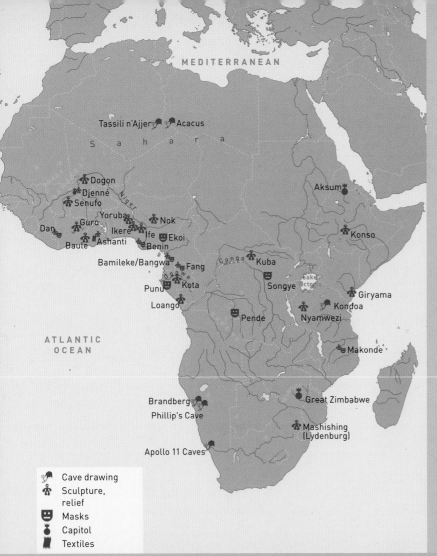

MEDITERRANEAN

S a h a r a

Tassili n'Ajjer Acacus

Dogon
Djenné
Senufo
Yoruba
Dan Guro Nok
Ikere
Baule Ashanti Ife Ekoi
Benin
Bamileke/Bangwa Fang
Punu Kuba
Loango Kota Songye
Pende
Nyamwezi Kondoa
Giryama

Aksum

Konso

Lake Victoria

Makonde

ATLANTIC
OCEAN

Brandberg
Phillip's Cave

Great Zimbabwe

Mashishing
(Lydenburg)

Apollo 11 Caves

Cave drawing
Sculpture,
relief
Masks
Capitol
Textiles

Chronology

ca. 10,500 BCE Settlement of the then-fertile Sahara. The region has been drying out since ca. 5000 BCE.

after 3000 BCE Egyptian civilization dominates northeastern Africa.

ca. 1500 BCE Agriculture spreads through all of Africa.

ca. 350 BCE–750 CE The Aksum Empire rules from the Horn of Africa, trading with the African interior.

8th–15th century The rise of the important West African empires of Ghana, Mali and Songhai. Most become Muslim after the tenth century as Arab-dominated city-states and trade centers spread along the east coast of Africa.

ca. 1100–15th century The Munhumutapa empire builds Great Zimbabwe in southern Africa.

12th–19th century The Edo kingdom of Benin rules in what is today Nigeria.

15th century The Portuguese found colonies on the African coast.

ca. 1680–1896 The Ashanti empire rules what is today Ghana.

Rock painting, Tassili n'Ajjer, Algeria,
after 7000 BCE

Seated figure, Nok, Nigeria,
500–200 CE

Lydenburg head,
South Africa, 500–700

Seated figure, Djenné,
Mali, 13th century

| 7000 BCE | 500 BCE | 700 CE | 1250 |

Africa

African Art

Produced by a wide range of ethnic groups, most of which survive today, the broad category of African art is made up of a variety of cultural artifacts produced under a wide range of conditions. Most African art comes from sub-Saharan tribal groups, and does not include art produced by the Islamic-influenced peoples of North Africa. Rock engravings and paintings are important examples of traditional African art, many dating back to prehistoric times. Wooden sculptures, masks, jewelry, carved ivory, brightly dyed, finely woven textiles, elaborate weaponry and other status symbols are also important. West Africa is famous for its prehistoric ceramic and bronze figures. The African climate and termites make conservation of older, wooden works of art particularly challenging. Where the meticulously detailed and finely carved masks are concerned, it can be difficult to separate the work of art from its practical role in religious ceremonies or initiation rites. In general, the wooden sculptures can be integrally connected to gods, spirits, ancestor worship, creation myths or fertility rites of the peoples who created them. Most sculptures represent humans or human-like beings, with the masks also occasionally depicting hybrid creatures that are part animal and part man. Other works of art function as fetishes with magical uses that protect a tribe by warding off the powers of evil. African works of art first found their way to Europe as "curiosities" via colonial collections. Over time, however, the wooden sculptures of human figures with their tendency toward abstraction and emphasis on specific body parts fascinated European artists who, under their influence, developed their own "primitive" style. African art, they explained, reduced art to its essentials.

19th century The race for African colonies begins between Great Britain, France, Belgium, Germany and Italy.
1884/85 The Berlin Congress. The Congo will remain the private property of the Belgian crown until 1908.
1910 Founding of the Union of South Africa in the wake of the Boer Wars (1899–1902)
1940–1945 North and West Africa become war zones.
1948–1990/94 Apartheid government in South Africa
1957–1970 Nearly all African nations gain their independence.
1960–1964 and 1996–2003 Civil war in Congo claims ca. 6 million lives.
1975 After bloody wars of independence, Angola and Mozambique win their independence from Portugal.
1994 Free elections in South Africa and genocide in Rwanda

Queen mother, pendant mask, Benin, 16th century

Mwete head sculpture, Kota-Mahongwe, ca. 1840

Lefem portrait figure, Bangwa, 19th/20th century

Ikere palace portal by Olowe of Ise, ca. 1916

1550   1800   1900   1950

At a Glance

Woodcarving and Other Sculpture

Statues, mostly carved from wood, but sometimes made of bronze or terracotta, are closely related to the rich, complex creation mythology of tribal peoples. The sculpted figures can represent primordial beings, ancestors or protective spirits of individual clans. Many tribes revere their most ancient ancestors as semi-divine heroes who set the existing social order in place, or who brought new techniques like hunting or farming to mankind.

Cave Paintings

Rock painting inside caves is particularly common in Namibia, where the famous Apollo 11 Cave in the Hunsberg mountain range shows signs of settlement from at least 100,000 BCE. Among many paintings of local animals, experts date the stone slab with a representation of a predatory big cat to ca. 25,000 BCE, making it the oldest known cave painting in Africa. Brandenberg cave has over 45,000 rock paintings showing animals, human figures and hunting scenes, among them the famous representation of the "white lady." Phillip's Cave in the Erongo Mountains includes rock paintings dating to 3400–3300 BCE.

Masks

In African culture, shamans often wear masks. The masks symbolize mythological powers, and can portray animals, ancestors or nature spirits. Wearing a mask bestows special powers that protect against danger. Many masks, like other carved figures, also symbolize fertility. Some tribes have their own mask societies associated with secret rites, dances, and other events open only to members.

Jewelry

Brilliantly colored African jewelry, like the textiles, can occur in an unending variety of forms and materials. Precious metal and stone, ivory, pearl, coral, wood, ceramic, dried fruit, and more are all incorporated into jewelry that is often worn by both men and women. Women in particular often wear jewelry for reasons that go beyond aesthetic appeal, with the style and material of the jewelry used to display their wealth and social position. In addition to other functions, some jewelry serves as talismans warding off evil.

"Primitive Art"

Since the late nineteenth century, European painters and sculptors have had a strong attraction to the art of the people of Africa and the South Pacific, which provided them with a wealth of formal inspiration.

While Paul Gauguin was wandering through the islands of the South Pacific, artists belonging to the Expressionist and Cubist movements, chief among them Pablo Picasso, were soaking up influences from African art.

In addition to their appreciation of the uniquely African formal qualities of the art, a certain "nostalgia for the primitive" also played a large part in the acceptance of African art.

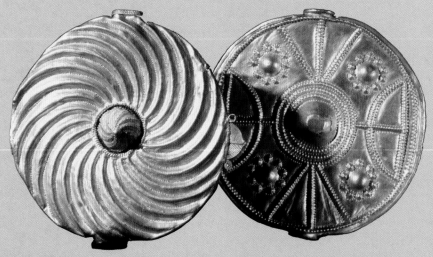

△ Jewelry worn by high status individuals in the court of the Ashanti kings as insignias denoting their rank. Ghana, 19th century. Gold, 3½ in (9 cm) diameter. The British Museum, London

Africa

The Stone Walls at Great Zimbabwe

The empire that built Great Zimbabwe became fabulously wealthy through trade in gold, iron and tin. Around 1200 BCE, this led to the construction of magnificent stone walls of granite blocks laid entirely without mortar. Elliptical in plan, the walls enclose huts and houses that may have served as a sanctuary. The walls are some 800 ft (244 m) long and up to 30 ft (9 m) high, with massive blocks up to 16 ft (5 m) wide. European colonial powers long viewed the ruins as the remains of an ancient, lost "white culture," perhaps the residence of the legendary Queen of Sheba.

△ View of the stone walls at Great Zimbabwe, 11th–15th centuries

Textiles

Textiles in brilliant colors with large scale, mostly geometric patterns are among the most recognizable of all African arts. Most are either woven or batik, with colors from plant-based dyes like indigo. Like African jewelry, textiles fulfill both aesthetic and social functions, representing both the artistic tastes of the owner and his or her social status and level of distinction. Textiles are not only used for clothing, but also as carpets, mats, and wall hangings that beautify the interior of a home while expressing the family's place in the social hierarchy. They are a common barter good, and a valuable part of the gifts exchanged during marriage negotiations. Many ethnic groups produce textiles as an important trade product. African textiles originally reached Europe via the Islamic countries where they had long been prized. Today, the indigenous textile market of many African countries faces stiff competition from cheap imported goods from Asia.

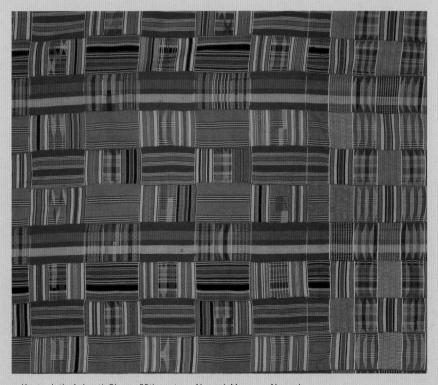

△ *Kente* cloth, Ashanti, Ghana, 20th century, Newark Museum, Newark

Key Terms

Rock Painting

Rock paintings and engravings are found all over the world in caves and under rock overhangs, wherever people found shelter. This art form begins so early that its very existence —and why it was created in the first place—is intertwined with origins of the magical act of representation itself. Ancient rock art serves as the basis for a new phase of cultural development.

Rock art in Africa is primarily found in the mountain ranges of the Sahara Desert, such as Tassili n'Ajjer in Algeria and the Acabus mountains in southwest Libya. In prehistoric times, these were fertile regions rich in game. The earliest phase is dominated by images of wild animals (Bubalus period, ca. 10,000 BCE). The following phase includes large scale representations of people with large,

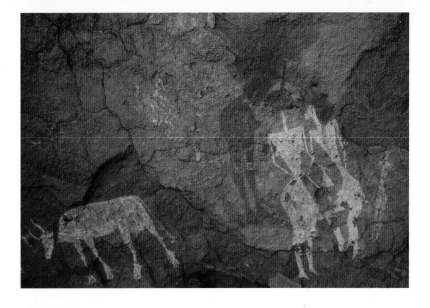

round heads (Round Head period, ca. 7000 BCE). The Judean King Herod, who visited the Roman province of Libya, raved about art from a later phase that was characterized by images of galloping horses (Horse period, ca. 1500 BCE). Around 200 BCE, the camel was domesticated in the Sahara and began to appear in the art (Camel period). Eastern and southern Africa (primarily Namibia) also have large numbers of rock paintings, most dating to relatively recent times. Some are still used in rituals and are frequently repainted.

◁ **Two Round Head figures with detailed heads and bodies,** rock wall of the Grotto of Tanzoumaitak, Tassili n'Ajjer range, Algeria, Round Head period, after 7000 BCE

▷ **Trio of men dancing in a trance,** rock painting from the Kondoa site, Tanzania. Many rock art sites in the Kondoa region are still used ritually today, making the dating of the paintings uncertain.

◁ **Dance scene with a multi-headed bull,** Tassili n'Ajjer, range, Algeria, Cattle period, after 5000 BCE

◁ **Painting on a cliff face in the Acacus range,** Libya, Horse period, ca. 1500–200 BCE. The painting is dated based on the double triangle representation of the human body and schematic representation of the head.

Sculptures In Terracotta and Bronze

Nok sculptures, named for the village where they were found in northern Nigeria, are the oldest securely attributed sculptures from sub-Saharan Africa. Dating from sometime after 500 BCE, Nok sculptures are defined by their naturalistic modeling and expert firing technique. In addition to animal figures, there are also human figures with oversized heads and facial features that, despite stylization, seem individualized. These are thought to be ancestor portraits of the ruling tribe. The highly developed Nok culture disappears archaeologically around the third century. A new culture emerged in southwest Nigeria in the tenth century. Ife was a

△ **Seated male figure**, Nok. Terracotta, 15 in (38 cm) high. Musée du Quai Branly, Paris

▽ **Memorial head**, Ife, 12th–14th century. Terracotta, 6¾ in (17 cm) high. Musée du Quai Branly, Paris

△ **Upper body and head of an** *Oni* (priest), Ife, with crown and ruler iconography, 10th–13th century. Cast bronze, 14 in (35 cm) high. National Museum of Ife

theocratic kingdom with a significant court culture. Its central sites remain sacred to the much later kingdom of Benin. While terracotta continued to be an important medium, Ife is most famous for its highly developed casting technology, which produced bronze and brass sculptures of exceptional quality. Ife figures are also thought to function as part of the ancestor cult of the ruling dynasties. Although increasingly naturalistic and clearly rejecting geometric forms (compare the ears with those of the Nok figures), Ife emphasis on the head is characteristically African. Faces are often covered in regular hatching or parallel lines, perhaps representing ritual scarification or tattooing.

Sculpture

As early as the fifteenth century, impressed European travelers were bringing back reports of the size and magnificence of the south Nigerian capital of the kingdom of Benin. Located some 100 miles (170 km) southeast of Ife and established as early as 1200, Benin was a regular feature on European maps and trade routes from the sixteenth century until its conquest by the punitive British expedition of 1897. Following its overthrow, countless works of art produced for the Benin's highly structured court culture found their way into museums all over the world.

The objects of ivory and cast bronze served a cult that worshipped godlike rulers. Heads and figures of deceased kings and queens, depicted in idealized form despite some effort at individualization, were placed upon ancestor altars. Benin's technologically advanced bronze relief panels covered the columns of the palace courtyard with scenes showing kings, people of high rank and victorious war heroes. Europeans also occasionally appear. The finely engraved leopards probably guarded a king's throne.

△ **Queen mother**, pendant mask, 16th century. Ivory, 9½ in (23. 8 cm) high. The Metropolitan Museum of Art, New York

△ **Memorial head of a king**, 19th century. Cast bronze, 18¼ in (45.7 cm) high. The Metropolitan Museum of Art, New York

▷ **Pair of leopards**, 16th–18th century. Cast bronze, 20 in (ca. 50 cm) high. National Museum, Lagos, Nigeria

△ **Relief panel with warrior king (Oba) and four companions**, from the palace of Benin, 16th/17th century. Cast bronze, 19 in (47.6 cm) high. The Metropolitan Museum of Art, New York

Art of the Yoruba

The origins of the Yoruba extend back to the time of the Nok culture (500 BCE–200 CE). Living primarily in what is now Nigeria, they are the most populous ethnic groups south of the Sahara, and one of the most important. Over the long course of their history, the Yoruba were often subdivided into small states. Their traditional arts, formally and conceptually rich, are dominated by the wooden sculpture typical of all African tribal art. Art in metal was reserved for kings. The depiction of faces with stylistically exaggerated, large and protruding eyes characterizes Yoruba art. The wooden sculptures are painted according to a complex, symbolic use of color regulated by taboos that are not easily explained. Many figures are ritual in function. Yoruba gods are organized in a hierarchal pantheon. Religious societies maintain masks with supernatural powers in rituals that honor ancestors or historical heroes. In the Gelede society, for example, the thematic center is the ritual closeness of its membership to the mother goddess. Doors and posts of palace-like buildings were dominated by richly carved representations of aristocratic power.

▷ Helmet mask with *olompupo* (mother with children), Yoruba. Wood with polychrome paint, 48 in (120 cm) high, weight 13½ lb (6.6 kg). Musée du Quai Branly, Paris

△ Helmet mask belonging to the Gelede society, Yoruba, ca. 1900. Wood with polychrome paint, 10½ in (26 cm) high. The Metropolitan Museum of Art, New York

▷ Olowe of Ise (ca. 1875–ca. 1938), **Door to the Palace of Ikere**, ca 1916. Painted wood, colored, 7 ft (213 cm) high. The British Museum, London. Unusual about this palace door is that its early 20th-century Yoruba sculptor is known by name. Olowe specialized in secular subjects that gave him greater creative freedom than more traditional ritual pieces. The arrival of a British colonial administrator is depicted on the right panel; the Ogoga (ruler) of Ikere is on the left. The meeting looks like a casual visit, although the country had long been a British colony and the Ogga hardly retained any authority.

Wood and Terracotta Figures

The mosque of Djenné in Mali, built around 1300, is the largest mud brick building in the world. Older still is the under-investigated thirteenth- to fifteenth-century culture that produced some of the world's most unusual human figures in terracotta.

West Africa occupies the savannah between the Sahara and the rain forest, extending east to west from Nigeria to Mali and north to south from Burkina Faso to Côte d'Ivoire. Most of the cultures living there are famous for their wooden sculpture. Among the most influential are the Dogon and Bambara in the north and the Senufo in the south. The tendency of African wooden sculpture toward symmetry and basic geometric forms may have something to do with the fact that they are made by carpenters, who tend to lean toward simplicity.

▷ *Tyiwara* (headress mask), Bambara. Wood, private collection. This is a stylized representation of a horse-antelope, the form the water spirit Faro took when bringing millet to the Bambara people.

▽ **Seated figure**, Djenné, 13th century. Terracotta, 10 in (25.4 cm) high. The Metropolitan Museum of Art, New York

◁ Master of Ogol, **Female figure with lip peg**, Dogon, before 1935. Wood, 28 in (70 cm) high. Musée du Quai Branly, Paris. Figures like these were kept in sanctuaries under the protection of the Hogon (head priest). The deceased were laid down next to their ancestor figures to bind their souls together.

▷ *Kpelie* mask, Senufo. Wood, Entwistle Gallery, London. Kpelie type dance masks are among the best known Senufo works of art. Similar motifs also appear carved in relief on doors. The heads frequently have horns and stunted legs emerging from beneath left and right side projections.

△ **Mask**, Dan, Côte d'Ivoire. Wood and horsehair, 8½ in (21.5 cm) high. Castello Sforzesco, Milan

△ **Mask**, Dan, Côte D'Ivoire, 19th century. Wood, 11¼ in (28 cm) high. Musée du Quai Branly, Paris

Woodcarving

Tropical rainforests and humid savannas make up the West African coastal region once known as the Ivory Coast (today the Côte d'Ivoire). The village communities of the Dan, Baule and Guro share a rich and varied woodcarving heritage.

Most Dan masks depict bush spirits: the mythological landowners who first allowed the founders of the villages to settle and farm the land. Today, the masks help the bush spirits communicate their wishes to the villagers. The mask aesthetic makes use of clear forms interspersed with curving elements that can be soft or sharp. Proportions are usually harmonious.

Baule figures represent a kind of spiritual sex partner. The Baule believe that up until the moment of birth every man is joined with a female spirit (biolo bla), just as every woman is joined to a male spirit (bialo bian). After birth, the lonely spirits, feeling abandoned, send their human partners erotic dreams. Following instructions from a soothsayer, the wooden figures are carved to satisfy the spirits.

Free-flowing lines characterize the masks of the Guro secret society. Human and animal features are often combined. Another favorite site for art is the pulley block from a narrow band loom, often carved with a mask-like face.

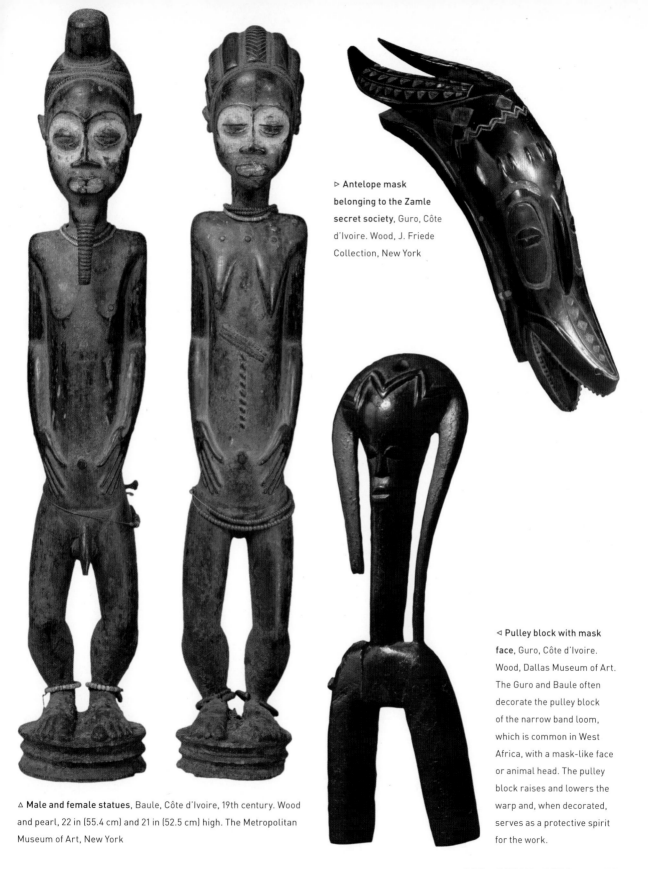

▷ Antelope mask belonging to the Zamle secret society, Guro, Côte d'Ivoire. Wood, J. Friede Collection, New York

◁ Pulley block with mask face, Guro, Côte d'Ivoire. Wood, Dallas Museum of Art. The Guro and Baule often decorate the pulley block of the narrow band loom, which is common in West Africa, with a mask-like face or animal head. The pulley block raises and lowers the warp and, when decorated, serves as a protective spirit for the work.

△ Male and female statues, Baule, Côte d'Ivoire, 19th century. Wood and pearl, 22 in (55.4 cm) and 21 in (52.5 cm) high. The Metropolitan Museum of Art, New York

Gold and Woodcarving

At the beginning of European trade with West Africa, the coast of what is today Ghana, the so-called "Gold Coast," was the focal point of trade in gold. In 1481, the Portuguese founded a trade colony here, bringing wealth and power to Akan peoples like the Ashanti. Countless beautifully made, mostly figural gold dust weights and containers survive as proof of the enormous quantities of gold that passed through the region. Gold also serves as medium in representational art and ritual contexts.

The best known pieces of Ashanti woodcarving are abstract figures (akua) dominated by a large, flat, circular head. These apparently female figures are the receptacles of divine power that helps those who want to bear children. The long neck is also an ideal of feminine beauty. If the akua has been successful, it will be housed in the shrine of the god. The similarity of the akua to the ancient Egyptian Ankh sign, a symbol of life, has yet to be fully explained.

▽ **Kuduo (lid vessel)**, Akan. Brass, 11 in (27.5 cm) high. Musée du Quai Branly, Paris. Kuduo vessels were used to store gold dust and other valuables.

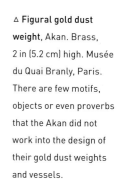

△ **Figural gold dust weight**, Akan. Brass, 2 in (5.2 cm) high. Musée du Quai Branly, Paris. There are few motifs, objects or even proverbs that the Akan did not work into the design of their gold dust weights and vessels.

△ **Akua ba (fertility figure)**, Ashanti. Wood, 16 in (40 cm) high. Private collection

◁ **Gold mask from the treasury of King Kofi Kakari** (reign ca. 1870), Ashanti, 19th century. Gold, 7 in (17.5 cm) high. Wallace Collection, London. This was probably the burial mask of a king or a trophy mask depicting a defeated enemy. The latter interpretation is supported by the ring underneath the beard, which could have allowed the mask to be attached to a throne post or other symbol of power.

◁ **Headdress mask of the Eekkpe society**, Ekoi, 20th century. Wood with polychrome paint, antelope skin, woven fiber, metal and bone, 29 in (72.5 cm) high. Musée du Quai Branly, Paris

▷ **Dance mask**, Bamileke. Wood, 35 in (89.3 cm) high. Musée du Quai Branly, Paris

Ritual Objects

The Ekoi, from the border region between Nigeria and Cameroon, make naturalistic dance masks that used to be covered with human skin. This may refer back to a headhunter tradition in the distant past. That said, many have female features, and "horns" that resemble the elaborate hairstyles of marriageable young women. They likely represent honored female ancestors.

The Cameroon grasslands are home to the Bamileke tribe, famous for a mask style that is less organic, more geometric, and expressive to the point of being grotesque. These gigantic masks, probably once worn exclusively by kings, are virtuoso pieces displaying an almost pure interaction between material and sculptural form.

During ceremonial dances, the lifelike portrait figure (*lefem*) of a Bangwa chief represents an honored royal ancestor in all his dynamic power and authority, underlined by neck bands made from leopard claws. The figure holds a large tobacco pipe and a palm wine calabash in its hands, objects with political as well as ritual significance.

In contrast, the figural throne from the Bekom group makes use of simplified, but still naturalistic forms, its balanced proportions exuding calm. It is thought to have held a bowl or calabash containing the bones of royal ancestors.

▷ **Bowl stand**, Bekom. Wood, 22 in (55 cm) high. Musée du Quai Branly, Paris. The figure would have been attached to a carved wooden seat and carried a large vessel atop its knees.

▷ **Lefem (portrait figure)**, Bangwa, 19th/20th centuries. Wood with polychrome paint, incrustation and raffia fiber, 40¾ in (102.2 cm) high. The Metropolitan Museum of Art, New York

Masks and Sculptures

The Fang are a large ethnic group, but stylistically, the name has come to define art by the Pangwe tribes from Gabon, Equatorial Guinea and the Congo. Barely sculptural, the heart-shaped, slightly convex face masks are distinguished only by a few details and an extremely overlong nose. The white colored surface is further decorated with the characteristic tattooing of an individual clan. Fang masks are worn during the Ngil ritual to ward off evil spirits. Punu masks, named for the Pangwe tribe along the Ogowe River, are also painted white, but are much more sculptural and rounded in form. The gentle planes of the face,

with eyes closed and lips brightly colored, give an almost naturalistic impression. Marks indicating scarification are frequently visible on the forehead and cheeks.

Fang reliquary figures constructed to house the bones of ancestors are both sculptural and heavily decorated with metal attachments. Those of the Kota are so heavily stylized and flat that they are almost two-dimensional. Many are almost entirely covered with sheet metal. Among their more defining characteristics are the concave face with almond eyes, crescent moon hairstyle and cheek flaps extending out on either side. There is usually no mouth. Shoulders

△ *Mwete* (head sculpture), Kota-Mahongwe, ca. 1840. Wood, brass and copper/plant fiber, 22½ in (56 cm) high. Musée du Quai Branly, Paris

▷ *Mwete* (head sculpture), Kota. Wood, brass and copper. Friede Collection, New York. The Kota sculpted heads are reliquary figures.

◁ *Bieri* (reliquary figure), Fang. Wood and pearls, 2 ft (60 cm) high. Musée du Quai Branly, Paris. This type of figure stood on containers for the bones of ancestors.

angle sharply to form one half of a rhombus with "arms" extending downward. These headdresses were found together with skeletons. The figures made by the Kota-Mahongwe were even more abstract. The basic form is a concave oval wrapped in metal wire. Only the button-like eyes and the highly stylized nose show that this is a face. These figures were used to protect the bones of ancestors, the shine of the metal marshalling the power of light to keep away the black magic of the night.

△ **Neck support with figures**, Luba or Shankadi, 19th century. Wood, 7½ in (8.5 cm) high. Musée du Quai Branly, Paris. The artist of this piece, which depicts characteristically 19th-century hairstyles, is known by the name "Master of the Cascade Coiffure." Hairstyles like these were so elaborate that neck supports were necessary to sleep.

◁ *Kifwebe* **mask**, Songye, ca. 1890. Wood with polychrome paint, 2⅓ in (53.3 cm) high. Philadelphia Museum of Art, Philadelphia. Raffia fiber was originally fastened to the holes around the edge, giving the mask a "beard."

▷ *Gitenda* **mask**, Pende. Wood with polychrome paint, raffia, 15¾ in (39.5 cm) high. Musée royale de l'Afrique centrale, Tervuren, Belgium

◁ **Figural drinking vessel**, Kuba. Wood, 7½ in (19 cm) high. Musée royale de l'Afrique centrale, Tervuren, Belgium. Kuba beakers like this one were used to drink palm wine. Many neighboring groups copied them.

▷ *Chibinda Illunga*, Chokwe. Wood, hair and pelts, 16¼ in (40.6 cm) high. Kimbell Art Museum, Fort Worth. With his hunting skill, Luba prince Ilunga won the heart of the Lunda queen Lweji.

Art in the Congo

The term "Congo" refers to the rainforest region alongside the Congo River and its tributaries. When the first Europeans reached the Congo in the fifteenth century, they encountered a culturally sophisticated kingdom. Like the interior empires of the Luba and Kuba, it continued to exist into the colonial era relatively intact. In contrast to West Africa, very few art objects from that period in the Congo survive, with the exception of those made for rulers.

The Pende and Songye peoples both had a highly developed mask culture. The face was depicted as a series of bold, arcing surfaces that dissolved into abstract forms similar to cubist art before coming together again symmetrically. The tendency toward symmetry also characterizes the figural representation of ances-tors and heroes even when, as is the case with the Chokwe, a noticeable naturalism is also present. Luxurious everyday objects also become works of art. The famous neck supports of the Luba empire protected the elaborate traditional hairstyles. The Kuba palm wine beakers carved to resemble heads were also eminently useful.

▽ *Nkisi nduda* (fetish figure with mirror), Loango. Wood and other materials, 23 ¼ in (58 cm) high. Musée du Quai Branly, Paris

△ *Nkisi* (fetish figure), 19th/20th century. Wood and other materials, 24 in (58.8 cm) high. The Metropolitan Museum of Art, New York

◁ *Nkisi nkondi* (fetish animal figure), Loango, early 19th century. Wood and other materials, 17½ in (44 cm) high. Musée du Quai Branly, Paris

Fetish Sculpture in the Congo

Nkisi (plural *minkisi*) figures are found throughout the Congo. When fetish figures like these are covered in mirrors, they are called *ndud*. The "nail fetishes" are called *nkondi*. All of them ward off evil spirits and black magic. During their manufacture, the artist adds a *bilongo*, which he receives from a *nganga* (medicine man). A bilongo can be any kind of material with magic powers. It is enclosed in a mirrored box set into the chest of the figure, after which the figure itself has supernatural powers. The term nkisi refers not only to the figure itself, but to the power it possesses, a power that can be released by driving in a nail. Most of the nkisi known today date to between 1885 and 1920. Many others belong to the period of the Loango empire (fourteenth–nineteenth centuries). Surprisingly, the distribution of these figures in the sixteenth and seventeenth centuries is identical to the regions where Christian missionaries were most active. This raises the question of the possible influence of Christian motifs, like St. Sebastian pierced by arrows, or Christ nailed to the cross, or any of a number of Christian reliquaries in bust form. As yet there is no satisfactory answer.

▷ *Nkisi* (fetish figure), Loango. Wood and other materials, 24½ in (61 cm) high. Musée du Quai Branly, Paris

Ritual Sculpture and Masks

The oldest evidence of human existence comes from East Africa, which is the region between southern Ethiopia and Kenya (or Tanzania). The earliest material culture also comes from here, in the form of tools like the stone hand axe. Paradoxically, East Africa is art-poor compared to other regions. Based on what can be seen in collections today, its peoples do not seem to have created much art at all, let alone a sculptural tradition. Much of this is probably due to colonial politics. The colonial powers were collecting African art from the very beginning, but focused on the sculptures of West and Central Africa, more or less ignoring East Africa.

Many of the larger pieces of East African sculpture have a funerary context. The grave figures of the Konso people of southern Ethiopia were probably only for chiefs and their families. The carved burial posts of the Giryama in Kenya are not so much monuments to the dead as a place for their spirits to reside. Individuals of high rank from the Nyamwezi in Tanzania would be raised off the ground by an intricately carved stool, or by a figure sitting on a stool in their place. The Makonde from the Tanzania-Mozambique border carve naturalistic helmet masks and special body masks for initiation rituals.

△ *Muti wa Lipiko* (helmet mask), Makonde. Wood and hair, 10¾ in (27 cm) high. Private collection. The addition of human hair enhances the naturalism of the piece.

Early Sculpture in South Africa

Like the rock paintings of the Sahara, the rock engravings and paintings from South Africa are well-known masterpieces of prehistoric art. Most were created by the San (Bushmen), and are still in ritual use today. The dates of these works of art are difficult to determine due to repainting and later additions.

The oldest known example of South African sculpture comes from Mashishing in the province of Mpumalanga (formerly Lydenburg in the Eastern Transvaal). These so-called Lydenburg heads have been dated by radiocarbon to between 500 and 700 CE. The upside down U-shaped heads made of terracotta resemble ceramic vessels. They have large mouths and eyes that look like cowry shells with hatched lines on the neck resembling jewelry. Notched lines may refer to scarification. The hairstyle terminates with an animal figure on the top. Some of these heads have holes in the neck area, perhaps to attach clothing or drapery of some kind, making the heads a kind of helmet mask.

◁ **Lyndeburg head**, 500–700 CE. Terracotta, 15¼ in (38 cm) high. African Museum, Cape Town

△ *Ndimu* (body mask), Makode,
ca. 1890. Wood, 24½ in (61.2 cm) high.
Private collection. Body masks are
worn by dancers during initiation
ceremonies that recreate the pain of
birth, thus preparing the initiate for his
or her new responsibilities.

▷ Stool figure of an upper class
female ancestor, Nyamwezi. Wood,
37½ in (94 cm) high. Private collection

◁ *Waaqa* (funerary figure), Konso,
mid-19th century. Wood, 79 in (198 cm)
high. Musée du Quai Branly, Paris.
These figures representing the dead
are often displayed surrounded by
figures representing dead enemies.
They are found most often at gravesites of the wealthy and heroes.

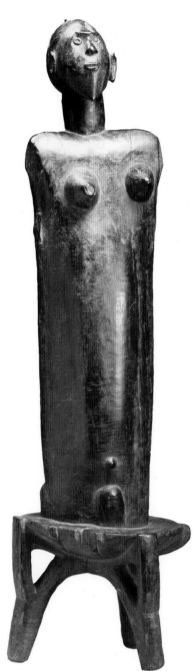

▷ *Kiqanqo* (burial post), Giryama.
Wood, ca. 65 in (ca. 160 cm) high.
Burial posts are often erected some
time after the death of the deceased
in order to placate a distressed spirit
mourning the loss of its body.

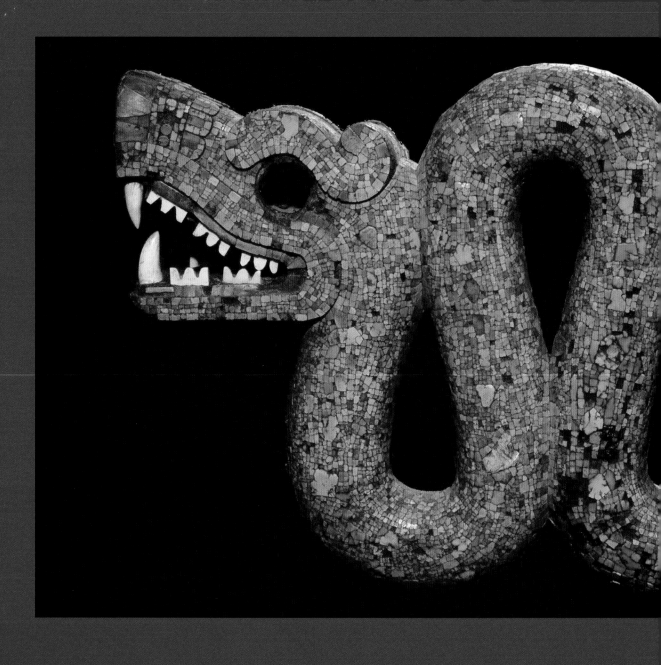

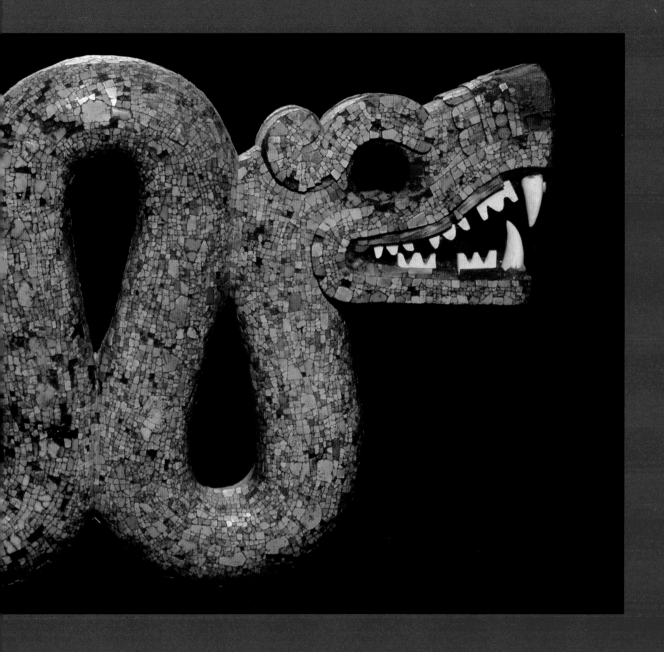

Pre-Columbian America

Pre-Columbian America

ca. 3000 BCE–250 CE Pre-classical epochs of the Maya

ca. 1200–400 BCE Olmec culture in Mexico

after 1000 BCE Huastecs and Zapotecs in Mexico

ca. 1000–200 BCE Paracas in Peru

ca. 900–200 BCE Chavín in Peru

ca. 400 BCE–60 CE Nazca culture in Peru

ca. 100–700 CE Moche culture in Peru

ca. 200–900 Classical epochs of the Maya

ca. 690–1519 Mixtecs in Mexico

ca. 720–1150 Toltecs in Mexico

ca. 900–1519 Post-classical epochs of the Maya

ca. 1200–1572 Age of the great Inca rulers (Sapa Inca)

ca. 1200 Founding of the Inca capital, Cuzco

ca. 1325 Founding of the Aztec capital, Tenochtitlán

ca. 1371–1520 Age of the rulers of Tenochtitlán

Colossal head from San Lorenzo Tenochtitlán, ca. 1200–900 BCE

1200 BCE

Pre-Columbian America

Ancient America

The North American continent was permanently settled from around 18,000 BCE. The earliest inhabitants probably came from East Asia across the Bering Strait. Around 10,000 BCE they also began settling Central and South America, developing the first advanced civilizations there. The earliest of these in Central America was the Mexican Olmecs, whose art and government shaped those to come.

Other peoples, such as the Huastecs, Zapotecs, Mixtecs and Toltecs, founded city-states and cultural centers in Mexico.

In Peru, the Paracas, Chavín and Moche established themselves as the earliest advanced civilizations, building pyramids and monolithic sculptures. Along the southern coast of Peru, the Nazca drew gigantic lines in the earth (geoglyphs), often in the form of human beings or animals.

The agrarian societies of the Maya, which endured through several epochs, were the longest-lasting of these advanced civilizations. There was war-like rivalry between their highly developed city-states.

In Mexico, the Aztecs established a strictly hierarchical empire centered around their capital, Tenochtitlán. They subdued their neighbors in violent campaigns and made them into tributaries.

The Inca of Peru possessed the most highly advanced political system in all of the ancient Americas. It included a strictly organized bureaucracy, news and postal services, outstanding road and walkway networks and a socialist-style planned economy with universal compulsory labor. Thanks to their thoroughly organized system of administration, they are often referred to as the "Romans of South America."

In the sixteenth century, within a period of just a few years, all these empires succumbed to the armed expansionist drive of the Spanish Conquistadores.

1440–1469 Montezuma I expands the Aztec Empire into a great power.
1471–1493 Heyday of the Inca Empire under Topa Inca Yupanqui
1493–1527 The Inca king Huayna Cápac conquers portions of Colombia.

1519–1544 Spanish campaigns of conquest
1527–1532 Civil war between the brothers Atahualpa and Huáscar weakens the Inca Empire.

1533 Atahualpa is executed by the Spanish Conquistadores.
1570–1572 Túpac Amaru leads final Inca resistance movement which is bloodily suppressed by the Spanish.

Jaguar, mural on red ground, Teotihuacán, ca. 400 CE

Statue on the Temple of the Morning Star Pyramid, Tula, ca. 950

Inca idol, ca. 1450–1532

Inuit mask, ca. 1850

400 CE   **950**   **1500**   **1850**

At a Glance

The Mayan Calendar System

The importance of the priesthood caste, the scholarly class of the Maya, was primarily linked to their knowledge of the ceremonial calendar. The Maya, who regulated their lives according to cycles of time, employed two different calendar systems: for everyday life, they used a solar calendar consisting of 365 days which they probably adopted from the Olmecs. This calendar divided the year into eighteen individually-named sections of twenty days each; the five extra "nameless" or "unlucky" days were added on at the end.

In addition, however, the Maya had a ceremonial calendar for ritual and divinatory purposes (bean oracle). This calendar consisted of 260 days, divided into thirteen units of twenty days each. Every 52 years or 18,980 days (= 52 yearly cycles of 365 days each or 73 oracle cycles of 260 days each) the two systems would start again simultaneously. For the Maya, this calendar cycle represented the highest unit of time calculation.

Quipu

From around 1400, the Incas developed the quipu—a system of "writing" using knots for recording statistical information in government and economic administration. Different colored strings with varying formations of knots were attached to a main cord up to 13 ft (4 m) long. These represented numerical values which could then be read and combined.

Maya stucco glyphs displayed in Palenque Museum, Mexico

Mayan Script

The hieroglyphic writing used by the lowland Maya (but not by those living in the mountains), employed logograms (specific symbols or pictures) for many names or terms as well as syllable symbols which were divided into vowels and consonants and combined (primarily with one another) to form square hieroglyphs. Owing to the wide variety of shapes and many possible combinations used for depicting specific words and names, the hieroglyphs that have been preserved in stone or manuscripts are extremely difficult to decipher.

Nazca Lines

The geoglyphs which the Nazca people scratched into the desert earth of Peru between 200 BCE and 600 CE consist of lines up to 12½ miles (20 km) long, geometric shapes, and figures of animals and people ranging in size from 30 to several hundred feet (10 to several hundred meters) long. Their meaning has not yet been fully explained: possible interpretations range from a calendar system or astronomical images to ritual paths used for religious ceremonies.

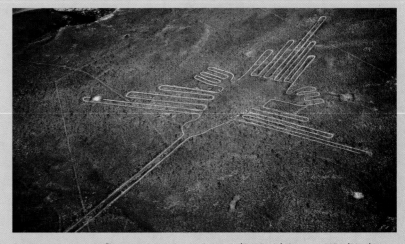

Geoglyph known as the "Hummingbird", Pampa Colorada (Red Plain), Peru, ca. 295 ft (90 m) long

Pre-Columbian America

Pyramids

Nearly all the pre-Columbian cultures constructed tiered pyramids, often monumental in size. The oldest were built around 3000 BCE. A central stairway led up to the pyramid's platform, where a temple or a ritual area for human sacrifices was built. The pyramids were also used as astronomical observatories. They were usually located in the center of a temple district and were part of an ensemble made up of a number of ritual structures. New, larger pyramids were frequently constructed on top of earlier ones—sometimes repeatedly—and the older pyramids remained intact inside the newer structures. The 200-ft (60-m) high double pyramid in the Aztec capital of Tenochtitlán (now Mexico City) was particularly famous.

Pyramid temple on the main square of Monte Albán, Oaxaca, Mexico

Ball Games

Over 1500 ball game sites have been discovered in the ruins of such pre-Columbian cultural centers as Copán, Monte Albán and Chichén Itzá. The object of the game, played in two teams, was to put a rubber ball through a stone ring mounted 8 to 11 ft 6 in (2.5 to 3.5 m) high on the side. Players were only allowed to touch the ball with certain parts of their bodies. Such competitions were apparently held during public celebrations; however, prisoners of war were also made to play for their lives.

Site of the sacred ball game, Monte Albán, Oaxaca, Mexico

Human Sacrifice

Life-and-death struggles and blood sacrifices feature especially predominantly in Aztec myths. The legendary forefather of the Aztec people was Huitzilopochtli ("Hummingbird of the South"), god of war and the sun. Human sacrifices were esteemed as "debt payments to the gods." Although the Maya also practiced human sacrifice, the practice was more frequent among the Aztecs. The Aztecs sacrificed prisoners of war, slaves and children; there are also accounts of voluntary sacrifice among warriors and blood sacrifices by rulers. Victims were placed on altars on the pyramid platforms and their hearts cut from their bodies while still alive. The bodies were then thrown down the steep stone steps, and parts of them were ritually eaten. Scholars still debate to what extent the many human sacrifices may have been a symptom of the empire's downfall in the face of natural catastrophes.

Human sacrifice ritual in the Tudela Codex, 16th century, parchment, 8 × 6 in (21 × 15.5 cm), Museo de America, Madrid

Chinampas

Chinampas (the name means "square made of canes") were a unique method of agriculture developed by the Aztecs: rafts or "artificial islands" made of wattle measuring up to 650 ft (200 m) in length were fastened to wooden poles placed in the shallow water near the banks of lakes. These floating garden plots were then filled with the fertile mud of the lake bed and could produce up to four harvests each year. The Aztecs cultivated corn (maize), beans, tomatoes, sweet potatoes, avocados, chili peppers and even flowers in this way.

"Floating garden," Xochimilco, south of Mexico City

Key Terms

La Venta Culture

The Olmecs—the "people of the rubber land," who left artifacts of their culture that were sometimes monumental in scale on the Mexican Gulf Coast as well as on the Pacific Coast from around 1200 BCE—may also have referred to themselves as the "jaguar people." The jaguar appears to have played a central role in their religion, as did a mixed jaguar-human creature.

The jaguar people of the rubber region were already familiar with the calendar and number symbols later used by the Maya. They built pyramids and held ritual ball games. They made sacrifices of painted wooden figures shaped like human beings.

Too little written history remains for us to do more than speculate about their culture. The significance of their colossal head sculptures remains just as mysterious as that of their chubby, genderless child figures. Both artifacts depict a similar type of human being: with a wide head, narrow eyes, flat nose and sumptuous, almost pouting lips.

At the same time, we see naturalistically formed figures with more slender bodies and narrow heads. The artifacts of the jaguar people represent the first recognizable artistic style of Central America as well as the earliest truly monumental art.

△ **Jaguar head**, Mexico, ca. 1200–600 BCE, flat relief (detail), Museo Nacional de Antropología, Mexico City

△ **Child figure with helmet**, Las Bocas, Mexico, ca. 1200–900 BCE. Fired clay, 13 in (34 cm) high. The Metropolitan Museum of Art, New York

▷ **Wrestler from Santa María Uxpanap**a, Mexico, ca. 400 BCE. Basalt, 26 in (66 cm) high. Museo Nacional de Antropología, Mexico City

◁ **Colossal head from San Lorenzo Tenochtitlán**, Mexico, ca. 1200–900 BCE. Basalt, 9 ft 4 in (285 cm) high. Museo de Antropología de la Universidad Veracruzana, Jalapa

▷ The rain god
Tlaloc, detail of a
relief decoration
on the **pyramid
of Quetzalcoatl**,
the god of nature,
ca. 250 CE, near
the citadel of
Teotihuacán,
Mexico, at the
south end of the
Street of the Dead
(all names come
from the Aztec
language).

Where People Became Gods

In the fourteenth century, the Aztecs
believed they had found the seat of the
gods in an abandoned city. In fact, they
had discovered one of the first large
cities on the American continent. During
its heyday around 500 CE, Teotihuacán
had an estimated 120,000 inhabitants—
approximately the same number as in
the simultaneously declining Rome.

Teotihuacán (outside of Mexico
City), was the center of the trade
routes which extended as far as the

◁ **Figure with a statuette embedded in its ribcage,** Teotihuacán, Mexico, ca. 200–500. Fired clay, 5 in (13 cm) high. Musée du Quai Branly, Paris

▽ **Death mask,** Teotihuacán, Mexico, ca. 300–650. Serpentine, turquoise, mother-of-pearl and obsidian, 8 in (21 cm) high. Museo Nacional de Antropología, Mexico City

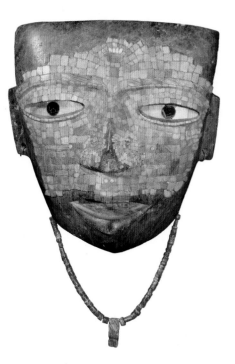

Maya region in what is now Guatemala. The most important commodity was the obsidian that was mined in the region, which was used to produce razor-sharp knife blades. The city's spiritual center was its north-south axis, with its monumental temples and gravesites. For centuries, constant streams of visitors apparently travelled to Teotihuacán as a pilgrimage site, no doubt contributing to an increase in local ceramic and textile production.

The cityscape was colorful: its façades were decorated with murals—an intense red was the favorite color—both on the official buildings and the unique living complexes. The latter were gigantic bungalows providing work and living space for up to 100 members of a family clan or ethnic group.

Archeological digs have revealed the skeletons of sacrificed human beings and animals at the foot of the pyramids. They were divided according to gender and killed in a variety of ways (some were buried alive) and carefully laid in place.

Around 650, the city's inhabitants abandoned the site, burning down the temples on top of the pyramids.

Temples and Palaces

The elements of Mayan architecture that survive are temples, palaces and government buildings. Many ordinary people lived in huts made of wood and leaves, of which nothing remains. Those of higher status did not reside at ground level, but made their homes on rectangular platforms elevated on banks or staircases. The higher the home, the more important the person; the temples of the most powerful gods were thus the highest buildings of all. And they were continually growing: on festive occasions such as the crowning of a new ruler, the temples were rebuilt higher and larger. The Maya used the magnificent stairways of their pyramids to great effect, letting the blood of sacrificial victims flow down them, or arranging the entire complex in such a way that especially sacred "snake shadows" would fall on them twice each year.

The pyramids were sacrificial sites, serving a second purpose as gravesites. Dignitaries were also buried inside the platforms of their palaces. These low, elongated buildings consisted of rows of high, narrow, windowless sleeping chambers; cooking and daily life took place in the open courtyards on the platforms.

△+◁ "Governor's Palace," Uxmal, Yucatán, Mexico, 600–900, western façade with relief frieze and view into a false archway of projecting brickwork.

▽ Temple of the Sun, Palenque, Chiapas, Mexico, 642. The latticework roof comb was covered in stucco; it appears massive but is light enough to stand on the roof.

△ **Temple I**, Tikal, Petén, Guatemala, ca. 700. The pyramid symbolizes the transition from the earthly world to the heavenly sphere; the ritual site is located on the upper platform.

▷ **"Palace,"** Palenque, Chiapas, Mexico, view from the southwest, 600–900. Elongated buildings set on artificial platforms are grouped around an inner courtyard. The tower may have been used as an observatory.

Images of Rulers and Gods

Among the Maya, art also served a purpose. With the rise of individual chiefdoms and royal dynasties, which began around 200 CE in the Mayan lowlands and the Yucatán Peninsula, the legitimation and preservation of power became important issues. Beginning around 400, information about rulers and their accomplishments was publically recorded on columns placed in the squares in front of the temples. More and more frequently, however, it was also illustrated in figurative relief panels on building façades. The lintel reliefs from Yaxchilán, which date to around 700, are a unique form of docu-

△ **Yaxun Balam (ruler of Yaxchilán) preparing to sacrifice a prisoner**, Lintel 16, Temple 21, Yaxchilán, Chiapas, Mexico, 770. Limestone, 31 in (78.8 cm) high. The British Museum, London

◁ **Vessel in the form of a god**, 600–900. Fired clay, Museo Nacional de Antropología, Mexico City

mentation: they were attached in such a way that selected individuals could only see them when they stepped through the gates with their heads raised high. They illustrate a ruler's duties in sacrificing enemies, ritual self-mutilation and visions received during a trance—repeating the same images with various different rulers. The figures' clothing, tools and gestures are depicted in intricate detail. It is unclear whether these vivid images were intended to glorify the Mayan rulers or to pacify their gods.

In the noble burial grounds on the island of Jaina, near the Gulf coast of Yucatán (and also on the mainland), 10–26 in (25–65 cm) high clay figures have been unearthed which were used in the cult of the dead. The styles range from naturalistic to caricature, and the figures seem to bear no thematic relationship to the dead individuals who held them in their hands or wore them on their chests.

△ Wak Tun, one of the wives of Yaxun Balam, facing a Vision Serpent after a blood sacrifice, Lintel 15, Temple 21, Yaxchilán, Chiapas, Mexico, 770. Limestone, 34½ in (87.6 cm) high. The British Museum, London

◁ Dignitary with a large hat, Jaina, Campeche, Mexico, 600–900. Fired clay, 10½ in (27 cm) high. Museo Nacional de Antropología, Mexico City

▷ Sacrificial stone altar depicting the god Chac Mool, Chichén Itzá, Yucatán, Mexico, ca. 987–1185. Limestone, 41 in (105 cm) high. Museo Nacional de Antropología, Mexico City. This stone sculpture dates from the post-classical period.

◁ Celebration introducing an heir to the throne, Building 1, view into Room 1, 790–792, murals, Bonampak, Chiapas, Mexico. The other rooms depict the military campaign and sacrifice of prisoners required for the occasion, as well as the blood sacrifices performed by the royal family.

▷ Vessel with five figures, ca. 750–800. Painted clay, 10¼ in (25.8 cm) high. Kimbell Art Museum, Fort Worth

▷▷ Vessel with scenes of a ball game, ca. 750. Painted clay, 8¾ in (22.2 cm) high. Kimbell Art Museum, Fort Worth

▷▷▷ Vessel with palace scenes, ca. 600–900. Painted clay, Edward H. Merrin Gallery, New York

Stories in Pictures

The largest wall painting cycle discovered to date was preserved (if poorly) in an otherwise fairly insignificant temple. It is surprisingly colorful, densely filled with 200 fantastically illustrated figures, but it also depicts deeply religiously motivated atrocities. With the discovery of these murals, the image of a peaceful Mayan people that had prevailed in research up to that point was made obsolete. The Mayan gods fed on blood, which their subjects shed for them (either their own or that of others). Burned together with paper and resins, it was sent to the heavens in the form of smoke. In exchange, the gods granted the people support and prophecies.

Other duties, pleasures, and vanities of the priests and aristocratic classes are illustrated on highly informative paintings on jars. The containers were useful in this world and indispensible for the journey to the next world. The few surviving artifacts of Mayan book art testify to their knowledge of mathematics and astronomy, prophecy and religious rituals, agriculture and beekeeping.

▷ *Codex Dresdensis*, Page 36, depicting the activities of the rain god, ca. 1200, copy of an earlier compilation. Paint on stucco-coated bast fiber paper, 8 × 3½ in (20.5 × 9 cm). Sächsische Landes- und Universitätsbibliothek, Dresden

◁ **Vessel with palace scenes**, ca. 600–900. Painted clay, Edward H. Merrin Gallery, New York

Reliefs and Sculptures

Mayan culture was rooted in images of gods which the Olmecs had cultivated as early as 1000 BCE. The earliest settlements of the Zapotecs also date from this time. The latter culture experienced its heyday in Monte Albán between 300 and 900 CE. The early bas-reliefs of dancers from Monte Albán I are well known. From the Zapotecs, the Mayans inherited knowledge of what are called "false arches," layers of bricks that project outward row by row (see illus. p. 676). The Zapotecs chose this building method to provide their deceased with a structurally safe space in their underground mausoleums. For their journey into the hereafter, they supplied the dead with skillfully crafted figurative urns. The Zapotecs had a written language, but although they also occupied a section of Teotihuacán around 400,

▷ Urn in the shape of Cocijo, god of lightning and rain, Monte Albán IIIa, Oaxaca, Mexico, ca. 400–500. Fired clay, 28½ in (72.4 cm) high. Kimbell Art Museum, Fort Worth

◁ Danzantes (Dancers) building, Monte Albán I, Oaxaca, Mexico, ca. 300 BCE. Stone, 4 ft 6 in–5 ft 1 in (137–155 cm) high

they do not seem to have used any writing there.

Some time after the fall of Teotihuacán, the Toltecs ruled over the high valley of Mexico, where, according to Aztec writings, they founded their capital city, Tollan—today called Tula—in 856. They were skilled in agriculture and had a written language and a calendar, but they were a warlike people.

The image of themselves and their gods which they propagated in their primarily blocky artwork is fearsome, as exemplified by the columns in their assembly halls. Even the Aztecs mourned the death of their legendary king Quetzalcoatl (974–999), who bore the name of an ancient Meso-American deity and was killed by jealous gods.

△ Statues of Toltec warriors on the platform of the Pyramid of the Morning Star (Temple B), ca. 950, Tula, Hidalgo, Mexico

◁ Zoomorphic vessel, Tula, ca. 900–1150. Fired clay and mother-of-pearl, 5¼ in (13 cm) high. Museo Nacional de Antropología, Mexico City. A warrior looks out from the throat of a coyote.

The Culture of the Mexica

Just a few centuries after the fall of the Toltec empire, the equally warlike Aztecs dominated the high valley of Mexico. The war and sun god Huitzilopochtli advised the people, who called themselves Mexica, to settle in a place where they saw an eagle perched on a prickly pear cactus. They founded their first settlement, Tenochtitlán, on an island on the still-large Lake Texcoco; it soon grew to become their capital city. From then on, representatives of the highest military rank were called "eagle warriors"; they were also the embodiment of the rising sun. A *cuauhxicalli* is an "eagle bowl," used to contain sacrificial human blood which forged a contact to the gods, who took their nourishment from it.

Through the shedding of their skin, snakes represented the natural core of life, from which a new existence was constantly being formed. Tlaloc, a god whose origins date back to Olmec archetypes, had his sanctuary next to Huitzilopochtli at the Templo Mayor in Tenochtitlán; his blue-green color identifies him as the god of rain.

When the Spanish Conquistadores, led by Hernán Cortés, arrived in 1519, Tenochtitlán's population was approximately 700,000. Three years later, this army of around 500 men with 14 cannons and 16 horses had not only destroyed the city, but they had annihilated the entire Aztec empire. Today, the ruins of Tenochtitlán have almost completely disappeared beneath the buildings of Mexico City.

◁ **Eagle warrior**, ca. 1440–1469. Fired clay, stucco and paint, 67 in (170 cm) high. Museo del Templo Mayor, Mexico City

△ **Coiled rattlesnake**, ca. 1300–1512. Granite, 14 in (36 cm) high. Museo Nacional de Antropología, Mexico City

△ **Vessel with a mask of the rain god Tlaloc**, ca. 1440–1469. Painted fired clay, 14 in (35.5 cm) high. Museo del Templo Mayor, Mexico City

▷ **Eagle-shaped** *Cuauhxicalli*, ca. 1502–1520. Basalt, 55 × 33 × 30 in (139 × 83 × 76 cm). Museo del Templo Mayor, Mexico City

Calendars and Codices

The foundation of Aztec religious practice was the reliable calculation of time. Like the Olmecs and the Maya, the Aztecs used a calendar which combined a longer solar year with a shorter divinatory year. In each of these systems, every day had a unique name. When both were combined, it took fifty-two years until the name of day was repeated, a new cycle began and everything was renewed. The sun stone contained not only the calendar but also a depiction of the epochs of the world. The protruding tongue of the central sun god, Tonatiuh, was shaped like the obsidian knives used in sacrifices and symbolized the god's craving for sacrificial blood. Symbols for the rays of the sun, glyphs of the eras of the world and calendar symbols are arranged in concentric circles and finally encircled by a snake with heads on both ends of its body, representing heaven.

▷ Tezcatlipoca (night and fate) and Quetzalcoatl (feathered serpent), Page 12 of the *Codex Borbonicus*, before 1500. Bast fiber paper, 15 in (38 cm) high; total length 56 in (142 cm). Bibliothèque de l'Assemblée nationale, Palais Bourbon, Paris

▷ Sun stone, also called the Aztec calendar, 1479. Basalt, 11 ft 10 in (360 cm) diameter, weighs almost 25 t (27.5 tons). Museo Nacional de Antropología, Mexico City

The few "dangerously pagan" Aztec codices which survived the Spanish flames are filled with myths, historical illustrations and genealogy, and instructions for rituals and ceremonies; others are divinatory calendars. The first third of the *Codex Borbonicus* contains the Tonalamatl ("pages of days") from which prophecies could be derived from the name symbols for the individual days. (Latin symbols and words are commentaries that were added at a later time.)

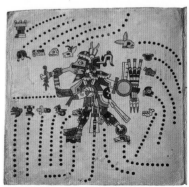

▷ **Tezcatlipoca and the 20 weeks of the Tonalamatl** (divinatory calendar), Page 44 of the *Codex Fejérváry-Mayer*, before 1521. Animal skin, 7 in (17.5 cm) high; total length 13 ft 3 in (403 cm). World Museum Liverpool, Liverpool

Early South American Art

Probably the oldest city in the Americas, Caral, in the Peruvian highlands, which was settled between 3000 and 1200 BCE, was only rediscovered in the 1990s. Beginning around 2000 BCE, large religious and cultural centers subsequently developed in Cerro Sechín and somewhat later in Chavín de Huántar, the city that lent its name to this culture: the Chavín (ca. 900–200 BCE). Evidence of human sacrifice can be seen even in Cerro Sechín. As in many ancient American (and other) cultures, the practice was based on the idea that buried body parts would give rise to new life in the form of wellsprings or useful plants.

The scratched landscape drawings of the Nazca culture (400 BCE–600 CE), known as the Nazca Lines, are

◁ **Stone relief depicting warriors and cut-off heads,** Cerro Sechín, Peru, 2000–1000 BCE. The old adobe brick temple of Cerro Sechín is surrounded by a wall with a circular frieze depicting a procession of dignitaries and body parts.

▷ **Drum**, Nazca, 1st century CE. Fired clay, 17¾ in (45.1 cm) high. The Metropolitan Museum of Art, New York

◁ Scratched drawing of an orca, Nazca, 150 BCE–600 CE, 85 ft (26 m) long

▽ Stirrup-handled vessel, Moche, ca. 200–500. Painted fired clay, 11⅓ in (28.7 cm) high. Yale University Art Gallery, New Haven

as famous as they are mysterious. Setting aside the many creative interpretations that have been proposed, researchers today assume that the animal drawings (which are also found on Nazca ceramics) represent venerated mythical beings. The engraved line drawings may have been paced out in processions, perhaps as part of a ritual requesting rain or fertility. The straight lines, which are barely visible today, lead to special assembly sites.

The Moche people (100–700 CE) are famous for their figurative clay jars whose faces, sometimes containing nearly portrait-like features, bear witness to the artists' skill in observation. Other vessels depicting multiple figures illustrate daily activities as well as revealing the culture's enjoyment of anecdotal situations or erotic scenes.

△ **Machu Picchu**, Inca, 1450–1562, view of
the city; Huayna Picchu towers above; Peru

Machu Picchu

In 1450, for reasons that no one can explain today, Pachacútec Inca Yupanqui (reigned 1438–1471) had a settlement built between the sacred Andean mountains of Machu Picchu and Huayna Picchu, at an altitude of 7743 ft (2360 m).

The Inca culture developed around 1000 in what is now the province of Cuzco, Peru. By around 1400, its capital Cuzco ("navel") had imperial characteristics, and the Inca dominated the region extending from Colombia far beyond Chile. The highest position in their society was that of Sapa Inca, who was assigned by the highest-ranking sun god to rule the world.

Machu Picchu ("Old Mountain"), located 47 miles (75 km) northwest of Cuzco, was more than simply a royal estate. Thanks to its ingenious irrigation and drainage systems and systematically planned stratification into an agricultural and a residential sector, it was, in fact, a self-contained and self-sustaining community.

The natural rock is partially integrated into the buildings; some of the walls are constructed of custom-fitted blocks layered without mortar and designed to withstand earthquakes. 600 people lived here permanently. When the Sapa Inca and his royal household were in residence, the population grew to 2000. In 1562, fearing the approach of Pizarro's Spanish army, the residents abandoned the still-unfinished city.

◁ **Machu Picchu**, view of the city and terraced fields from the summit of Huayna Picchu

▷ **Machu Picchu**, wall of the "Temple of the Three Windows"

Inca Ceramics and Idols

The Spanish, who conquered every part of Central and South America that they explored, searched doggedly for the immeasurable golden treasures of which persistent rumors continued to circulate. They never found El Dorado ("The Golden City"), but everything they did find was thrown into crucibles and converted to gold bars to fill the empty coffers of their homeland. While the Spanish sought gold for its monetary value, the Incas revered it for its sun-like radiance. As descendents of the sun, they saw this as their birthright. Objects such as small idols made of gold were also seen as appropriate offerings for the sun god, Inti, or valued as burial goods, as were those made of silver.

The aryballos (or aribalo)—named after similar vessels produced in ancient Greece—with its mostly geometric patterns of black, white and red is typical of the ceramics produced by the Inca. The farmer-shaped vessel is a good example of the way in which a person could carry an aryballos on his or her back using a cord drawn through the handles.

An indispensible item for everyday life was the *kero*: a cup used for libations in a wide variety of rituals. Every kero was intended to commemorate a particular person. Keros were made of wood and decorated with carved designs which were then filled in with brightly-colored resins. Geometric designs often appeared in combination with subjects from nature.

◁ **Female idol**, Inca, ca. 1470–1532. Gold, 9½ in (24 cm) high. National Museum of the American Indian, Washington, D.C.

▷ **Male idol**, Inca, ca. 1450–1532. Silver and colored paste, 7¾ in (19.5 cm) high. Musée du Quai Branly, Paris

△ **Aryballos with geometric pattern**, Inca, ca. 1450–1550. Fired and painted clay, Museo Nazionale Preistorico Etnografico "Luigi Pigorini," Rome

◁ **Vessel in the shape of a farmer carrying an aryballos**, Inca, ca. 1450–1550. Fired clay, 7¾ in (19.5 cm) high. Ethnologisches Museum, Berlin

▽ **Drinking vessel (kero)**, Inca, ca. 1430–1532. Painted wood, private collection

Kachinas and Bison Paintings

The traditional societies of North American Indians were highly distinct, and their cultures correspondingly varied. In general, however, similar living environments gave rise to comparatively similar cultural developments. Long before European exploration of North America, its southwestern section (today Arizona and New Mexico) had evolved into an important cultural center. The tribes who lived there were called Pueblo Indians, after the Spanish word for "village." Under protective overhanging cliffs, the Anasazi built multistoried structures from a mix of natural stone and adobe. Many of the pictures engraved in the rocks depict male and female figures with exaggerated genitals, perhaps referring to initiation or fertility rituals. The Hopi of Arizona, a tribe of Pueblo Indians, practiced Kachina rituals in which they summoned the rain-bringing spirits of their ancestors through dance and offerings in the form of small wooden figures or dolls. As we can see from Max Ernst's collection of these Kachinas, African masks were not the only source of inspiration for the Modern Art movement that included Picasso and cubism.

Plains and prairie Indians such as the Sioux (North Dakota) preferred movement-filled depictions of hunting scenes, which were painted on bison skins and used as ceremonial robes.

△ **Cliff Palace, Anasazi**, 1100–1300, Mesa Verde, southern Colorado

▽ **Rock engravings (petroglyphs)**, Rio Grande Gorge, New Mexico

△ **Bison robe**, Sioux, ca. 1890. Painted bison skin and porcupine quills, 97 × 44 in (247 × 111 cm, detail). Musée du Quai Branly, Paris

▽ **Max Ernst with his Kachinas**, photographed by James Thrall Soby on the terrace of Ernst's New York apartment, ca. 1942

△ **Kachina**, Hopi, ca. 1900. Painted wood, 10¾ in (27.4 cm) high. Musée du Quai Branly, Paris

The "Salmon Cultures"

On the Pacific Northwest coast of the North American continent, it was primarily the estuaries of salmon rivers that provided a viable location for human settlements. The Tlingit and Tsimshian Indian tribes maintain settlements to this day in southern Alaska and northern British Columbia (Canada); the Kwakiutl still live in the central region of British Columbia. The Chilkat blankets produced by the Tlingit are worn only for ceremonial occasions. They are woven on vertical looms with the warp threads—made of cedar bark wound with mountain goats' wool—hanging freely; the weft threads are wool. The design patterns are wooden tablets painted with geometric animal motifs constructed of standardized individual elements. The entire design often follows an axially symmetrical pattern around

▽ **Headgear**, Tsimshian, British Columbia, ca. 1900. Wood, graphite, abalone shell and paint, 6⅓ in (16 cm) long. Musée du Quai Branly, Paris

▽ **Chilkat blanket**, Tlingit, southern Alaska, ca. 1890. Dyed mountain goats' wool and cedar bark, 4 ft 7 in × 5 ft 6⅓ in (137.7 × 165.8 cm). Musée du Quai Branly, Paris

The Inuit

The art of the Inuit is first and foremost the art of hunters. In their hunting rituals, the shamans confirmed the community's relationship to the animal world. Their prey should allow themselves to be hunted down; in return, their souls would be safely guided back to their origins.

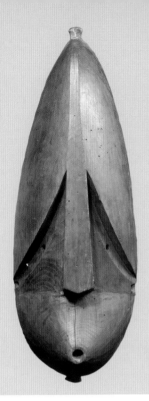

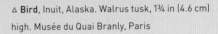

◁ **Mask**, Inuit, Alaska, ca. 1850. Wood, 19 in (49 cm) high. Musée du Quai Branly, Paris

△ **Bird**, Inuit, Alaska. Walrus tusk, 1¾ in (4.6 cm) high. Musée du Quai Branly, Paris

a central animal head. The colors are white, yellow, ochre, blue and black; it seems essential for the design to fill the entire surface. "Potlatch" festivals, held mainly in the wintertime, include masked theatrical performances. At these gift-giving celebrations, the host presents his or her guests with Chilkat blankets or other valuable items for the purpose of obligating them to play host and offer gifts in return. The masks and headgear worn by high-ranking members of the tribe also contain animal motifs or symbols. Depending upon the context, they may represent the animal itself, the spirits of its species or an entire legend.

▷ **Chief's mask**, Kwakiutl. Painted wood with abalone shell inlays, private collection

Index

Artists

Picture credits

Gift, 1987. Inv. 1987.16), 571 r. (H. O. Havemeyer Collection, Mrs. H. O. Havemeyer Bequest, 1929. Acc.n.: JP1847), 574 b. (Rogers Fund, 1943. Acc.n.: 43.25.4. Photo: Lynton Gardiner), 577 l. (Charlotte C. and John C. Weber Collection, Gift of Charlotte C. & John C. Weber, 1992. Acc.n.: 1992.165.19. Photo: Seth Joel), 582 l. (John Stewart Kennedy Fund, 1926. Acc.n.26.123), 582 r. (Rogers Fund, 1938. Inv. 38.158.1), 583 l. (Rogers Fund, 1919. Acc.n.: 19.186. Photo: Lynton Gardiner), 591 t. (John Stewart Kennedy Fund, 1913. Inv. 13.100.102), 591 b. (Gift of Mr. e Mrs. Wango H. C. Weng, 1990. Inv. 1990.318), 593 b. (Gift of Florence & Herbert Irving. Acc.n.: L.1996.47.14. Photo: Lynton Gardiner), 594 (Purchase, Lita Annenberg Hazen Charitable Trust Gift, 1987. Inv.1987.16), 596 t.r. (Purchase, Walter and Leonore Annenberg and The Annenberg Foundation Gift, 2003. Acc.n.2003.222), 596 b. (Purchase, The Vincent Astor Foundation Gift, 1999 Benefit Fund, and The Rosenkranz Foundation Inc. Gift, 1999. Acc.n.1999.263), 610 (H. O. Havemeyer Collection, Mrs. H. O. Havemeyer Bequest, 1929. Acc.n.: JP1847), 615 2nd from l. (The Michael C. Rockefeller Memorial Collection, gift of Nelson A. Rockefeller, 1972. Acc.n.: 1978.412.730), 615 2nd from r. (The Michael C. Rockefeller Memorial Collection, gift of Nelson A. Rockefeller, 1972. Acc.n.: 1978.412.725), 617 l. (The Michael C. Rockefeller Memorial Collection, Gift of the Estate of Kay Sage Tanguy, 1963. Acc.n. 1978.412.826), 624 c. (The Michael C. Rockefeller Memorial Collection, gift of Nelson A. Rockefeller, 1972. Acc.n.: 1978.412.730), 626 t.l. (The Michael C. Rockefeller Memorial Collection, gift of Nelson A. Rockefeller and Purchase, Nelson A. Rockefeller 1970. Acc.n.: 1978.412.1558), 627 b.r. (The Michael C. Rockefeller Memorial Collection, gift of Nelson A. Rockefeller, 1969. Acc.n.: 1978.412.796), 628 t. (The Michael C. Rockefeller Memorial Collection, Nelson A. Rockefeller Bequest, 1967. Acc.n.: 1978.412.1510), 628 b.l. (The Michael C. Rockefeller Memorial Collection, gift of Nelson A. Rockefeller, 1972. Acc.n.: 1978.412.725), 629 l. (Rogers Fund, 1978. Acc.n. 1978.7), 633 b.r. (The Michael C. Rockefeller Memorial Collection,Nelson A. Rockefeller Bequest, 1979. Acc.n.: 1979.206.1470. Photo: Schecter Lee.), 634 c.l. (Acc.n.: 1984.526. Photo: Schecter Lee), 638 r. (Gift of the Buckeye Trust & Mr. & Mrs. Milton Rosenthal, Joseph Pulitzer Bequest & Harris Brisbane Dick and Rogers Funds, 1981. Acc.n.: 1981.218), 639 2nd from r. (The Michael C. Rockefeller Memorial Collection, Purchase, Nelson A. Rockefeller Gift, 1965. Acc.n.1978.412.576), 639 l. (The Michael C. Rockefeller Memorial Collection, gift of Nelson A. Rockefeller, 1972. Acc.n.: 1978.412.323), 646 t.l. (Gift of Mr. and Mrs. Klaus G. Perls, 1991. Acc.n.1991.17.3), 646 t.r. (The Michael C. Rockefeller Memorial Collection, gift of Nelson A. Rockefeller, 1972. Acc.n.: 1978.412.323), 647 (Gift of Mr. & Mrs. Klaus G. Perls, 1990. Acc.n.: 1990.332), 648 l. (Gift of Martin L. Schulman, M.D., 1983. Inv. 1983.603.6), 650 l. (Gift of the Buckeye Trust & Mr. & Mrs. Milton Rosenthal, Joseph Pulitzer Bequest & Harris Brisbane Dick and Rogers Funds, 1981. Acc.n.: 1981.218), 653 l. (The Michael C. Rockefeller Memorial Collection, gift of Nelson A. Rockefeller, 1969. Acc.n.: 1978.412.390-.391), 657 r. (The Michael C. Rockefeller Memorial Collection, Purchase, Nelson A. Rockefeller Gift, 1965. Acc.n.1978.412.576), 658 c. (Gift of Louis V. Bell Fund & the Fred and Rita Richman Family Foundation & James Ross, 2000. Acc.n.: 2000.177), 662 r. (The Michael C. Rockefeller Memorial Collection, gift of Nelson A. Rockefeller, 1979. Acc.n.: 1979.206.127), 673 l. (The Michael C. Rockefeller Memorial Collection, gift of Nelson A. Rockefeller, 1979. Acc.n.: 1979.206.1134. Photo: Schecter Lee), 689 b.l. (Gift of Mr. and Mrs. Raymond Wielgus, 1964. Acc.n.: 1978.412.111); ©2010. Kimbell Art Museum, Fort Worth, Texas/Art Resource, NY/Scala, Firenze: 15 t.r. (AP 1969.16), 406 b. (AP 1966.08), 548 (AP 1986.06), 570 l. (AP 1985.16), 574 t.r. (AP 1985.16), 577 b.r. (AP 1994.07), 579 t. (AP 2001.01), 592 t.r. (AP 1995.07), 592 b. (AP 1969.16), 596 t.l. (AP 1996.05), 598 t. (AP 1972.02), 598 b.l. (AP 1971.15), 599 b.l. (AP 1981.19), 599 b.r., 606 (AG 1971.02. Anonymous gift), 607 c.l. (AP 1971.12), 607 t.l. (AP 1969.09), 607 t.r. (AP 1971.10), 615 l. (AP 1989.04), 621 t.l. (AP 1989.04), 660 b.r. (AP 1978.05), 680 b.l. (AG 1979.02. Gift in memory of John William and Mary Seeger O'Boyle), 680 b.c. (AP 1989.05), 682 t. (AP 1985.09); ©2010. Marie Mauzy/Scala, Firenze: 91 t.; ©2010. Munson Williams Proctor Arts Institute/Art Resource, NY/Scala, Firenze: 390/391 (Museum Purchase, 54.38); ©2010. Musée du quai Branly, Photo Hughes Dubois/Scala, Firenze: 13 b.l. (Precedente collection: Samir Borro), 613 l. (Inv.: 70.1999.5.3), 613 c. (Inv.: SG.53.287), 614 r. (Inv.: 71.1878.30.15), 632 l., 632 c. (Inv.: 71.1879.10.11), 632 r. (Inv.: 71.1933.2.1), 633 t.l. (Inv.: 71.1878.30.15), 633 t.r. (Inv.: 71.1887.50.1 Oc), 633 b.l. (Inv.: 71.1878.30.8), 634 b.l. (Inv.: SG.53.288), 638 2nd from l. (Inv.: 70.1998.11.1), 639 2nd from l. (Inv.: 71.1886.77.2)644 (Inv.:70.1998.11.2), 645 l. (Inv.: 70.1998.11.1), 645 b. (Inv.: 73.1996.1.4), 658 l. (Inv.: 71.1965.104.1, prov. Musee de l'Homme), 658 r. (Inv.: 71.1898.1.1), 659 l. (Inv.: 71.1886.77.2), 660 t.l. (Inv.: 70.1999.9.1), 663 l. (Inv.: 71.1892.70.3), 696 t. (Inv.: 71.1951.35.3); ©2010. Musée du quai Branly, Photo Jacques Viot, DR/Scala, Firenze: 623 t.l. (Inv. Iconotheque: PP0004155); ©2010. Musée du quai Branly, Photo Patrick Gries/Bruno Descoings/Scala, Firenze: 15 c.l. (Inv.: : 73.1969.7.1), 507 c. (Inv.: : 71.1969.103.44), 612 l. (Inv.: SG.84.433)612 r. (Inv.: 72.1980.1.1), 617 t. (Inv.: 71.1909.19.1 Oc), 622 r. (Inv. 70.2001.27.520), 624 l. (Inv.: 72.1966.2.8), 624 r. (Inv.: 71.1894.77.1), 628 b.r. (Inv.: : 72.1999.7.3), 648 r. (Inv.: 73.1969.7.1), 652 r. (Inv.: 71.1952.59.1), 656 l. (Inv.: 71.1948.8.2), 657 l. (Inv.: 73.1992.0.47), 662 l. (Inv.: 71.1892.70.2), 695 b.r. (Inv.: 71.1885.78.149), 696 b. (Inv.: 71.1885.78.450); ©2010. Musée du quai Branly, Photo Patrick Gries/Scala, Firenze: 503 r. (Inv.: 71.1967.111.165), 519 b. (Inv.: 71.1967.111.165), 612 c. (Inv.: 72.1984.2.2), 615 r. (Inv.: 72.1964.9.79), 618 b.l. (Inv.: 72.1964.9.79), 622 l. (Inv.: : 71.1887.31.52), 630 b. (Inv.: 71.1943.0.406 X), 630/631 t. (Inv.: 71.1932.32.20), 651 l. (Inv.: 71.1935.60.371), 655 r. (Inv.: 73.1963.0.441), 663 r. (Inv.: 71.1892.52.22), 675 c. (Inv.: 70.2001.14.1), 697 t.r. (Inv.: 71.1905.31.64); ©2010. Musée du quai Branly, Photo Patrick Gries/Valérie Torre/Scala, Firenze : 626 c. (Inv.: 71.1961.103.318), 655 b.c. (Inv.: 71.1965.17.1, prov. Musee de l'Homme), 665 l. (Inv.: 70.2001.4.1), 669 2nd from r. (Inv.: 71.1887.114.90), 692 r. (Inv.: 71.1887.114.90), 695 t. (Inv.: 71.1886.17.1); ©2010. Musée du quai Branly, Photo Patrick Gries/Vincent Chenet/Scala, Firenze: 633 2nd from r.b. (Inv.: 71.1964.24.1.1); ©2010. Musée du quai Branly, Photo Thierry Ollivier/Michel Urtado/Scala, Firenze: 656 r. (Inv.: 73.1990.5.1); ©2010. Musée du quai Branly/Scala, Firenze : 504 r. (Ancienne collection: Paul Eudel), 631 b. (Inv.: SG.53.291. Depot de: Musee d'archeologie nationale. Precedente collection: Musee national des arts d'Afrique et d'Oceanie), 637 l. (Inv.: 73.1967.1.9 D. Collecteur: Pierre Verger. Depot de: Universite de Dakar (I. F. A. N.). Precedente collection : Musee national des arts d'Afrique et d'Oceanie), 669 r. (Inv.: 70.1999.1.1 D. Ancienne collection: Alphonse Pinart. Depot de: Chateau-musee de Boulogne-sur-Mer), 697 t.l. (Inv.: 70.1999.1.1 D. Ancienne collection: Alphonse Pinart. Depot de: Chateau-musee de Boulogne-sur-Mer); ©2010. Museum of Fine Arts, Boston. All rights reserved/Scala, Firenze : 337 b.r. (Gift of Robert Jordan dalla collezione di Eben D. Jordan. Inv. 24.217), 352 r. (Hayden Collection, Charles Henry Hayden Fund. Acc.n. 35.1953), 364 r. (Purchase Fund 1951. Inv. 56.147), 365 r. (Lee M. Friedman Fund. Inv. 68.721)368/369 t. (Tompkins Collection, Arthur Gordon Tompkins Fund. Inv. 36.270),541 r. (Marshall H. Gould Fund. Acc.n.: 64.2025), 566 t. (Gift of John Goelet. Acc.n. 67.818), 567 l. (Harriet Otis Cruft Fund. Acc.n.: 17.73), 567 t.r. (Marshall H. Gould Fund. Acc.n.: 64.2025), 567 b.r. (Acc.n.: 14.46), 575 (Maria Antoinette Evans Fund. Inv. 31.976), 608 t. (Fenollosa-Weld Collection. Inv. 11.4000), 609 b. (Fenollosa-Weld Collection. Inv. 11.4584), 611 t.r. (William S. & John T. Spaulding Collection. Acc.n. 21.6610), 625 l. (Gift of William E. & Bertha L. Teel. Acc.n.: 1992.414); ©2010. The Kyoto International Culture Foundation Archives/Scala, Firenze: 568/569; ©2010. White Images/Scala, Firenze: 18 t.r., 218 b., 240 t., 259 b., 268 l., 273 t., 280 t.l., 290, 316 b., 334 b., 345 b., 346 b., 355 t., 374, 375 t.l., 376 l., 376 c., 389, 400 b., 410 c., 411 b., 421 t., 448/449, 504 l., 505 b.r., 512 b., 515 t.r., 515 b., 675 b., 687 t.; ©2010. Yale University Art Gallery/Art Resource, NY/Scala, Firenze : 319 t.c. (Everett V. Meeks, B.A. 1901, Fund. Acc.n.: 1982.120.4), 392 2nd from r. (Gift of Katherine S. Dreier to Collection Société Anonyme. Acc.n.: 1948.209), 433 t. (Gift of Katherine S. Dreier to Collection Société Anonyme. Acc.n.: 1948.209), 435 b.r. (Gift of CollectionSociété Anonyme. Acc.n.: 1941.548), 462 b. (Gift of The Woodward Foundation. Acc.n.: 1977.49.22), 468 c. (Gift of Collection Société Anonyme. Acc.n.: 1941.629), 583 r. (Gift of Winston F.C. Guest, B.A. 1927. Acc.n.: 1956.39.1), 689 b.r. (University Purchase. Acc.n.: 1956.27.7)

Bridgeman Art Library: 24/25, 32 t., 33 b., 102/103, 107 l., 115 b.l., 195 2nd from l., 211 t.r., 217 t.l., 228 2nd from l., 244 t., 244 b., 248, 260 t., 271 t., 289 t.r., 306, 317 b.r., 338 t., 342, 344 t.r.,350 l., 362/363, 366, 375 b.r., 379 b.l., 384/385, 393 r., 414 b.r., 417 t.r., 417 b., 430 r., 435 c., 444 l., 465 t.r., 473 b., 478 b., 490 t., 498 b., 510 t., 510 b., 523 b.c., 529 b., 553, 619 b., 68 l., 92 t.; © British Library Board. All Rights Reserved: 275 t.r.; © Crane Kalman, London: 469 l.; © Gerard Degeorge: 522 t.r., 642 c.; © Julian Chichester: 523 t.l., 526 t.; © Michael Graham-Stewart: 627 b.l.; © Staatliche Kunstsammlungen Dresden: 320 b.l., 349 b.; Alinari: 423 t., 445, 464 b.; Archives Charmet: 344 b.; Bildarchiv Steffens: 163 t.r., 179 t., 537 t.; Bildarchiv Steffens/Paul Mayall: 614 l., 618 t.; Cameraphoto Arte Venezia: 135 c., 154; Daniel P. Erwin Fund: 623 b.; Funds provided by the Alice Pratt Brown Museum Fund: 625 r.; Gift of Charles Lang Freer: 607 c.r., 607 b.r.; Giraudon: 94 l., 160 c., 170 t.l., 303 t., 312 b.l., 344 t.l., 345 t.l., 443 b., 444r.; Lauros/Giraudon: 345 t.r.; Peter Willi: 192/193; Photo © AISA: 81 r., 103 b.r., 242 b.r., 469 r., 535 b.; Photo © Bonhams, London: 664 t.; Photo © Christie's Images: 572 t.r.; Photo © Heini Schneebeli: 629 c., 655 l., 665 2nd from l., 665 2nd from r.; Wolfgang Neeb: 495 t.

© BEDNORZ-IMAGES: 18 c.r., 78/79, 81 c., 104/105, 109 b., 124, 134 c., 135 r., 146 t., 147 t., 148 b.r., 157 r., 160 l., 160 r., 161 l., 161 r., 162 t., 162 b.l., 162 b.r., 163 b.r., 164 t., 165, 166 t., 168 t., 169 t.r., 169 b.r., 172 t., 172 b., 173 t., 173 b., 174 l., 174 c., 174 r., 175 t., 176 t., 176 b., 177, 178 t., 178 b., 179 b.l., 180, 182, 183 t., 185 t.r., 187, 188, 189 l., 189 r., 190, 191 t., 196 t., 196 b., 197 b.r., 199, 201 l., 208 r., 209 t.l., 209 t.r., 209 b., 212 t., 213 b.l., 238 b.l., 239 t.l., 239 t.r., 291 t., 292 b., 293 t., 294, 296/297 t., 313 l., 313 r., 318 t., 328 b., 381, 382 t.l., 382 b.l., 382 r., 383 t., 383 b.l., 418, 419, 426 t.l., 426 c.l., 426/427, 429 t., 488 t., 488 b., 489

ARTOTHEK: 350/351; Blauel/Gnamm: 216; Joseph S. Martin: 230 c., 249; U. Edelmann - Städel Museum: 326 b.; Westermann: 343 b.

Atlas of the Valley of the Kings , The American University of Cairo, © The Theban Mapping Project, 2000, 2003, 2005, Gesamtplan Valley: S.13 sheet 1/70, Grab KV7 – S. 48/49 sheet 19/70: 70
© Georg Baselitz: 490 b.
© 2010 Hilla Becher:498 t. and c.
Photograph by Maggie L. Kundtz, courtesy PaceWildenstein,
New York. © Chuck Close, courtesy PaceWildenstein, New York: 479 b.
© 1999–2009 Getty Images, Inc. Bobby Haas: 670 b.
© Keith Haring Foundation. Used by permission: 495 t.
Bowness, Hepworth Estate: 469
Photo: Prudence Cuming Associates/© Hirst Holdings Limited and Damien Hirst. All rights reserved, DACS 2010: 495 b.
© David Hockney: 476 t.
© Allan Kaprow Estate. Courtesy Hauser & Wirth: 482
© Ellsworth Kelly. Gift of the artist, 1969: 470 t.
©Jeff Koons: 494 l.
© Estate of George Platt Lynes: 433 b.
Reproduced by permission of the Henry Moore Foundation: 467 b.
© 1961 Claes Oldenburg (The Sidney and Harriet Janis Collection, 1967): 477 b.
© 2010 Bridget Riley. All rights reserved. Courtesy Karsten Schubert, London: 471 t.
© 2010 Gerhard Richter: 491 t.
Courtesy of the Artist and Metro Pictures (Cindy Sherman): 499 b.l.
Foto Thomas Stephan, © Ulmer Museum: 38 r.
Photo: Kira Perov: 492 r.
Jeff Wall Courtesy of the artist: 499 b.r.